Here's what reviewers said about Paul Reese's first book
written with Joe Henderson

Ten Million ~~Steps~~ *urney of Paul
Reese, who ra* ~~~~ *arathon a day*

"Talk about role mode ... my vote as first centerfold for *Modern Maturity*! ... Truly, the running shoe has replaced the rocking chair as a national symbol for healthy aging."

**– Arnold Schwarzenegger
(then) Chairman, President's Council on Physical Fitness and Sports**

"There are numerous observations, anecdotes, yarns, experiences and discoveries made by Reese, who, with Henderson's help, tells it in such a way that you will find it hard to put down the book once you've started it. It's both inspiring and entertaining."

– Mike Tymn, *National Masters News*

"The best reason for a read of this book is that it reminds us that every now and then in our lives we should do something different."

– *Running and Fitness News*, American Running and Fitness Association

"Reese's daily journal became the basis for this inspirational and entertaining book."

– *Health News and Review*

"The tale is both a biography and an adventure saga. ... Entertaining and inspiring, the authors speak of running, determination, character. Theirs is primarily a statement of aging gracefully."

– *FootNotes*, Road Runners Club of America

"It is casually written, providing a relaxing bit of reading. ... A good book for us older folks. 'Getting old' doesn't mean 'dying.' There are challenges, and we can meet them – some better than others."

– *Leatherneck* magazine

"Paul Reese has produced a travel/adventure log (with the help of running writer Joe Henderson) that occasionally is every bit as inspiring as the works of Kerouac and Steinbeck."

– *New York Running News*

Go East
Old Man

Adventures of a runner in his 70s
traveling 22 Western states

PAUL REESE
with Joe Henderson

Foreword by Covert Bailey
fitness expert and best-selling author

Published by:
  Keokee Co. Publishing, Inc.
  P.O. Box 722
  Sandpoint, ID 83864
  Phone: 208/263-3573

Cover design by Randy Wilhelm

Printed in the United States of America
10 9 8 7 6 5 4 3 2 1

Publisher's Cataloging-in-Publication Data
Reese, Paul, 1917-
    Go east old man : adventures of a runner in his 70s traveling 22
  western states / by Paul Reese with Joe Henderson
      ISBN 1-879628-15-5
      1. Reese, Paul. 2. Running – West (U.S.) – Biography. 3. Elderly –
  Physical Fitness – West (U.S.)– Biography. I. Henderson, Joe, 1943-
  II. Title.
  796.42' 092–dc20

Contents

TO ELAINE

Who makes these adventures possible
and whose sharing enhances the enjoyment.

Foreword

Paul Reese practices the Gospel of exercise that I have been expounding for many years. In fact, he is somewhat of a zealous practitioner.

He has run more than 118,000 miles (6812 of them while running across 22 states) during the past 33 years. Think about that a moment: On foot, he has traveled more than four and a half times around the world. Maybe *zealous* is an understatement.

In this book, Paul tells about his feelings and adventures during his many miles on the road. The remarkable thing about these runs is not the number of states crossed, not the miles logged, but rather that Paul did most of this running between the ages of 73 and 79.

That sure blasts the stereotype of older citizens belonging in rocking chairs. It is proof positive that people are capable of considerably more physical activity than most believe possible.

A basic lesson to be learned from Paul's achievements is that there is much hope for all of us to lead full and productive lives as we move into our sunset years. Who would think it possible that a person in his 70s could run 296 days without sustaining any injury?

If this has you thinking that Paul is an exception, endowed with super genes, think again. He has been troubled with asthma for 50 years, at age 70 he underwent dozens of radiation treatments for prostate cancer, and he has a back problem called "spondylosis."

There is still controversy over whether or not exercise will help people live *longer*, but there is little doubt that participating in regular physical exercise will help people live *better*.

The message of this book – a message that applies regardless of age – is this: If you want to maintain your zest for life and enjoy life to the fullest, get fit ... and stay fit.

COVERT BAILEY
fitness expert and best-selling author

Prologue

This Don Shepherd is my kind of guy, I kept thinking as I read his book, *My Run Across the USA*. At age 48, he had come all the way from South Africa to attempt a record-breaking run across the United States. The guy had little money, no logistical support or pit crew, no sponsor.

Wearing a T-Shirt, Bermuda shorts and running shoes, and carrying a light backpack, Shepherd simply ran out of Los Angeles on May 12th, 1964, and arrived in New York City a then-record 73 days later. Along the way, he often mooched meals, sometimes slept in barns, occasionally got lost, sometimes endured miserable weather and continually enjoyed himself.

His enjoyment, I might add, wasn't entirely related to running. He dedicated his book to 31 ladies he met along the way, which causes me to add hastily that I have neither the energy nor inclination to identify with him on that score. But I did identify with Shepherd in that I was a late-bloomer as a distance runner, not having come to the sport until age 47. This coincided with my retirement from the Marine Corps, at which time I needed an outlet to compensate for the active life I'd led in the Corps.

At age 55 (which at my present vintage of 79 seems like only yesterday), I read of Shepherd's exciting adventure and thought, "I've got to try this someday." *Someday* was a long time coming because I had to keep working at my civilian job until retirement and couldn't take four months off for a jaunt across the country.

Also I was not about to emulate Shepherd and take off solo. My battle plan called for a pit crew, which meant I had to wait until my wife Elaine retired. When finally we both were free to go, I was blessed that Elaine was willing to go along with my wildness, providing I met two conditions: we buy a new motorhome for the adventure, and she would get a black Labrador puppy after we finished. The motorhome was easier for me to accept than parenthood.

The adventure we called "RUNXUSA" began on April 21st, 1990. We departed the Pacific Ocean at Jenner, California, and headed east, arriving 3192 miles and 124 days later at the Atlantic. At age 73, I became the oldest person to run across the country.

Every one of our days on the road, I wrote in a journal, and by the end of our run this tome reached 400 single-spaced typewritten pages. It was intended as a memento for our family and a few friends.

Luckily for me, the dean of American running writers, Joe Henderson, saw this journal at the home of our mutual friend Pete League. Joe told me, "If this journal were trimmed and toned, I'm sure it could be published."

I knew that revision could be done only by a pro, so I told Joe, "Be my guest." No stranger to challenges, he accepted, and that's how we teamed up to publish the book *Ten Million Steps*.

This brings us to the story behind the book you now hold. The day after I finished RUNXUSA, an editorial appeared in the *Hilton Head Island Packet*, the newspaper of that South Carolina resort community. It ended with the line, "Dare we ask what's next for Reese?"

Even before Elaine and I read that editorial, we had asked ourselves, "Is this the end of it, or are we going to keep doing runs like it?" We knew for sure we wouldn't try crossing the USA again, but we also knew we wanted to continue this sort of exploring on foot and motorhome.

For a year after RUNXUSA, we busied ourselves writing the account of it and catching up on chores around the house after being gone for more than four months. But always on our minds was: What next? Maybe run from Canada to Mexico? How about the length of California, our home state?

Finally we hit upon the idea of running across all the states west of the Mississippi River. We'd already crossed eight of them – California, Nevada, Utah, Colorado, Kansas, Oklahoma, Missouri and Arkansas – on the USA run. This left the other 14: Oregon, Washington, Idaho, Arizona, New Mexico, Wyoming, Montana, Nebraska, Iowa, Texas, Louisiana, South Dakota, Minnesota and North Dakota. (Alaska and Hawaii didn't figure in.)

To limit our time away from home in any one stretch, we programmed these runs over five summers: Oregon in 1992; Idaho, Washington, Arizona and New Mexico in 1993; Wyoming and Montana in 1994; Nebraska and Iowa in 1995; Texas, Louisiana, South Dakota, Minnesota and North Dakota in 1996.

Go East Old Man focuses on our adventures in the Western states. Putting the book together (again teaming up with Joe Henderson), we faced a decision on what to do about the eight states we'd already covered in *Ten Million Steps*. We didn't want to ignore them or repeat the material already published, so we made a third choice: Summarize those early experiences in a fresh chapter of the new book.

Chapter One contains summations of our 1990 runs across California, Nevada, Utah, Colorado, Kansas, Oklahoma, Missouri and Arkansas when running across those states was part of our Grand Design to cross the USA. We put these states first to maintain the chronological order of the running. We combine the eight states into one chapter because the run across them all was continuous. A reader who wants complete accounts will find them in *Ten Million Steps* (which can be ordered from Cedarwinds Publishing, Box 351, Medway, OH 45341; phone 800/548-2388).

Chapters Two through 15 carry day-by-day accounts of our adventures in

Oregon, Idaho, Washington, Arizona, New Mexico, Wyoming, Montana, Nebraska, Iowa, Texas, Louisiana, South Dakota, Minnesota and North Dakota. These reports tell what we saw, felt, experienced and thought as I ran across those 14 states.

What you read here will, I hope, put you in my mind and in my moccasins. After you've finished reading this book, you may ask, "What's next?"

I will say that, God willing, there will be a *next*. At the moment, Elaine and I are kicking around a few ideas – which ties in with our philosophy that one key to aging gracefully is always to have an agenda.

PAUL REESE
Auburn, California
March 1997

Chapter 1

California, Nevada, Utah, Colorado, Kansas, Oklahoma, Missouri, Arkansas:

It All Began Here

California: Off and Running

April 21st to May 1st, 1990 – 260.3 miles

Day	Overnight	Miles	Notes
1	Duncan Mills	5.4	Started RUNXUSA at Jenner
2	Santa Rosa	26.1	began 26-mile-a-day routine
3	Saint Helena	26.2	
4	near Winters	26.9	
5	West Sacramento	26.5	
6	Plymouth	31.0	
7	Sacramento	17.8	ran one segment in High Sierra
8	Plymouth	31.1	started Slice 100-K
9	near Hams Station	31.1	finished Slice 100-K
10	near Woodfords	25.1	crossed Carson Pass in snow, temperature dipped to 22 with winds 40 to 50 MPH

(first 13.2 miles in California on Day 11; last 11.9 in Nevada)

What a relief to finally get this thing underway! That was my dominant thought as I stepped out of the Pacific Ocean at Jenner, California, and headed for the Atlantic, about 3200 miles east by my calculation. The date was April 21st, 1990, and at age 73 I was embarking on a transcontinental run that I had been thinking about for 18 years.

This is the way football players in the Super Bowl must feel at the kickoff, I told myself: relief over finally having the hype end and the game

Word had leaked out about the run, and a couple of reporters wanted to do a preview story. But I refused, saying, "Hey, at this point, I'm merely running with my mouth."

Getting underway, I had reason for more than a little doubt about whether or not I'd ever plant my tootsies in the Atlantic. The perils were many: getting hit by a car, either Elaine or me taking ill, maybe encountering an unfriendly rattlesnake or critter, or possibly some unforeseen incident arising at home and compelling us to return.

Atop all that I wasn't sure of how I would hold up running. In the three months of upping my training for this transcon adventure I had logged no run longer than 15 miles. Now here I was setting out with a battle plan called for running 26 miles a day for 122 consecutive days.

Note the word *consecutive*. I wanted one of the byproducts of this run to be living proof that older people are physically capable of much more than they or others believe possible. I felt that by running every day I would prove this more strongly than if I were to take days off.

While I was jubilant to finally launch, I was not too enthralled with running across California. The entire route was old hat to me, since I had driven over all segments of it numerous times. A sense of adventure was missing, because we already knew what was around the corner and over the next hill.

Our route took us from Jenner on the Pacific through Duncan Mills, Guerneville, Santa Rosa, St. Helena, Winters, West Sacramento, Sacramento, Plymouth, Fiddletown and through Carson Pass along Highway 88 to Nevada. Two hundred sixty miles of familiar territory.

While in high school I had attended summer camps near Duncan Mills and Guerneville, and had logged many miles walking and running in both areas. In the Santa Rosa and St. Helena areas I had run a number of races.

I'd lived in Sacramento many years and knew the area. Plymouth, Fiddletown and Highway 88 were part of the routing for a 166-mile, four-day race Dr. Ralph Paffenbarger and I had romped through together. Besides, Plymouth and Fiddletown were landmarks on a 100-kilometer race Paff and I had run several times. For good reason, then, the luster was off California for me.

But this was not true for my running companion, George Billingsley, a 68-year-old highly regarded ultramarathon runner. For several years George and I had been training together a couple times a week. When I told him about my plans to run across the USA, the temptation was irresistible to him and he wanted to get into the act.

His wife Georgia agreed to pit-crew for him on two conditions: They would buy a motorhome (that sounded familiar), and she would bring along her four cats. George would have agreed had she said she wanted to bring along a baboon.

As for the mere act of running across California, the going was all pretty routine. Its three most distinctive features (apart from our not sustaining any injuries) were George's banter, the camaraderie of other runners as we participated in a 100-kilometer race and some tough sledding through Carson Pass on Highway 88. Let's take those one by one.

George was a good running companion because he was a talker and his talk was usually upbeat. Since the scenery was all too familiar to me, his chatter helped to inject some variety.

When we encountered hills, he said, "I love hills." If there were a mosquito attack, he shouted, "I love mosquitoes." While we ran in rain, he chanted, "I love rain."

The most fun George and I had on the road in California was tied in with a 100-kilometer race, run over two 50-K days. For nine years Hal Stainbrook, Ray Mahannah and I had directed this event. Ralph Paffenbarger and I had run it every year of its existence, and we wanted to do so again this year.

The only way we could manage that, with my being on the road with the USA run, was to tie the race in with our transcon route. This we did with a course that went from Sacramento to Hams Station on Highway 88.

As a sendoff to George and me, many of our veteran 100-K runners showed for the race – speedsters like Jerry Blinn, Roland Martin and Steve Galvan. I enjoyed visiting with them.

It was more fun, though, to have all the young, pretty women runners – Toni Belaustegui, Joan Bumpus, Linda Elam, Joann Hull, Dee McKim and Sharlene Kelley–give me a hug. Hugging a sweaty old man showed the respect they had for a guy running across USA. My God, think of the scenario if I were a handsome young stud!

Seriously, I carried the warmth and good wishes of all these runners with me all through RUNXUSA. I appreciated their gestures of friendship in coming to this 100-K race to wish us well.

In the two days of the 100-K race, we had an uphill climb of more than 4000 feet. But that was a piece of cake compared to what happened the next day, when we fought the fury of the mountains and tasted their majesty.

Until now we had been running in T-shirts and shorts. But we started this day bundled in polypropylene tops and tights, covered with Goretex jackets and pants.

The temperature was 22 degrees, and a strong wind made it feel much colder. This wind persisted all day, gusting to 50 miles per hour at times.

In the miles approaching 8573-foot Carson Pass, we encountered heavy rainfall and were apprehensive that it might turn to snow. This would have made the going dangerous, if not impassable, for the motorhomes. We couldn't allow them to become stranded on the mountain.

George and I had barely reached the summit when light snow began falling. We told Georgia and Elaine, "Drive down as fast as you can safely go. We'll catch up with you below the snow line, no matter how far away that is."

For George and me, going down the mountain was every bit as taxing as going up. Because of the wind and slippery highway we had trouble keeping our feet under us.

When a car approached, we had to plant ourselves and not move to keep from sliding into its path. Luckily, few cars were on the road.

This was undoubtedly our toughest day to date. But despite these difficulties, the beauty of the area wasn't lost on us. El Dorado Forest, Silver Lake and Caples Lake – no matter how many times seen – are always inspiring.

It was also inspiring to me, after the struggle through Carson Pass, to know that we had only a half day and 13 miles left in California. I was ready for a change of scenery.

Nevada: Coldest and Hottest
May 1st to 17th, 1990 – 405.2 miles

Day	Overnight	Miles	Notes
11	Minden	25.1	day's first 13.2 miles in California, last 11.9 in Nevada
12	near Carson City	25.0	George injured
13	Fallon	25.4	first taste of desert
14	Fallon	25.5	
15	east of Fallon	25.0	temperature hit 106
16	west of Frenchman	25.3	adopted earlier starting time
17	west of Cold Springs	25.0	temperature dipped to 25
18	west of Austin	26.1	temperature 20
19	east of Austin	25.4	temperature 10 to 91!
20	east of Eureka	25.1	completed 500 miles, temp. 29
21	near Eureka	26.0	
22	east of Eureka	26.0	temperature 25
23	west of Ely	26.0	temperature 22
24	Ely	25.0	
25	Majors Place	26.2	temperature 26
26	west of Baker Jct.	26.2	temperature 19

(first 10.5 miles in Nevada on Day 27; last 14.5 in Utah)

My first reaction, on stepping into Nevada: Well, finally we've left home. We've cut the umbilical cord to California, my home state.

This was like Joe Montana going from the San Francisco 49ers to the Kansas City Chiefs – no more of same-ol'/same-ol'. Instead, like Montana (and here begging pardon for linking myself with football deity), I was on a new playing field.

This afternoon, after concluding our first day in Nevada, we headed for

Minden to spend the night at an RV park. I thought, "All's well on the Nevada front."

But as I found out the next morning, all was not well here. When the Billingsley's arrived in Genoa to start the day's run, I jumped out of our motorhome, ready to run.

George came over and said, "We've got to talk!"

"Sure," I told him, "we can talk as we go along."

"No, you don't get it," he said. "This is important. We've got to talk *now*." He hit the "now" like a tom-tom beat, so I knew something unusual was cooking.

In short order he related that his shin splints had him in deep trouble. He could barely walk.

He said, "I've given it some serious thought, and I want Elaine and you to go on ahead. I'll try to catch up in a few days if I can."

I told him, "Hey, you're dealing with a Marine, and Marines do not leave their wounded on the battlefield. Somehow I am going to keep tabs on you."

And that's the way it was the next five days, when I did all my running solo. Periodically during each day, Elaine and I would check on George's progress, then at the end of the day we would rendezvous at some camping spot.

I admired George's courage and tenacity for hanging in. Had such an injury befallen me so early in the run, I might have folded my tent.

Both the coldest day (10 degrees) and the hottest day (106 degrees) of RUNXUSA came in Nevada. Gladly, though, would I trade some of the 90-degree-plus days that came later in the South for the 106-degree-desert day.

Highway 50 through Nevada turned out to be a good running route, mainly because it lived up to its billing as "The Loneliest Highway in America." The light traffic was a blessing.

I had not studied the topography and had thought the route would be all flat desert. It came as an unhappy lesson in geography to learn that after we left Fallon we would have to run over eight summits, none less than 6000 feet.

The people we met in Nevada were friendly. People like the gent in his mid-50s, bearded, looking like an outdoor type, who stopped his battered green coupe adorned with the words "Spirit Wolf" to ask if I needed help. Or like the guy from Colorado who parked his car, got out, walked a half-mile with me while briefing me on what to expect in his home state.

Each of the three transcontinental bicyclists I encountered stopped for a chat. I had to admit it was a mite discouraging to hear them tell of covering 100 miles a day, while I'm plugging away at 26.

Even the two Nevada Highway Patrol Officers who stopped to check on me were quite friendly. Neither of them was any good, though, at camouflaging what he was obviously thinking: "This old geezer must be crazy to be out here on the desert running like this."

Maybe the desert sun did get to me a few times. I do recall having a very one-sided conversation with a black mustang as he cavorted nearby and put on a show for me.

Another time I left the highway to trample in the boondocks and run on the actual Pony Express Trail. My thinking was: If there is such a thing as reincarnation and if I were ever a Pony Express rider, it would all come back to me. If not, I'm at least treading on history.

Fallon, Austin, Eureka, Ely, each of the small towns I went through in Nevada left an impression. Fallon, for example, with all its greenery and abundance of water, was like an oasis after we had been on the desert for a few days.

Living on the desert, parked roadside at night (no campgrounds for miles), we had to ration our water. That alone sparked appreciation for the amenities of Fallon. After the barrenness of the desert, this town of 4000 appeared metropolitan to us.

Austin, which perches on the side of a mountain at 6800 feet, is a hamlet of 400 souls – quite a shrinking from the 10,000 it had at the height of the mining boom.

This western town has a personality of its own. I can still visualize Stokes Castle, which sits on the west edge of town. It is a replica of a Roman tower, three or four stories in height and made of hand-hewn granite slabs. I was also impressed with the International Hotel and Cafe, which had been moved from Virginia City to Austin piece by piece.

"You are entering the loneliest town on the loneliest road in America." So read the sign that greeted me as I came into Eureka. More eye-catching were the two red buildings with white trim, one an old three-story hotel and the other a theater.

From Ely, Elaine and I took two pleasant memories. One was of mechanic Bill Sanford who, learning we were on a rigid time schedule, dropped his task at hand and did some delicate wiring to repair the burglar alarm on our motorhome and also aligned the front wheels. The other pleasantry was dinner at the Jailhouse Restaurant where (despite Ely having a population of only 4882) the food, service and setting would rival any big-city restaurant.

George's shin splints stayed with him almost a week. Then about the time they waned, he began to have trouble with a knee on which he had arthroscopic surgery three years before.

Seeing George's stoic behavior and watching him in action, I had little doubt that he would get across the country. I also felt that much of it would be a painful journey.

As we brought down the curtain on Nevada, I did some quick calculating and found that we had spent 15-1/2 days covering 405.2 miles, which meant that we were still on our 26-mile-a-day pace. We were 605.5 miles into the

3200-mile run across the country.

Oh my God, 2595 miles to go! Better not think about that.

Utah: "Sir, Do You Need Help?"

May 17th to 30th, 1990 – 338.5 miles

Day	Overnight	Miles	Notes
27	near Utah border	25.0	day's first 10.5 miles in Nevada, last 14.5 in Utah
28	west of Delta	26.5	
29	west of Delta	26.2	
30	Delta	25.5	
31	near Holden	25.1	RUNXUSA one month old
32	Salina	25.0	
33	east of Salina	25.0	
34	near Emery	26.0	winds 35 to 40 MPH
35	west of Green River	25.0	temperature 29
36	west of Green River	30.5	
37	Green River	25.0	
38	east of Green River	25.1	George found $135
39	near Cisco	26.5	ran in first heavy rain

(first 11.1 miles in Utah on Day 40; last 15.4 in Colorado)

My most lasting impression of Utah centers on the solicitude so many people had for my welfare. Never a day went by without some folks stopping to ask if I needed help.

These were trusting folks too. A young family – mother, father, three girls – in a station wagon stopping in the morning darkness to ask, "Do you want a ride?" A lady with two small children also stopped to ask if I needed help.

Then there was Irish Anderson. He saw us on the road one day and the next day made a 38-mile round trip from his farm just to bring us some fresh asparagus.

On one day alone 13 drivers inquired about my welfare. Of the 21 states I've run across, Utah was an easy winner for extending the most Christian charity.

Another distinct memory from Utah was the heavy rainfall on our last day in the state, the first rain since leaving California. I launched at five o'clock in the morning and ran all day in the rain. After I finished, the motorhome looked like a laundry with my wet running gear hanging all about.

As George and I ran along the highways, we were often surprised with some of the items we found or saw. The three most prevalent items were baby diapers, discarded cassette tapes, and beer cans.

We also found such items as a new bar of Sweetheart soap, a new pair of cellophane-wrapped jockey shorts, combs, new rolls of paper towels, screwdrivers, pliers, knives. But the memorable find was George's discovery of a money clip containing $135.

Our routing in Utah took us through several small towns: Hinkley, Delta (our favorite in this state), Holden, Scipio, Salina and Green River. They were all pleasant, but for some reason none was as personable as the towns we had passed in Nevada.

After about a week in Utah George's problems with shin splints and his knee had virtually disappeared. Most of the way through this state, we ran separately.

While he was mending, we were going at different rates. He prudently exercised caution by taking long pit-stops.

While I ran frontage roads, George preferred freeways. When we did run together, we both marveled over the beautiful desert scenery in Utah, particularly in the area that the Utah Tourist Bureau calls "Panoramaland," and justifiably so.

The bad luck that George had with injuries reminded me to continually assess my injury status. In Utah I seemed to have four potentials: the metatarsal bone on the outside of my left foot, left hip joint, left knee and right groin.

I suspected that the foot and hip could possibly be arthritic. From time to time, each of these injuries was irritating – never debilitating but always a cause for concern.

All told, I decided, I was holding out better than expected. No injury threatened me.

My asthma seemed to be on vacation. In 39 days I had to resort to only one allergy pill.

I felt somewhat tired but also strong. I had weathered one 30-mile day without undue strain, the longest distance since my three 31-mile days in California.

Above all, the morale flag was flying high. Finishing Utah, we had logged 1003 miles – almost a third of the distance to the Atlantic – and all systems were clicking smoothly as we continued to average our 26 miles a day.

Colorado: Climbing to New Heights

May 30th to June 17th, 1990 – 468.1 miles

Day	Overnight	Miles	Notes
40	Fruita	25.5	first 11.1 miles in Utah last 14.4 in Colorado
41	near Grand Junction	25.2	
42	near Delta	25.0	winds 40 MPH-plus
43	near Montrose	26.1	temperature 25
44	Cimarron	25.0	
45	Lake Mesa	27.7	

Day	Overnight	Miles	Notes
46	Parlin	27.8	
47	east of Sargents	23.4	temperature 28
48	Salida	25.0	crossed Continental Divide
49	near Coaldale	25.3	
50	Royal Gorge	25.0	
51	near Penrose	26.4	
52	Pueblo	25.7	
53	Fowler	26.2	parted with George
54	Sugar City	26.0	
55	Haswell	26.1	
56	Eads	26.3	
57	Sheridan Lake	26.1	
58	Tribune, KS	26.4	

(First 15.4 miles in Colorado on Day 59; last 11.1 in Kansas)

My first day in Colorado I felt like I was in Fantasyland. Elaine and I took the advice of a highway maintenance worker and left I-70 to follow old Highway 50 into Fruita, Colorado. Once we got onto old Highway 50, we saw we were in for adventure because we read signs about a hazardous road and no state maintenance. On the 20 miles on this semi-deserted road, we met three cars – one driven by a senior couple who were lost.

It was a thoroughly delightful day for us. We saw abundant wildlife. Elaine could drive slowly down the middle of the road, and I could run alongside the motorhome and visit with her. There was nothing here but the road, the sound of the wind, the motorhome, the birds chirping, the desert and us.

George elected to stay on the Interstate. He said it was shorter and less hilly and, besides, he was not too sure of the old road's condition.

In Mack, on a road leading to I-70, we were surprised to run into George and Georgia. "When I entered Colorado on the Interstate, a sign read 'No pedestrians,' so I got off here," George explained.

Each of the towns we went through in Colorado left an impression of one sort or the other. Mack is typical of so many small towns dying because an Interstate bypassed them.

In Fruita what caught my attention was the number of trees – mainly, I'd guess, because I had not seen any trees for many miles. The town takes its name from the fact that the valley in which it is located has been producing fruit for more than 100 years.

After all the small towns Elaine and I had passed through the past month, Grand Junction was almost overwhelming. The impression we got was "big city," and we got into the spirit by spending time in a shopping mall.

Delta advertises itself as the "City of Murals." My favorite was the one depicting Indians, buffalo and an Indian encampment.

I was impressed with the cleanliness and orderliness of Delta. It reminded me very much of the way small towns used to be before the birth of shopping malls and Interstates.

Going through Montrose, I noticed that the town had a heavy concentration of motels and restaurants. Maybe that was because they were all located on my route.

Gunnison surprised me. I had expected to find it among hills but discovered it was in a flat area. What surprised me more were some of the sophisticated clothing, jewelry and art stores I saw when I took time out to check bookstores for maps and information of Monarch Pass.

Salida boasted that it has the highest concentration of peaks 14,000 feet or more in the continental USA and the fact that it enjoys 300 days of sunshine per year. Hear that, retirees!

What caught my eye the most in Canon City was the state prison which dates back to 1876. I ran through the prison parking lot in order to stay off the busy road.

Pueblo, where the population is 104,000, ranked second to Sacramento, California, as the largest city on our USA route. This is not kind to say, but after seeing Pueblo I feel sorry for every one of the 104,000 souls who inhabit it. Depressing city that it is, Pueblo needs to go back to square one and start over.

The high point in Colorado was literally the highest point of our journey, meaning our romp over Monarch Pass, 11,312 feet. From the outset of our trip, we harbored concern about this pass.

Were the road conditions conducive to running? How would we fare at this elevation? Would the motorhomes have any trouble with the passage?

All my efforts to get detailed advance information failed. So we were flying by the seat of our pants.

The highway up Monarch Pass from the west had no bike lane. But there was a shoulder of gravel approximately three feet wide.

The going was easier than anticipated, except for one problem which occurred at least a half-dozen times. Whenever the road made a sharp bend, the shoulder narrowed to 12 inches between the rocky mountain and the very edge of the highway. I had to pussyfoot around the corner and be ready to instantly embrace the rocky cliff if a car was approaching.

The climb itself, George and I agreed, was surprisingly easy. We celebrated at the crest by visiting the gift shop and buying some silly gifts.

The scariest incident that I experienced since leaving California happened on our third day in Colorado. I was rounding a corner on a ledge with a 150- to 200-foot dropoff. The road had absolutely no shoulder, only a foot or so of road edging.

The wind was blowing 40 to 50 miles per hour, pushing me all over the road. I saw two semi trucks approaching. They couldn't move over because cars were in the fast lane.

I was already having trouble staying on the road because of the wind. The force of these semis passing by would most likely push me over the edge of the road and into the dropoff.

Sizing up the situation, I realized that an instant decision was in order. I dived for the edge of the road and hugged the ground there next to the ledge in order to be off the road and to nullify the blowing by the trucks.

Seeing all this, the truck drivers gave me what few inches they could. The trucks passed perilously close, and I heard the deafening thrump of the tires and felt their warmth.

Shaking from the experience, I scrambled up and ran 50 yards down the road to the safety of a guardrail. After I ridded myself of the heebie-jeebies and regained my composure, I again headed down the road, thanking God I was still numbered among the living.

In Colorado George decided he wanted to shorten the time of the USA run by cutting the distance, this by taking more direct routes than some of the back roads Elaine and I had charted. He pointed out that his routing would save at least 165 miles, or about 6-1/2 days at our 26-mile-per-day rate.

George said, "By the combination of taking direct and major highways, and by extending my day a few hours, I can finish several days earlier. I need to get home to manage some business affairs, and Georgia misses her grandchildren."

Elaine and I took a different approach. We favored the quiet back roads, and we were in no particular hurry to finish.

George and I parted on the morning of our 53rd day. I understood why he wanted to accelerate, and he understood why I wanted to stick with the planned route, so we went our separate ways at Pueblo, Colorado. (He did indeed accelerate, finishing a week ahead of me.)

Exiting Colorado, I had come 1471.1 miles since stepping out of the Pacific in California. As I entered Kansas, the West was behind me ... for now.

Kansas: Midway Through RUNXUSA
June 17th to July 6th, 1990 – 499.9 miles

Day	Overnight	Miles	Notes
59	Leoti	26.1	completed 1500 miles
60	Lake Scott	26.5	
61	Amy	26.3	
63	near Kalvesta	26.5	RUNXUSA 2 months old
64	Dodge City	26.2	
65	Ford	26.1	
66	Greensburg	26.3	temperature hit 100
67	Coldwater Lake	26.4	temperature 101

Day	Overnight	Miles	Notes
68	Medicine Lodge	26.2	temperature 100
69	Attica	26.3	temperature 102, winds 35-40
70	Anthony	26.1	
71	Caldwell	26.2	
72	Arkansas City	26.1	
73	Cedar Vale	26.3	
74	Chautauqua	26.2	temperature 103
75	Caney	26.1	temperature 100
76	Coffeyville	26.2	temperature 102

(first 16.2 miles in Kansas on Day 77; last 10.0 in Oklahoma)

Kansas was an ocean of wheat and corn fields. The only variance in this oceanic setting came on one of the 20 or so occasions when I passed through a small town or city along the route. Kansas went on for 19 days, 499.9 miles and at times I wondered, "Will Kansas ever end?"

The dominant impression I took away from Kansas was a reaffirmation of an opinion I had formed – this back in 1958-61, when I spent three years on the staff of the University of Missouri in Columbia, Missouri – about the character of Americans who populate the Midwest. These are caring people, people of solid values, people of good moral fiber and people who pay more than lip service to "love thy neighbor."

As I plodded through the state, many times I found myself wishing that I could say nice things about the state's roads just as I had about its citizenry. Truth was, if I were to compare the state's roads with some citizenry, and be honest about it, the comparison would be with some notorious skid row.

The state highways were narrow and without bike or breakdown lanes. Trying to find better road conditions for running, Elaine and I sought out back roads. Unfortunately they existed for only a short distance of our route.

In addition to the roads, I ran into two other problems in Kansas. One was flies that bit with a vengeance.

Elaine ran into the same problem. "They're biting unmercifully," she complained.

Best I could do was to say, "Welcome to the club."

We tried two repellents, Off and Cutter's, and they were about as effective as a .22-caliber gun against a tank. We did have some success using Avon bath oil.

A second problem came about when my feet, responding to heavy mileage, swelled to the point where my shoes no longer fit. My only recourse was to cut the toes out of my shoes and to make a couple desperate phone calls to order bigger shoes.

I am lucky in being able to manage heat. Otherwise the seven days over 100 degrees could have been a problem.

Being in Kansas during harvesting season, we were treated several times to watching harvesting crews at work. Usually we'd see three threshers, two trucks and a pickup drive into the field, line up in their harvesting formation and begin the operation. Their teamwork was precise with no wasted time or motion.

Another farming operation Elaine and I became well aware of because of the noise was the irrigation system. The first time I heard the noise, it sounded like the prop noise of an old airplane, a noise heard from a half-mile away. We soon learned that the noise came from big V-8 engines that operated water pumps.

One farmer told us, "It's a noise we live with, because it brings the water that we need to make a living out here."

Of all the Kansas cities we passed through, Tribune won our award as being the most impressive and pleasant. It was clean, well-managed, and had several very nice homes and every service we could require – except an RV park. Like all the small towns, its location was signaled by a water tower, grain elevators and a grove of trees.

One of the disappointments with Kansas towns was that few of them had any RV parks. Leoti was a good example. Here the temperature was 96 degrees (quite warmish in a motorhome!), and the best we could do was overnight under a shady tree by the high school.

With the exception of the hamlet of Horace, all the towns were neat in appearance. Horace, though, looked like it was once hit by a tornado and the folks there subsequently neglected to clean it up.

Cimarron brought back memories. I could recall seeing Richard Dix in a movie by that name, a recollection dug up from the distant past. A guy has to have been around quite a while to know who Richard Dix was.

I left Cimarron with a couple of lasting impressions: Never saw so many trees anyplace else in Kansas, and judging from all the unlocked cars and bicycles on front yards, folks hereabouts must be honest. I left wishing I had time to explore the Cimarron Hotel, established in 1886, and Clark's Pharmacy with its old-fashioned soda fountain characteristic of drugstores of my youth.

We appreciated Medicine Lodge on a couple of counts. The town had a comfortable RV park, and dinner at the Hereford House was a treat and at price hard to beat.

For $4.75 we had a salad bar, chicken fried steak, mashed potatoes and gravy, and toast. My iced tea, cheerfully refilled, was 40 cents.

We even played tourist long enough to visit the home of Carrie Nation, now preserved as a museum. Brought back memories of the sign in some bars in her day: "All nations welcome except Carrie."

Oh, if that's not clear, she was an active prohibitionist. By active I mean that, with ax in hand, she liked to invade bars and start chopping!

One of the biggest cities en route was Arkansas City (population 13,201), often called "Ark City" by the natives. Having been in the boondocks so long, we found the place overwhelming in size.

In the town of Caldwell, while searching for an RV hookup, we ran into a unique situation. No RV parks about, but we were referred to a private home where, for $10, the owner hooked us up to electricity and water. That was a once-and-only.

Coffeyville was distinctive for several reasons. For one thing, population 15,000, it was the biggest city on our Kansas route.

Another distinction: When the people at the city park where we were overnighting heard about our run, they wowed us by saying, "We're pleased that you decided to stay here. We can't charge you."

Also distinctive was a reporter showing up to write a story about our run, the first such story in 2-1/2 months on the road. The reporter was Gretchen Pippenger, a graduate of the Journalism School of the University of Kansas.

Going across the state, we had a number of people encounters. On one of the 100-plus-degree days 13 drivers stopped to check on me.

The usual remark was, "It's kind of hot out here. Sure you're okay?"

Frazzled as I looked, I got the impression some of them might think I was a fugitive from Shady Pines Rest Home.

One encounter came when I was leaning against some mailboxes tying a shoe. The mail carrier drove up, saw my "RUNXUSA" T-shirt and commented, "RUNXUSA? You're too old to be doing that!"

My reaction, unspoken: Them's fighting words, partner, and they'll carry me another 500 miles!

The most interesting encounter was with a farmer in a pickup who pulled up alongside me and asked how old I was. After I told him, he said he was 83 and that for the past 29 years he's had a prosthetic hip joint that has given him no trouble.

He went on to say that he and his children still own much of this land.

A couple of the encounters were mildly amusing. A lady in a rather large car stopped to ask, "Are you just out hiking?"

Ye gods, lady, I'd rather be hiking on the Matterhorn than on this narrow-gauge road, I thought. Politely, I briefed her on our mission. After she drove away, I had the feeling she didn't get it.

The second incident happened when a woman driving a Cadillac with Oklahoma plates stopped and asked me if the motorhome a ways back was mine. When I said it was, she asked, "Are you interested in selling it?"

Lady, I'm thinking, you could have that Cadillac stuffed with money and it wouldn't be enough to buy my lifeline to the Atlantic. Her surprise question left me so flabbergasted that I was wordless, just shook my head to signify, no, not interested.

With 1970 miles logged after leaving Kansas, I have come to a major conclusion about a long trek like this: A runner has to take the ups and downs and work around them. But the psyche should remain constant. By that, I mean upbeat.

An upbeat thought: After finishing Kansas we had 1970 miles completed. Another 1222 and we would be splashing in the Atlantic at Hilton Head Island, South Carolina. Mission accomplished!

Oklahoma: At Least the Dogs Were Friendly!

July 6th to 8th – 44.0 miles

Day	Overnight	Miles	Notes
77	Miami	26.2	first 16.1 in Kansas, last 10 in Oklahoma
78	Miami	26.1	completed 2000 miles

(first 7.9 miles in Oklahoma on Day 79; last 18.2 in Missouri)

As if to perform a geographical balancing act, we immediately followed our longest-mileage state (Kansas, 499.9 miles), with our shortest (Oklahoma, 44 miles). We were merely cutting across a corner of this state to get from Kansas to Missouri.

In past trips to Oklahoma I'd enjoyed visits to Tulsa and Oklahoma City, but on this foot crossing naught did I find to enjoy. The best part of Oklahoma was that I had to endure only two days there.

In my last half-dozen miles in Kansas I got two offers of help, more than the total I got in some states I've run across. Not so with Oklahoma; no offers of help.

After we crossed into Oklahoma we saw nothing but farms until we came to the town of Welch. Approaching Welch, I followed a habit born of Kansas and looked for the water tower and grain elevator signaling the town's location. Neither appeared, a reminder that we weren't in Kansas anymore.

I did not escape Oklahoma without a dog incident. But this was a friendly encounter that started when an Australian Shepherd charged out toward me from a farm.

I yelled to the nearby farmer, "Is he friendly?" and the farmer nodded yes. Not bothering to brake, the dog jumped on me, wanting to be petted and wrestled.

Each time he pounced on me, I was knocked back a foot or two, and marveled at his strength. A veritable Sherman tank, he was having a ball, and I was almost getting killed with affection.

I also didn't escape Oklahoma without getting attacked by some flies with nasty bites and dispositions. Apparently they were after any blood the mosquitoes neglected to get.

Near Miami (talking Oklahoma here, not Florida) the traffic was so thick that I made a career of jumping into the weeds. Here, as throughout the state, not a single driver gave me any consideration.

As I waded through the weeds, I muttered at the primitive highway conditions. Could it be that too much of the Oklahoma tax money goes into the Sooner football program?

I was ticked with the Oklahoma drivers because they were the most inconsiderate and discourteous I've encountered in the 2000 miles so far. The traffic, drivers and road conditions made Oklahoma stressful for Elaine too.

On the plus side I went past many farmhouses, and dozens of dogs barked at me. But not one left the property line to pursue me.

Oklahoma's dogs are well-trained and disciplined. I wish I could say the same for its drivers. We were more than glad to exit Oklahoma and enter Missouri.

Missouri: A Stroll Down Memory Lane

July 8th to 14th – 169.3 miles

Day	Overnight	Miles	Notes
79	Neosho	26.6	first 7.9 in Oklahoma, last 18.7 in Missouri
80	near Cassville	26.2	
81	Cape Fair	26.6	
82	Walnut Shade	26.2	
83	near Theodosia	26.2	
84	Bull Shoals Lake	26.2	

(first 19.2 mile in Missouri on Day 84; last 7.0 in Arkansas)

Missouri was somewhat of a homecoming for me. Returning to the state for the first time since 1961 conjured up memories of the three years I spent there as an associate professor at the University of Missouri while serving as executive officer of the Naval Reserve Officers Training Corps (NROTC).

I had not been in Missouri very long when I noticed a difference here from the rural areas in Kansas. In Missouri I was seeing 10 houses for every one I saw in Kansas.

In Missouri I also was not seeing any high-powered farm equipment on the farms like that I had seen in Kansas. The conclusion: larger holdings, more affluence in Kansas.

During the six days in Missouri I had only one unpleasant experience. I was going past a black pickup parked beside the road when the driver beckoned to me like a teacher motioning to an elementary student.

"I have a complaint about you jumping in front of a gravel truck," he announced.

Seeing the radar on his dashboard, I asked if he was a police officer and got confirmation. I was irked – first because of his motioning to me as if I were a child; second because the report was stupid (I crossed the road safely to escape the gravel the truck was spewing); third because this guy was flaunting his authority, Mr. Superior.

Exercising remarkable restraint, I listened to him lecture me that "this is not a good road to jog on," then dismiss me by saying, "You may leave now."

Leaving, I suspected this clown was from the local sheriff's department and not the Missouri Highway Patrol. The Patrol has more class than that. The guy left me so sizzling that I pumped enough adrenalin to ease through the rest of the day.

Offsetting this was a light-hearted incident. It started when I felt something licking my ankle, looked down and saw a little Welsh Terrier. Afraid a car might hit him, I picked him up and carried him back to his home, a quarter-mile lugging a pooch – not once but twice because he had a mind of his own and was intent on accompanying me, which he wound up doing.

When the two of us came upon Elaine at a pit stop, I told her, "Meet Mr. McGillicuddy. The guy loves me. I can't shake him."

We devised a plan to jettison him, and it worked. When Elaine took a piece of meatloaf to the rear of the motorhome to distract him, I sneaked out the front and down the highway. I prayed that the elegant little gentleman would made it home safely on the highway, and I had to admit I missed his company.

In all the cities I passed through – Neosho, Cape Fair, Reed Springs, Walnut Shade, Bull Shoals – the most impressive sight was a luxury home in the middle of Reed Springs, a town that gave the impression of being an overgrown concession stand. One of the distinctive features of the home was its high metal fences, designed so that a team of German Shepherds – I saw four of them on duty – could patrol.

A second feature was a huge waterfall design with an enormous eagle ornament sitting atop it. Also evident were surveillance cameras. All of which made me wonder: What retired Mafia man lives here?

As I went through Missouri, the opinion I formed of the rural folks during the three years I lived there was reinforced. They are sturdy people, they can weather a storm, their basic values are good, and they are people of character.

As I crossed a long bridge over Bull Shoals Lake, out popped the humorous thought that a transcon run could be enlivened with the requirement that the runner swim all bodies of water encountered. Crossing the country my way is taxing enough, thank you.

On that score somebody recently asked, "Do you ever think about quitting?"

I simply replied, "Not yet, at least." Truth of the matter is, the only stopper would be if I could not move forward. That includes moving on crutches if necessary.

Around the time we had logged the first 1000 miles, I asked Elaine, "What would you do if I said I was going to quit?"

She answered, "You mean because you were ill or injured?"

"No," I said, "just tired of running."

Her reply: I'd kick your butt out the door and tell you to get running." Hey, that's my kind of girl!

Arkansas: Into the South
July 14th to 23rd, 1990 – 238.9 miles

Day	Overnight	Miles	Notes
85	Lakeview	26.2	first 19.2 in Missouri, last 7.0 in Arkansas
86	Norfolk Dam	26.3	temperature hit 103
87	Melbourne	26.5	
88	Batesville	26.2	
89	near Newport	26.1	
90	near McCrory	26.2	
91	near Brinkley	26.3	
92	Clarendon	26.6	RUNXUSA 3 months old
93	Helena	26.3	crossed Mississippi

(first 21.4 miles in Arkansas on Day 94; last 5.0 in Mississippi)

Arkansas had significance at both beginning and ending. Beginning, we started a trek through the South that would finish at Hilton Head Island, South Carolina. Ending and exiting Arkansas, we would cross the Mississippi River at Helena.

I drew few lasting impressions from the 10 or so Arkansas towns I passed through. In Mountain Home I thought it somewhat unbelievable when I went past a furniture store at 7:07 A.M. and, although the store was closed, 20 or more new outdoor furniture pieces sat on the sidewalk in front and no security evident. What gives – honest citizens or an efficient police force?

We took away two favorable impressions from Melbourne. When Elaine stopped to buy propane and told the owner about our run, he refused payment. When we inquired at City Hall (one small room, one desk) about RV hookups, we were told only water and parking were available, but to make ourselves at home under the water tower in the city park.

Our evaluation of Cotton Plant was that in all our travels we've never seen such a dilapidated town. There were about 15 storefronts on each side of the main street, and all were in various stages of deterioration, vandalism and abandonment.

One thought on my mind these days was that running across the USA is a pass-or-fail course. You make it, or you don't. There's always the anxiety that some latent injury or some illness will pop out to stop you.

In Arkansas, as in some other states, I've harbored the urge to take a day off and rest. But I don't for three reasons:

1. It would skew the physiological test of what a 73-year-old can or can't do.

2. It would take some of the challenge out of the enterprise.

3. If I did skip a day, I might have a helluva time restarting. Rest could be habit-forming.

Our most memorable experience in Arkansas was crossing the Mississippi River at Helena. The bridge was under construction and, by prior arrangement, the police were scheduled to provide an escort. However, they got tied up in court, so Elaine and I were on our own.

Arriving at the bridge and seeing no cars approaching from the left lane, I busted my butt running the hill and got two-thirds of the way before the first cars appeared. I stopped, hugged the bridge rail and waited until they passed.

I ran again until reaching a 12-inch ledge – almost a sidewalk – that ran the length of the center span. I then ran on the road whenever possible and jumped to the ledge as cars drew close.

After the last car went through the stoplight at the end of the bridge, I took off as fast as I could before the light turned loose another flock of cars, an all-out effort that cost me dearly as the miles mounted later in the day. But I was triumphant, reaching Mississippi unscathed.

Only 800 miles to go now. At one time I would have regarded 800 miles as frightening, but this point the thought of running this distance did not faze me at all. Good Lord, maybe I've been out here too long!

Overview of
OREGON

September 2nd to 15th, 1992
296.9 miles

Day	Overnight	Miles	Notes
1	near Midland	9.2	start at 4000 feet elevation; sudden decision to run nonstop in Oregon, no walking
2	Hagelstein Co. Park	22.4	through Klamath Falls
3	Collier State Park	22.0	good-bye to Klamath Lake
4	Klamath Forest	22.5	first wildlife seen in Oregon
5	Klamath Forest	22.5	through Chemult
6	south of La Pine	22.8	through Crescent and Gilchrist
7	Bend	23.4	through LaPine
8	south of Redmond	23.1	through Bend
9	Culver	22.6	through Redmond
10	north of Madras	22.5	through Madras
11	Shaniko	23.0	ghost town of Shaniko
12	Grass Valley	22.5	passed 45th parallel
13	Moro	22.1	morning temperature 20
14	Culver	16.4	rainy finish at 350 feet elevation

Chapter 2

Oregon:

On the Road Again

Thoughts on driving to the start for Day One: As I start this run through Oregon, I can't help but note the already readily apparent contrasts between this run and the 3192-mile run I made across the USA in 1990. Maybe the most apparent contrast is the presence of our two Labradors, Rebel and Brudder. In our 1990 run Elaine and I were alone in the motorhome. Now we have two 90-pound hunks who are boldly claiming their share of real estate within the already tight quarters of the 20-foot motorhome.

Another obvious contrast – this one by absence rather than presence – is that George Billingsley, who ran the first 1300 miles of USA with me, is not along this trip. When we made the USA run, George's wife, Georgia, brought along her four cats. These days she has nine cats. Could be a reason they aren't here this time. Or it could be that back in 1990 George was a mere kid of 68. Now that he's 70, maybe he's shedding a few wild hairs.

Another contrast is the routing. Going across the country, Elaine and I studiously plotted a course that took us on backroads and avoided metropolitan areas, even though this added mileage.

However, with Oregon our schedule allows only 15 days to get across the state and that means I have to take a route of no more than 300 miles at 20 miles per day. Luckily that is exactly the distance across Oregon, California border to Washington border, on Highway 97. So we'll have no navigational problems – simply follow 97 all the way.

There's a contrast too in the mileage backgrounds that I brought to the runs. Starting RUNXUSA, I had a 13-mile daily average for the preceding month. Starting Oregon, my average for the previous month is six miles. That should prove interesting.

DAY ONE. Our battle plan called for Elaine, me, the trusty Mallard motorhome, with Labradors Rebel and Brudder also embarked, to arrive near the California-Oregon border today and to begin running tomorrow, northward on Highway 97 through Oregon. The strategy called for covering 20 miles a day, arriving at the Washington border in 15 days.

Our plans went down the tubes when we arrived at the border around 2:30 in the afternoon and, itchy-footed, I decided to sneak in a few miles early. Good equity, I told myself, in case of rain or other possible setbacks.

Actually this was the second change in our battle plan, because my original intent had been to run Highway 97 from north to south. That was before I received this enlightening information from Warren Richards.

He said, "The elevation at the California border is nearly 4000 feet higher than at Biggs near the Washington border. Running from south to north would obviously involve less climbing of grades." Mr. Richards is an operations support engineer with the Oregon Department of Transportation. Bless the man for pointing me to the downhill route!

From the California border to the Oregon Tourist Information Center the distance was only 9.2 miles. But we decided to spend the night at the Center because we were told that we could stay parked for as long as 18 hours.

Good deal in an attractive area with water, lawns and restrooms. The price, gratis, was right too.

DAY TWO. We did not start bright eyed and bushy tailed because our sleep last night was sabotaged a number of ways. For one, the trucks parked at the Tourist Center kept their generators running. Sounded like a cluster of washing machines in motion.

Secondly, on the tracks paralleling the highway a train went past so thunderously loud it sounded as if a volcano were erupting. For sure, Brudder and Rebel erupted with blood-curdling barking.

Around midnight, it rained heavily, followed by hail the size of marbles, bouncing off the motorhome and creating an infernal racket. Then about four A.M., the early travelers began stirring, noisily completed their preparations, and launched from the Center.

After that, Brudder and Rebel went into their, "It's time for breakfast ritual," so Elaine and I suited up for another day. By five o'clock, I finished breakfast and my ablutions, and was geared to run.

But as I looked out and saw pitch dark and a heavy tule fog, I said, "No way. We will wait for a civilized hour."

By 6:30 today the fog had lifted somewhat, so I had no excuse for not starting. Soon afterward I saw, barely distinguishable through the fog, a sign telling me Klamath Falls was eight miles away. I wondered what adventure would running through Klamath Falls bring. Because the breakdown lane was half the size of yesterday's and because the fog was hanging, I stepped off the road onto the gravel when cars approached. Unlike Alan Seeger I do not have a rendezvous with death. On second thought that's not quite right. I have one but just don't want it to be here and now.

Many a time I've smiled at the thought that the race through life is the only race I'll finish faster than I want to. Most of us cross the Great Finish Line too soon, or sooner than we'd prefer. Could be a sign that we're living a fairly happy life.

Going through Klamath Falls, a city of 18,000, I encountered a lady out with her small dog. It was the size of an overgrown jackrabbit.

I told her, "It looks like a miniature Doberman."

She replied, "Well, to be technical, it's a Manchester Terrier." That's what she said, but her tone was more to the effect, "Idiot, if you had any smarts, you would know what this dog is."

She further contributed to my canine education by adding, "This type of dog was originally bred to control rodents."

Out of Klamath Falls, when I came to a new bridge under construction, I asked the foreman of the project, "Is it okay for me to run on this?"

After appraising my vintage body, he replied, "Well, you can walk across it but don't run – and be careful."

After I took a look at the many reinforcing steel rods protruding in all directions, I concluded he was right. Even a Kenyan steeplechaser would hesitate to run through this maze.

The railroad tracks that parallel Highway 97 and go along Klamath Lake resurrected memories of an Amtrak trip Elaine and I once took from Sacramento to Portland where I ran the Portland Marathon. We boarded the train in Sacramento, and, with two suitcases in hand, headed for our roomette.

The attendant suggested, "You might want to leave those suitcases in the storage area below."

"No, we'll take them to the roomette," we replied.

"Are you sure about that?" he asked.

Elaine and I nodded affirmatively, and the attendant answered only with a broad smile. We knew why when we saw an Amtrak roomette for the first time. The two bunks were made up, since it was 11:30 P.M., time to go to bed. As we went into the roomette, we immediately discovered there was less than 18 inches of space between the edge of the bunks and the roomette door, and no space for storing the suitcases.

After looking around, laughing, then conferring, Elaine and I decided, "Retreat, hell! We'll stack the suitcases on the top bunk and sleep on the bottom bunk." Kind of a cozy evening, I might add.

After finishing today, we were lucky enough to find our-selves only three miles from Hagelstein Park that has restrooms, camping spots (without hookups), pleasant grassy surroundings and a small lake. All this for $5.

For Brudder and Rebel, the event of the day was swimming in the small park lake. Of course, it would have been enhanced if we had turned them loose to pursue some of the ducks and geese inhabiting the lake.

When we went to bed, my mood was upbeat. "Cheez, no sweat, no pain, and I've already completed more than one-tenth of this trip." Piece of cake.

DAY THREE. The scene as I started this morning, under an umbrella of overhanging dark clouds, was the railroad track to the west and beyond that, Upper Klamath Lake. Eastward was a small mountain range.

I was not the only one stirring this early hour. The shores of Klamath Lake were lined with white and gray cranes eyeing the water for breakfast. Klamath Lake, I'm told, is the second largest body of fresh water west of the Rockies.

At my first two pit-stops, I brought surprises for Elaine. The first was a Swiss Army knife that I found on the roadside. It was practically new, in excellent condition with the blade out when I found it.

While I'm always glad to find such goodies, at the same time I feel some remorse for the person who lost them. Elaine was delighted with this find, to the point where she confiscated it.

My other find was a pair of pliers. When I handed them to Elaine, she paraphrased Stanley, saying, "Dr. Paffenbarger, I presume."

She was referring to our good friend Dr. Ralph Paffenbarger. On our ultraruns Paff cannot resist picking up any gems (defined as nuts, bolts, screw drivers, etc.) that he spies on the road.

When I came to the junction of Highway 62, leading west to Crater Lake, I was reminded of the two times I ran the demanding marathon there (about 7500 feet elevation, if I recall correctly). Elaine's favorite pastime there was to stay awake in the tent and watch for bears foraging in the campground. One night she witnessed one tearing apart a plastic water bottle we'd left on our picnic table.

One of the best laughs I had there was the night a guy left the restroom and was headed back to his tent, at which time he suddenly discovered he was being trailed by a black bear. Not sure of what to do, he started singing, just making up words. "There's a bear following me. Make some noise. Noise, noise, noise. Bang something. Distract this bear. Help if you can hear me. There's a bear following me ... "

Luckily he was carrying no food, which would have brought on a bear encounter. The bear was on a food mission and continued on its way when the man turned into the campground. By then the man was ready for another trip to the rest room.

I scored a first today. My jock strap had been chafing me for quite a while, and the rawness it caused had become so uncomfortable that I decided it was time for action.

Leaving the road, I went into the woods, hid behind a tree and took the damn thing off. As I threw it away, I wondered how some varmint would react when stumbling across it. That's a scene I would like to see played out.

After I finished, we backtracked to Collier State Park to spend the night. For $13 we had a RV hookup and the shower was so clean it could have passed Marine Corps inspection.

The California State Park system could take a lesson here. In the first place it charges $16 just to pitch a tent. Secondly very few of its parks have RV hookups. And finally their restrooms would fail any inspection.

Something is amiss in my home state. Calls for an investigation!

DAY FOUR. Today I continued with two experiments, neither of which I did on RUNXUSA. Every day I change brands and models of shoes. This time I tried the Nike Air Pegasus, and that resulted in a shoe mystery.

Yesterday when I wore the Saucony shoes, my feet hurt as they pounded the corrugated road. Today, same type of road with the Nike Air Pegasus, my feet did not hurt. Ironically these conditions should be reversed because the Saucony model is a training shoe and the Nike model, a racing shoe.

My other experiment is trying to see if I can run the entire distance without any walking. Actually what this amounts to is that I run from one pit-stop to the next, three miles away, then docking for grub and grog before running to the next stop. The amount of revigoration that comes with the pit-stop is amazing. As I do my intervals, I am not pooped, whereas if I were running a continuous 22 miles, no pit-stops, I would be enervated.

Four days into this I am now getting the feeling that I just might be able to run across the entire state. When I started, I thought I'd be lucky to make 100 miles before I introduced some walking.

A shaky experience early in today's run. A semi truck passing a car edged near the fog line which I was hugging. The noise, wind swishing and nearness of the truck were frightening. My guess was that the truck driver did not see me. Well, one thing for sure: If hit by a semi, I'd have no painful lingering moments before crossing the Great Finish Line of Life. The feeling was like having a house pass by in a tornado. The experience spooked me all day, and I stayed tuned for vehicles approaching me from the rear.

Today Highway 97 was a concrete carpet through a forest, and since I was on the outer edge of this carpet, almost against the forest, I was not too visible to motorists. Actually, though, given the bike lane, I considered the running conditions about as good as they get for a main thoroughfare.

In stark contrast to the lush green forest that I ran through most of the day, I passed through two areas of desolation. One was a half-mile or so of carnage, not a tree standing, just stumps and branches, rape of a forest. Enough to drive the Sierra Club up a tree if there were any standing here.

The other depressing sight was the scarred remnants of a forest fire. The area, about a mile in length, was blackened ground and charred pine trees, looking more like posts than trees. Seeing all the adjacent forest, I was left wondering how the fire was ever contained.

Early in the day, I decided that when I finished today's run I wanted a fried egg sandwich. Where that idea was born, I don't know, especially since fried eggs sandwiches are rarely on my menu. But today we were talking about a *must*, which brought up this thought: What would a psychiatrist do with material like this?

Another wild thought as I ran along: When I return home, I am going to suggest to Abe Underwood and Dennis Scott, race coordinators for the Buffalo Chips Running Club (with more than 500 members) they consider organizing a race across Oregon on Highway 97 for interested club members.

Sure, American pioneer spirit at low ebb, they'll probably get only 10 or so adventurous souls. But these runners would harbor the experience for a lifetime. I'll suggest to Abe and Dennis that they extend the race over 10 days, say 30 miles a day. Just far enough to be a challenge, just short enough to be achievable.

Time now to report on some of the snacks Elaine has been feeding me at pit-stops: oatmeal cookies and peanut Kudo bars, pork and beans, spaghetti, rice pudding, pudding over peaches or bananas, jello and cookies, peanut butter and jelly sandwiches, turkey sandwiches. I've been sticking with two drinks: ice tea and Koolaid.

I seem to thrive on this refueling every three miles. Immediately after eating and drinking, I am back on the road running, and since I am doing only a 12-minute mile there is no problem with this digestively. I have yet to lose any weight.

Since there were no RV parks anywhere in the vicinity, we again overnighted in the forest. Brudder and Rebel exhausted themselves exploring the real estate bordering the motorhome. Elaine tells me how much she is enjoying the company of "my boys."

DAY FIVE. My thought, as I came to the junction of Highway 138 and saw a motel, cafe and gas station: That's a heap of civilization compared to what I have been seeing. Everything's relative, I guess, because when I came to Beaver Marsh and found a motel, gas station, deli market, cafe and RV park, I considered it almost metropolitan.

But the topper was when I rounded a corner, entered Chemult and saw two blocks – two entire blocks – of business district. Half a dozen gas stations, motels, a hardware store, markets and a restaurant. I was overwhelmed. As I ran through the city, I was asking myself, What's different with this city from all the small southern towns I ran through a couple of years ago? What's missing?

Then it hit me. Not a church did I see here, whereas in the South I would have seen three or four.

Elaine was elated with her logistical successes today. At Beaver Marsh deli she was able to buy lettuce and tomatoes. At a rest area she was able to fill the motorhome with water. At Chemult she was able to buy propane. Such is life on the road.

I was startled when I saw the name on the mailbox: Russell Simpson. It opened a floodgate of memories of World War II, particularly Bougainville. Russell Simpson, a member of my intelligence section, was killed there.

When we landed on Bougainville, half of the section was on one APD (a destroyer modified to transport troops) and the other half was on another APD. The APD Russ was on was hit with a torpedo bomb, and several Marine and Navy personnel on it, including Russ, were killed. He was only 18, an upbeat kid who loved sports and the Corps.

Oh God, the memories of Bougainville:

• That first night when daisy cutters (anti-personnel mines) from a Japanese plane landed 20 yards or so from my foxhole and killed a dozen of my comrades.

• The boldness of the operation, simply going in, establishing a perimeter, building an airfield within it, with a Japanese force four or five times as large as ours barely 50 land miles away.

• One patrol, where so intent on following an azimuth, that I misjudged distance and went twice as far as ordered. Scary when I realized how far out we were, the danger of being hit by our own artillery and aircraft as much as being hit by the Japanese.

• The screaming of a fellow Marine officer through most of the night. He'd been captured by the Japanese who, at nightfall, placed him on their side of the river, tortured him, hoping to induce Marines to cross the river into their lanes of fire at night. Next morning, the Marines did cross the river, found the officer tied to a tree with a bayonet up his rectum.

• On a jungle path, going by the aftermath of a battle and seeing dead bodies blackened by the jungle weather, bodies with hordes of maggots crawling out of eye sockets and ears. Welcome to war!

• Rain, jungle rot and itching, 45 nights of sleeping on the damp, sandy soil of a foxhole.

• Malaria for the third time. I was evacuated to a med center in the rear and given a cot in a tent. The luxury of that cot, along with an increased dose of atabrine, was the treatment.

Since I did not test malaria-infected the first day, the young corpsman said, "You know, I doubt if you have malaria." I marveled at my patience in explaining to him that malaria was tertiary and that it would show within the next couple of days. On day three, it did show and on day three I was out of there and back to friends in my unit.

When we were evacuated, our trip back to base camp at Guadalcanal was sheer luxury. We were clean, out of the daily downpours of Bougainville, dry, fed, and survivors. And we were laden with memories that would forever linger. Not the least of which was of Russ Simpson whose body was never found. When I visualize him, I still see his infectious, somewhat mischievous smile. Dead at 18. Shit.

As I finished today – with a cumulative total of 98.5 miles in Oregon – I thought, Already I'm about one-third through this trek. It's a cakewalk compared to 124 days across America afoot.

DAY SIX. By now Brudder and Rebel have worked out a routine. About 4 A.M., they start stirring.

First they stretch, then they shake violently, rattling dog tags and generating enough noise to wake even the soundest sleeper. Next, they put a paw or two on us as we lie in bed. If that doesn't get us up, the next step is to put their entire head and chest atop us, dead weight.

All this dog language is meant to say, "Hey, I need to go out. My bladder is in urgent need of draining."

As I ran along on the first leg this morning, I kept hearing a strange sound that I tried to identify. Odd as it may sound, it took me a while to realize that it was my own wheezing.

Which reminded me that I had neglected to use my Ventolin inhalant before I began running. When I reached the motorhome that was my number-one priority, and it got me out of asthma alley.

Today's jaunt was punctuated with two settlements: Crescent and Gilchrist. Crescent consisted of little more than a ranger station, two motels, cafe and Crescent Oregon Church of Community Fellowship. The most surprising aspect of the town to me was the sidewalk through it.

Gilchrist is home to the Crown Pacific lumber plant that sits on the lake to the west of the highway. What surprised me there was the modern Gilchrist mall on the east side of the highway.

It did not catch Elaine by surprise, though, because when I ran by I saw the motorhome parked in the mall lot. This meant she was on a shopping spree in the first supermarket we've seen in 100 or so miles.

The name Gilchrist stirred a memory with me. Twenty or so years ago, while running in a race I was hit by a car driven by a guy named Gilchrist.

This was a three-day race at 33-1/3 miles per day. We were into the second day of the race on a course along the Sacramento River.

To minimize the wind and cold of the river frontage, I was running near the shrubbery, which dictated that, not too wisely, I was running with traffic instead of facing it. When I heard the impact of Gilchrist's car hitting something, I was distinctly aware that something had been hit, but in that split second I did not realize that something was me, even as I was flying through the air.

When I thudded against the pavement, I knew damn well that I'd been hit. In the first moments as I lay there, I had dreadful visions of never walking or running again. Yeah, I remember Gilchrist. We both made a mistake: I was running with traffic; he had been drinking.

Today when I passed an American Indian and his family and their car stalled alongside the road, I regretted that, mechanical moron that I am, I was not able to help. He was trying futilely to get it started and seemed in desperate straits. If he took any notice of me passing by, he probably thought, "Just another white man who doesn't care a damn about helping an Indian." Care I did; help I could not.

Once again we overnighted in the forest, this time at a spot three miles south of LaPine. Privacy we have, unless we are invaded by varmints of some type.

DAY SEVEN. When this weary old road runner descended on LaPine, he found that all the business district is located on Highway 97. The entire strip was about five blocks long. I had expected more.

Elaine had succumbed to the first supermarket she saw, Alpine on the south end of town. But Erickson's Sentry Market on the north end of town appeared bigger and better. As I went past Erickson's, I suspected she might make a second stop.

After being in the boondocks for a few days, I was engulfed with civilization today. Like at the Wickiup Junction where there was a gas station, a motel and, Lawdy me, a Dairy Queen, and a bowling alley. The Master Host Motel hereabouts is one of the best I've seen in quite a spell.

Never would I have guessed, say 30 years ago, that I would be out running in my BVDs at age 75 – let alone running all the way across a state. Frankly, if anything, I figured I'd be dead before age 75.

And for sure, I would never have guessed that, attaining 75, I'd feel so young or have such zest for life. No doubt about it, living an active life style has provided a number of benefits.

I can't help but contrast myself to others my age who don't exercise. Though we're the same age, I know I feel younger and think younger.

I have more vitality. I eat better and sleep better. I even think my mind is sharper. I suppose that sounds a little superior, but that is not at all how I mean this. Rather, I'm trying to say how grateful I am for what exercise and running have done for me, how I love and appreciate just being alive, alert and active at age 75.

After a day of 23.4 miles, and being about 10 miles south of Bend, we headed there to find an RV park. On the southern edge of town, we located John's Mobile RV Park. Checking in, we were made to feel welcome by John Wilson, a minister from Sonora, California, who was tending the store while his 47-year-old son was on a honeymoon with his 44-year-old bride.

Mr. Wilson did not mention his denomination (at least we knew he was not Roman Catholic!), but he had been a minister all his life. When he learned about our run, he said, "I read a book about a fellow who ran across the United States. He met this girl along the way and was converted."

Since I'd read all the literature about runs across the USA, I was puzzled for a moment trying to think of which runner, which book he was talking about. Then I stopped struggling and asked Wilson, "You said he met a girl and was converted. Isn't that true?"

"Well, yes," he replied.

"Oh, then, that's Peter Jenkins and the book was *Walk Across America*. He walked from Alfred, New York, to New Orleans where he met this girl, named Barbara as I recall. Not only was he converted, but he also married the girl."

The book was a bestseller, but every time I hear the title, I think it a bit of an exaggeration: New York to New Orleans is hardly across the USA.

While expressing interest in our run, Mr. Wilson was every bit as interested that we use a pooper-scooper if the dogs left any messages. We assured him that we would.

They did, and we did. His concern was understandable, because the park was fastidiously clean. Elaine and I enjoyed frolicking in the shower and being rehabilitated. Lest there be any doubt, those were *separate* showers.

DAY EIGHT. As I hit the road this morning, a quote from a German pathologist came to mind. It's called Wolff's law: "The robustness of bone is in direct proportion to the physical forces applied to that bone."

Could be why my legs and knees have held up so well. They've had more than their share of physical force. I'm adding to that physical force by trying to run all the way across the state, with no walking.

As I thought about that, I had to admit if I am successful who really knows but me that I actually did it. It would be easy to sneak in some walking. But, aye, there's the rub: *I* would know.

So many things in life are judged comparatively. On Guadalcanal when I was trained in a small cub plane for air scouting, it was more or less like stepping into a car.

Then came the transition to torpedo bombers (TBMs), the plane we had to use to fly on and off carriers. The first time I climbed into the greenhouse of a TBM, it felt as if I were climbing a three-story building. Comparativeness.

The same today when I came into Bend after having been in the boondocks a few days. Bend was overwhelming, a bustling city, humming with activity, the fastest growing city in Oregon, Mr. Wilson told us last night.

Since Highway 97 goes right through the heart of Bend, I was able to see much of the city. As I went past a Fred Meyer's supermarket, I spotted the trusty Mallard parked there. Predictable.

What impressed me most about Bend, besides the place brimming with action, was the number of motels. I swear they could house an entire city. Nobody had to tell me that Bend is a springboard for vacationers.

I could hardly believe the plushness of the River House Motor Inn, which is spread out on both sides of the Deschutes River. I estimated 400 rooms, but when I detoured into the lobby (feeling a bit self-conscious in my scanty and sweaty running duds) and talked with the desk clerk, I was told 254 rooms. Guess the convention facilities made it appear larger.

In midtown Bend, as I ran by a 24-hour donut shop, I stopped to study the goodies. My expression must have been akin to Brudder's when he eyeballs me for a handout when I'm eating.

History was made when I decided to pass up a donut treat, because rarely does this junk food addict miss a chance at a yummy greasy donut. Must be an index of my being tired. Just as I made this decision and started to mush onward, I saw Elaine parked up ahead. Had I bought a donut, she would have caught me eating it and likely cut me off from snacks at the next pit-stop. Indeed the fates are kind.

Since I had to navigate through Bend without benefit of a bike lane, street work being in progress, I was delighted on leaving the city to again meet up with a big lane. "Mine, all mine," I exclaimed, which stirred in my mind a classical line of Cyrano de Bergerac's about his nose.

But struggle as I might, I could not recall the wording of that line, though at the same time these Cyrano words about his nose came clearly to mind:

> "Know that I glory in this nose of mine,
> For a great nose indicates a great man
> Genial, courteous, intellectual, virile, courageous –
> as I am ... "

Being endowed with a prominent proboscis, I find those words somewhat of a defense mechanism, and maybe that's why I remember. So what, if in my case, they are gross exaggeration!

Our day finished six miles south of Redmond and with 23.1 miles logged. Our spot at the Green Acres RV Park was adjacent to a huge shed. Brudder and Rebel thought it was heavenly, since it provided many gopher holes to explore.

DAY NINE. It's remarkable what a good night's sleep brings about on this run. I am tired at the end of each day, but sleep refreshes me and I am ready for the next day. Contrarily, when I ran across the USA , after a month or so on the road I was exhausted at the end of each day. Sleep did revitalize me enough to get through the next day, but the deep feeling of exhaustion never left me. On this run, after a good night's sleep, I find myself through the first 12 to 15 miles the next day without feeling tired.

All kinds of impressions as I went through the city of Redmond. If there was any doubt about this being a farming area, it was dispelled as I passed through town and saw a farm implement store that extended over two blocks. I saw Highland, Freeman, and other products, but missing was John Deere. Where art thou, John, and why thine absence?

Amused by a sign in front of Wilson's furniture store: "Hunting for a sofa? Furniture season now open."

Unbelievable, in 1992, to see a sign reading "Coffee 5 cents" – and they mean it. The building did not house a restaurant but instead a True Value hardware store.

Going with traffic through town, I was forced to run on the sidewalks, which involved a lot of ups and downs. Another drawback of sidewalks is that, uneven as they often are, the chances of tripping are high.

Which reminds me: Not yet on this run, nor all the way across the USA, has the weary old road runner once tripped or fallen. A feat unto itself.

Out of town, once again on the open road, my relaxation was rousted when I heard an eerie noise. What the hell was that? I turned in its direction, then discovered it came from a small jackass alongside her mother. Guess she was hungry. Looking at the scene, I discovered I had a vocabulary lapse. No problem with horses; youngsters are fillies and colts. But what is the word for youngsters that are jackasses?

My highway adventures today were enlivened with two happenings – the first with some teenagers, the second with what I'll call road conditions. A speeding car filled with teenagers approached me, swerved into the bike path, prompting me to make a hurried exit to the dirt, and as the car sped by the kids were yelling and waving, I thought. On second look, that was wrong; they're waving with an extended middle finger.

Now with inner-city kids, that would not have surprised me. But to see it from these farm kids (almost a repeat of an incident a day or so ago) has me worried about the state of the nation. What are we coming to? There's nothing wrong with these kids that a couple of months of boot camp would not cure.

Speaking of which, one hell of a good argument could be made for one year of required military service following graduation from high school. No exceptions, not for pre-med, not for farmers, not for college-bound.

I sensed the second bit of enlivenment as I approached it. Uh-oh, I thought, now this has to be the spot Joe Henderson, an Oregon resident, told me about. He said, "You'll come to this spot where there is a very narrow bridge across a gorge. On the bridge you look down to either side and see a drop of 600 feet or more."

Fearful of heights as I seem to be with old age, the very thought of this scared the living caw-caw out of me. I can't understand this fear. I can fly a small plane without any fear, look out the window of an aircraft without fear, but when I stand on the edge of a cliff or at the window of a tall building, I get shaky knees.

Besides, I almost find myself suppressing an urge to jump and that has the concomitant thought that, some wild moment, I might not be able to suppress that urge. And here I was facing that exact situation.

My God, I thought, seeing the bridge, it is dangerously narrow. There is no space whatsoever for a car and me to occupy the one lane, and there is no bike path, no sidewalk. If two cars and I met abreast, and if they could not stop, I'd get smashed.

I studied the bridge and estimated it was 80 to 100 yards across. I could see 100 yards or so behind me and about 200 yards north of the bridge.

I formulated a battle plan. First I would make sure the road was clear in both directions. Then I would sprint full-out across the bridge. Since the guard rails were so low and since I was so shaky about the height, I would run smack in the middle of the bridge and would look neither to the left nor right in an attempt to ignore the height.

As I waited for the traffic to evaporate, I sneaked a quick peek into the canyon. Goose pimples and suppression of an urge to wet my pants. Rocky walls and a drop to eternity.

I saw a suspension bridge to the west and wondered how I'd make out trying to cross that train bridge. I noticed a sign telling me this is Crooked River Canyon. I knew this crossing would be a bear. I'd be gasping for breath, my legs would ache, and I might have to take sudden drastic action to avoid traffic from either direction. I knew the longer I waited, the worse the situation would be.

I kept monitoring the traffic, geared to go when the road was empty. The moment that happened, I took off. Tennyson's words, "Into the valley of death rode the 600" came to me.

With all the effort I could muster, I fought for air, pumped my arms, struggled to maintain fast leg rotation, not daring to glance off to the side and the vertical drop. I listened intently for cars approaching from the rear and watched the road ahead.

Everything – head, arms, legs, heart – was pounding. I wasn't sure that so geared I could make it all the way across the bridge. The farther I went, the more apprehensive I was that a car would descend upon the bridge. By the time I was three-quarters across, I was so wobbly that I was not sure I could take proper evasive action if confronted by a car.

Body beat and bursting, but mind now at rest, I escaped the bridge and came to the road at its northern end. Spent, I staggered to a safe spot roadside to regroup. I dared not look into the canyon. I did have enough presence of mind to say a prayer of thanksgiving.

DAY 10. Oh, pity, a sad story: a child's toy elephant, pink nose and red ears, forsaken here on Highway 97. Somewhere a child cries.

Sort of reminded me of my youngest daughter, Susan, who as a child had a Humpty Dumpty to which she was inordinately attached. More than once on our trips across country, Susie left Humpty in a restaurant and, once the discovery was made, we had to retreat, miles be damned, to retrieve him.

One of these trips, I vividly recalled, bordered on 40 miles. You can write the scenario: Susie crying, mother sympathizing, father with smoke coming out of his ears. A story with a happy ending, though: First, never again was Humpty left because father made sure he left with the family. Second, Susie is now 35 and that same Humpty is one of her prized possessions.

Last night Tom, our KOA host, told us that from where we finished yesterday to the Washington state boundary was a distance of 105 miles. Thinking about that, I suggested to Elaine that we wrap up this run in four days by running 26 miles a day.

Her answer to that was an arched eyebrow. Presto, I dropped the subject. The cardinal principle here is: Don't ruffle the pit-crew.

As I crested a hill today, I looked ahead and spotted Madras nestled in the trees in the valley below. This is the last town of size we will pass through. The Mad Shopper probably has a list a mile long, I thought.

As I jogged down a hill and into Madras, hayfields to the right and left, it was evident as I looked ahead that once out of Madras, still heading north, I'd be in the foothills.

In town I took time out to buy some postcards in the local pharmacy, apologizing to the clerk in the process for my attire.

"Well, to tell the truth," she said, "it's rare that we see an older gentleman in here wearing just shorts and a T-shirt." At least I came out a gentleman.

Out in the boondocks shortly after leaving Madras, I came up with a wild idea and was anxious to spring it on Elaine. We're both San Francisco 49ers fans, and each week we record their games to watch later at our convenience.

Remembering that the 49ers were playing this Sunday, a couple of days hence, I got the bright idea to suggest to Elaine that Sunday afternoon we find a motel with TV reception of the game and that we watch it live. I knew she'd scream that she would rather sleep in the motorhome, but I'd counter with, "We'll just watch the game on TV in the motel and take a shower there. We can still sleep in the RV."

Despite that clever strategy, I did not win. Her reaction: "Let's wait until we get home and see the game recorded."

End of subject. Remember, never ruffle the pit-crew, O Runner, for we are speaking of thine life blood.

At dinner Elaine told me that Rebel has taken a new stance. Once she parks for a pit-stop and gets out of the driver's seat, Rebel takes it over. Then he looks in the outside rear mirror, watching for my arrival. Once I arrive, he comes to the motorhome door, awaiting my entrance.

Now lest you think this is inordinate affection, his motivation is this: He knows that I'm there to eat and drink, and this means a handout for him. Once I am seated at the dining table, he parks on his haunches nearby and, as he drools, he waits for his handout.

DAY 11. The major highlight of this day started stirring for us when, a bit past the junctions of 97 and 197, we saw a sign advertising the Shaniko RV Corral. We had resigned to overnighting at some roadside spot.

Now, Eureka! Only three miles or so from where we would finish, there was an RV park with hookups and showers. Manna from heaven.

After we finished the day's run and drove the three miles to the RV park, we discovered the ghost town of Shaniko. Maybe one reason it was so delightful was that it was so unexpected. The whole town, or what remained of it, was a museum out of the old west. The centerpiece is the restored Hotel Shaniko. Actually this hotel was originally called the Columbia Southern Hotel, a two-story brick building that took two years to build. An elite establishment for the times, it was referred to as "Queen of the Highland Hostelries."

Elaine and I were invited to tour the restored hotel. We were impressed with the quality of the original woodwork, somewhat remindful of the woodwork in the Coronado Hotel across the bay from San Diego.

All the rooms, about 20 in number, were on the second floor. The first floor housed a restaurant, gift shop, lobby and kitchen. The restaurant, this Saturday, was doing a bustling tourist business.

After our evening dinner in our RV, we made a second trip to the hotel for purchases from the gift shop and to treat ourselves to apple pie à la mode, which turned out to be homemade pie with a generous scoop of ice cream for the reasonable price of $2 per serving.

We learned that, at one time, Shaniko was the world's largest inland wool-shipping center. A couple of the old wool warehouses still stand, 75,000 square feet each, enough space for four million pounds of wool.

In 1902, five million pounds of wool were sold in Shaniko. Wool buyers from all over the world came here to bid for wool and to ship it out on the Columbia Southern Railroad. Shaniko, where August Scherneckau located in 1879, zoomed into prominence in 1900 when it became a railroad terminus. A few years later, another railroad was built up the Deschutes Canyon, going through Madras (in 1910) and through Bend (in 1911), and this was a death blow to Shaniko. A short while later many of the buildings here were destroyed by fire.

Back in the heyday of Shaniko, hundreds of wild horses roamed the plains, sheep were everywhere, and the friendly Indians had scatterings of small teepee settlements on the high-desert plateau. The Indians called these settlements Sim-pa-te, meaning summer camp grounds.

The town once had six full blocks of hotels, saloons, gambling houses, livery stables, bawdy houses and law offices. In fact, by actual count at one time there were 13 houses filled with "sporting girls."

There was even a department store in town, and at one time as many as three newspapers. Some of the historic buildings still standing are the watertower built in 1900, the jailhouse in 1900, the schoolhouse in 1903 and the city hall in 1901. S.R. McCarthy built that narrow, two-story city hall for $865. Just try to get a bargain like that today! The water tower does not look such at first blush, because it is a blockhouse-shaped building.

The town was unusual in that it never had a church nor a cemetery. Its name came about in an unusual way too. It was founded by August Scherneckau, but the Indians could only pronounce his name as Shaniko, and that name stuck.

One of the town's museums has a large collection of buggies and buckboards. I am of such vintage that the collection of old cars and fire engines brought back memories of my youth.

One thing that remains unchanged about Shaniko, now home to somewhere around 60 folks: The cold desert wind still whips inhospitably through this high-desert plateau, just as it did when Shaniko was in its heyday. Which gave us something to share with the pioneers.

DAY 12. At breakfast this morning, I had some new companions. As I was cooking Cream of Wheat, I noticed some weevils.

"Don't worry about them," Elaine said. "They're good protein."

So I continued cooking. Neither of the dogs, who habitually share my breakfast, noticed any immediate ill effects.

Those companions came to me courtesy of Nabisco in Modesto, California. Since the Cream of Wheat was individually packaged, it was evident that the weevils weren't from our kitchen. Take that, Nabisco!

Shortly after starting, I saw an odd sign that told me I'm at the 45th parallel, halfway between the Equator and the North Pole.

Early today I encountered a pipeline under construction that runs from Canada to San Francisco – or so a construction worker told me. A trench about 10 feet deep is being dug, and often through much rock, to lay the pipe. The worker said the pipe is 47 inches in diameter and that each section is 40 feet long. I was also told this will be a natural-gas pipeline costing billions of dollars.

After leaving the site, I thought I should have asked the name of the pipeline. You know, if I'm correct, this thing is under pressure. What would happen if there were an explosion?

At one point today, for no reason at all, I suddenly thought of my first exposure to long-distance running. I was a child of but 12, and my Uncle Paul took me to witness a 17-mile road run from Healdsburg to Cloverdale, California. I marveled at men able to run that extraordinary distance.

Good Lord, come to think of it that was back in 1929 or '30. What I most vividly recall was that, trying to follow the race, my uncle got a ticket from a Highway Patrol officer. I felt absolutely miserable because Uncle Paul, struggling to raise a family in Depression times, could ill afford a ticket, and he got it because of trying to do me a favor.

At one pit-stop today Elaine fed me rice. Eating it, I commented, "Gohan, Rebel-san and Brudder-san."

"Oh," Elaine replied, "I see you're thinking of Miss Polka Dot again."

Which is sort of an in-house joke. She was referring to a character (who in one scene wore a polka-dot dress) in a novel I wrote years ago. The novel centered on a Marine officer during a 14-month tour of duty in Japan. The book never got published. The highest compliment about it I ever received was Elaine's, "You can't fool me. I know it really happened, you and Miss Polka Dot."

Kent was the only town, if such it can be called, that I passed through today. The only activity I saw there was at the Sagebrush Cafe, which advertised fresh cinnamon rolls. I saw a couple of bicyclists emerge with rolls in hand.

On my last leg, two bicyclists approached me, and I waved a hello. They paid no attention whatsoever.

Hard sometimes to understand the unsociability of some people. Something akin to when I'm out running and encounter another runner, say hello to him, and he utterly ignores me.

Note that I said *him*, because these days I never first say hello to a woman (unless I know her). Can't be too careful with the sexual-harassment banner flying and that coupled with the dirty-old-man syndrome. In this case, ladies, I'd rather be tagged unfriendly than intrusive. Sign of the times.

I finished near mile-marker 38 today. Quickly by higher math, I calculated if I can do 22 miles tomorrow, I'll have only 16 our last day. True, I could split it 19-19 (more higher math) but feel it's better to stick with 22-16.

DAY 13. With a certain amount of sentimentality, I wore the New Balance 840 shoes today. I felt sentimental because this shoe (well, seven pairs of them) carried me 3192 miles across the USA and because this is the last pair I own; they cannot be replaced since they are no longer manufactured.

Which is the story of running shoes: Find a pair you like, and the manufacturer – New Balance, Nike, Reebok, Adidas, Saucony or whoever – discontinues that model. This is known as merchandising. Keep the customer coming back in search of the perfect shoe!

With the Washington border nearby I can almost smell the spoils of victory – which is precisely the trouble with too many athletes. They taste the spoils before the victory, which sometimes does not materialize.

From a distance today I was able to distinguish the location of Grass Valley, signaled by a grain elevator and clump of trees. My impression is that the town is misnamed. It should have been called "Wheatland."

As I entered town, I was greeted by two barking dogs. A sign informed me that the town's population is 160. Elaine was parked in midtown Grass Valley when I arrived there for a pit-stop. She was at the center of the town's activity: the local market and Carol's Cafe, both gathering spots.

My next town was Moro. As I swooped down its main street, I saw that most of the residences sit on a ridge line that is on the west side of the main drag; that Sherman Hospital is located on a hill up Bidwell Street, that the town's motel offers budget rates, color TV and air conditioning, and that the Sherman County Courthouse dates back to 1899. With only 300 people, Moro is the smallest county seat in Oregon. While running through town, I also noticed an old two-story hotel now converted to a collectibles store and made a mental note to check it out when I finished running.

That turned out to be an interesting visit. All two stories were filled with an interesting collection of bric-a-brac, dated clothes, uniforms, household items, jewelry, plus an assortment of other paraphernalia. Some of the upstairs hotel rooms were preserved as they had existed 75 or so years ago.

The proprietor, seeing our vintage and motorhome, asked, "Are you part of the snow-bunny migration?"

We briefed him on our run across Oregon. He then went on to explain snow bunnies as older folks who, living in motorhomes, spend the summer in Oregon and Washington, some even in Canada, and then in late fall migrate to Arizona.

We'd been settled in our RV spot for about an hour when two shots suddenly rang out. We looked out the motorhome windshield and saw two men, rifles in hand, running toward a corral. They stopped, aimed and fired into the corral.

"They must be shooting cattle," I said. About then the two shooters and a couple of other guys climbed atop the corral fence, looked in a moment, then climbed down and started retreating to a nearby truck. Soon the truck appeared near the corral gate. We began to get an indication of what was going on by reading the sign on the truck, "Mid-Columbia Mobile Slaughter."

A man jumped out from the truck, opened the gate, carried a small cable from the truck winch into the corral. The next thing we saw was one of the dead cattle attached to the cable being dragged out of the corral. This done, a second was winched out. Both were lying there limp. Then one of the men pulled what appeared to be a hose out of the truck. As we watched, we saw that it was an air hose, and in a short time both cattle were inflated with air. Flat on their backs, with their legs rigidly extended, they lay there.

Just as I was wondering, Why this?, a man with a skinning knife approached them and Elaine said , "Oh, they stretched them out so they would be easier to skin."

Obviously the skinner had been through this many times. He wasted no motions, working with rapidity. In a matter of minutes, he had skinned both animals. By now, the truck driver and fellow with him had donned butcher aprons and white hats. Using a hydraulic hoist, they raised the cattle into the truck and started the butchering process.

They worked for two hours or thereabouts, all this within a hundred yards of our RV. Evidently it was now time for a different phase of the operation, because they moved the truck a short distance to another part of the fairgrounds where they had access to running water and a disposal pit.

Because of the direction the truck was parked, we could not observe this phase of the butchering process. But they were busy for almost another two hours, most likely attending to the detailed butchering.

When the butchers were finished, they exited the truck, ceremoniously removed their aprons and went over to a man who had just driven his Cadillac onto the fairgrounds. My guess was he had bought the beef at the fair that had closed the day before. Soon the Cadillac and truck left. A man finished hosing down and cleaning the drain pit, locked up the area and also departed. We had nearly four hours of entertainment, if such it can be called. I was grateful that we were not having steak for dinner.

DAY 14. Alive in my mind was the thought that today I'd be touching on American history. When I reached the Columbia Gorge, I'd be in the same general area that the Oregon Trail and Lewis & Clark Expedition had passed through. Back years ago when I was into reading and teaching American history, the Oregon Trail never did excite me very much, despite its role in the Westward movement. Maybe my enthusiasm was dampened because the Trail was the freeway from Independence, Missouri, to Oregon.

Between 1841 and 1860 about 200,000 people, best as I could remember, started on the Trail. Along the way, about one out of 20 of them wound up in a grave beside the Trail.

Funny thing about the Trail. A lot of people don't realize that it led to California as well as Oregon. The way that worked was this: At Fort Howard in Idaho, the trail pioneers had to decide whether to turn south and head for California (and the lure of gold) or to continue to Oregon.

The incentive for Oregon was the fertile Willamette Valley where each single male pioneer was granted 320 acres. A married couple got 640 acres. But a single female was entitled to zero acres.

With all the people and traffic on it, so heavily traveled was the Trail that the deep ruts cut into the earth by the iron-wheeled wagons are still visible today in many places. Elaine has often reminded me of these ruts through her family's farm in Idaho.

We awoke this morning to the sound of rain. One look outside, and it was readily apparent that no sun would we see today. What the hell, I thought, in Oregon we were lucky to get through 13 days without rain. Sixteen miles in rain today wasn't any strain, because I knew that when finished this is it – no more encores.

Closing out my last day, I smiled when I thought about how Brudder and Rebel will adjust after this trip. Right now they are used to a snack at each one of my six pit-stops. What's going to happen when that ceases tomorrow? The way they beg, each has his own style. Brudder looks at me despairingly, almost saying, "You can't eat all of that without giving me some. How dare you." Rebel often lowers his head moodily and just waits, confident he'll get a handout. Brudder fixes a yellow-eyed stare on me. Rebel seldom looks me in the eye.

At the last pit-stop I changed from my trousers to my sweaty, smelly, dirty Sporthill tights that have faithfully kept me warm much of the Oregon run. Ever the sentimentalist I felt they deserved the victory lap.

'Twas a beautiful sight when I saw that last highway marker, one mile to the border. I was still holding my hellfire blazing pace of a nine-minute mile, not an undue effort since the day's route was downhill.

To finish our run, we needed to run to the Washington boundary, located midway in the Columbia River. Elaine decided to accompany me so she could take a picture. The narrow ledge that passed for a sidewalk was difficult to negotiate. The semis racing across the narrow bridge and stirring up rain water did not add to our enjoyment. It was a bit foggy and misty, but we took our pictures, despite doubts as to their quality.

When we returned to the motorhome and the waiting mutts, we decided it was celebration time. What to do? We descended upon Dinty's Restaurant for bacon and eggs served with potatoes and toast.

Elaine and I felt pleased with ourselves. We did what we set out to do, did it faster than planned, did it more comfortably than anticipated and finished with bodies, human and canine, in good shape, and with the motorhome still intact and purring.

As we left Biggs, headed west on Interstate 84, it felt damn comfortable to park my butt in the motorhome, watch the rain, feel no wind, to just lean back and relax. Thinking back on the run, what astounded me most about the adventure was I was able to run all the way across Oregon. No walking between pit-stops.

All of which left us thinking about our future runs across Arizona, Idaho, New Mexico, Montana, Washington and Wyoming. Can we hack that in two summers? Where to start? When? After we run these six states, we will have run across every state west of the Continental Divide. Beyond which, I dare not think!

Overview of
ARIZONA

April 19th to May 7th, 1993
389.6 miles

Day	Overnight	Miles	Notes
1	west of Duncan	21.3	underway at Arizona/New Mexico border
2	Safford	22.4	
3	Fort Thomas	21.0	still fighting asthma
4	east of Globe	21.0	met bicyclist from Montreal
5	Globe-Gila RV Park	21.0	visited historic Globe
6	Claypool	21.7	left Highway 70 for Highway 60
7	Boyce	21.8	ran through Queen Creek Tunnel
8	near Apache Junction	22.5	
9	Tempe	21.3	began detour of Phoenix complex
10	Scottsdale	21.5	over 200 miles
11	Turf Soaring RV Park	21.1	back to open spaces after Phoenix
12	Turf Soaring RV Park	21.8	temperature continues in 90s
13	Wickenburg	22.0	wedding anniversary
14	Aguila	22.0	over 300 miles
15	east of Wenden	22.0	
16	Wagon West RV	22.0	met dentist biking USA
17	Quartzsite	23.5	now on I-10
18	near Blythe, CA	19.7	mission accomplished at Arizona/California border

Chapter 3

Arizona:

Fun in the Sun

DAY ONE. Driving across Arizona to the start of the run was somewhat intimidating, because I kept wondering, How in God's name am I going to be able to cover all this on foot? But like so many other things in life, the trick is piece by piece, bit by bit, one step at a time, like building a house.

Getting underway, I wondered what will unfold across Arizona. Anything can happen.

Speaking of things encountered, we saw four dead snakes in Arizona on our drive to the start. How many will I see when running?

Not anxious to see any since I've been told that there are nine species of vipers here: Western Diamondback, Mojave, Black-tailed, Tiger, Rock, Twin-spotted, Ridge nosed, Western and Sidewinder. Sounds like a rattlesnake convention!

My step-daughter Kathy Blume, a surgical nurse, tells me that sautéed rattlesnake is delicious. Yeah, sure. And have Dr. Kevorkian standing by!

I can't imagine actually eating this. But, on the other hand, how many people can imagine a 76-year-old adorned in a T-shirt and shorts romping across a state?

This endeavor launched, I thought about my three goals: to get across Arizona in no matter what condition, to clear up the asthma now plaguing me and to get rid of the chest pain that has bothered me for weeks.

From the border to Duncan, not much unusual happened, just a couple of dog encounters. At mile 1.5, a big German Shepherd barked, moved toward me, then obeyed my command, "Stay!" Or did he back off because it was hot and he was lazy?

As I looked west ahead of me, all I saw was the desert valley in which Duncan sits, sage brush and sand, and a small ridgeline about 15 miles away. Duncan itself is a town whose time has come and gone.

On this run, unlike my run across the USA and across Oregon, I am carrying a camera for the first time, a lightweight Olympus Stylus. Another toy to play with.

Also because of the glare, I am wearing dark glasses for the first time on a cross-state run. If this expansion of outfitting continues, I'll wind up carrying a portable TV!

Dr. Wayman Spence, the guy who invented Spenco shoe inserts, will be pleased to hear that on this jaunt I am wearing one of his newly developed sacroiliac belts. A good investment for 45 Yankee dollahs, because it is lighter than any of the other five belts I've worn, it is cooler, does not raise sweat like the others, and the compression is good.

Even with this lightweight sacro belt, I'm carrying about five pounds because my fanny pack is loaded with cassette recorder, camera, water and an assortment of goodies (asthma inhalant, mace, toilet tissue, handkerchief, Blistix, Lifesavers, small knife, etc.). Through the process of higher math I calculate that five pounds as one-twenty-eighth of my body weight (Bingo! He weighs 140). I don't know what it means except that race horses are handicapped with 15 pounds, and that's miles removed from being one-twenty-eighth of their body weight. And, moving up the scale, does a jet airplane carry one-twenty-eighth of its body weight?

The day is not complete without a historical marker, this one around mile 20 and reading, "In memory of Horatio Harris Merrill, born January 3rd, 1837, and his daughter, Eliza Ann Merrill, born July 27th, 1881, who while traveling by team from Pima, Arizona, to Clinton, Arizona, were ambushed and killed by Indians December 3rd, 1895, shortly after sundown."

Which left me with two thoughts: The girl was only 14, and why is "shortly after sundown" so important as to be memorialized?

Time on the road, and reminders like this of death give a man occasion to peer into his soul. At age 76 it is prudent to start checking the books, because the books will be closed soon. Cheery thought!

DAY TWO. So after all the planning for Arizona and after an introductory half-day on Arizona highways, today I faced my first full day of running in this state. Starting, the primary question on my mind was: Will I be able to handle our programmed 22 miles? After all, yesterday was the only day since the Honolulu Marathon in December that I'd gone over 10 miles.

And just how tired will I be when finishing? The effort today was undue, and I was achingly exhausted but did manage to log 22.4 miles, which brought me to the eastern edge of Safford.

From past experience I had learned that the first three or four days of a run like this are the most tiring. My consolation was in knowing that if I could hang on for a couple more uncomfortable days, I would groove into running 22-mile days without strain.

Elaine and I had picked 22 miles daily as a target for several reasons: That distance was challenge enough; it moved us through the state at a reasonable rate; it allowed us to have all afternoon for recreation and rest.

Approaching Safford, I saw that it is surrounded by three mountain ranges, which afforded me some entertainment because I would think about climbing each range, study its configuration, then try to decide on a route up it. Thankfully these ascents were not on my agenda, because I calculated it would take a day to get on top, where the temperature would be freezing, and another half day to get down.

This fantasizing about climbing these ranges did revive memories of my climb up Mt. Fuji in Japan. Two nights before I was to end a 14-month tour in that country, I was having dinner with a couple of my company commanders at our camp near Gotemba.

Captain Ed Deptula, who commanded the weapons company, turned to me and said, "Colonel, do you realize today is your last chance to climb Mt. Fuji? Tomorrow you have change of command and a social farewell. It's now or never."

I don't know if it was, because I felt a gauntlet was being passed of whether it was a case of seize the opportunity, but I heard myself saying, "Let's do it!"

We drove to the base of the mountain and started the climb at eight P.M. In the light packs, we carried we had a beer and a cigar to celebrate our arrival on the top.

It was an adventure of a lifetime with about 8000 Japanese on the trail and 14 stations to pass through. The stations serve two purposes: Hikers can buy hot tea and have the hiking sticks purchased at the start branded at each station.

Awesome is the best word I know to describe the scene when the sun popped out in early morning and in unison 8000 Japanese gasped. About five A.M., Dep and I reached the top of the crater. Too pooped for our beer and cigar, we settled for hot tea and rice.

Coming down on the volcanic ash side of the mountain was a piece of cake. We made it in two hours.

Back to the present, just before I entered Safford I stopped to read a historical marker (Hey, these things are prime time out here on the desert!) that told me Coronado had been in these parts back in 1542 when he was searching for the seven cities of Cibola.

I had only a couple of human encounters on the road today. The first was early in the day when a fellow from Duncan asked if I needed help.

The other encounter was with a transcon bicyclist going with traffic and moving fast. I saw he had "Boston" emblazoned on his shirt.

I yelled, "That's the way to go. Good luck!" He waved back but did not stop.

Several times today my thoughts went back to an article I read last night. "You don't know what it's like until you've been there," said the old lady as she lamented the nullity of old age.

No, no, these are not the golden years, she said, because there's nothing to look forward to, no goals to set, age keeps her from the hiking-swimming-biking she once enjoyed. These are not the golden years, because her whole being is controlled by inertia.

She had about a half-dozen other indictments of old age, but I could not recall them. The more I mulled her remarks, the more I thought, God, lady, I do feel sorry for you. You've surrendered to aging, and you are rotting away years!

You should meet Esther Stanton who lives down the street from me. At three score and 10, Esther this past summer took a ride in a hot-air balloon, enjoyed a glider flight and braved a white-water rafting trip.

Esther knows that the secret to successful aging is having an agenda, having goals and doing what you can do at whatever pace you can do it. When I think about Esther, maybe what I'm doing at age 76 isn't so wild after all.

DAY THREE. Today I walked and talked a while in Safford with a native American, Ray Mara. He was very articulate and most gentlemanly. In fact, he called me "Sir" so many times, I thought he might genuflect at any moment. All part of his Indian heritage, most likely – respect for age.

My thought as he departed, "Why hasn't some program picked this guy up and sent him to college?"

Even in these small towns, Safford/Thatcher, nobody waved to me. Yet once I exited town, 60 to 75 percent of the drivers waved.

Take this as a rule: The more remote the area, the higher the ratio of waving. Make of that what you will.

The setting west of Thatcher is agriculture and well-kept farms. Tourist that I am, I detoured 200 yards off the road to read a historical marker. It told me that it marks the location of the first home of Eastern Arizona College, founded in December 1890, and that in 1891 it moved to Thatcher. Hardly worth my 400-yard detour.

What I related to more were two black puppies nearby, scrounging for food, looking semi-starved and making me wish I carried some sort of handout for them. Besides food, they are in dire need of a bath. Boy, those guys could have done severe damage to a McDonald's Big Mac.

The town of Pima prides itself on being the pioneer town of Gila Valley, which I thought sort of ties in with the historical marker I had read about a man and his daughter being ambushed by Indians while traveling between Pima and Clinton. As I went past the Pima Market and the nearby Tastee Freeze, I heard cars stop 10 yards behind me. I turned around to see that a bulldog was in the middle of the road and cars were trying to avoid him.

The most dramatic incident of the day also featured a dog. It occurred near my 13-mile mark when a dog ran out from a ranch house. As he approached the highway, I yelled, "Stay!" but he ignored me and kept coming.

At the same time, a Chevy van, traveling at a high speed, hit the dog and I saw him bounce three times on the road. I prayed he was dead and not lying there suffering.

The woman driver of the van stopped, hurried back, crying and shaken. About this time, the owners of the ranch house, an Indian and his wife, rushed out from the house.

The wife recognized the driver and called, "Don't worry, Sharon. It wasn't your fault. We know he's been running out on the road."

Yes, that might be true, I thought. But had I not been on the road, had I not come along at this time, he would not have run out. I was saddened to feel indirectly responsible for his death.

This is the saddest incident that has happened to me in 3600 miles of running across states. I will have a hard time wiping out the vision of that dog bouncing on the highway and the thudding sound as he impacted with the vehicle.

Like so many tragic accidents, it happened in just a twinkling of time. I was also left wondering why the driver, who should have been able to see the dog for at least 50 yards, didn't slow down.

It's remarkable how aware we often are of our shortcomings, yet do nothing to correct them. Case in point: On each three-mile leg, I drink about two ounces of water, whereas I should drink all eight ounces in my bottle. But I rarely seem to get around to doing that.

Sort of reminds me of when I started running marathons. In my first three marathons, rather than slow down to take a drink of any kind, I just ran the 26 miles drinkless.

Then came the Ocean to Bay Marathon over King's Mountain one hot day during which, while going up a hill, I keeled over. Out cold (or was it hot?). Ever since, I don't bypass marathon waterholes.

All I thought of on the last leg today was the pain in my chest. I am not sold on the diagnosis that it is muscular-skeletal. My legs are fine, my breathing is passable with the asthma inhalant, but this mysterious chest pain is draining. I don't suffer well.

DAY FOUR. We instituted a new procedure today. After coffee and a bit of sweet roll, I hit the road. The plan is that I will have breakfast at the three-mile pit-stop.

This change in M.O. is a time-saver, because we clear our overnight camping spot very soon after rising instead of staying there until Elaine whips up breakfast. At the three-mile pit-stop, she has time to prepare breakfast. This arrangement also gives me something to look forward to at three miles.

We spent a comfortable night in the LDS parking lot in St. Thomas last night. This Mormon church was small, befitting the community, but new and well built.

Now that I think about it, all the Mormon churches I've seen while traveling the country are relatively new and very well built. Credit the LDS with smart business management. Associatively, of the 14 states I've run through, I saw more concern for my welfare, more offers of help in Utah, a Mormon stronghold, than in any other state. Mormons believe fervently.

At 6:31 A.M., a school bus filled with kids went past. You know, boarding a school bus so early this time of year isn't so bad weather-wise, but what about mid-winter? And compare the character development here of these bussed kids – up, breakfasted, loaded on bus around six A.M. – with urban kids whose mothers wake them around eight A.M., have breakfast on the table, then drive them to school.

For the first eight miles from St. Thomas, my route was though an agricultural valley, and many farmers were out working their fields. In the hamlet of Geronimo, not much remained. The main edifice was a dilapidated motel of 1940 vintage.

Just past the town, west that is, I read a historical marker that called Geronimo a rebellious leader who led the Apaches. I mulled that as I ran along and found myself objecting.

Why rebellious? I'd call the man *courageous*. He fought for what he believed in. I considered it disgraceful that such a rinky-dink hamlet is named after him and there is nothing in it, least as far as I could see, to commemorate him.

All over the USA we have Martin Luther King buildings, streets, etc., and I see little difference between these two men, each a leader, each fighting courageously. Geronimo needs to be eulogized more. Besides being a leader, the guy was, by the way, a brilliant military tactician.

Speaking of Geronimo, much of my run was through the San Carlos Indian Reservation territory. As I saw many modest homes in the area, I pondered: Why do people stay here? Are they on dole? Or are they tied to their ancestral homeland? What's the attraction out here in this day and age?

A highlight of the day was meeting a bicyclist from Montreal and having a 20-minute conversation with him. Denys Savaria, a banker, decided at age 48 to take a time out in life and live a dream of his: Starting in Seattle, he would bicycle much of the USA, then return to Canada.

"I'll be on the road for a year and will travel close to 5000 miles," Denys told me. Looking at his bike with 100 pounds of gear, I concluded he was prepared.

"I stay in motels whenever I can," he said. "But I am prepared to sleep by the roadside if necessary."

I would have guessed Denys to be in his late 30s rather than his actual

48. At 5-11 and 175 pounds or thereabouts, full head of hair and full beard, he looked to be in excellent shape.

I remember him saying, "I don't have to ask you why you're doing this running. You're doing it for the same reason I am biking, because you enjoy it. It's that simple."

Near the end of our conversation, Denys jolted me by suddenly asking, "Are you close to God?"

Caught off guard, I responded, "I think so."

He replied, "You have to be. You have to have somebody to talk to out here."

On parting, Denys and I took pictures of each other and exchanged addresses. He said he would write me a note when he finished his trip.

(A postscript here: On November 11th, 1993, I did receive a note from Denys telling me that he had successfully completed his trip, asking for a copy of my first book and noting, "The dream is over. Up to the next one!")

Following up on what Denys asked, "Are you close to God?" and mentioning talking to Him out here, I have a confession: I sure do. But, to be fully honest about it, I also talk to some of my dead friends and relatives.

If the going gets tough, I call upon guys like Jerry Conway, Dan Halvorsen and Dub Carter – all deep into athletics, all dying young because of cancer – for some help. Or I might ask my uncles, Paul and Prosper Hontou, both great athletes in their day, "What do you guys think about this crazy stuff?"

Similarly, I might ask my mother if she thinks this is a bit strange for a 76-year-old. I almost get tearful when I think of the many things this dear lady did for me. This is the sort of stuff that gets my mind off running, and distracts me from aches and pains.

When I finished this fourth day, I felt that I am gaining in strength and the chest condition, while painful, is not as excruciating as the previous two days. The prognosis at the moment is that the patient will survive.

DAY FIVE. Early today I reflected on the question Denys Savaria raised yesterday: "Are you close to God?" Denys, I'd say this: If a man out here in the loneliness, quiet and beauty of this desert can't associate with God, I don't see how he ever can.

Look at this setting, and you sense a divine presence. You get the feeling of omnipresence. You are under the eyes of God.

In the setting of the concrete jungles of our cities, rampant with materialism, such feelings flourish not. That's one of the reasons that, were I writing the ideal high school curriculum, it would require every student as part of graduation to live in the wilderness or desert for a week – no running water (fetch it from a stream), no plumbing, no electricity. Just live close to the earth.

For certain they should gain some appreciation for the modern conveniences they now take for granted. Hopefully they might be inspired to do some thinking on what life is all about. They may even find God.

Most of today, I was in foothills or the open desert, no habitation, much sagebrush and bushes. As I went through the area, I realized how easy it would have been back in the 1800s to wait and ambush a passerby. The bushes here about are big enough to conceal a horse.

Running through the San Carlos Indian Reservation today and thinking about Indians, I reflected on the Navajo in the Marine Corps in World War II. They were used as radio operators, because nobody could decipher their language.

They made a major contribution to the Marine Corps war effort. Now, come to think of it, why didn't the Army use some in Europe?

Some sights along the way today: I went past a sign reading Bo Gritz for president in 1992. News to me.

An Arizona Highway Patrol officer, the fifth on this run to date, went past, and he was not curious enough to stop. Now look here, Officer, I am a curiosity piece; in five days on the road, I've seen nothing similar.

Then, moments later, I did meet a police officer who stopped to inquire about my welfare. This solicitous young officer, an American Indian with the unlikely name of Jerry James, is from the San Carlos Police Department that has jurisdiction over the entire reservation.

Adrenaline pumping, pure excitement here, as I saw a sign indicating a historical marker ahead. But it merely told me that an old Indian cemetery once existed down by what is now San Carlos Lake.

Not much to see in Peridot, mainly a cluster of 100 or more Indian homes in the area. The only business in the area was a general store. Peridot, I'd learned somewhere in life, refers to some sort of gem. But how that refers to this community, I did not find out.

Another sight west of Peridot was a grandstand. A sign told me this is the setting for the All-Indian rodeo held every Veterans Day.

About midday, I saw an interesting table-top mountain to the southwest. Would like to be able to explore it. My guess is that a small plane could land atop it.

At the last pit-stop today, Elaine reported that our water tank registered empty, which meant that we had to exist on bottled water until we reached Globe where we overnighted. Globe, 17 miles from our finish, was the closest spot with an RV park, the Gila County RV Park.

In the afternoon, after settling at the RV park, we caught up on a bit of Globe's history. The town, which sits in a narrow valley located between the Apache Mountains to the northeast and Pinal Mountains to the south and west, sprang up around 1875 when silver was discovered in the area. By the time silver mining ebbed, copper mining had taken over.

At the RV Park we were given a city map that showcased a walking tour of historic downtown Globe. Not wanting to leave the dogs alone too long in the RV, Elaine and I made a whirlwind tour that included Holy Angels Catholic Church, First Presbyterian Church, Woolworth's, old steam engine number 1774 that sits in a downtown park, and what was formerly the Gila County Courthouse and now houses the Cobre Valley Center for the Arts, founded in 1984 to help local artists and to preserve and restore the historic courthouse.

Elaine, an artist herself, was more appreciative than I of the works of art displayed. Thus overwhelmed with culture, we trod back to the RV park to be warmly greeted by two lonesome Labradors. Could such affection mean feeding time? You betcha!

DAY SIX. One discovery we made in Globe last night: The town has motorcycle races on Friday nights, the noise from which sabotaged our getting to sleep early.

Another discovery was that the San Carlos Indian Reservation extends, on the west boundary, to four miles east of Globe's city limits. Curious about how big the reservation is, I inquired at the local Chamber of Commerce and learned that it includes almost two million acres. I was told that nearly 10,000 Apaches live on the reservation.

I was also told that the Apache tribe contains seven different bands, these being Aravaipa, Chiricahua, Coyotero, Mimebreno, Mongollon, Pinaleno, San Carlos and Tonto, none of which I'd ever heard of before (discounting Tonto and the Lone Ranger). Learn something all the time.

Actually my main concern with Indians was at a point when, on Highway 70 and running through the reservation, I heard shots coming from an area near the road, and I thought, "I hope these Indians are not thinking, 'Hey, boys, we got ourselves a white eyes. Zero in and shoot for effect.' "

Many vehicles on the road this morning are dragging boats, about 50 or so in the first couple of hours. Once again proof that Saturday and Sunday are the worst days for road runners. Most of the boaters appear uptight as they race for water. Some gave me a, "What the hell is this?" stare.

Another thing about weekends and recreational traffic: Watch out for those beered-up drivers.

Example: When we were stopped for breakfast, a pickup towing a boat stopped beside us at seven A.M., a guy hopped out of the pickup and grabbed two beers from a cooler in the boat, then scooted back into the pickup. These guys could be dangerous on the road later.

This was another day enlivened when I met a bicyclist on a cross-country jaunt. Only 25 and the owner of a computer business, Joe Machalat said he was taking time out at this point in life to make an eight-week bike trip from San Diego, California, to St. Augustine, Florida.

The remark I remember most from the 20-minute conversation with Joe was his saying, "An experience like this makes you humble. I'm talking about the vastness of the country and what I can do by way of time and distance."

Lord, if he's humble knocking out 50 to 100 miles a day, what am I with only 21 a day in Arizona?

Joe and I exchanged road information. I confirmed from him that I could go into the Phoenix area on Highway 60 as far as Apache Junction and that I was not restricted from running on I-10. In return I gave him information about motels and stores ahead for him.

As I go across states, a question I frequently get is, "Who's sponsoring you?"

"No one, " I reply, "just going on my own." An answer which surprises most people.

Back in 1990 when planning our run across the USA, I tried to get sponsorship, mainly from shoe manufacturers. I was given not a glimmer of hope.

So I backed off. Now I am glad that it worked out that way. It is somewhat nice to be my own person and not owned by the company store.

When I ran through Globe today, I got a good feeling for how this town is channelized between two mountain ranges. I realized how going through a town, even a small one like this, gives appreciation for the tranquillity, purity, spaciousness of the desert.

Let me quickly point out here that I do not mean by inference to knock Globe. This town, parked at an elevation of 3500 feet and harboring around 6000 souls, is impressive for its history, its cleanliness, its spirited citizenry.

I worry about Globe, though. A short distance west of the town, I went past a Wal-Mart store. Now by some standards that would be a mark of progress, the importing of this cut-rate giant.

But I think not. Wal-Mart, I fear, will mean the demise of small shops I passed though in Globe – the stationery store, Wool-worth's, the little drug store and others. One by one they will close and storefronts will be vacant. The evaporation will begin.

After finishing our day, we overnighted at the Apache RV Park, located at the junction of Highways 60 and 88. As Lowell Thomas (and that's going back quite a ways) used to say in his travelogues, "We bid fair adieu" today to Highway 70 that we had followed from the New Mexico border to Globe. Our new traveling companion became Highway 60.

DAY SEVEN. Today is Sunday, meaning church day (more piously put, Remember thou keep holy the Sabbath). As far as church is concerned, I truly believe I get closer to God out here on the road than in the four walls of a church with all its distractions.

However, I do more penance in a church, because I must endure the typically dull and incoherent sermon of some priest, which always leaves me wondering: What in the hell did this guy learn during all his years in a seminary.

I say "priest" because I do attend Catholic mass with a modicum of regularity. But, in fact, I am not what would be called a "practicing Catholic," that being defined as one who receives the sacraments frequently and who subscribes to all the tenets of Catholicism, which I don't.

For one thing I have trouble with the Catholic dogma of no divorce. For another the Catholic teaching that it is a mortal sin to eat meat on Friday, and mortal sin can result in being sent to hell for eternity

Again, to miss mass on Sunday is a mortal sin. That sounds like a business arrangement to me.

I just can't buy that eating meat or missing mass is grounds for eternal damnation. God is too merciful, too just to let that happen. I can live with the 10 commandments but not with the six commandments of the church.

As with combat, time out here on the road alone leads to meditating about God, death and afterlife. Such thinking was more intense in combat when a guy's two main focuses were on survival and on what happens after death. In those days most Marines in combat thought there was a good chance that they might cross the Great Finish Line.

On Highway 60, three miles west of Claypool, I went through Miami (population 2018) and my impression was that it looks like a town on the verge of collapse. Only the mining economy keeps it alive, I'd suspect.

A sign told me that by 1915 Miami was a boom town, producing more copper than anyplace in Arizona for the next 15 years, and it still ranks as one of the state's major copper producers. Why, then, I wondered, all the vacant storefronts?

Just a short distance west of Miami, I came across a sight I've never seen before in all my more than 4000 miles of running across states. Beside the road was a small religious shrine housed in a white stucco building maybe 15 feet by nine feet.

The altar was adorned with religious statues, flowers and lighted candles. I took timeout for a picture and then asked the Innkeeper to watch over me.

Another stop I made just west of Miami was to read a sign about the Blood Tanks Wash, a name that came from the massacre of some Apaches in 1864 by whites and Maricopa Indians. The blood of the Apaches in the creek turned the water red, and that is factual – but how this came about is uncertain, because a different account says that blood flowed after a shootout between U.S. cavalrymen and Pinal Apaches.

As I worked my way up the hill to Queen's Tunnel, located between Miami and Superior, 20 or so bicyclists passed me while whirling downhill. Some were grimly focused on speed. Others, relaxed and enjoying, exchanged greetings with me.

The danger level of these bikers is certainly higher than mine. First they travel at a considerably faster speed. Secondly they literally trust their lives to the alertness of the drivers approaching them from behind. Finally only with a tiny mirror can they see what is approaching them, whereas I can observe approaching vehicles.

Despite which, one woman biker yelled to me, "And I thought we were crazy!"

I approached Queen Tunnel with caution, even to the extent of carrying a flashlight that I pointed at traffic to be seen. Near the tunnel entrance, I made what the Marines call an estimate of the decision: Tunnel about 600 yards long, dimly lit with yellow lights, moderate traffic. If I waited until no cars approached and ran like hell, I could probably get halfway through before a car joined me.

When I saw no approaching traffic, I took off with the fervor of an Olympian and got 400 yards before a big RV bore down on me. I screeched to a halt and, standing on an eight-inch shoulder, hugged the tunnel wall. Once the RV passed, I again revved up.

I did have one scare: A guy going my direction, approaching from the rear, tooted his horn, making me think I was about to get clobbered, and almost moving me to reach for the Charmin. He turned out just to be some clown playing in the tunnel. After I emerged unscathed, I realized I'd heard an eerie noise all through the tunnel, probably from the air-circulation system.

My next town, Superior (population 3468 and reportedly being named after Lake Superior), began as a silver-mining center and lasted as such until 1912, at which time Superior might have faded out of existence had it not been for the discovery of copper, which is still being produced on a modest scale.

I did not see much of the town's business district, because it was located about a third of a mile off the highway to the north. Superior, from what I did see, can best be described as a tired town. What I hoped to see, what I scouted for – an RV park – did not exist.

We wound up at the Cactus Country RV Park, where the manager told us, "Make sure the dogs are in the RV at night, because there are coyotes in the area."

DAY EIGHT. During the drive to the start this morning, Elaine was still fuming over the encounter she and the dogs had with the Teddy Bear Cholla on their walk yesterday afternoon.

"Those cactus spines are kind of like fishhooks," she said, "and they're a real mess to get out of the dogs."

Speaking of cacti, by now I've come to recognize some. The Teddy Bear Cholla, for sure. Probably the easiest to identify is the Saguaro, the tall sentinel (sometimes as high as 40 feet) with branches that all spring out at the same level.

Another cactus easy to recognize is the Beavertail, because its pads are shaped as such, it lacks spines, and it's blue-gray in color. Can't get much simpler than that. I never did learn the name for one cactus growth that looked like bananas growing.

After I worked my way out of the mountains this morning, I saw a flat desert valley extending maybe 20 miles and reaching to the eastern boundary of the Phoenix complex. These flats brought the protection and comfort of a bike lane.

Several times today, I went past white crosses alongside the road. The crosses had the name and date of death of the deceased.

Good Lord, I thought in each instance, what happened here? Did the driver fall asleep? Was he drunk? Did some other driver cross over and hit him?

About nine miles into the day's run, I saw signs to the south of the road warning about live artillery fire and unexploded rounds in the area. The idea here is that if you see a red flag, expect live fire, in which case it would be prudent to avoid the area if you cherish life.

When a Highway Patrol officer, feminine in this case, passed me about 16 miles into the day, I was reminded that I've been on the Arizona highways 170 miles and have yet to witness a ticket being issued. Rarely have I gone that far in California without seeing a ticket being issued.

In another mile, I stopped to examine a tag on a van left on the highway. The tag, issued by the Highway Patrol, read, "This is not a citation..." That too is different from California where vehicles left on the freeway are cited.

One observation that always amuses me is to come into the motorhome on a pit-stop and to see how pooped Rebel and Brudder are after the desert walks with Elaine. I suspect they'll welcome some R&R in the kennel in three weeks when Elaine and I go to Canada.

But maybe not, because they like to be in on the action or lack of it. They just want to be members of the family, which isn't asking much.

Life is so simple out here on the desert. The coolness of the breeze as it flows through a mountain pass, the shade of a tree, fast-flowing clean water, the refreshing pure air – these are the luxuries out here. Our contaminated cities testify that we are the creators of our own disasters.

Out here, I have a strange feeling, one I can't articulate very well, but it goes like this: After being out on this desert for many hours over a week's time, I feel like I am part of this desert, integral to it, woven into it. Hell, if you believe in reincarnation, maybe I was a cactus at one time.

The Japanese who spend endless hours admiring the cherry blossoms – "Saguri mo sukoshi," I can hear them saying – would be in ecstasy out here in this land of wonderment.

Marvelous the way the Japanese and many Europeans take timeout to enjoy beauty, whereas we Americans, in the mainstream at least, are so preoccupied with the superficial and materialistic that we don't get into any in-depth analysis of nature. We don't study the beauty of a tree, the majesty of a mountain. Good Lord, many if not most Americans don't even take time out in life to ask, "What am I doing here on earth?"

DAY NINE. Last night was miserable. For some undecipherable reason, I did not get to sleep until one A.M.

I wasn't edgy or anything like that. Just couldn't sleep. Had a hankering to get up about 11 P.M. and go for a swim in the KOA pool but refrained, knowing management would not approve.

As I started, this old body's theme song seemed to be, "Hey, how about a day off?" Heretical!

I had a little difficulty when starting to run because my asthma acted up, and I had what I called the asthmatic dry heaves. Otherwise, far as injury assessment was concerned, I was doing fine. My only problem was with my right big toe that had an irritating toenail about ready to drop off.

Once in the built-up area, with traffic in all directions, I had to be more alert, less relaxed than when on the open desert. The relaxation, if such it can be called, in the built-up area was checking out places as I went past them.

For example, on old Highway 60, the Barlene Family Country Music Theater and the thought that having dinner there with Elaine would be a change of pace. Not sure, though, that the dogs would approve our leave of absence.

Then, near Tomahawk Road, I passed by the KOA RV Park where we stayed last night, and the thought that it would be relaxing to be floundering in the pool there, especially since the temperature today was in the mid-90s.

Down the road a short ways, and out from Lawdry's Automotive Repair, a Rottweiler charged out toward me. I was saved when someone in the shop called to him, and the thought: Damn, they make those Rottweilers big!

When I came into the Apache Junction area, I almost felt like I was in familiar territory. Maybe that's because Apache Junction is nestled at the foot of the Superstition Mountains about which I'd read and seen TV shows, such as "Unsolved Mysteries."

Just about all the stories centered around Jacob Waltz – "the Dutchman" – who was thought to have located a rich gold mine in these mountains. When dying, so the reports went, he revealed the location of the mine, saying the key to finding it was Weaver's Needle, a towering rock monolith.

An avalanche of prospectors subsequently descended on the mountains. But the mine was never found, leaving unanswered the question: Did Waltz actually discover a mine?

The signs and symptoms are evident: The newly opened freeway, 360 through Phoenix, is playing havoc with the economy of this strip. Some of the business names are interesting: the Feed Bag for a restaurant, the Happy Hooker bait shop, for example.

As I went past Greyhound Park, a huge complex for dog racing, a sign told me races are held Tuesday through Sunday. There was the customary charge for parking but this was a new wrinkle: Patrons who don't park but walk through the lot to buy their admission tickets are charged 50 cents for this walk-through. Now that's slicing the cheese pretty thin, I thought.

Next to the Greyhound complex was the American Swap/Pawn Shop. Now that is what could be called tactical location or seizing the moment.

A dog-grooming place called Smoochie Poochie. That's not arf but *barf*! No self-respecting dog would be caught in there.

Today I came very close to being hit by a car. Distracted by thinking about my water bottle being empty while I still had two miles left, I crossed a street and was oblivious to the red light.

A car, traveling about 50 miles per hour and making no attempt to stop, flashed past me, eight yards away at the most. Had I been a wee bit faster, I would have been clobbered. If I am hit someday, I hope it will not be the result of my own stupidity like that maneuver.

After leaving the tranquillity of the desert and descending into pell-mell traffic, crammed-together housing, the hustle and bustle of commercialism, I realized that we are like ants crawling around in the makings of our own civilization.

The major conclusion I reached today was that, like being sick makes a person appreciate wellness, today's running through the hurly burly of citification made me appreciate the beauty of running under nature's umbrella of mountains, forests, deserts, open spaces.

DAY 10. Maybe the big deal today was navigating through – or was it around? – the Phoenix complex. The routing put us in built-up areas for the first 18.5 miles of the 21.5-mile day.

Running through built-up areas is more stressful, less scenic, less enjoyable than running in the great outdoors. In fact, it is a genuine pain in the ass, albeit a necessity at times.

At long last, I was once again in open space when I reached Frank Lloyd Wright (also known as Bell) Road and saw grass, bushes and small trees but, somewhat surprisingly, no cacti. I suspected that I was in an area of affluence, since the cars that went past me were a flashy red Mercedes convertible, a white Morgan and a couple of BMWs.

However, the two car dealerships recently located here, probably signaling the startup of a new automobile row, are Ford and Chevrolet. They are disturbing the hell out of the local jackrabbits, and the gophers have a major relocation problem. The locals in quest of these dealerships are probably asking, "Where in the hell is Frank Lloyd Wright?"

I noted that along the side streets of the Ford dealership, many of the employees' cars were parked. They were mainly Toyotas and Nissans. There's a lesson here.

Carried me back to the days when, fresh out of the University of California in Berkeley, I started teaching in Sacramento. One condition of employment was to live within the city limits. Maybe the Ford people should hire only employees who drive Fords.

"Blessed be the Lord," as we used to say in the Benediction services when I was a grammar-school boarder at Christian Brothers School in Sacramento and the Brothers would round me (and a few other dissenters) up for this evening service and require us to attend. Blessed now because I left Frank Lloyd Wright and, crossing over the canal, headed for the boondocks.

Our day finished, we drove to Westworld, which is primarily an equestrian center. There we overnighted at the RV park that has 400 spaces, only about a dozen of which were filled.

Westworld occupies more than 15 million square feet on the Sonora Desert at the base of the rugged McDowell Mountains in Scottsdale. The facility represents a mix of the old and new West, from polo to rodeo, classic cars to monster trucks, trail rides to hot air balloons, country music to symphony concerts. In a word, this place is prepared to make a buck!

Westworld has a polo field of approximately 12 acres, seven outdoor arenas, an upscale restaurant, equidome (a covered stadium that seats 10,000 people), amphitheater with 8000-seat capacity, riding stable, many barns and an RV park. Now don'tcha agree the place is armed to make a buck?

If not, let me add that all the facilities are first class. We were lucky to stumble into this luxury just off Pima Road. To which Brudder and Rebel, who frolicked happily around the polo fields, would add a hearty "arf!"

DAY 11. When I started a bit early, 6:01 A.M. to be precise, I was a bit chilly wearing only T-shirt and shorts. But this was somewhat refreshing compared to all the sweating I've been doing in 90-plus temperatures.

I ran all day in shoes with the toes cut out; no problem. But since I was on a dirt shoulder all day, I had the problem of rocks invading my shoes, and I had to stop several times to dump them.

The rock and dirt shoulder I followed all day was at least six feet wide. So I played it safe, staying away from cars and, as a result, did not once resort to cussing a driver. A record there.

Like many other tourists, I took time out to take a picture of the Rawhide Town and Country Western Steakhouse, a place that features staged gun fights, stagecoach rides and an array of shops. The place must get a lot of action, because the parking lot is three-quarters of a mile long.

This area, but a short time ago open desert, is now beginning to be invaded by housing as evidenced by the Pinnacle Peaks Villas adjacent to the new Pinnacle Peaks Shopping Center. But the desert is still there, because down the road at Desert Foothills Drive is a sign advertising the most beautiful desert drive in the world, a 17-mile scenic loop to Cave Creek.

When I went past Milton Drive, I asked myself, "Can I remember any poem by Milton?" Ah yes, the sonnet on his blindness, the first lines of which go, "When I consider how my time is spent in this dark world and wide/and that one passion which is death to hide ... "

The concluding line: "They also serve who only stand and wait." All the lines in between eluded me years ago.

At the 12-mile pit-stop, Elaine was somewhat animated because of a radio report about guns in Australia. She recited the case of a man who woke up when he heard a burglar in his home.

Able to get his gun, he shot the intruder. The net result was that the burglar got three months for robbery, and the home owner got 10 years for attempted murder.

That sounds Clintonesque. Or maybe reflective of the type of colony that would have Jerry Brown as governor.

All kinds of action at the pit-stops. At my final one, the radio reported that Clinton just passed his first 100 days in office. I'll refrain from comment, since he is not my kind of guy. Just suffice it to say that if in 1776 we'd had a nation full of Clintons, we'd still be under the British flag (yeah, and Hillary would be busy sewing Union Jacks!).

On my last leg, as I came out of a mountain pass, I saw a valley below and in the distance, about four miles away, a heavy flow of traffic moving north and south (okay, if your sympathies are with the Confederacy and you want top billing, south and north). Hello Highway 17.

We finished, then drove 10 miles to overnight at Turf Soaring RV Park, located adjacent to a glider airport. Without any effort whatsoever we abstained from taking a glider flight.

DAY 12. On the road at 5:50 A.M., making this our earliest start in 12 days on the road. Considering that we got out of bed at 5:10., then had to dress, unhook the motorhome water and electric connections, piddle the dogs, button up the RV for moving and then drive eight miles to the start of our running day – all within 40 minutes – I'd say we have our act together. We even made a pot of coffee that fortified me for the pre-breakfast leg.

Traffic at this early hour was unusually heavy. But that did not send my blood pressure up as much as when I almost stepped on a dead snake, four feet long. My biggest objection to the traffic was that it blasted the tranquillity of the desert.

On the Highway 17 overpass I looked south, hoping to get a view of the Phoenix complex. But a mountain range masked any distant view in that direction.

A nearby sign read, "Prison area: Do not pick up hitchhikers." A quarter-mile later I passed the Ben Avery shooting area. Sounded like a convenient arrangement for an escaped prisoner: Waylay some shooter and steal his gun, then back in business.

At the three-mile breakfast pit-stop the best parking Elaine could find was only two feet from the white fog line. When the semis passed by, they rocked the RV. Every now and then, when the RV rocked more violently than usual, the dogs scampered about the RV looking for the epicenter of this earthquake.

One thought I often harbor in heavy traffic: In the mood of Carl Sandburg's "Chicago," someone should write an epic about the people grimly driving, pell-mell to work, coffee mugs in hand or on dashboard, radio blaring, frenzied looks, some pacifying themselves with cigarettes, long on anxiety and short of temper.

At eight miles into our run, Highway 74 made a right turn, which was somewhat dramatic in that to this point it had been a straight-line road. Turf Soaring RV park, where we stayed last night, is located at this junction.

A sign indicated that Sun City was to the left. Seeing that sign reminded me of my 7th ROC classmate Ed Schlutter, now a resident of Sun City, who gave me some help with navigation through the Phoenix area.

I have not seen Ed since 1942 when he and I, in company with other gallant young Marine officers, were chasing girls in the Grant Hotel in San Diego prior to going overseas in World War II. We were both adventurous bachelors, friends in officer training in Quantico, Virginia.

Ed, Bob Reynolds and I were a triumvirate while in the 7th ROC. After Quantico, my path never again crossed with Bob, whereas Ed and I were cavorting in San Diego.

The irony of Bob Reynolds was that, unbeknownst to the Corps, he went through Officer Candidate Class while married, an offense for which some candidates were caught and dismissed. And while Bob would have been ousted if discovered, he emerged from the training ranked number one in the class.

When I entered the RV today at the 15-mile pit-stop, Elaine asked, "Well, what do you want?"

Trying to be humorous, I responded, "Same setup as last time, bartender," meaning in this case a Pepsi, half of a ham sandwich and some jello.

That didn't go over too well, because I heard her saying, "Don't be a smart ass, and tell me what you want." She gave me that look as if to say I am talking about food, which unto itself is quite a tribute to a 76-year-old geezer.

A slow learner, I tried the same routine at the 18-mile pit-stop: "Same setup as before, bartender."

Prepared, she quipped, "I've never seen you before. What's your pleasure?"

This time, I gave her the look. The one I received back would be enough to sizzle this page.

After finishing our 21.8 miles, we drove back to the Turf Soaring RV Park, where we had spent last night. Overnighting alongside that small airport, I found myself thinking back to the days when I learned to fly after World War II. When I was scouting in the torpedo bomber, I was not the pilot but a tactical air observer (TAO). I was in tactical command of the plane (except for air-to-air combat), and the pilot was in charge of flying.

My 91 missions left me wondering if I could fly. Curious and having some governmental educational funds after the war, I went to the Dupen

Flight School in Sacramento and learned to fly. I still remember my flight instructor, Jack Emahiser, who was a cool cat.

I did not truly appreciate Jack until one day when he was sick and I had a replacement instructor who was Mr. Panic himself. I could not touch any control but what he would start screaming bloody murder, "Do this!" "Don't do that!" Had Mr. Panic been my instructor from the beginning, I probably would never have learned to fly.

Shortly after getting my license, I had to abandon flying because my GI funds were exhausted and I could not afford it. One thing about flying is that it is akin to skiing in that if you cannot maintain your efficiency through frequent application, you had better abandon it, because you will lose your skill. In skiing you might break a leg. In flying, you might lose your life.

DAY 13. The major achievement today was completing our detour of the Phoenix complex and rejoining Highway 60, which we had left at Apache Junction. This made us feel as if we were on the home stretch. How did Browning put it? "God's in his heaven, and all's right with the world..."

The most important personal aspect of this day for Elaine and me was that it is our anniversary, which resurrected a host of memories starting with our wedding in the chapel at the Presidio in San Francisco. From there we went on to a camping honeymoon in the Humboldt Redwoods and many, yet too few, years of happy companionship.

To celebrate our anniversary, I offered to take Elaine out to dinner. But she declined, saying she had already planned a steak dinner.

I was lucky this day in finding places to shop for a gift. My first stop was near 15 miles at Hank's Antiques to buy a piece of blue glass for Elaine's collection.

At another antique shop just down the road a bit, a little old lady, seeing that I was a runner (how could she miss with me in shorts, T shirt, and Reeboks), said, "You know, when I lived in California, we had this fellow who ran by our house and he looked like Jesus Christ.

"Well, one day a lady friend of mine was visiting me about the time this runner usually came by. So I went to the window to look for him. Watching me, my friend asked, 'What are you doing?'

"I told her, 'I'm looking for Jesus Christ.' Honest, you could never believe the expression on my friend's face. She thought I had flipped."

For me there was more to the story than she told, more than she knew, because she was talking about a time frame and an area where an acquaintance of mine, Gordon Ansleigh, ran. At that time, with full beard and long, flowing hair, he did indeed resemble Jesus Christ.

And here I quickly add, resembled Christ in appearance only. This is not the time nor place to cite the multitude of reasons why the resemblance stopped with just appearance.

Anyway, back to anniversary, after we finished in Wickenburg, I was able to buy Elaine a nice piece of Indian jewelry there. It at least showed that I remembered our anniversary and earned me much-needed brownie points.

The running part of the day was relatively easy, because the bike lane that began at Lake Pleasant continued all day. Leaving the RV park, we were somewhat worried by the strong winds and their effect on the RV, but they abated by the time we reached the mountains.

We started in a valley and reached the foothills in seven miles. Contrasting this desert with the Nevada desert, I would say that in the morning Nevada has more beauty, whereas in the evening the Arizona desert has more.

At eight miles, a big RV, Bounder by name, was intruding into the bike lane and heading for me. I pointed to the bike lane line, and the driver's response was an obscene gesture, typical of the mentality of the guys who drive the oversized RVs (Southwinds, Bounders, Pace Arrows).

Fact is, three miles farther down the road, a Southwinds taking the bike lane forced me into the weeds. Driving these massive RVs, these drivers must develop self-aggrandization and then drive accordingly.

On the outskirts of Wickenburg, I looked down a hill and saw the Horsepitality RV Park, a very neat facility of 100 units and tempting enough that I detoured off course to make a reservation for the night.

Playing tourist, I stopped to take a picture of the Wickenburg city-limit sign, telling me that the town was founded in 1863 and the elevation is 2093. Elsewhere I had read that the population is 4515 and Phoenix is 58 miles southeast.

Another sign told me that Wickenburg is the home of Cody Custer, the 1992 world champion bull rider. Yippee hi ho! Damn, Cody Custer is a colorful name for a rodeo performer.

After crossing a long bridge, maybe a couple hundred yards, over the Hassayama River, I came into downtown metropolitan Wickenburg. At this point the river could be used in a Hollywood movie to pass for the Rio Grande. Give credit here, though, for this is the first bridge I can remember crossing in a long time with a wide pedestrian sidewalk.

Downtown I passed the Swiss Chalet Restaurant. Ever curious, I stopped at the Swiss Chalet to scan the menu: escargot, shrimp avocado salad, filet mignon, New York steak, fresh salmon, lobster.

Now, Elaine, are you sure you don't want to go out for your anniversary dinner? She didn't.

DAY 14. A minor disaster late yesterday afternoon when our air conditioning went out in the 90-degree weather, causing us to drag out all our user's manuals and ferret out the problem. We finally figured that the problem was with the switch connection, corrected that and returned to normalcy.

Experienced a first last night when a chest pain came on me just before dinner and stayed with me the better part of four hours. Unanswered questions here.

I must confess that early this morning the idea of taking a day off did pass through my mind. I was cozy in the RV and surrounded by creature comforts, not the least of which was Elaine.

I did not succumb to the temptation (of taking a day off!) for a number of reasons. For one, it is easier to run when I have an equity (i.e., ahead of schedule) as now. Another, suppose that air conditioner goes out again. We'd feel silly sitting here in 90-plus weather, downright uncomfortable.

And besides, there are the laws of inertia and momentum. Hit the road, Jack!

Starting, I reflected on the good feeling to know I could count on the fingers of one hand the days remaining on this run, providing all went well. Not so anxious that the run get over but rather more concerned with successfully completing it.

Getting underway and in a meditative mood, I found myself mulling over a bit of sad news reported yesterday in the sporting pages of the *Arizona Republic*. Dave Waymer, 35, was reported dead. Killed by his own hand.

There was a touch of I-know-this-guy here, because he played football for the 49ers, and Elaine and I had watched him play in many games. The paper reported a trace of cocaine was found in his system.

I was left wondering: How many players knew this guy was on drugs? And from that, how many others are using drugs? Good Lord, these guys are making a half-million or more a year, they're on top of the world. Isn't that enough to savor?

Why drugs? How terribly tragic.

Playing tourist, I stopped on our drive through Wickenburg to take a picture of a bronze sculpture of a cowboy and his horse. The kneeling cowboy is saying "Thanks for the Rain," which is the title of the sculpture that stands in front of the Desert Caballeros Western Museum. It captures Wickenburg's wild west days, and contains western paintings by Remington and Russell.

All kinds of roadside entertainment this morning. A short ways after breakfast, I went by the Flying A Ranch, and a sign told me it is an authentic dude ranch, a member of the National Dude Ranch Association, and it is on the American Plan. I always have to do a slow take on the "American Plan" to remember that, unlike the European plan, it includes meals and lodging.

And more entertainment: a historical marker commemorating the Wickenburg Massacre that occurred on November 5th, 1871, when the Wickenburg-Andberg stage was ambushed by Apache Indians and seven people were murdered, one of whom was a woman. I did not understand the motive for the ambush, but I readily understood how the rolling hills and gullies hereabouts made an ambush easy.

I knew at 22 miles today that I was feeling good, because I was thinking of how much I'd enjoy a deep-pan veggie pizza with a Sharp's beer. A good sign, because when I think about food, I feel good. Maybe that's why finishing in 96-degree weather at 2400 feet elevation did not faze me at all.

The milestone of our day was that we went over the 300-mile mark.

DAY 15. Tragedy struck last night when our RV air conditioner collapsed and died a natural death. Try as we might, we could not revive it.

We are in for some uncomfortableness until its revivication. The trick now is to find an RV repair facility along our way, and this will not be easy.

Shortly after I started today, I went past a dead king snake, the first of the breed I've seen in Arizona and too close to come to a snake, even a dead one. About as close as I like to come is when I cross over a bridge with a sandy, dry creek below and look down to see if I can spot a snake.

I can still vividly recall the shivers up my back years ago when I almost stumbled on a rattlesnake. This was on the sandy banks of the Russian River in California.

I came upon a scene were a rattlesnake was hypnotizing a cottontail and appeared about ready to strike. I clapped my hands loudly, startling the cottontail who scampered away. Ungrateful little sucker didn't realize I'd saved his life.

Today the king was not my only snake encounter, because not too much later my blood pressure screamed, "Snake! Snake!" And there he was curled up under a shady bush alongside the road.

My eyeballs, like beacons, focused on him, my blood was gurgling, and I did not register a studied look. Instead I headed west, pardner, with rapidity.

The snake stirred not one iota as I went past him. Bless him.

It was a somewhat dull day, and I found myself entertaining all kinds of thoughts from the silly to the sublime. One thought was that had I been a solitary scout going through this territory back in the days of Indian attacks, I would have preferred, if given a choice, a pair of binoculars over a rifle. Evasion would have been better than encounter.

One guy with a rifle would not have lasted very long when attacked by 15 armed Indians, especially since this was in the days before movies. Guess the Pony Express had somewhat the same idea when it would not allow its riders to carry rifles.

So many thoughts here in the course of a day on the road. Like thinking about the TV program I saw last night that showed surgeons at Johns Hopkins Medical School installing a device (fibrillator was as close as I could come on making out the name) in people to control their heart rhythms, thus adding another 10 years to their lives.

Ah, longevity, which had me thinking about my own. I really don't think I'll last another 10 years (no tears, please!), yet if I could sign a contract guaranteeing me 10 years – but not a day more – I would not sign. Which seems contradictory.

The day was broken by a few incidents. When Elaine was parked at a pit-stop, a guy in a pickup towing a fifth-wheel stopped dead in the middle of the highway, got out, came over to Elaine and asked, "Do you know where you are?"

Seems he had wanted to take a particular turn off, missed it and was now lost. Elaine gave him the necessary navigational help. The guy had so much difficulty turning around that Elaine concluded the fifth-wheel was a new experience for him.

At one point today, a senior citizen and his wife in a pickup saw me, drove into the bike lane to get a closer look and waved cheerfully as they passed close by. Hey, folks, nice to be so friendly, but suppose I had not been alert?

For the first time in my 3800 miles of running across states, a trucker, this one from Texas, stopped to ask if I was all right.

"I don't believe it," he said when I told him what I was up to. "Good luck," he added when driving away.

Seeing the direction he took, I realized that the guy had passed me and then was concerned enough to stop his semi, turn it around, come back and check on me. I'll tell you something, pardner, that raises my estimate of Texans.

One final incident, just to show how a guy's mouth can get him into trouble. At a pit-stop Elaine and I were talking about getting the RV air conditioner fixed.

Unthinkingly and innocently I asked, "If they gave us a good deal on a trade in for this one, would you take it?"

Attached as she was to the faithful Mallard, I expected a quick, "No way." Instead I heard an assertive, "Yes, providing the new one had radials."

Good Lord, I realized, I have ignited in her the thought of trading in our RV.

DAY 16. With the air conditioning defunct last night, we were uncomfortable until about 10 P.M., when the weather cooled. The heat was especially hard on the dogs.

As I approached the town of Wenden today, there was some diversity in scenery in that the area was lined with agriculture. Crossing over the long bridge over the Centennial Wash on the east end of town and entering Wenden, I saw that the only updated building was the Exxon gas station. Judging from two prominent businesses – the Anderson Clayton Western Processing Division and the McMullin Valley Gin – cotton must be the chief agricultural product hereabouts.

Down the road a piece and a sight had me thinking, Lawdy me, I've seen it all now. A burly, bearded semi driver with a wide load on his rig was cuddling a miniature poodle. What next – Arnold Schwarzenegger eating Twinkies?

At the pit-stops this morning Elaine, was making chatter about trading in our RV. All this set off by my innocent, joking remark of yesterday. Should teach me to keep my big mouth shut.

Speaking of RVs, considering the cost of purchase, gas, maintenance, RV parks, depreciation and all such, traveling by RV is every bit as costly as moteling/restauranting. The pluses of RVing are its convenience, sleeping in your own bed and better food at less expense. The biggest advantage of an RV for our purposes is that we always have sleeping and eating facilities with us, no matter how remote we are from a motel or restaurant.

While in the foothills, I was able to look down into a valley four miles ahead and make out Salome, a cluster of white buildings at the base of the foothills. Salome, the name kept reverberating, then the dawning: Wasn't this the dancer who wanted the head of John the Baptist and wound up with an "I gotcha!"

Elaine had driven ahead into Salome to locate Moe's RV Repair and see if she could get our air conditioner fixed. When I met her, she told me that Moe did not repair air conditioners, but he did recommend a place in Quartzsite, which he said was 11 miles away. As I studied the map, I saw that Quartzsite was 36 miles distant, which made me glad that Moe did not work on our air conditioner.

I saw a bicyclist coming from a distance and hoped he would stop for a visit, which he did.

"Hi, where are you going?" I asked.

"To Virginia Beach, and I've got to be there by August 6th for the 60th wedding anniversary of my wife's parents," he said.

He volunteered that he had just retired from the Navy. "I'm a periodontist and I just completed 20 years."

I said, "I see from your T-shirt that you're from Marine Corps Air Station, El Toro. You're talking to a guy who spent 23 years in the Marine Corps."

"Oh, is that right. I've spent a few years with the Marines. One tour of duty had me at Parris Island for three years."

"Oh, God forbid!" I exclaimed.

"And I had four years at El Toro where I was the XO of the dental company there. I just had to do this cross-country before I get any feebler. I've got some neck and back problems that are not getting any better."

He added, "I sort of envy you running. I can't do that anymore. That's why I took up cycling."

As we talked, I learned that he wanted a year's leave of absence from the Navy to make this bike ride, but the Navy would not grant it. If he wanted to make the ride, he had no choice but to retire.

And that, I thought, is where we are today. college professors by the dozens get paid sabbaticals, and yet this guy in the Navy – where doctors and dentists are needed – can't get a year's leave of absence without pay. Now that's a Yankee doodle dandy!

It was not until we had finished talking and were taking our leaves that we introduced ourselves. His name was Ken Clark.

After finishing, we were lucky in having to drive only four miles to the Wagon Wheel RV Park. A comfortable spot with showers, laundromat and recreation hall, and all this for $7.43.

The owner was away in Laughlin to try his luck and, on the honor system, we had to register ourselves and leave a check. Trusting soul.

DAY 17. The two features of this day were running on the interstate (I-10) and tracking down a repair facility in Quartzsite to get our air conditioner repaired. Although I-10 was 12 miles from our start, I was apprehensive from the beginning about running on it.

My two concerns: Would the Arizona Highway Patrol order me off it? And how dangerous would it be with the heavy volume of 70-mile-per-hour traffic?

Well, I thought, at worst if the Patrol ordered me off I would have to return to Highway 72 and follow it to Parker and the California border. This would mean I'd lose the distance and time I had run from the junction of Highway 72 to I-10.

A somewhat unusual encounter this morning when I met an older gentleman peddling his bike from Ehrenburg to Ashfork, Arizona. He told me his name is Lee McGuire.

"How far is it that you're biking, Lee?" I asked.

"About 200 miles."

"How long will it take you, four or five days?"

"Oh, a bit longer than that. I am kind of fooling around, looking for a place."

"What do you mean, looking for a place?"

"An acre or two of ground I can buy," he explained.

Changing gears, I asked, "Do you bike like this very often?"

"All the time. It's my form of transportation."

"No wonder you look in such good shape."

"I feel good."

I asked, "How old are you, anyway?"

"Sixty-seven."

"That makes you nine years younger than I am. I have to tell you that, besides myself, you're the only other fossil I've seen on the highways in hundreds of miles."

Lee was the most unusual bicyclist I've met on the road. Unlike the others decked out in biking gear, he was wearing a flannel shirt, khakis, boots and a cowboy hat, and strapped to his waist was a pistol. He had a sleeping bag across his handlebars.

"I sleep on the ground," he said, "and the pistol is for rattlesnakes. I have a special shell just for snakes."

He impressed me as the kind of a guy you'd like to have alongside you in a foxhole in combat. And that, lest there be any doubt about it, is an accolade.

As I approached the access ramp to the Interstate, I was a bit shaken to see a sign with a bicyclist on it. My first thought, at a distance, was, Good Lord, bikes are prohibited. That means pedestrians too.

But when the sign became readable, I saw, "Bicyclists use shoulder only." Okay, I'll buy that.

After a mile on the freeway, I crested the top of a mountain pass and was moving downhill at a fair clip when suddenly my nightmare materialized as an Arizona Highway Patrol officer braked to a stop in front of me. Uh-oh, I thought, he's gonna say, "Get your ass off this freeway."

The officer got out of his vehicle, approached me and asked, "Are you okay?"

After I explained what I was up to, he said, "Okay, just wanted to make sure you were all right."

Ever the diplomat and knowing a good thing when I see one, I thanked him for stopping.

"No problem," he replied.

Hallelujah! I'm now sure it's okay to run on I-10.

Quartzsite was a rarity in our travels, because we did not have to search for an RV Park. The town was loaded with them.

Reading a Chamber of Commerce brochure, we found out why: The town is the scene of an annual gem and mineral show, and from mid-January to mid-February the town of 1000 jumps to nearly one million in population. According to one report, the U.S. Bureau of Land Management counted 272,000 RVs parked on the desert for the 1993 gem and mineral show.

The best luxury in Quartzsite was finding a facility to repair the RV air conditioner. It did not take the mechanic long to diagnose that the trouble was in the switch.

As he was repairing it, he commented, "You're damn lucky this thing did not catch on fire."

DAY 18. Starting today, I had two apprehensions: one about the Arizona Highway Patrol, the other about the heavy semi traffic. Elaine was concerned too about stopping on the freeway for a pit-stop and getting ticketed. Breakfast was not dull, because Elaine was parked in the breakdown lane and as we ate, semis buzzed by only three feet away from the motorhome, rocking it none too gently.

In my book, following a freeway is not the way to run across a state. With so many passing vehicles, I feel as if I am under a microscope and the solitude of the open road is lost. So obsessed am I with watching the road and traffic that I do not get a chance to study the scenery.

At about six miles, I got my first Arizona Highway Patrol feedback. A state trooper came toward me, slowed a bit (sending my blood pressure into orbit), and as he looked I waved.

He returned the wave and kept going. Oh, baby, there's good news today!

On her side of the freeway, Elaine was not quite so lucky in dealing with the Patrol. Seeing her in the breakdown lane, an officer stopped to ask her what she was doing. When she explained, he told her that she could not park in there. Following his orders, Elaine stayed out of the breakdown lane and instead parked in the median. She was on her second median pit-stop when the same officer came by, saw her, stopped, got out of his car, then bowed his head and looked to the ground as if to say, "What am I going to do about this?" To Elaine it was obvious that he was fighting frustration.

Advancing toward her, he said, "In no way, under no circumstances should you park in the median. When you do, we get all sorts of calls about a motorist in trouble. I'll tell you what you do, go ahead and park on the shoulder – in the breakdown lane – but use your judgment in getting all the way off the road."

At one point today I told myself, You should be enjoying more. But in truth, there was not too much to enjoy on this Interstate. My theme seemed to be, Let's get it over as soon as possible.

Because it was my last day, I could afford to extend myself and ran many miles at a nine-minute pace, like there was no tomorrow. I knew there would not be one.

Finishing, I took a picture of the Colorado River and Arizona state boundary sign. I could not take one of the California state boundary sign, because there was none. What's this, economy, Guv?

Elaine could not pick me up at the border on the bridge. So we had to rendezvous at the California Agriculture Inspection Station – a somewhat anticlimactic finale.

Heading home, I felt satisfied that we had completed our mission, made it across Arizona. But I did not feel any sense of great accomplishment.

Nor was I overcome with jubilation. I simply felt that running across Arizona was something I knew I could do, and I did it.

These feelings were a sharp contrast to what I experienced after running across the USA. Then, Elaine and I felt the accomplishment was so great that we could hardly believe we did it. We were jubilant, jumping with joy.

It was still a good feeling – a damn good feeling – to have finished a 389.6-mile run across Arizona at age 76.

Overview of
IDAHO

June 28th to 30th, 1993
63.0 miles

Day	Overnight	Miles	Notes
1	Trestle Creek	15.0	start at Montana/Idaho border
2	Sagle	22.2	
3	Oldtown/Newport	25.8	finish at Washington/Idaho border

Chapter 4

Idaho:

Adventures of a Panhandler

DAY ONE. In football if your opponent fumbles, you make a desperate effort to get the ball. If you do, it's called a "turnover."

It's also called a "break of the game" or "taking advantage of the situation." In all sports it's an axiom of the game that you capitalize on all the advantages you can – height, weight, speed or smartness (better play-calling, better execution).

Similarly with running across a state. For one thing "across" means a north/south or east/west route and, all things being equal, the trick is to take the shortest one.

That's taking advantage of the situation. Better yet, if the state tapers in size at one point and has a narrow passage across it, run this passage and take advantage of the situation.

When I studied Idaho, looking for the best route across, the northern panhandle jumped out as the easy way across. I measured the distance there and found that it was only 63 or 64 miles.

I chuckled, then felt sort of guilty, like I'd be cheating running this as an across-Idaho route. But then again I told myself it is technically across Idaho, and this is taking advantage of the situation. What the hell; go for it!

We did not arrive at the Montana/Idaho border on Highway 200 until one P.M. Since there was no place to park the motorhome at the borderline, we drove 400 yards into Montana before parking.

When I hit the road, headed west for the Pend Oreille scenic highway, I was dressed in half-tights, a T-shirt and a windbreaker. In the intermittent rain, I was a bit cold. In 400 yards I went past the Cabinet Gorge dam viewpoint but did not detour for the view, as I was running late and wet.

Five miles from the Idaho-Montana border I saw a young couple bicycling and asked them where they were headed.

"To the East Coast," they responded.

Since they were struggling uphill, none of us made a move to stop for conversation. However, I think had this been a solitary biker, he would have stopped for a pow-wow.

I've noticed that the soloists are always more hungry for conversation than the couples. This particular pair appeared to be novices. Oh well, five hundred miles or so on the road will get them out of the novitiate.

When I came into Clark Fork, population 448, I met another bicyclist going cross-country. His name was Neil Curry, and his home town was Boulder, Colorado. He was self-sufficient.

Neil said he started outside Seattle. "At Mukilteo, I went across on the ferry up to Anacortes and then on Highway 20."

"What route will you follow from here?" I asked.

"Most of it will be on Highway 2."

"It goes all the way across, then?"

"Yeah," he said, "all the way across. I'll follow the Bike Centennial route into North Dakota, then cut across and kind of straighten out to go through Minnesota and so forth."

"How many miles do you do a day?"

"About 70 to 75," he told me.

"That's quite a few for being self-sufficient and loaded with gear like you are."

"It's enough," he said. As we parted, I wished him good luck on his way to Boston.

Highway 200 today paralleled Lake Pend Oreille, and the size of it would have amazed me had I not read about it being the largest body of fresh water in Idaho and one of the largest in the western states. It's 42 miles long, 6.5 miles at its widest point, and has 111 miles of shoreline.

I was not too far out of Clark Fork when I heard a strange noise behind me. Turning around, I saw an attractive lady (hey, a guy never gets too old to look!). Red hair flowing, she rode a trotting horse, and in her hand was a rope attached to another horse she was leading.

Both gray sorrels looked like thoroughbred horseflesh. And, as inferred, the young lady, herself, was a thoroughbred!

Pooped after only 15 miles, I finished somewhat worried about how I would fare in the San Francisco Marathon July 18th after running across Idaho and Washington. A week before Elaine and I departed for the Idaho/Washington runs, we had a call that I was one of four runners chosen in the Master Card Masters of the Marathon.

The program includes all masters runners (those over age 40), men and women, in 11 western states. From a host of nominees two men and two women are selected as winners.

Because I was one of them, Master Card would host Elaine and me to a weekend at the San Francisco Hyatt Hotel and give me an award. In return I was committed to running the San Francisco Marathon, sponsored by Master Card. After finishing today, just the thought of chugging through a marathon over San Francisco hills tired me.

DAY TWO. In our beautiful overnight setting beside a creek and under a grove of pine trees as the rain pounded on our motorhome, I was severely tempted this morning to stay in our cozy, warm bed and to postpone hitting the road. But, realizing that we were under pressure to get across Idaho and Washington and to be in San Francisco on July 15th, I reluctantly got underway.

In East Hope, population 215, I passed a young, rugged individualist laden with a backpack so heavy it had him bent over, attributable mostly to his having it overloaded on the top. He was carrying a six-pack of beer.

Greeting him, I (ever the brilliant conversationalist) said, "Looks like you've got a heavy load."

"Yeah."

"Where are you going?" I asked.

"Don't know. Just going crazy. Yeah, going crazy." And with that he went past, to be seen nor heard no more.

When I came to the town of Hope, my thought was, "Here's a throwback in history." Hope sits on a small hill on a side road, about 80 yards from Lake Pend Oreille. I saw a post office, what was once a hotel, a general store and a few other buildings that were in the throes of death.

The side road on which the town sits was undoubtedly the main road before the lakeside highway was built. Hope, which hugs the hills of the northeast shores of the lake, dates back to 1882 and the construction of the Northern Pacific Railroad.

In its heyday it was a booming railroad town. Today it doesn't do much more than offer a good view of the Monarch Mountains.

One attraction that caught my eye, almost directly opposite Hope and in the lake, was an island, about a mile long by my guess, with a scattering of luxury homes nestled beneath groves of pine trees. Some easy living out yonder, I thought.

My one dog encounter today was at five miles when I went past a roadside home and a huge black Shepherd, scratching himself, saw me, interrupted his scratching to growl menacingly a couple of times, then returned to his scratching. I couldn't help but love those fleas!

My pucker-up experience of the day came at 12 miles when a Corvette, going about 65 miles per hour and passing another car, came to my side of the road, even edged over the fog line and thus came close to the 18 inches of off-road real estate in which I was running.

He came upon me so suddenly and unexpectedly that all I experienced was sort of a blur and the swirl of his engine noise as he went past. I was spared meeting St. Peter by 18 inches. The message I took away from that scary experience was stay clear of the fog line.

At a couple of pit-stops today, Elaine reported that Brudder and Rebel are hard to control on their walks because the pickings are too rich in this area. On one walk they found a dead bird, some animal intestines, some horse dung and a discarded burrito. Just how good can it get!

After Hope, the only other town on the way to Sandpoint was Kootenai, population 320, as I was informed by a road sign. There were some residences here to the north side of the road and not much else, or if there was I did not see it.

My impression running into Sandpoint was exactly what it was when we drove into it from the south on our way to the Idaho/Montana border: For a town of 5300 folks, this is a bustling burg.

The local economy revolves around the lumber industry and tourism, and there is much evidence of both. The town's two major activities are the Winter Carnival in January and The Festival in August, the latter centered on classical music.

Sandpoint dates back to 1880 when Robert Weeks opened a general store and dealt in furs. Later railroads and lumber sustained the town.

But what speeded up its growth was the construction of the Farragut Naval Base in World War II. The base was located at Bayview on the southern tip of the lake.

A boot camp, Farragut turned out 300,000 Navy seaman for duty in World War II. All of which, at least to me, seemed a bit incongruous: seamen being trained in Idaho. What next, mermaids in Salt Lake?

The run from Sandpoint to Dover, where we ended our 22-1/4-mile day, was uneventful. The last six miles I ran in the rain. If rain it must, the best timing is when my day winds down, so in this respect I was lucky.

DAY THREE. Ah, sweet mysteries of the road: At nine miles, I was running along when, quite suddenly and without warning, my right foot went out from under me and buckled, and I thought it might break.

As it failed to support me, I found myself going into a kneeling position, sort of genuflecting and barely recovered before falling. Back upright again, I jogged along as if nothing had happened, which left me puzzling over what that, a happening of only a handful of seconds, was all about.

I got some history education at 11 miles when I stopped to read a sign at a place called Seneacquoteen. "Long before white men discovered this river," the sign reported, "Indians used to camp here at this important early crossing. Seneacquoteen is a Kalispel word meaning crossing the river. Fur traders, surveyors and miners used to cross the river at this place. Then during the Kootenai Gold Rush in 1864, a wagon road came from Walla Walla, Washington, to a ferry here."

My next stop was at Laclede, and a short stop it was because the town's only edifices were a general store, the Laclede Community Church and a lumber company.

At 15 miles I passed by a mountain of rocks stacked one atop another, some looking as if they might tumble down onto the highway at any moment. The scene reminded me of the time a few years ago when I was running a leg in the Lake Tahoe 72-Mile Relay and Elaine was driving a Toyota and pit-crewing for me.

As I came around a turn in the road above Emerald Bay, I saw this huge boulder in the middle of the road, and strewn by it were pieces of metal that I recognized as being from a Toyota. I knew that rock had tumbled onto the road, hit a Toyota and knocked it over the edge of the road, down the rocky ledge three or four hundred feet to Emerald Bay.

My first thought: My God, it's Elaine! I ran to the edge of the road, looked down to the Bay and saw sitting at the water's edge a battered yellow Toyota – a different color than ours.

My instant reactions were relief that it was not Elaine and pity for the victim. I was surprised at how intact the car was after that descent, yet no way could that driver still be alive. The next day, reading a newspaper, I learned that the victim was a music teacher from the San Juan School District in northern Sacramento.

My day brightened considerably today around the 13-mile mark when I picked up a bike lane that continued all the way to the Washington border. I was also lucky in being able to talk Elaine into letting me stretch out to 26 miles today so I could finish today and head into Washington.

The only town of any size that I passed through today before reaching Washington was Priest River. Highway 2 extends about a mile through this town of 1560 souls. Residences and businesses are sprinkled side by side with no evidence of any kind of zoning.

In the last four miles, I experimented with a soft drink called "Jolt." It advertises double the caffeine of Pepsi or Coke.

The stuff jolted me, all right. I'm wired! Where's the party?

Around Albeni Falls Dam, almost to Washington, I had trouble making my way through the major construction project. Otherwise the last 13 miles, thanks to the bike lane, were smooth running, though I did feel tired from upping today's mileage to 26.

When I approached the Oldtown/Newport complex and crossed the bridge over the Pend Oreille River, I came to the best pedestrian path across a bridge that I have seen in 15 states. As I ran west, on my left was a four-foot cement wall of the bridge and on my right was a cement retainer between the cars and me, and the footway was about six feet wide.

Today's finish was somewhat anticlimactic, since the distance across the state was a mere 63 miles. Nonetheless to celebrate I suggested to Elaine that we dine in Oldtown at Fay's Steakhouse with a view of the river.

She said she did not want to go to the trouble of eating out. Now it can't get much more anticlimactic than that!

In truth she wanted to stay and enjoy the setting we had and to cook the steak dinner she had already planned as a finish celebration.

While the run distance was only 63 miles, I saw enough of northern Idaho to be knowledgeable of the natural beauty of the area. Someone once said, "If you want to find God, look to creation." Northern Idaho is a region where you can do that.

Overview of
WASHINGTON
July 2nd to 11th, 1993
212.0 miles

Day	Overnight	Miles	Notes
1	Bear Creek RV	17.0	start at Clallam Bay
2	Bogachiel State Park	23.75	framing a talk for Masters of Marathon
3	Kalaloch Campground	24.25	Fourth of July
4	Lake Quinault	23.0	Lake Quinault
5	near Humptulips	23.0	checking out shake factory
6	Artic	24.5	through Hoquiam and Aberdeen
7	Raymond	23.5	Elaine and motorhome have a near-miss
8	Bay Center	23.0	featured on CB radio
9	near Astoria Bridge	18.5	leaving Highway 101 for 401
10	Camp Kiwanda, OR	11.5	finish at Oregon border

Chapter 5

Washington:

An Olympic Run

DAY ONE. Ray Nicholl. That's the name I thought of instantly when I started planning a run across Washington. Each of the past 10 years Ray has run the Gold Rush 100-kilometer race (50-K on Saturday, 50-K on Sunday) that Hal Stainbrook and I direct.

Ray, a 56-year-old ultrarunner, thrives on romping over our hilly course in the California gold country. Over the past decade, S&W, the company for which Ray works, has transferred him from Modesto to Petaluma and now to Bellevue, Washington. Even the more than 700 miles from Bellevue to our race has not kept Ray from making the trip and competing in the 100-K.

Ray Nicholl knows running, Ray Nicholl knows Washington, so my thinking went: Why should I grope for a running route across the state when, with little effort, this guy can do a better job than I? Easy, then, was the decision to ask Ray to suggest a route.

Come to think of it, *suggest* is the wrong word. *Plot* a route might be better, because I intended to follow whatever route Ray outlined.

Ray's response to my request was enthusiastic, because he called me the day he received my letter. "There's only one way to go," he said. "Run the Olympic Peninsula. It's beautiful, it's short, it's safe."

"How many miles are we talking about?" I asked.

"Oh, 215 to 220, by my estimate," Ray answered.

"Sounds good. What's the routing?"

"You'd start at Clallam Bay on the north end of the Peninsula, follow Highway 113 south to 101, then take 101 south to the Oregon border."

"Sounds pretty simple," I said.

"Yeah, it is. A great run. I have only one problem with it."

"What's that?" I asked.

"That I can't get some time off to run some of it with you."

I found myself thinking, Well, I'm kind of glad you can't. That was nothing against Ray, because he is an upbeat guy and would be fun to run with. The problem here would be that this 56-year-old kid would want to set a faster pace than my 76-year-old body would appreciate.

Committed to Ray's routing, Elaine and I arrived in Clallam Bay around noon. To make sure I technically started on the northern border of Washington, I walked through Clallam Bay Spit Park to the water's edge. Standing there looking north, I could see the Strait of Juan De Fuca marking the border between the USA and Canada, across the water, and Vancouver Island.

As I got underway today, my mood was different from when I started the Idaho run. There I was eager to get started, to launch the campaign. Here I had to force myself to move out, and six miles went by before I grooved in.

The expectation was that after a couple day's off, I'd be fired up and ready to run, but that was not the fact. I felt tired and sluggish.

While I was almost a reluctant warrior, Elaine was, as she reminded me at each of today's four pit-stops, delighted to get back to a pit-crew mode and 22-mile days after driving 430 miles from Idaho to Clallam Bay in two days. She makes no secret about the fact that she enjoys our low-mileage days when I am running, and she and the dogs are cavorting. She is not fond of the days that require driving over 200 miles in one day.

By the time I had logged six miles, I did get to feeling that it was nice to be back on the road. And I counted among my blessings that I had no injuries, not even a flicker, and that the weather, in the 60s, was kind. After last night's deluge I had anticipated running in heavy rainfall today.

After finishing, we were lucky to find the Bear Creek Motel and RV Park only two miles south of where the run ended. The RV park did not offer much more than electrical and water hookups, but that was luxury enough.

DAY TWO. The traffic on this narrow, two-lane road with bike lane was sparse this morning. I was thankful for that, because I had some thinking to do. I had to frame a three- to four-minute talk to be given at the Masters of the Marathon awards ceremony.

Mark Beal, a New York publicist handling PR for Master Card, sponsors of the San Francisco Marathon and Masters of the Marathon, had told me, "When you receive your award, you'll be expected to say a few words." I assigned myself this topic for thought today.

When I went through Forks, everything was humming for the Fourth of July weekend. Motels, restaurants and gas stations were doing a brisk business, and the city park was swamped with people and cars.

The action in Forks was easy to observe, because this town of 3000 has only one main street. Forks has two things going for it: It's close to the west side of the Olympic National Park, and it's close to the Pacific beaches.

At the 15-mile pit-stop, the baked potato Elaine served me fired me up for the next leg and set me to thinking about my feeding habits. "One thing I would like to have learned more about," said Trevor Smith in *Running and Fitness* News when he reviewed the book (*Ten Million Steps*) about my transcon run in 1990, "was nutrition." So there'll be no doubt about it this time, here is an outline of my nutrition pattern:

• After rising and dressing and while driving to the start of the day's run, I have a cup of coffee and some sort of sweet roll.

• At the first pit-stop, mile three, comes breakfast, which always includes coffee, juice and fruit. The main course could be oatmeal or Cream of Wheat, or hot cakes, or bacon and eggs, or hash browns, or occasionally (Look Away to Dixie) grits.

• Thereafter I take on food and drink at three-mile intervals. At mile six, usually just coffee and sweet roll or toast ... at mile nine, iced tea or Koolaid, cookies, maybe homemade pudding, or jello, or fruit ... at mile 12, some non-carbonated drink (iced tea, coffee, lemonade, etc.), half a sandwich, and a cookie or piece of candy ... at mile 15, a Pepsi or Coke and some carbohydrate (spaghetti, beans, macaroni, rice), and a piece of candy or cookie ... at mile 18, another Pepsi or Coke, other half of sandwich, maybe some pudding or jello ... at the end of the run (miles 21, 22, 23), a root beer float (if Elaine thinks I am deserving) or some other drink.

• Dinner always includes a big fresh salad. The entree could be chicken, pasta, chicken fried steak, a roast, steak or hamburger (in one of many disguised forms!), some form of potatoes or noodles, country gravy, a vegetable, rolls with butter and jam, and dessert.

My guess is that my food intake is 7500 to 8000 calories a day. On this diet regimen during the 124-day, 3192-mile run across the USA I lost only five pounds.

It was hard to believe that on a Fourth of July weekend we could find a camping spot at Bogachiel State Park, just off Highway 101. It even had hookups for an RV.

I was told that Bogachiel covers 200 acres, but my energy level took me no farther than 50 yards from our motorhome. I was also told that Bogachiel is an Indian word meaning "muddy waters," none of which I saw.

About the talk I planned to think about today, here's what I came up with: I feel lucky to be here today, and lucky to be a runner. Beyond that, I feel lucky just to be alive at 76, let alone somewhat active at that age.

To appreciate that statement, that kind of luck, you need to have lost – as in dead – a number of friends as I have, or to know others who are ailing, infirm, stagnant or crippled. I'm lucky to have discovered running is a great medicine to keep me going.

One of the best features of running is that everybody is welcome, even fossils like me. Over the past 30 years in different races I've been lucky enough to line up behind Olympians several time, whereas I'd be jailed if I tried to get on a football field with Joe Montana or a basketball court with Michael Jordan.

I should acknowledge that I am lucky, very lucky indeed, to have the full support of my wife, Elaine, in my running endeavors. I say lucky because contrastingly I have friends, young and old, who want to run and race but whose wives throw roadblocks in the way. Unfortunately these wives do not heed the advice of Helen Hayes, "We do not stop playing because we are old. We grow old because we stop playing."

Even when I have had misfortune, running has been a good friend. Case in point, when I had radiation for prostate cancer, running helped me get through the experience relatively easily.

Another lucky fallout from running is that through it I've formed some lasting friendships and met many interesting people. Both Elaine and I have been lucky with running by having a lifetime of memories from travel associated with it.

The sum total of all this luck is that running gives me a zest for life. Enjoying my sunset years as much as I do, there are days when I almost feel guilty. If you are lucky, you too will grow old. So if you are into exercise, I urge you to keep it up.

If you are not exercising, I urge you – plead with you – to take it up. Your sunset years can be beautiful if you are lucky enough to be active and are lucky enough to have a zest for life.

DAY THREE. A most unusual Fourth of July in that I did not hear a single firecracker. I'd have to stretch all the way back to World War II to remember the last time that happened. Even when I ran across the USA in 1990, I heard plenty of firecrackers on the Fourth of July. In fact, I even had some teenagers in a passing pickup throw some at me.

A sign along the roadside today told me about the Hoh River and Destruction Island. The sign read: "In 1775, while at anchor under the lee of this island, the Spanish explorer Bodega y Quadra, commanding the schooner Sonora, sent seven of his men ashore for wood and water – all of whom upon landing were killed by the Indians."

In memory of this incident, Quadra named the island "Isla de Dolores," the island of sorrows. In 1787 Captain Barkley anchored here in the Imperial Eagle and landed six men who met a similar fate at the mouth of a nearby river he called "Destruction River." The Indian name of Hoh has since been restored to the river.

Compared to Barkley's six sailors, I had an easy time crossing over the mouth of the Hoh. The sign did make me curious about the meaning of the Indian word "Hoh." At the same time it answered how Bodega Bay, 30 miles or so north of San Francisco, got its name.

Around 15 miles today I had a moment of excitement when a wallet on the roadside caught my eye. Money! I picked it up to examine it, found it was empty and concluded it was a discard from a robbery.

I tossed the wallet back on the road. Then down the road a ways, I found myself regretting that my fingerprints were on it.

Until this point I have forgotten to mention that the Idaho and Washington runs are the baptism for our new Four Winds motorhome.

Going across the USA, and subsequently Oregon and Arizona, we had a 21-foot Mallard Sprinter.

Near the end of the Arizona safari we somehow got to talking about a "slightly bigger" motorhome. The net result (which usually happens when people begin talking about new cars or just looking at new cars) is that, returning home from Arizona, we traded our Mallard for the Four Winds. It is 23 feet and loaded with amenities, such as built-in generator, microwave, shower with small tub, double bed six feet in length.

Brudder and Rebel give it high marks, because the dinette makes into a comfortable bed for them. Like I've said before, one version of heaven: Die, become a dog, and get adopted by Elaine.

One thought I tangoed with today was the idea that if we are on earth but to live our lives and once they are lived, we are obliterated – no body, no soul, no onward movement – life would be meaningless. I went so far as to try to synthesize this into a four-line poem, but I could not line it up the way I wanted. The closest I came was: If there is nothing after death, Life is but for naught. For what have we wrought, With living and each breath?

Felt lucky today not to find myself running in rain, lucky to have moderate traffic, lucky to stay free of injury signs or symptoms, and lucky – this being July 4th – to find a camping spot near our finish.

We finished one mile south of Kalaloch, then drove back to check out the Kalaloch National Park Campground that has 130 campsites – but, we soon learned, no RV hookups. The campground adjoins the ocean, which made for a pleasant setting.

The only drawback: This camp area was self-service. You find your camping spot and register, which is easy enough. The problem is there is no surveillance, and camp rules are violated. For example, the rule is one vehicle per camping spot. A short ways from us, two spots had six vehicles.

The shower/toilet areas, unsupervised and studiously avoided by us, were downright messy. Likewise, some of the campsites showed damage. Overall, considering damage and vandalism, the government is probably losing money by not having supervisory personnel on hand.

DAY FOUR. Starting, I was apprehensive about whether I'd make it today, because I was awake much of last night with a lower left quadrant pain and left shoulder pain. Something was wrong, most likely a pulled muscle, but I worried about gall bladder or a kidney problem. My plans did not call for being on an operating table in the near future.

Luckily my stomach pain, which was distressing the first three miles, settled into just being uncomfortable and stayed with me as such most of the day. This, it seems, is part and parcel of life after 70 – every day some chink in the body armor. My day fell into two grooves: a mile-by-mile reckoning of my travels on the road, and a dwelling on the one failure of my life. First, about the travels.

As I ran south, I could hear the ocean to my right, but could not see it because a forest of pine trees obstructed the view. To the east what I mostly saw was a heavy growth of Douglas fir.

On my fourth mile I crossed over the Queets River and off a bit to the east caught sight of the decaying hamlet of Queets. From my study of the map, I knew that Highway 101 would now swing east and depart the ocean's edge, and that in fact I'd not catch sight of the ocean again until I reached South Bend.

Across the Queets River bridge I was greeted with a barrage of signs. One told me I was now in Grays Harbor County. Another said Aberdeen was 64 miles away. A third read, "Buckle up. We Love You."

A fourth sign: "Use your ash tray." My reaction to that was, hell, if you love them, tell them to quit smoking rather than to use an ash tray.

Must admit to not being too alert around nine miles, because I saw a sign that I thought read, "Olympic Convention Center, nine miles." Then, on second glance, I correctly made it out to read, "Olympic *Correction* Center." Oh well, the way correctional facilities operate these days with all their amenities (recreation centers, television, individual dress codes, prisoners' unions, etc.), maybe convention is just as appropriate.

At the 18-mile pit-stop I had just left Elaine and the motorhome parked atop a hill and was a short ways down the hill when some idiot, coming uphill over the double line and passing four cars, was headed directly for the area where Elaine would be accessing the highway.

If she has started out onto the road, I thought, this guy will cream her. Stopping on the right shoulder, I anxiously turned around to check on Elaine and was relieved to see that she had not yet moved the motorhome.

From relief I went to anger and a wish that I had a rifle in hand to fire at the idiot who could have killed her or other people. But in fact the idiot left the scene without any awareness of what could have happened and without any punishment for putting lives in jeopardy. He left probably congratulating himself for being a good driver and getting past all that traffic.

So went my travels this day. As I moved down the road, I found myself dwelling on the one failure of my life. I don't know why, but I focused on not being promoted to colonel in the Marine Corps. I could write a chapter, if not an entire book, about this episode.

Space doesn't allow that here. In brief, I shouldered the blame for an incident that wasn't my fault to protect two other officers involved. I felt compelled to protect them because they were two of the best officers in the battalion, and I lived by the dictum that the commander is responsible for all that his unit and subordinates do or fail to do.

I well knew that this decision meant I would get an unfavorable fitness report and would fail my promotion. That's the way the system works; one bad incident takes precedence over, say, 45 days of successfully commanding 1600 men in a jungle operation.

My goal in the Corps had been to make colonel. I failed, and that failure will always haunt me, regardless of the reason. Maybe that is why I dwell upon it every now and then.

However, not for an instant do I regret the decision I made. And in no way am I bitter with the Marine Corps. In fact, I still love the Corps and the multiple admirable men I met while serving in it.

DAY FIVE. When I got underway this morning, I sensed that something was different from my other four days in Washington, but I could not immediately figure out what it was. Then it dawned on me: The sky is clear and sunny, much different from the usual overcast of the past four days.

Unlike yesterday I encountered some edifices along today's route. A small shake factory at mile three, a Standard station and garage at mile 3.5, and at mile 4.5 (the entrance to the north shore of Lake Quinault recreational area) Brennan's Cafe and Grocery and JJ's Cafe, and about 25 trailers parked at this road junction.

When I was wondering if Brennan and JJ speak to each other, a motorist stopped to ask me, "Where's the Salmon Fish Hatchery?"

My first impulse was to say, "How the hell should I know?" (Yeah, it was one of those kinds of days!). With remarkable restraint, I replied, "Sorry, I don't know."

With all the frantic logging activity I saw on the road, I continued to get the impression that the timber industry is going all-out to beat some sort of timeline or restrictions imposed by the Clinton administration. Despite their haste all the truckers approaching me this morning pulled over to give me running space. But I would have been willing to bet, even give odds, that if I had been wearing a Clinton/Gore T-shirt (may lightning strike me dead!), I would have had some close calls.

The hamlet of Amanda Park sits in sort of a swoop and contains a cafe, motel, Texaco station, mercantile store and Timberline Library. The Quinalt River flows past the town.

A poster in town told me that a guy named Jim Hargrove was running for state senator. I played on a high school basketball team with a Jim Hargrove. This guy looked about the right age. Could there be a connection?

On any run across a state, there are emotional peaks to be enjoyed and valleys to be weathered. At nine miles today, I was in a stormy emotional valley, being concerned about a lower left quadrant pain since I knew not what caused it, worried about being devoid of energy and slowed by a pull in my left calf that I had to tape.

Then at 10 miles, the same damn thing I experienced yesterday: a pull in the tendon of my big toe, so severe a cramp as to be painful. The only remedial action I could think of was to walk and work it out.

At about that time I came across Elaine parked in front of a store. That made sense, since it was "Elaine's Neilton Store."

In candor I must admit that around 12 miles today my ornery streak came out. The road was empty except for an approaching small motorhome and me. I was off the road running the fog line, which the approaching motorhome was also hugging.

"Damn you," I thought, "I'm not giving you an inch." I continued solid on the line as the driver came closer. Had he not moved over, I would not be narrating this. I had to be thoroughly ticked to take such a chance, and I was. All I wanted was the fog line; he had the rest of the road.

Having run by several small shake factories the past three days, I stopped near 12 miles today to check out the J&J Shake Company. Like all the other shake factories, it included a huge shed containing a small mill and a good-sized furnace. The product exits the mill on a conveyor belt.

I learned they don't manufacture the shakes from logs. Instead they use blocks, a stockpile of which are kept outside the mill.

I thought today about the question I quite often get: "When are you going to quit running?"

My standard reply is, "I hope not until the day I die."

Now as I think about it, that is a lie – because my first day in heaven I intend to break four minutes for the mile and 2:10 for the marathon.

DAY SIX. As I ate breakfast at the three-mile pit-stop, I thought about a talk Elaine and I gave last month. Someone in the audience asked, "How soon do you start running after eating at a pit-stop?"

My answer surprised the person: "I start running as soon as I've finished eating."

Case in point, at this breakfast pit-stop I had scrambled eggs, hash browns, toast, fruit, orange juice and coffee, then immediately hit the road. Well, almost immediately 'cause I had to pause for Elaine to give me a hug and a caution to be careful.

"What do you enjoy more, racing or running across a state?" I was recently asked.

"Going across a state," I answered unhesitantly. I went on to explain that in racing there is the excitement of competition, some hurting from strain, good companionship, much focus on performance, and spectators and recognition. But usually the race is over a familiar scene, it is on someone else's time schedule, and when the race is over there's no tomorrow.

Going across a state, I get to share with Elaine, the only competition is to complete the day, we set the timelines, each step of the way is a new and different territory, there is always an aura of adventure, there is time for meditation and observation, and when the day's run is over there is always tomorrow.

The parade of logging trucks was unusually heavy this morning. Out of curiosity, from mile seven to eight I timed the flow of trucks and found there was one every 90 seconds. This was the flow north only, and had nothing to do with those moving south.

Speaking of truckers, at one pit-stop today Elaine told me how she listened to two on the CB radio complaining about how the Indians are violating their treaty regarding elk hunting. The treaty calls for the Indians to hunt with bow and arrows. Instead they are using high-powered rifles with telescopic sights and are killing an inordinate number of elk. The truckers' gripe was that there are few elk left for them to hunt.

There were variations in temperature today at various spots along the route. I was warmed by the sun in open spaces and chilled when on the road shaded by forest growth, albeit the growth was not as thick as the previous few days.

These variations matched my running mode, wherein at times I felt fired with energy and then at other times drained of energy. I had no insight as to what brought on these surges and slumps.

Given the comfort of a 3-1/2-foot bike lane, this was one of the easiest days for running in Washington. Another bright aspect to the day was realizing that I have not used an asthma inhalant since I began running in Washington. Sometimes I think the key to controlling my asthma is to hit the road for 20 miles a day.

The biggest change of pace to today's run was going through Hoquiam and Aberdeen, two adjacent cities and the biggest we will see on this jaunt. The first thing I noticed as I hit downtown Hoquiam was that the gas prices were down 15 cents a gallon from what we have been paying. When you're feeding a thirsty motorhome, that's good news.

The major tourist attraction in Hoquiam is Hoquiam's Castle, a 20-room Victorian home built in 1897 by Robert Lyle, a lumber baron. Completely furnished to resemble its heyday, the mansion is open to the public for tours.

As I went from Hoquiam (population around 9000) and Aberdeen (population around 18,000), the only way I knew I was going from one of these two contiguous cities to the other was by a sign reading, "Welcome to Aberdeen." Navigating Highway 101, which runs smack through the middle of Hoquiam and Aberdeen, was not easy. The road is a bottleneck, and it makes a couple of turns that are hard to detect.

Elaine and I were successful, though, in rendezvousing at the Aberdeen Visitors' Center. There we learned to our surprise, considering the area had so many motels, the nearest RV park was eight miles south at Artic, which left us no choice but to drive.

It took little time for Elaine and me to conclude that this RV park owner is an unusual breed of businessman. We had a lovely spot under the pines, full hookup, and were charged only $10. This guy has no nearby competition and would, if he were the typical businessman, be charging $15 to $20.

Even with his low rate he invites guests to pick vegetables and fruits from his garden. He was an interesting conversationalist, and what intrigued Elaine and me was his resemblance to Garrison Keillor, even to the point of having some of his mannerisms. He said he has never seen Keillor on TV and, in fact, he doesn't even own a TV. That was a bit strange since he has cable hookups for all his RV spots.

DAY SEVEN. This was hardly a day packed with exotic scenery or fast-paced action. There were, though, a couple of moments of excitement, the major one involving Elaine who experienced the scariest moment of the day.

Driving downhill, she rounded a curve and saw approaching her in her lane a lumber truck racing uphill and, over the double line, passing another lumber truck. Instantly Elaine realized she had but one course of action: pull far off to the shoulder.

Simultaneously the driver being passed made the same decision. And in this posture – the two lumber trucks and Elaine all abreast – passed each other. A trembling experience for Elaine, but with a happy ending. Well, not altogether happy, because justice truly being served the truck driver doing the passing should have been flogged.

My major element of excitement came when I was going through Cosmopolis, a hamlet contiguous to the southern boundary of Aberdeen. I was sort of daydreaming when I looked down the sidewalk and was agape to see a deer 25 yards away and headed straight for me.

Suddenly aware of my presence, the deer stopped momentarily, then panicked and ran onto Highway 101. I grabbed my orange cap and, waving it, ran onto 101 to warn drivers not to hit the deer.

The deer safely reached the other side of the road. Then, seeing no place to go and with the traffic yielding to my waving, he retreated to my side of the road, cut across a grassy field and escaped to the riverbed. All this action was so fast that I did not get a chance to whip out my camera and take a picture. It was gratifying, though, to see the deer escape unharmed.

This was another of those days when, because of a drive to find an RV park, I had already been over much of the day's route – a happenstance that usually dampens the anticipation. However, I did get more impressions of Aberdeen. For one thing I saw a disproportionate number of chiropractic offices. My guess was this was tied in with the lumber industry. A guy certainly can't throw his back out while smoking a joint!

Downtown I stopped to peek into a Washington state liquor store. Neat, clean and sterile was my impression. The Merck Apartments, now a bit seedy, on K Street were a reflection of how a city changes. It was evident that at one time this building housed one of the city's better hotels. Ever the tourist I stopped to take a picture of a mural across the street from the Merck Apartments. The mural reflected the early railroad days in Aberdeen.

Going past a husband and wife, tourists and senior citizens, I greeted them with a cheery, "Good morning." Their response was a vacant stare. I got the impression that seeing me – a fossil in windbreaker, Sporthill pants, ball cap, fanny pack, running shoes – they thought I was some kind of weirdo. Come to think of it, by some standards I probably am.

Elaine got much of her entertainment today from listening to truckers on the CB radio. At three different pit-stops, she gave me reports.

The first was two guys in wheelchairs on 101 and the trouble they were having going up and down hills, which was understandable to me since our route today was lined with four big grades. The chairs also had tough sledding in some areas where the bike lane was only a foot or two wide, which left them no choice but to use the road. Not to worry, though. Wheelchair athletes are gutsy, and these guys would make it.

A second CB report Elaine gave me was that a number of truckers were trying to get another trucker to slow down, and for good reason. He was so drunk that he was barely intelligible on the CB. Hearing that, my thought was, Not in my neck of the woods, I hope.

The CB report that stirred Elaine to action was hearing the truckers report that a person was lying on the highway, writhing in pain.

One trucker asked, "Does he belong to the motorhome that was parked along the road?"

That did it for Elaine. She roared out from her pit-stop parking place, retreating back down the road to where I should be, and worried that she might find me clobbered along the roadside. When she spotted me in my red shirt, sprinting down a hill, I looked powerful good to her.

After finishing our 23.5-mile day, the only RV park we could find was the KOA Timberland in Raymond. A somewhat sterile place, all it offered was a hookup. Fact is, Elaine was not allowed to walk the dogs in the park and even had to keep them in the motorhome.

"We're not supposed to take dogs over 17 pounds," the manager said. "But since we are not busy, we'll take yours." After saying that, she was somewhat appalled to see our two 90-pounders.

DAY EIGHT. Adrenaline is beginning to surge a bit with the realization that, including today, I have only three days on the road to complete our Washington run. That in mind, I found myself thinking about my commitment to Master Card to run the San Francisco Marathon on July 18th.

I harbored two concerns: I'd be tired from this long run in Washington so near the marathon, and I'd be slowed because I'd been grooved in long slow distance in Washington with no speed work. Besides that, I knew the SF Marathon course would be sprinkled with a series of nasty hills. Oh what the hell, that's tomorrow. The task today is to crank out 23 miles.

Our first adventure this morning was to migrate through the town of Raymond that sits in a small valley surrounded by foothills. The Willapa River flows through the middle of the town.

The Raymond city sign read, "Waterfront park. Antique machinery. Wood statue carvings. Museum murals. A great place to retire." Odd, I thought, that the sign made no mention of the huge lumber plant I saw just ahead on the west side of the road.

After seeing much heavy ship-loading equipment at Port Willapa, I concluded that much shipping must be done out of Raymond. South of Raymond, Highway 101 swings west and follows the Willapa River directly to the ocean, going through South Bend that sits on the ocean. When I entered South Bend, my thought was, The name sounds familiar. Why? Finally the light shone: South Bend, Indiana, Notre Dame and football.

Boy, 'dis ol' boat am a-movin' slow this morning. Gonna have to tune those mental gears.

Speaking of Notre Dame, I read in yesterday's *USA Today* that the Notre Dame football team graduates 92 percent of its players, much better than Stanford's 80 percent and phenomenal compared with some other colleges down to 20 percents. If the NCAA were oriented to academics and not dollars, there would be a penalty for each player not graduated.

South Bend, Washington, is proud of two things: It is the oyster capital of the world, and it has a classic architectural attraction in the Pacific County Courthouse built in 1910. A lady I talked with in downtown South Bend told me that the county recently restored the dome of the Courthouse and that restoration cost more than the original courthouse.

When the story in yesterday's paper about some guy in Wisconsin winning $110 million in a lotto crossed my mind, I wondered: If that had happened to me, would I be inspired to run faster today? Or would I even be running? Not a second's hesitation with that one: Sure, I'd keep running and, yeah, I'd probably be zipped up a bit today.

The story went on to say that the winner was a teacher and he intends to keep on teaching. There I part company with him. The world is filled with too many things to see, too many places to travel, too much to learn for a person with $110 million to be giving eight hours a day to the company store.

My day was brightened by an encounter with a bicyclist, Ray Williams from Huntington Beach, California. "I was originally a backpacker," he said. "I've done the Pacific Crest Trail and the Appalachian Trail. This year I'm biking the Pacific Coast from Seattle to San Diego."

Ray, outfitted in the best of biking gear and equipment, and streamlined for the road, was a sharp contrast to his companion, a good-looking guy with reddish beard who said he wanted to remain anonymous and who gave no information about himself. It was evident that he was a novice at bicycle traveling. His bike was antiquated, he carried a heavy sleeping bag, he did not wear biking gear, and what gear he had was not stowed aerodynamically.

He said he did not want to be compared with his companion who had an adventurous background. When they pedaled away after our conversation, I was impressed with how fast they moved, even the guy on the ricky-tick bike.

At the 15-mile pit-stop, Elaine gave me another report on trucker chatter on the CB radio. What she heard was, "There's this old guy on the road, and I can't figure out what he's doing. He's down at South Bend today, and I saw him up north of Aberdeen a couple of days ago."

Another trucker: "Yeah, I've seen him too, and I can't figure it out."

Third trucker: "Hey, I know who you're talking about. I got pretty close to him on a curve yesterday. I don't know what he's up to."

All this was too much for Elaine. Unable to resist any longer, she injected herself into the conversation to explain what I was doing. Of course, she also had to go into all the gory details of my being 76, my running across the USA and all that.

She said she reported all this to me to alert me to be on the lookout for truckers honking as they passed by. Which is exactly what happened.

DAY NINE. We had to make a command decision today about our routing. Our choice was whether to continue on Highway 101 to the Astoria Bridge or whether, about 10 miles north of the town of Naselle, to take Highway 401 that also led to Astoria Bridge.

At the breakfast pit-stop, I told Elaine that I had no preference, since either route got us to Oregon. So the decision was hers.

Without any hesitation she chose 401. She thought it might be easier to drive, especially since it would not have the beach traffic that would be a fallout from 101. With 401 being nearly eight miles shorter than 101, I thought her decision was brilliant.

All day, I passed by only two communities, Nemah early in the day and Naselle at the finish. Nemah sits in a small, pleasant valley, and all I saw there was a small cafe, named appropriately enough the Nemah Cafe, and a community church built in 1917. The church didn't look as old as I.

By comparison Naselle was metropolitan with its Sentry Market, Timberline Library, Bank of the Pacific, City Park, two churches of vintage, three small businesses and Little League baseball park. From a couple of signs, I learned that Naselle is a Chinook Indian word meaning protective shelter or hidden.

With few distractions today, I had much think time. One thing I thought about was writing a letter to Rush Limbaugh. I am ticked off that President Clinton did not re-appoint Arnold Schwarzenegger as Chairman of the President's Council on Physical Fitness and Sports, because he has been the best chair in the 25 years that I have followed the work of the Council.

In his campaign, Clinton vowed "to appoint the best people available regardless of party." In Arnold's case, he lied.

What Clinton did was appoint two people, man and woman, as chairs to replace Arnold. That did seem appropriate for a couple of reasons: Arnold was so good that it will take two people to come close to matching his work. Secondly, why not co-chairs, because after all we have co-chairs today as President and Mrs. President of the USA.

Trying to be philosophical about this PCPFS appointment, I was at least thankful that Clinton did not bring about my worst fear and appoint Jane Fonda, for if he did we would all be doing the Hanoi squat. (Sorry, but after losing some good friends in Vietnam, I cannot forgive Jane Fonda or her ilk for Hanoi.)

The only human contact I had today, other than with Elaine (which is about as good as it gets!), was with a bicyclist who told me he was on his way to Aberdeen, 55 miles away. I envied him being able to cover so many miles in one day. With his helmet tightly on, he seemed to have trouble hearing, so our conversation was short-lived.

I surprised Elaine at one point today when, at the 12-mile pit-stop, I asked, "Are you interested in seeing a herd of 10 Roosevelt elk?"

"What do you mean?" she asked.

"Well, a half-mile back, I saw 10 elk about 40 yards off the road and grazing under some trees. If you want to drive back, I can point them out."

Excited to see the animals, Elaine drove to where I had spotted them, but there was some letdown as we could locate only three. We knew the rest were close by, but we could not see them. This must have been the day for wildlife, because only 400 yards or so from the pit-stop at 12 miles, a doe and two fawns crossed the road 20 yards ahead of me, then stopped in the grass and played tourist as they watched me amble down the road. They were probably thinking, "He needs two more legs if he is ever going to get into high gear."

In the Naselle area we made a futile effort to locate an RV park, then decided to drive 12 miles to Mauch's RV Park on Highway 101 a half-mile north of the Astoria Bridge, overlooking the bay and Columbia River. It was not a very attractive place, but it did afford hookups.

Well, on second thought, I should amend that. It was not attractive to Elaine and me, but to Brudder and Rebel it was four-star, because it was loaded with gopher holes and they dug halfway to China.

My first action when we came to the Astoria Bridge was to stop and read a sign that confirmed that pedestrians are not allowed on the bridge. The Washington/Oregon border was about a quarter-mile out on the bridge, and that is where I wanted to finish tomorrow.

As I studied the bridge and found it to be a narrow two-lane road without a sidewalk, I realized there was no way Elaine could stop and pick me up even if I could manage to run there without being hit. That meant my only other course of action would be to run the quarter-mile out, turn around and run back, risking life and limb in both directions as well as a heavy traffic fine. In this case, I decided discretion was the better part of valor. I'd not risk the quarter-mile to the border but stop at the bridge entrance tomorrow.

Hell, I must be getting old. Where is my spirit of adventure?

DAY 10. I was caught a bit off balance last night when Elaine, after reading over my notes for yesterday, said in a voice coated with some emotion, " I'm pleased that you said some nice things about me."

I must remember to say more nice things about her. My God, I think a thousand such thoughts.

• Like the quickening of my pulse, the added adrenaline just when she holds my hand.

• Like the joy of going somewhere, anywhere with her and not having to fly a lonely solo.

• Like knowing she is around to lean on, to share with. Yes, sharing with words, with glances, with expressions, with touching, thoughts often on the same frequency.

• Like our sharing and caring on these runs, which are fun with her and because of her and inconceivable without her.

• Like detecting, at times, the suspicion of a sparkle in her eyes and the hope that I put it there – damn good trick for a 76-year old!

• Like appreciating the dozens of small things she does for me in the name of love, and realizing how lucky I am to have found her and how she fills my life with meaning.

Maybe I am prompted to say all these nice things about her since her comment sort of made me think I don't say often enough the thoughts I harbor. Well, for sure, with all my years, with all my meditative thinking on the road, I have learned that man's greatest gift, most precious commodity is love.

Well, now, I don't believe I've ever started any day on the road on such a romantic note. Even an Elizabethan troubadour would have trouble matching that mood. Could it be that I am that ecstatic about my last day on the road in Washington?

One thing on my mind today was a visit to Fort Clatsop after we finished. Yesterday I asked a fellow in Nessler for some information about the fort.

His reply was, "Oh, I don't know anything about that. It's in Oregon."

This was a somewhat provincial attitude, I thought, with the fort less than 50 miles away and a landmark in U.S. history. Well, I didn't know a whole lot about it myself, other than that Lewis and Clark had wintered there in 1805-06, that they had spent much of their time there working on their journals and maps, that there were about 40 people in the party and that they were lucky enough to have friendly relations with the Indians. In fact, the fort was named after an Indian tribe.

At the breakfast pit-stop, Elaine was still excited because a few minutes before a herd of 25 to 30 elk had crossed the road in front of her motorhome. She had stopped for them, was enjoying watching them leisurely cross the road when some screwball, driving about 65 miles per hour, approached and made no effort to slow, passed her and startled the trailing elks who bolted across the road. Luckily they all were across by the time the idiot reached that spot.

Today's finish was similar to the one in Oregon, with rain most of the run. Like the Oregon rain, this one was no drizzler; it was a drencher. In no way, though, did the rain dampen my satisfaction over being able to complete another run across a state.

Washington is the 16th state that I have run across, and from those experiences I have learned a number of lessons and encountered some problems. Many lessons, many problems. But if I had to synthesize to one lesson, I would name this:

The major lesson is that if a person has a wish to accomplish one major thing in life (like my run across the USA, or building a house, writing a book, traveling to a destination, taking a sailing expedition – anything), he should select a time in life to stop the world and fulfill his wish. If he has to wait, like I did, until retirement, that is fine, but program it. The earlier it can be done, though, the better, because thereafter it can be savored longer and the benefits and experience will apply longer.

When I first began long distance running in July 1963, I thought three miles was a long run. I never dreamed that I would someday run races as long as 166 miles. Nor did I anticipate that some day, as happened today, I would stack up a total of 106,751 miles on the road.

Now I wonder where it will go from here. Well, New Mexico in September, God willing.

But meanwhile, in a week's time and 800 miles of travel, there is the San Francisco Marathon. How do I get into these things?

Overview of
NEW MEXICO
September 6th to 24th, 1993
413.3 miles

Day	Overnight	Miles	Notes
1	Folsom Falls	10.1	start at New Mexico-Colorado border
2	Sierra Grande	22.3	Folsom and a fossil lesson
3	Clayton	23.0	blessings on the N.M. Highway Patrol
4	Clayton	23.4	Elaine adopts Minus One
5	Jct. Hwys. 104/402	23.1	meeting Albert Barnhardt
6	north of Nara Vista	23.0	wind, horses and cattle for companions
7	Logan	23.0	a plumbing problem
8	Tucumcari	24.0	a coyote sighting
9	Caprock Amphi.	23.0	tour of Caprock Amphitheater
10	Clovis	22.1	plumbing restoration
11	Clovis	22.0	metropolitan Clovis
12	Wagon Wheel RV	23.0	a friend (All Four) for Minus One
13	south of Portales	23.0	fighting headwinds
14	north of Tatum	23.7	easy, uneventful day
15	Lovington	23.0	first antelope sighting
16	near Hobbs	22.5	fond farewell to Minus One, All Four
17	Hobbs	22.5	passage through Hobbs
18	Jal	24.0	grasslands, pump-jacks, refinery fields
19	Carrizozo Sands RV	13.0	finish at New Mexico-Texas border

Chapter 6

New Mexico:

Grasslands Galore

DAY ONE. The guy's crazy, absolutely crazy, was my first reaction after reading the letter from the New Mexico Department of Transportation. Then, still holding the letter, I thought, But, good Lord, if this is true, I'll never be able to run across the state.

I had written the Department, just as I write the Department of Transportation of each state we plan to run across, asking for road information and regulations. The essence of the reply that I received said that in order to run across the state I would need: a permit, insurance in the amount of $1 million and, while running, a vehicle with a flashing yellow light preceding me as well as one following me.

For a few seconds as I held the letter, I wavered between disappointment, anger and disbelief. If I were inclined to panic, this guy would have me deep in the heart of Panicville.

Then reason began to set in, and I thought, This guy is berserk with authority. The state of New Mexico would not go overboard with such requirements. Why, Mr. Officious has even sent copies of his letters to six info addressees. I've run across 16 states, and no state has anything even remotely resembling what this bozo is prescribing.

Calming down, I decided to call the legal office of another state agency. I explained to the attorney who answered the phone that I planned to run across the state, but this letter from the Department of Transportation seemed to be a stopper.

"I don't know what the guy's talking about," were the first words from the attorney. "New Mexico has no such regulations or laws applying to an individual running on its highways, including freeways. In fact, I'm a runner myself, and I often run on the highways."

A contrast to the letter I received from Mr. Nincompoop was the letter I received from Sgt. Linda Wrasman of the New Mexico State Police. She answered legal questions I asked, and gave me routing and weather information.

In planning for New Mexico, I also had one other secret weapon: Dr. Royce Jones of Clovis who filled me in on the area I planned to run, particularly alerting me to the ever-present wind conditions (boy, was he right!).

Driving from home to the start of the New Mexico run, Elaine and I retraced approximately 1200 miles of the route we ran across the USA. Speeding over all this territory at 60 miles per hour, I found it difficult to believe that I had run every step of it.

We arrived at the Colorado/New Mexico border near Branson, Colorado, in early afternoon. Eager to get the show on the road, I set forth south on Highways 561/456 to log 10.1 miles, which brought me to a point four miles north of the town of Folsom.

As I ran through some canyons flanked with rocky ledges on both sides, my dominant thought was that this was great mountain-lion country, they might just be hungry, and it's possible I could be considered tasty. As a result of such thinking, I found myself picking up the pace.

There was a touch of history along this road, as I discovered when reading a historical marker that read: "Tollgate Canyon. Between 1871 and 1873, Bazil Metcalf constructed a toll road from the Dry Cimarron through Tollgate Gap, providing one of the few reliable wagon roads between Colorado and northeast New Mexico. This road remained an important commercial route until the Colorado and Southern Railway came through this area in the late 1880s."

Since there were no RV parks nearby, we camped for the night at a roadside table area at a place called Folsom Falls. I made a point of walking to the falls, only 60 yards away, because I wanted to see the area that was a favorite gathering place for Indians. Standing on the cliff near the falls, I felt as if I were touching history.

DAY TWO. Today I learned something that I had not been taught in all my high school and college years. This discovery came about when I ran into the hamlet of Folsom and got a lesson in anthropology, or was it archaeology? What I learned was that back in 1925 a cowboy going through the Folsom area dug up bones from some animals extinct 10,000 years.

This finding, along with some flint spear points the cowboy unearthed, threw anthropologists and archaeologists into a tizzy, because the prevailing thought was that the earliest occupation of the Western Hemisphere had not been much before the year A.D. 1. The scientists who flocked to the cattle-grazing Folsom area confirmed that indeed the area had been inhabited as long as 12,000 years ago.

The result of all this research was that Folsom man was second only to the Sandia man in arriving in New Mexico, and both were ancestors to the Indians. I wanted to visit the Folsom Museum, which displays spear points and fossils more than 12,000 years old, but it was closed.

I did play tourist long enough to go a quarter-mile out of my way to take a picture of the defunct Folsom Hotel listed in the National Historic Register. It was easy to imagine what an oasis this two-story stone building once was. The town also housed a number of empty storefronts, such as the Folsom Supply and General Merchandise Store.

Until I reached Folsom, things had been quiet along the route. At times 15 or more minutes would pass before a vehicle went by on this country road.

The passing drivers, most of them in pickups, waved. One young farmer stopped to ask if I needed help, typical of rural America.

A few steps down the road, it was my turn to play Good Samaritan when I saw a worm wiggling and roasting on the highway now warmed by the sun. I picked him up and tossed him on the grass and safety. Only a worm, but I feel good about it.

As I left Folsom, and despite all its history, I still felt somewhat like a pioneer, because I'd guess that I could be the first person on foot to follow the exact route that I am taking to cross New Mexico from the Colorado border to the Texas border. Right or wrong, I liked the thought.

I stood smack in the middle of Des Moines at 11 A.M. and saw no one on the streets. I took time to count 15 empty storefronts. A sign at the fire department in midtown told me that the elevation was 6622 feet.

The terrain today consisted entirely of grasslands dotted with small, conical hills. Entertainment was hard to come by the last few miles.

The major attraction was a series of long freight trains passing by on the tracks adjacent to the highway. Out in this lonely territory even the engineers wave.

The day finished, my weary body reminded me that I have not run more than 10 miles on any day since the San Francisco Marathon on July 18th. It will take a few days to get comfortable with 22 or so miles a day.

DAY THREE. Last night was a bummer. We finished the day 35 miles from the closest RV park, so we had no choice but to spend the night roadside.

We chose to stay at the Sierra Grande rest stop, which we had judged to be a quiet, restful spot. Wrong. It was about as noisy as living beside the El in Chicago.

First there was lightning much of the night, accompanied by windstorms of 50 miles per hour or thereabouts, rocking the motorhome. Every so often a freight train would roar past on the tracks only 50 yards away. Interspersed with the lightning, the wind and the trains was a constant parade of semi trucks, all making noisy stops at Sierra Grande.

Elaine was fascinated with the lightning and stayed up to watch it. I was ticked that it kept me awake. The dogs were frightened by it and, seeking reassurance, deserted their comfortable bed to lie on the floor beside our bed and be closer to us.

The lightning, windstorms and thunderstorms of the past three nights have me worried about the New Mexico weather. Somewhere I read that the state averages eight tornadoes a year and that there were as many as 18 in a record year. As I looked at the black clouds this morning, I thought, I don't mind getting soaked by rain, but this tornado stuff is a different ball game and I don't want to get caught on that turf.

There were a surprising number of windmills on today's route. With the prevailing high winds, they spin around faster than Pinwheel Smith.

He was the guy who, on his dying bed, said to his wife, "If you're ever unfaithful to me, I'll turn over in my grave." For her subsequent activity, he earned the name of Pinwheel.

Whenever I see a town listed on our route, I wonder about what I will see there. At least a gas station and a grocery store, we hoped.

Not so with Grenville, a ghost town. For lack of entertainment I counted 26 buildings in various stages of decay and saw only six residences (and these in dire need of maintenance) still inhabited.

However, the town did have a small community center and rinky-dink post office. The scene left me pondering why the town was founded in the first place and then why was it now deserted.

All day, the sun kept swinging in and out behind the clouds. One moment it was chilly; the next, warm. Snap your fingers, and get a weather change in these parts. Luckily for me, it did not rain.

Spent my entire 23-mile day along Highway 67/84, which would have been free of litter had it not been for beer cans and some discarded license plates. Between miles 12 to 17, I could have reached into the grass and picked up California, Texas and New Mexico plates – all current.

In early afternoon, when a Highway Patrolman stopped in front of me, I wondered if he would bark, "What the hell are you doing on this road?" As I approached his car, I was glad to see a half-smile on his face.

"How're you doing?" he asked.

"Okay," I said. "It's kinda nice to have this wide breakdown lane to run in."

"How far are you running?" he wanted to know.

Whereupon I went into my song and dance about running across the state, even to the point of outlining my route for him.

"Well," he cautioned, "be careful to avoid the area about 20 miles west of Clayton. It's not entirely safe."

Which prompted me to tell him that when I was planning this run, I was forewarned to avoid the area around Vegas because of the crime rate.

"Yeah, I'd vote for that," he replied.

He went on to tell me that he has a 4000-square-mile area to police. Besides traffic control, one of his main tasks is to watch for cattle rustlers. We chatted for a few minutes more, and only then did I learn that his name was Mike Johnson.

After last night's dismal experience at the Sierra Grande roadside rest, we drove the 12 miles into Clayton and overnighted at a KOA campground.

DAY FOUR. My cup ranneth over this morning, when after 12 miles I approached the town of Clayton and saw an historical marker. Excitement prevailed, because first I am coming to a town, of which there are not many on our route, and secondly because historical markers are high entertainment out here.

The marker told me about Rabbit Ear Mountain: "These two striking mounds were the first features to become visible to Santa Fe traffic crossing into New Mexico from Oklahoma, and so became landmarks for caravans. From here, traffic on this major 19th-century commercial route still had about 200 miles to travel before approaching Santa Fe."

Down the road a piece I came across another historical marker, and the emotion of this discovery was almost more than I could handle. This one told me about Clayton:

"Population 2068. Elevation 4969. Trade caravans and homesteaders traveling the Cimarron Cutoff of the Santa Fe Trail passed near here. Clayton was founded in 1887 and named for the son of cattleman and ex-Senator Stephen W. Dorsey, one of its developers. It became a major livestock shipping center for herds from the Pecos Valley and the Texas Panhandle."

The elevation interested me, because I could compare it with the 6025 elevation at Branson, Colorado, where we started. Took me a while as I jogged along to figure that we had dropped 1056 feet in elevation since starting.

Another sign on the outskirts of town advertised Clayton as "the CO_2 Capital of the World." I didn't figure that one out until the manager of the RV park where we stayed told me that nearby is the Rio Bravo Carbon Dioxide Field, one of the largest CO_2 deposits in the world.

What's a barrel racer? I asked myself when reading the sign, "Clayton, home of Charmayne James, world champion barrel racer, 1984-1988."

Gave me something to mull over as I trod down the road. Then, harkening back to the rodeos to which my Uncle Paul took me, I recalled the barrel-racing event. Problem solved.

Strange sometimes how we human beings function, I thought as I went past the Union County Feed Lot where hundreds of cattle were penned and being fattened for execution. I felt some compassion for them, yet at the same time would have no hesitancy in embracing a juicy steak for dinner.

A sign told me that Nara Vista was 62 miles away. I stopped to ask three natives working on a fence if there were any stores in Nara Vista.

For my effort, all I got was, *"No comprende."*

After finishing 10 miles south of Clayton, we drove back there to spend another night at the KOA RV park. Was hoping it would be as peaceful as last night, the first of our three in New Mexico that we did not have thunder, lightning and windstorms. *Pax vobiscum,* as we used to say before the

Ecumenical days.

Just as life on the road is simple and uncomplicated for us, so too is it for the residents of Clayton if I judge correctly from what I read in the *Union County Leader*, the weekly newspaper of Clayton. Compare these juicy items with what goes on in inner urban city front page:

• Ron Reed, of Portola, won a coffee mug in the weekly drawing at the Hi Ho Restaurant.

• Bingo games will be conducted weekly at the local VFW post.

• The Girl Scouts will be selling candies Saturday.

• There will be an all-you-can-eat chili dinner Saturday before the boys' football game.

Happily missing from the *Leader's* pages: murder, rape, robbery, muggings.

DAY FIVE. My most interesting experience today happened about eight miles from our start when I met Albert Barnhardt. Running in the direction of his home, I saw him drive out from his house and do a wheelie around his mailbox. In the process, he spotted me.

Doing so, he parked and waited until I arrived. I sensed he was hungry for conversation. So I took time out for a visit.

"That's quite a hot rod you've got there," I said, referring to his flashy red Chevrolet S-10 pickup.

"Keeps me young, " said Albert, chuckling. He went on to tell me that he had been in these parts since 1936 and that he was 66 years old. What was keeping him young at heart, I quickly concluded, was his being so upbeat, his sharp sense of humor and contentment with his life.

Until I encountered Albert, I'd spent much of my running time reflecting on kids and sports in the USA, 1993. Last night in Clayton, I happened to wander past a baseball field where a Little League game was being played.

As I observed the scene, I thought, My God, this is certainly scripted since my days as a kid playing sports. These guys have umpires, coaches, score-keepers, bleachers of spectators, batting helmets and even a P.A. system. For sure, adults are in charge.

Back in my day, a couple of guys – we called them "captains" – chose sides from the kids present and played ball, be it football, basketball or baseball. No spectators, just us kids. We did the scoring, the umpiring and we even coached each other. Our uniforms were the clothes we were wearing when we showed up to play ball.

Here's a case when I look back that I would not trade our way for the Little League way. On the playing field, we practiced leadership, we learned how to organize, and we developed character. On those scores, we were major league, and comparatively the Little League is bush league.

Mon Dieu, having so spoken, I can expect the wrath of Little League parents to descend on me. I've sinned almost as much as attacking Momism and apple pie in America!

Lately I've been experiencing some pain in my shoulder blades. Best I can make out, this must be bursitis or arthritis. But having had prostate cancer, I always harbor the fear of metastasis.

When I think of my aches and pains at age 76, then think of Dr. Paul Spangler, 94, still running races, still driving to them, I wonder how he does it. A person needs to be at least 70 to appreciate his accomplishments.

At 55, 60 or even 65, you don't yet have the feel for it. I know; I've been there.

I'm encouraged somewhat today, because into my fifth day and picking up mileage at the rate of 23 miles a day, I am beginning to feel stronger. The going should become easier than when I started with a low-mileage base. My toughest days on these trans-state runs are the first three or four as I jump up to 22 or 23 miles a day, whereas at home I try to run around seven miles a day.

Elaine, who is already mothering two Labradors and a fish tank full of guppies, has now added to her collection. She rescued a turtle from the middle of the highway. She named this creature of unidentified gender "Minus One," because somehow he lost his front left foot.

So Elaine adds to her daily chores the job of feeding Minus One and of keeping his plastic-basket residence clean. She gives him raw hamburger and lettuce, and he munches noisily.

The landscape today was punctuated with a farm settlement about every mile, and I swear there were more windmills than trees.

When I came to the junction of Highways 402 and 102, saw a good parking spot under a clump of trees and realized we had but two miles left to finish our day, I thought, I bet this spot is where Elaine will decide that we overnight.

Right on, to quote Shakespearean prose, because the first thing Elaine said when I finished my 23.1-mile day was, "Let's go back to that clump of trees at 402/102 junction and stay there tonight." Proving that the lady and I are on the same frequency.

Parked roadside like this, we always have to be alert, because some kook might just come by and decide to make a hit on us. So thinking, I'd like to trade Brudder and Rebel for a couple of attack dogs.

To their credit, though, it's a sure bet that they would alert us to the presence of any intruder. It would be interesting to see how they would react if we were ever attacked. Hopefully that scenario will never develop.

Another thought: Parked beneath the trees in a motorhome with a generator providing air conditioning, I felt like a damn sissy compared with the pioneers who had only the shade of trees to shelter them from the sun and heat.

DAY SIX. Mark this as a singularly uneventful day in which I covered 23 miles along Highway 402 through the New Mexico grasslands in 85-degree weather and dropped to our lowest elevation yet, 4100 feet. With no distractions I had plenty of time to think and to observe. A couple of things my meditative wandering focused on were a summer experience at my uncle's ranch and my early days as a distance runner.

When I went back on the road after one pit-stop today, Elaine gave me a couple of plums to eat while I ran the next leg. Had these been a couple of plums back home, most likely I would have simply eaten them and that would have been that.

But being out here on the road and in a pensive mood, plums in hand, my mind harkened back to the summer when I was in the eighth grade and staying at my Uncle Paul's ranch. These were hard times, and Paul's family augmented its meager income by picking plums during the season.

Joining them, I learned what an arduous task this was. For one thing the plums were picked from the ground. This meant that the picker had either of two choices: Bend over from the waist and pick up the plums, or crawl on his knees and pick.

I was a crawler. Crawling along and picking, I put the plums in the bucket. When it was filled, I carried the contents to a 60-pound box.

Once the box was filled, I carried it to a central collection point, stumbling and straining all the way. For each 60-pound box, I was paid seven cents.

Mornings, I was a demon picker – crawling, filling boxes, carrying and always multiplying seven by the number of boxes filled. Then came lunch.

Aunt Agnes packed man-sized sandwiches and cake or pie and other goodies. Overwhelmed with food, I succumbed to a siesta and did little picking in the afternoon. Until I learned better, my siestas were often interrupted with an urgent dash to the field toilet, because I had sampled too many plums when picking.

While not in a siesta mode, I labored valiantly for seven cents a box. In a hurry, that taught me the value of money.

My other mental meandering today was a takeoff from yesterday when I dealt on how adults are taking over kids' sports and how, as a result, this adulterates a sense of responsibility for the kids. I also said the kids are being pampered. Except for salaries they have about everything the major leaguers have – uniforms, coaches, managers, umpires, spectators, well-groomed playing fields.

Today, putting the shoe on another foot, I fell to thinking about how distance runners are being pampered and shucking responsibility as compared to the time 30 years ago when I came to the sport. Back in my early days it was the responsibility of the runner to know the course. Today every turn – and often every mile – is marked for the runner.

In my baptismal days as a runner, if we wanted aid, we carried it, or we had a handler in a car or on a bike carrying it for us. Today aid stations dot the courses every two or three miles.

If we wanted to know our time along the way, we had to carry a wristwatch or a hand-held stopwatch. Today most races have clocks along the route that tell runners their times, and most serious runners have wristwatches that give (and even record) their times along the way.

Don't get me wrong: These changes add to the enjoyment of runners, and they are necessary with the hordes of runners in today's races (can you imagine, for example, 2000 handlers – in cars or bikes, yet! –following 2000 runners in a race?).

But the point is that all these refinements do pamper runners, and they call for no exercise of a sense of responsibility. Things as they were when I started running, I was weaned tough as a distance runner.

In Amistad, five miles into our day and the only town shown on our maps today, I had hoped to see some conveniences, at least maybe a grocery store or gas station. No such luck. The town consisted of a Methodist church, a school with a huge gymnasium and three dwellings.

I took a bit of a chance today by running the center yellow line and by running with traffic so my leg would not be on the down-hill slant when facing traffic. I have a slight muscle strain in my left calf, caused no doubt by my left leg being downhill too much.

The only other problem I have besides my calf strain is that my lips are chapped and cracked. These cut lips revive memories of RUNXUSA out on the Nevada desert, when eating and drinking was painful because my lips were raw. 'Tis time to break out the Blistix, Chapstick and bandanna.

DAY SEVEN. As I set about to describe one of the perils of a journey such as this, I grope to put this as delicately or euphemistically as possible. You see, we had a major plumbing breakdown last night.

The apparatus that opens our sewage disposal broke and can be fixed only at an RV facility. That means we cannot dispose of the (enter euphemism) sewage that is in there and, worse yet, we cannot use the toilet.

So what are we to do? It will be nearly five days to Clovis and the nearest RV repair facility.

After some deep thought and a couple of conferences on how to handle this problem, we hit upon a system of lining our toilet with a plastic bag (the kitchen trash type) and "emptying" (more euphemism) into the bag. We have to be careful not to get too much waste (again, euphemism) into the bag before we extract it from the toilet, tie it, then hunt for a place to dispose of it.

What was stopping the removal of the sewage was a valve with a broken handle. We hit upon the idea that if we moved this valve by unbolting it, the sewage would escape.

Doing this, Elaine and I were both under the motorhome, she holding the valve in place and I unscrewing the bolts. The more I loosened the bolts, the more sewage leakage we had.

When I had the bolts completely off, Elaine yanked on her pliers holding the valve cap and, *Geronimo!*, stuff (supreme euphemism) flew out. Though I moved fast, I could not escape getting sprayed. When the tank was empty, we flushed it with water and made it acceptable to take to a repair facility.

This Sunday, as with many Sundays, my thoughts strayed to church and God. You know, I thought, some of the people who doubt the existence of God might benefit by coming out to the New Mexico desert on one of the nights when the thunder and lightning run rampant. Maybe they could feel the power of God.

If God were to release the full power of the rain, the thunder, the lightning, mankind would be wiped off the face of the earth. The atomic bomb, the hydrogen bomb would pale by comparison.

Church on my mind, and a thought that would infuriate most Catholic priests and Protestant ministers: In my mind, there is not an iota of doubt that out here on the desert – or, say, on a road in the mountains – I feel closer to God than in a church.

Everything around me is the handiwork of God. Whereas a church is filled with all sorts of distractions: the way people are dressed, the way they look, their mannerisms, their activity. Praying, which is nothing more than talking to God, is so much easier, so much more felt in one of God's settings (desert, mountains, forests, etc.) than in the four walls of a church.

And the truth is that most often I leave a church service with a sense of disappointment. Invariably the priest's sermon (which they cutely call a "homily" these days) is all words, no ideas, usually pointless, little or no relevance, often something left over from his seminary days.

Enough about church, priests and sermons. I've probably put myself on the verge of excommunication.

As I logged 23 miles today, my enemy was the wind. When I first hit the road at 6:30 A.M., it was mild. But as I picked up miles it increased in tempo, getting up to 30 to 35 miles per hour.

The only town we went through all day was Nara Visa. I shuffled up a small gully, crested onto a knoll and there ahead of me lay this town with a population of 51. At least this is what Rand McNally lists, but from all the houses I saw that appears to be an underestimate.

A greeting committee of two black Labrador puppies met me in town and, nipping at my heels, followed me 75 yards to the junction of Highways 402/54, where Elaine was parked for a pit-stop. When I was in the motorhome, the puppies parked outside and waited my return.

Their presence caused Brudder and Rebel to roust about the motorhome and bark.

When Elaine was ready to drive off, we were afraid the puppies might get run over if they followed me on Highway 54. So I took two dog cookies and coaxed the puppies back 25 yards behind the motorhome while Elaine drove away.

They attacked the cookies with gusto, and it was evident that they were not accustomed to such goodies. As they did so, I slipped away on Highway 54.

At the nine-mile pit-stop, I told Elaine, "I have 14 miles to go against this headwind. You know, the smart thing to do would be to drive 14 miles ahead, then get out and cover the distance by running with a tail wind."

Her reply: "No way. You'd be avoiding conditions as they are."

"I kind of like to think of it as using my intelligence," I said.

"Your *what*?" she asked. No tea and sympathy from that girl.

Our day ended on a lucky note when we drove seven miles into Logan and found an RV park. Besides electricity and unlimited water, we saved ourselves a couple of plastic kitchen bags!

DAY EIGHT. Some variations in scenery did unfold with the day as I ran redline Highway 54, then switched to 409, a backroad, and in the process went through the town of Logan. Even the grasslands were varied at one point when, unlike previously, they were dotted with bushes, most of them about 15 feet in circumference.

Down the road a piece, a sign told me I was entering "Logan Village, elevation 3830." My reaction: the lowest elevation we've been since starting, and it's hard to believe that we have dropped more than 2000 feet since starting.

Coming into Logan, I was forced into a dangerous maneuver when I had to negotiate an underpass leading into the downtown area. There was only 12 inches of space between the fog line and the cement wall of the underpass.

If I met a semi in there, I could be in big trouble, like, "Hi there, St. Peter!" Assessing the situation, I made sure no traffic was approaching and then took off at full steam, managing to get through the underpass without encountering any traffic, but running tuckered and puckered all the way.

The most conspicuous business in town was the Bruhn Sand and Ready Mix Gravel Company smack in the middle of the business section. The local bar, Whiskey the Road to Ruin, was closed.

This cosmopolitan adventure added diversity to my day and Elaine's. She filled the motorhome with gas and descended upon the two local grocery stores and unleashed some spending fury, this more exciting than bargain day at Macy's.

Entering Logan, I had faced a booby trap in the underpass. Exiting, I encountered another when I was alerted to "narrow bridge."

Again I assessed the situation – a bridge about 150 to 200 yards long, two lanes, about 10 inches between the fog line and the railing. The only safe way across was to sprint when no traffic was approaching.

Luckily I could see a half-mile ahead. So when the road was clear, I took flight and got across safely.

I well know, though, that on a long haul across a state violent explosions of energy such as this could result in a debilitating injury. Once across, then, I paused to make an injury assessment.

All appeared well, or at least no component was complaining at the moment. So after taking a quick glance at the swift flowing Canadian River, I moved onward.

Elaine, ever the inventive one, has added a new procedure when I come into the motorhome for a pit-stop. She's waiting with a pair of pincher pliers, and she extracts all the stickers from my shoes.

This is not a kindness to me. Instead she wants to make sure the stickers don't get on the motorhome floor to be painful to the dogs' paws.

Late this afternoon, Elaine had a moment of panic. In Logan, she had bought a plastic basket as a cage for Minus One, her captive turtle. A couple hours after she put him in it, she went to give him some hamburger and discovered he was gone.

After a frantic search she located him, put him back in his "cage" and covered it. Now Minus One sticks his head through one of the holes in the plastic basket and observes all the goings-on. This boy has moved in.

The day finished, I asked myself, How do you feel? The answer: A bit tired but otherwise okay.

What the hell, if I were working around the house, I'd be tired. Tired is status quo for age 76.

DAY NINE. When the New Mexico state trooper pulled up behind our motorhome at our three-mile pit-stop, our first thoughts were, Can we be in some sort of trouble? Was that bozo in the Department of Transportation right – maybe we were not allowed to run this road.

Quickly I exited the motorhome and approached the officer just as he got out of his vehicle.

"Hi," he greeted me. "Just want to make sure you're not broken down." Instant relief.

"No, nothing like that," I replied. "We're just making our usual three-mile pit-stop." Then I quickly explained our purpose here.

"Good for you," he said. "We don't see many runners out here. But sometimes we get a number of bicyclists."

We exchanged introductions, and I learned that his name is Nathan Wallace.

"When you get on top of Caprock," he went on, pointing to a distant plateau, "stop and take a good look at the view, about as scenic a sight as you'll get around here." He informed me we'd get a good look at the town of San Jon from "the top of the cap."

A couple of miles later as I entered San Jon, I saw the mortal wound Interstate 40 had dealt. The midtown street that had once been a part of Route 66 was lined with closed motels, restaurants and assorted stores.

A sign filled me in on local geography, or is it geology? "Llano Estacado rises above these red dirt lowlands to the south, a high plateau covering 32,000 square miles in eastern New Mexico and adjacent areas in Texas. Topographically it is one of the flattest areas in the USA and rises to 450 feet above the surrounding Great Plains."

Just as I was exiting the town, another sign told me that the Caprock Amphitheater was 10 miles away. I wondered, now what's that all about?

Later in the day I had the pleasant experience of finding out. Caprock was not a mountain in the usual sense. Instead it stood out as a long plateau or mesa.

Looking at it, I thought that once we got on top, we would follow a plateau for a while, then dip abruptly from it down into a valley. This I was to learn in subsequent days of running never happened.

As I started up Caprock, I saw that the area is studded with heavy bush growth. The grade was about seven percent. About two-thirds up I saw juniper growth, sandy cliffs and all sorts of rock-lined canyons jutting out.

When I came atop the mountain, Elaine was parked by a sign giving the elevation at 4900 feet. Directly across from her was a road along a ridgeline leading to the Caprock Amphitheater.

At the entrance was a sign announcing that the play, "Billy the Kid," was presented here by the New Mexico Outdoor Drama Association from the end of June until the end of August.

Visiting at the pit-stop, Elaine and I had observed a pickup exiting the amphitheater and heading toward us. We gave it little attention until the driver came to the highway, drove across it and parked beside us.

Then Elaine and I went on full alert. At the same time Brudder and Rebel started barking, notifying the intruder that we had reinforcements. When the pickup driver started toward our motorhome, I went out to meet him.

"How're you doing?" he greeted me. "I'm Bill Strong. I'm the curator of the amphitheater. Do you have a problem?"

"No, no. Nothing like that. Believe it or not, I'm running across the state, and we're just parked here for a pit-stop."

"Running across the state?" he asked. "You mean on foot?"

Which once again called for me to explain what Elaine and I were doing. Bill was impressed.

"You know, I'm glad to hear that. Because the main reason I drove out here was to invite you to stay overnight."

This was another of those days that when starting we had no idea of where we'd spend the night. Now here was Bill offering us a home for the night. I think the expression is: Some days you just live right.

I was a bit curious about the theater. So I asked Bill what the nightly attendance was.

The average nightly audience was 261," he said. "I know because I just calculated the figure for a board meeting tonight.

"Our problem is how to increase the audience to reach our capacity of 950. What we need is an adjacent attraction, like river rafting or such, which in turn would attract an audience for us."

Bill seemed lonesome for conversation, and we were reluctant to take leave of him. But in Robert Frost's words we had "miles to go." Departing, we told him that we'd most likely be back for the night.

We finished on Highway 69, six miles north of the township of Grady, and decided we'd drive into town to make sure we were not missing an RV park. Grady offered no such amenity, so we returned to Caprock Amphitheater.

Bill Strong cheerfully welcomed us aboard and showed us where to hook up the RV. When Elaine was walking the dogs, he took me on a tour of the facility.

Elaine and I enjoyed the wildness of the amphitheater setting. We went to sleep hearing the howling of coyotes and prowling of deer nearby. No wonder Brudder and Rebel had a somewhat restless night.

DAY 10. Some days out here on the road are without any razzmatazz, and this was one of them. No interesting incidents, no people encounters, no spectacular scenery.

There were only three variances from seeing anything but grasslands. The first of these came early in the day when I went past Ed's Bar and Mac's Barbecue Sauce plant, both set side by side in what appeared to be an abandoned farm.

A sign advertised Ed's as a friendly family bar. The eye-catching attraction here was a metal pole at least 100 feet high with an antenna atop it and an observation platform about halfway up. It was also dotted with advertisements from eight different beer companies.

Mac's place was decorated with paintings of cows, which to me did not seem to relate too appealingly to barbecue sauce.

Seeing the township of Grady was also a diversion. As I entered town, I got a good look at the high school.

Checking out the rundown condition of the track and baseball field, my guess was that the present school administration is not into athletics. Time was, though, when this was different, and this I knew from reading a sign on the town water tank telling me that the Grady Broncos were the boys' state basketball champs in 1978 and 1980, and the girls' champs in 1985 and 1986.

The other diversion was the township of Broadview. Elaine was parked in front of an antique store for our pit-stop. We were both impressed with how extremely neat and clean Broadview was, a town in which every residence could have passed a Good Housekeeping inspection.

In all my day-dreaming today I was amused most when I thought back on the summer when I was in the seventh grade and got a summer job that paid me $1 a day and a free lunch. I did the leg work for a guy who drove a laundry/dry cleaning truck.

My job was to jump out of the truck and to pick up or deliver the laundry. That is, I did this in all instances except one.

That one was when it came time to pick up the laundry in Sacramento's red-light district. In all such instances Charlie himself, despite his frailty, hiked up the rooming-house steps to pick up the laundry, among other things.

Obviously this was the part of the route Charlie enjoyed, because he spent at least a half-hour in each rooming house before he returned to the truck with a huge bag of laundry. Much of it was small towels reddened with blood, raising a lot of questions in my young mind that had not been enriched with any sex education.

Probably the strongest memory from that job – now remember I was only in the seventh grade – was the day Charlie emerged from a rooming house accompanied by one of the prostitutes.

"You'll have to get in the back, Paul," Charlie told me. "I'm giving Flo a ride to the doctor."

During the entire trip I listened to Flo as she lamented to Charlie about how she'd gotten pregnant. She was still trying to figure out how she had slipped up. If nothing else, that did enhance my sex education somewhat.

Once we finished our running day, Elaine hotrodded the motorhome all the way to Clovis. She was eager to find the Bison RV repair facility and to get our plumbing repaired, an enthusiasm (kindled by our heavy use of kitchen plastic bags) I shared with her.

We were not sure when or if Bison RV could do the job, but we lucked out on both counts. Bison had the parts, the time and the expertise to do the repair quickly and competently.

Elaine and I felt like we'd discovered gold. It's not every day when you are on the road that you can get cheerful, competent and reasonably priced service for a vehicle. This was the time and the place.

DAY 11. The major entertainment today was our passage through Clovis. Compared to the hamlets on our southward route through the New Mexico grasslands, Clovis, population 33,000, was metropolitan.

About four miles north of downtown the Clovis built-up area began with a scattering of residences and businesses. The volume of traffic was the heaviest yet in New Mexico.

Talk about tragedies, I went by Daylight Donuts with a George Washington in my fanny pack and a craving for a donut fix. I instantly decided, I'll have one to raise my morale! Then, alas, as I approached the store my eyes did behold a sign: "Closed."

The sign told me that the building was in the National Register of Historic Places, because it was originally the first hospital in these parts. I studied the two-story white building that somewhat resembled a southern plantation home and was impressed with its fine condition.

Seeing that it now housed the Western Guns and Art Collection, I decided that I could afford five minutes of diversion inside. I left thinking that $950 for a Springfield rifle and $350 for a Colt made in Argentina was excessive.

Negotiating my way through heavy traffic, I crossed Highways 60/84 and caught Highway 70, heading south toward Portales. As I trod the overpass out of town and over the Sante Fe railroad tracks, I counted 13 sets of tracks, attesting to Clovis being a train terminus.

I bowed my head in reverence to the brilliant engineer who thought to put a sidewalk on this overpass and to protect that sidewalk with a three-foot cement barricade between it and the road. Too bad this guy did not wander into town, where 90 percent of the route I ran was without sidewalks.

I had one regret when departing Clovis, which was that I was not able to visit with Royce Jones, a local M.D. and runner who had been kind enough to give me needed advice about roads in New Mexico. He wanted me to stop and have dinner with him, but I had to bypass his invitation because of the logistics of handling the dogs and motorhome. Besides, I needed all the rest and sleep I could schedule to ready myself for the next day's run.

The most pleasant impression Elaine and I took from Clovis was from our experience with the Bison RV Center. The young service manager, Bill, said that he used to run considerably but now does only three miles every other day because he has a back problem.

I resisted the temptation to talk with him about his back problem. Years ago, when running a marathon and seeing a neophyte runner make some mistake – running on the slope, breathing improperly, clenching hands tightly, etc. – I'd try to be helpful and offer a suggestion. Nowadays I keep my mouth shut, realizing that the average young runner would think, "What's this old coot who's going so slow know about running?"

After finishing today, we toured Cannon Air Force Base to see the only active F-111 base in USA and a boon to the Clovis economy. With the lack of sense some base closures make, those sound like good criteria for closing Cannon.

DAY 12. Everything comes at a price. Example: The comfort of the KOA Kampground in Clovis where we stayed the past two nights was paid for by KOA being located much too close to the Sante Fe railroad tracks. As a result we were often rousted from our sleep by the loud whistles of passing trains.

Yesterday's issue of *USA Today* carried a lengthy article on how dangerous roadside rest areas have become. Knowing that, we are trying to play it safe much as we can by seeking out RV parks even if this means extended driving.

Oh, how this world changes. Last night I stepped into the modern world when I used our new cellular phone for the first time to call my son in Sacramento, California.

I was impressed with how clear the transmission was. What will this world be like in another quarter-century?

I was only eight miles into the day when I found a turtle midway in the road. Playing Elaine's game, I picked him up and carried him a mile to the pit-stop, hoping all along the way that he had good bladder control.

"Oh no," Elaine shrieked when seeing him.

"Well," I said, "you decide whether or not you want to keep him."

The turtle found a home. Minus One found a friend.

"What are you going to name him?" I asked.

She said, "I'll have to think about it."

I suggested Eureka, but she vetoed that. My guess was that she would have a name by the next pit-stop.

Meanwhile it never rains but what it pours, because a half-mile after the pit-stop, I stumbled across yet another turtle. "Sorry, fella," I told him, "but I can't adopt you. Elaine would have a conniption."

At the next pit-stop I was surprised not at all when Elaine told me she had found a name for the turtle.

"I'm going to call him All Four," she announced.

So now we have a family of six: Minus One, All Four, Rebel, Brudder,

Elaine, Paul. Such is parenthood at my age.

When I first saw the sign, "Greyhound Stadium," my reaction was surprise at greyhound racing being in these parts. I had not heard about that.

Then, closer and seeing a schedule of games, I learned that this was the football stadium for Eastern New Mexico University. Quite a layout, I thought, for a school with only 3800 students. I also thought there must be quite a traffic snarl as the cars from this stadium hit Highway 70 after a game.

I had read somewhere that the university, with 500 people working there, is the single biggest employer in Portales.

About 12 miles into my day a white pickup stopped, and the driver got out, ran over to me and said, "Hey, I hope you don't mind me holding you up." It took a couple of seconds for me to register that this was Bill Strong from the Caprock Amphitheater.

"Not at all, " I replied. "Always welcome a visit out here. What are you doing in these parts?"

Bill explained that he had a house in Portales, that he had attended the university there, and had graduated last June with a major in elementary education and drama. He was applying for a job as traveling drama teacher for five elementary schools.

"Well, I sure hope you get the job," I said. "I know you'd be great at it."

He seemed to appreciate my confidence in him, and he responded, "It sure would tie in with a major project I'm just starting to work on. What I want to do is to get a dormitory built at the amphitheater so we can have a summer program there for kids."

After Bill took leave of me, I found myself thinking of how many dollars are wasted funding worthless projects. Yet here is a guy with a worthwhile project and little hope of funding.

After 14 miles on the road I reached the outskirts of Portales. A roadside store featured new-crop peanuts, local sweet potatoes and pure sorghum salsa. The peanuts I knew about, because over the last three miles I'd seen a lot of peanuts that had fallen on to the road from trucks.

I had been told that visitors stopping by the local Chamber of Commerce would be given a free pound of peanuts. The local folks just want to prove how tasty their peanuts are, but I had neither the energy nor appetite for such diversion.

In town I stopped to take a picture of a sign that read, "Welcome to Portales, the home of 12,000 friendly people and two or three old grouches." Reflecting on that, I wondered if we don't have some age discrimination here. A person need not be old to be a grouch, and all old people are not grouches.

DAY 13. Today I came to the motorhome for the three-mile pit-stop and Elaine, barely opening the door, said, "Now don't get excited. Prepare yourself. I've had a slight accident."

Then she opened the door, and I saw blood dripping from her chin, her forehead was cut, her blouse was splattered with blood, and blood was dripping from her knee. Before I could ask her what happened, she explained that she was jogging with the dogs and tripped.

"Basically I'm all right, just scrapes and bruises," she said. "I've got a nasty cut under my chin, I'm pretty sure my little finger is broken, and I know I'm going to be uncomfortable for a while."

I lingered at the pit-stop for a while to make sure she was okay. Leaving, I cautioned her, "Don't be alarmed if I am slow, because I am not going to fight the wind."

Wind was a four-letter word today. It hit its full fury, 35 miles per hour, on my last leg. By the end of the day, I was understandably frazzled from 23 miles of running into this headwind.

I was also tired from a big mistake I made yesterday when I tried a new pair of New Balance 520 shoes. They were too heavy for me and not configured to my running style. Wearing them tired me, and then this feeling carried over to today.

It was hard for me to believe that the same company could manufacture the 840, a shoe extremely kind to me on my run across the USA. Well, maybe not too hard to believe, because this same company discontinued the 840, one of the best shoes to ever come out of their plant.

When a bus load of football players from Eunice High School went past, headed north for a game, it revived memories of my high school days when the weekend game – football, basketball, baseball – was the highlight of my week. Being in a Christian Brothers school, I had not yet discovered that girls were a more interesting sport. That was to come later.

In fact, today when I came to the junction of Highway 225, I was reminded of some of those girls when a sign told me that Rogers was off to the east. Yes, Betty Ann Rogers.

Now there's a story if I turn the clock back a little over 50 years. A very classy young lady, and we might have clicked, but a war (and some Air Force dude!) got between us.

I guess it is only natural to sometimes wonder about what would have happened had I gone down the path of life with Betty Ann. Or for that matter, with Jane, or Jean (both of them!), or Helene.

The only serious *affair d'heart* there was one of the Jeans. She was my first love, unknowingly my tutor in how to deal with the fair sex and the recipient of all my naiveté in such dealings. Good Lord, how did I get off on this?

As always when I see towns on our route, I am curious about what we will see there. Such was the case today with Dora and Pep (honest, those are the true names).

I knew I was in Dora because a red and white sign told me so. I could not resist stopping at Bill's Welding to take a picture of an iron ornament showing the Iwo Jima flag-raising. It was a bit difficult to take the picture and salute at the same time!

I knew the town was rural. But a guy leading a cow down the main street was overdoing it a mite, I thought.

The most distinguishing feature of the hamlet of Pep, eight miles south of Dora, was a grove of approximately 30 trees, all unidentifiable to this fugitive from botany. Pep even had a post office and a community store, closed this afternoon with this sign on the door, "Gone to the football game."

Elaine rewarded my day's performance by handing me a root beer float when I finished. As I took it, she said, "The best is yet to come."

"The best?" I asked, raising an eyebrow. For a split second, she gave me a this-is-unbelievable-look, then said, "I mean dinner."

Oh well, I thought, if she knew how I went down memory lane today with Ann and Jean I and Jane and Jean II and Helene – geez, I wouldn't even be getting a root beer float!

DAY 14. This day came close to starting on a calamitous note when I didn't see a piece of metal left on the edge of the road at a construction site and, as a result, tripped over it. I was lucky enough while staggering to retain my balance and not fall and incur an injury. As I regrouped, I realized that this was the closest I'd come to falling in at least 4000 miles on the road.

Elaine with her fall yesterday was not so lucky. Today one of her fingers is swollen and painful. She thinks it is broken.

This is not the time for either of us to get injured. I have yet to suffer a major injury when running across a state, which is the way it should be.

Out here I would have a hard time handling an injury. Back home, a different story.

Time was when I regarded injuries as an enemy. But now I regard them as a friend.

Why the change of heart? Because the net result of an injury is to whet my appetite for running and to increase my appreciation of the sport.

Sometimes it takes an injury to remind me of just how lucky I am to be able to run and race. Sidelined with an injury, I realize what I am missing and hanker to get back to it.

Running conditions don't get much better than they were this morning: newly constructed blacktop highway, temperature in the 60s, light traffic. The only setback all day was when the highway bike lane disappeared for a few miles.

The scenery – same old grasslands and some rolling hills – left a lot to be desired. The one variation came when we were in an area with a number of active oil wells.

A sign told me it was the Black Hills Prairie Chicken area. I saw neither chickens nor hills, but there were some sand dunes.

The biggest nuisance Elaine and I face in this area is some sort of sticker that is all over the bushes and grass. It sticks to my shoes, my shoelaces and to the dogs.

If touched by hand, it is prickly and painful. If the dogs get one on their paw, they limp in pain.

Elaine and I keep a pair of pliers handy to remove the stickers from us and the dogs. Check off another contingency not reckoned with in our planning.

The only community we passed through today was Milnesand. On this Sunday morning no one was in sight at the Milnesand Baptist Church. Near the post office were eight big shady trees, very inviting for a pit-stop in this hot weather, and an inhospitable sign, "Don't drive in here."

As is often my bent Sundays when on the road, my thoughts went to God and church. A man can do some profound thinking when he is in the arena of the open lands that God has created.

Much of my thinking today went to the Game of Life. A game we are all put here to play until, in Shakespeare's words, "we shuffle off this mortal coil" (so much more poetic than saying, "until we croak"). A game in which I for one am not sure of the rules.

Well, I know some of the rules. Sure, it's wrong to kill people, to rob people, to maim or rape people.

But how about some of the niceties? Is divorce wrong? Is abortion wrong? Is masturbation wrong? Is it necessary to believe and practice the dogma of some organized religion to play the Game right?

Above all, I asked myself, When the Game of Life is over for me, when I cross the Great Finish Line, will I wind up on God's team or Satan's team?

Plodding along alone in this outdoor setting with the sky as the dome of my church this Sunday, I enjoyed reviewing my life and how I have played the Game of Life. In that review I saw some good things and some bad things – just as God has, I am sure. I guess whether or not I make His team when the Game is over depends on how He weighs the good and the bad.

Yeah, about every Sunday running the roads I wind up saying the same thing: I feel that I get a lot closer to God while running the roads than I do when being in a church. To put it another way, I'm a better player in the Game of Life while running the roads than in church.

Amen.

DAY 15. As I started today, it was good to know that I can count the remaining days of this run on the fingers of one hand. It's not so much that I want to get the run over but rather that I just want to make sure I finish.

Fact is, in all honesty, I marvel at how I have avoided disaster (to wit, injury or illness) when running across 17 states. To put it in the hep language of the early Christians, *Deo Gratias.*

About the time I was thinking there was no wildlife in these parts, I spotted a herd of six antelopes in a field adjacent to the east fence. The antelope with horns started to run toward me and the fence.

Usually they run away, so I was thinking, Is this guy going to attack? Then he stopped at the fence and looked west across the road.

I followed his look and saw a single antelope on the west side. This guy must be on a *cherchez la femme* mission, I concluded – that or he thinks I have designs on the femme.

I kept going, hoping that if he planned to jump the fence he would wait until I got a respectable distance down the road. I scare easily!

I could not help thinking how nature has dealt these animals an unfair hand in that their white rumps make them so easy to spot. With that weakness and the telescopic sights hunters use, it's a wonder that any antelope survive.

As I looked at these peaceful and graceful animals, I knew I could never bring myself to shoot one. Maybe that's partly because I've been shot at a few times myself.

The only person I encountered today was a pickup driver who, going the same direction as I, pulled over to my side of the road and, facing traffic, drove along beside me. His first question was, "What'cha doing out here?"

To keep it simple I replied that I was running from Colorado to Texas.

"You mean all the way, all the way on foot?"

"Yeah, but only 23 miles a day," I explained.

"That's a helluva long ways on foot," he said. He seemed to get the picture of what I was doing, but as oncoming traffic forced him to return to his side of the road, his parting question was, "You don't need a ride, do you?"

Which left me not so sure that he did get the picture. As he drove off, I noticed a sticker on his rear bumper, "I stop for all pow-wows."

The only town we passed through today was Tatum. There I saw more trees than I had seen spread over the preceding 20 miles.

For the past 80 miles I had been seeing decorated ornamental wrought-iron signs at many homes and business. But the topper was here in Tatum where every street has one of these signs – of birds, or horses, or wagons, or such – posted about 15 feet high on a lamppost and indicating the name of the street. As I looked at these attractive signs, I thought, Good Lord, in most California cities these signs would be stolen minutes after being installed.

On the south end of town I ran past the school complex (elementary school, middle school, high school) and was careful to slow down and not exceed the speed limit (okay, okay, weak joke, weak runner). Observing the kids at recess, I noticed about an equal mix of Indians, Mexicans and Caucasians, but I did not see any blacks.

I was made to feel like a kid when we checked into the A-1 Mobile Village RV park in Lovington. That youthful feeling came about when I met 91-year-old Roy Dodson, who was taking care of the park in the absence of his 71-year-old son who owns it.

Roy was assisted by his wife Dot, age 89. They have been married 71 years.

Some excitement was injected into my day when I was a passenger in a golf scooter driven by Roy as he escorted me to our RV spot. On the way he carried on a monologue about his sons and about his living at various places all over the United States.

I was not listening too closely because I was more intrigued with wondering, How does a 91-year-old guy muster all this energy? That Roy was of the old school was evident when it came time to pay for the RV spot.

I started to hand him a Visa card, and he said, "You know, checks and credit cards are too much for me. I'd prefer cash."

DAY 16. On the run into Lovington today I saw enough pumpjacks and natural gas holdings to realize that oil and natural gas are the two main staples of the Lovington economy, or of Lea County for that matter. From what I could learn, the town – population almost 10,000 – did not hold any special tourist attractions.

And it did not seem to have any significant history. In fact, founded in 1908, it was not a lot older than I.

What saved the community, what injected life into it, was the discovery of the Denton Oil Pool, about nine miles north of town, in 1950. Those were my thoughts as I ran Highway 206 which coincides with Main Street in Lovington.

Today I had some of my best entertainment in running across 17 states. This happened when I went past an ostrich farm.

I'd seen an ostrich farm once before, this when I was in South Africa. There the birds were inactive.

Here the six I saw were running, not so unusual unto itself. What did make it unusual is that they were performing just like a group of runners in that they were running intervals on a straightaway.

A flight of three would take off and scoot down the stretch, soon followed by another flight of three. Then all six would walk back to the start and repeat another such interval.

I stood there watching them in awe for at least 10 minutes. I knew, from what I had been told in South Africa, that these flightless birds who spread their small wings when running can attain speeds up to 40 miles per hour. Today I was impressed with their speed and running form, remarkable for eight-foot-tall creatures that weigh 300 pounds.

In South Africa I had been told that ostriches are dumb, that their brain is only about the size of a walnut. The way these birds were running these organized intervals did not look dumb to me.

This day did not go well for Elaine. First of all she was on the binnacle list with all sorts of wounds.

A few days ago she had tripped and cut her face and fractured a finger. Then two nights ago, when we were parked roadside, she stumbled on the metal step when exiting the motorhome.

"It feels like I broke a metatarsal," she said.

But Elaine's wounds pale alongside of the momentous decision she has come to today. For the past two days, Minus One and All Four have thrown up the raw hamburger she has fed them, and they do not appear to be eating the lettuce she has provided.

"I think they'd be better off if I turned them loose," she told me. Now the time had come.

"This is a good place," she said after looking around at Harry Adams State Park where we were comfortably located for the night.

The park, about nine miles north of Hobbs on Highway 18, was an oasis compared to our usual grasslands, desert-like surroundings. Here were trees, manicured green grass and a good-sized pond.

"I hope I'm doing the right thing," Elaine told me as she took the turtle basket and started to leave the motorhome. "I know Dan would sure like to have them, but I'm not sure they would survive the trip home."

She was referring to our son-in-law, Dan Phillips, who is the devoted parent of four turtles. I was trying to think of something appropriate to say and was not succeeding.

Elaine went on, "I'm really going to miss seeing Minus One sticking his neck out of his basket and watching me when I cook."

In one way I was glad to see the turtles go. Attending to her wounds, to the dogs and me, Elaine already had too much to do. The turtles were an added burden.

Yet on the other hand fussing with them brought her a certain amount of pleasure. We can all use all of that that we can get.

I watched her, turtle basket in hand, favoring a broken metatarsal, as she limped 200 yards across the grass to the pond. Injury-battered and emotionally bowed, she was a pathetic figure.

I felt sorry for her. And I was a little ticked at myself for not thinking of some way to be helpful.

She knelt by the water's edge and, reaching into the basket, picked up the turtles one by one and released them. Then she lingered for a while before returning to the motorhome.

"I think you've done the right thing," I said. "It's best for them."

"I hope so," she replied. "You know, when I let them go, I gave each one of them a little pat on the shell.

"All Four scampered away as fast as he could. But Minus One just stayed with me a while. He did not seem too sure that he wanted to go."

As she spoke, I noticed that she had tears dripping down her cheeks. That's one of the problems with pets, I thought. You get emotionally attached, and sooner or later, one calamity or another, you're going to get wounded emotionally.

DAY 17. Scary beginning today when I felt a bit warmish and had signs and symptoms of catching some sort of virus. But I was buoyed by the thought of having only three days left in New Mexico.

I had been forewarned by Royce Jones, an MD and runner who resides in Clovis, that the prevailing wind in these parts was from the southwest. The reason I had started from the north and thus incurred a continual headwind was that after I finished I'd be closer to St. George, Utah, and as a result would get two more days of rest before running the marathon there.

In retrospect, not too smart a decision. Had I to do it over again, I'd start from the south and exploit and enjoy a tailwind.

I found it somewhat exciting to approach Hobbs, which to this point had been just a name on a map to me. Now I would see what it looked like.

Besides, I would go through the entire town on foot, and I'd be willing to bet that not five percent of the natives have done that. I didn't know zilch about the origin of the name Hobbs, but to me it had the bounce of a real Western sound.

Having been buried in the tranquillity of the plains and grasslands the past few days, I was overwhelmed by the hurly burly of this city of 35,000. The experience bordered on being culture shock.

I saw as many Texas license plates in Hobbs as New Mexico plates, but understandably so since the Texas border is only three miles away. What's more, so I learned, Hobbs was founded by a Texan. Which proves, dear folks in Hobbs, you can't win 'em all.

Almost out of Hobbs, I looked at my watch and saw that I was a half-hour past the time for a pit-stop. Something was wrong here.

I looked down the road, hoping to see the motorhome. Though I could see almost a mile, Elaine was nowhere in sight.

Coming to the junction of Highway 62, I realized I had taken a wrong turn and was now 2-1/2 to three miles out of my way. Wasted miles, wasted energy, wasted time.

I decided there was no way out of the dilemma but to retreat. I needed a ride back to Highway 18, so I resorted to hitchhiking.

After three drivers ignored me, Glenn Davis, a friendly farmer in his 60s by my estimate, stopped to pick me up. He kindly drove me back to the intersection of Highway 18 where I had missed the turn.

My first act when Glenn deposited me at the Highway 18 junction was to descend upon a nearby convenience store to buy a Pepsi. I was out of water and drained in the hot weather.

Thus fortified, I headed south on 18 and caught up with Elaine. After I apologized profusely to her for missing the turn, she was kind enough not to chastise me. I could not figure out whether her kindness was because I looked so ragged and frazzled or whether she was in a forgiving mood.

At Nadine, just a mile to the south of Hobbs, all I saw was a medley of residences ranging from mobile to modest homes to a couple of luxurious homes. D.K. Randolph, who had a farm nearby, told me that it's been unusually dry here lately, making it rough on the cattlemen.

When D.K. first saw me, he stopped to ask, "What are you doing out here?"

"I'm running across the state."

"You're doing *what*?" he replied incredulously.

After we got that settled, D.K. told me that the economy of Hobbs still revolves around the oil industry. "But it's nowhere what it was back in Prohibition days before the market went berserk. Back in those days, the town was real rough and tumble with a lot of prostitution, pool halls and such."

At the 20-mile pit-stop, when I entered the air-conditioned motorhome in the 90-degree heat, I found myself thinking, Damn, if I had not goofed off by taking a wrong turn and running extra miles, I'd be finished by now. But then I knew better than to dwell on that energy-draining thought.

Our only disappointment today was not being able to locate a nice RV park in town. In fact, the only place we could find was a mobile village filled with construction workers from a highway project.

We got the only available spot there. At least we enjoyed air conditioning in the 90-degree weather.

DAY 18. Always, it seems, when I start closing in on a run across a state, I get a bit edgy, spooked by the feeling that some-thing bad – an accident, an injury or such – might happen and keep me from finishing after I've gone so far. Feeling thus, I border on being over-cautious. Yet physically I feel fine.

My mind flashed back to the start of the Bidwell Marathon in Chico a few years ago. I was standing behind Doug Latimer, a superb athlete who finished the grueling Western States 100-Mile Endurance Run 10 times.

A runner beside Doug asked him, "How do you feel?"

"Strong but tired," was Doug's reply. Those words pretty much echoed how I felt today.

On a sociological note, there seemed to be three types of traffic on the road: oil workers in pickups, oil workers in oil tankers, and women driving cars and embarked on shopping expeditions. To a man, with the exception of one jerk, the pickup drivers were friendly. They all waved to me, and some stopped to visit.

The first asked, "Are you working out?"

"Well, a little more than that," I answered, then went on to explain my run across the state. "I'm about 390 miles into it with only 20 to go."

"Congratulations!" he responded. It was evident that he wanted to say more, but an influx of traffic made it necessary for him to move on.

Another positive experience when a pickup driver wheeled up behind me, stopped and yelled, "Hey, I saw you out here yesterday. How about a drink of water?"

"Thanks a lot," I said, "but I've got some." With a trace of a blush I waved my baby bottle of water. I would have been crimson if the bottle were pink instead of blue.

"Okay, " he yelled. "Good luck." He then made a U-turn and headed back down the road.

He had not been gone five minutes when another pickup driver stopped to inquire, "Do you need a ride?"

"No, I'm fine. Thanks."

"Okay." And he drove off.

By now I was asking myself, Why all this sudden concern? Was I dragging that much ass?

I had to admit that I was quite a sight out on the road – hat slouched down on my head, fanny pack dangling, left calf taped, decked out in running shorts and T-shirt, and a wee bit of vintage showing. Seeing me, a non-runner could conceivably think, What convalescent home did this guy escape from?

My bad pickup encounter was with some sadistic jerk whose duties for some reason required him to drive up and down the road. Every time he passed me, he edged close to the fog line, rode it directly to me, then revved his engine as he blasted by me.

The best way to get back at this jerk, I quickly concluded, was to ignore him. And that I did, at the same time staying out of his way as he roared down the fog line.

Today I fell to thinking about the annual reunion of my Marine Corps officer class that is coming up in three weeks in San Diego. Originally Elaine and I had planned to drive the 500 miles to the reunion, but after all the New Mexico driving we decided flying would be preferable.

Ah, this modern world! Once we made the decision to fly, I picked up the cellular phone and called our travel agent, Jackie Camey in Sacramento, who made all the flight arrangements.

More than anything, though, when I think about my Marine classmates today, I think about the camaraderie that flows when we are together, and it spreads to our wives who also attend the annual reunions. We are closer now than when we were second lieutenants, and as our numbers dwindle we seem to get closer.

I did one other bit of reminiscing today. That came about when I reflected on a story in yesterday's newspaper that told about an earthquake in Klamath Falls, Oregon. I had reason for association, because exactly one year before that earthquake Elaine and I went through Klamath Falls when I ran across the state.

Elaine and I were surprised after finishing today when we found Jal to be considerably larger than reported to us by the natives. Best of all, and most unexpected, the city park had free camping and RV electrical and water hookups in a grassy area alongside a small lake.

Brudder and Rebel enjoyed a swim in the lake, but their swimming was not without incident. Emerging from the lake, Rebel saw some boys fishing 100 yards away and decided to socialize by running over to them.

Never having been around a fishing scene before, he managed, with a modicum of effort, to get in the middle of the act and in the process got a fishhook stuck in him. By then Elaine and I had dashed to the scene. Extracting the hook as Rebel wiggled and Brudder tried to help was no easy task. Such are the perils of parenthood!

DAY 19. The final performance today as the curtain comes down on New Mexico, a play (double entendre there!) that falls into three acts.

Act I, preparation and planning, which seems to get more complicated with each state we run, because we have learned as we go along and that, in turn, involves more factors in the planning considerations. Act II, the running and crossing of the state itself; the fun part once the show gets underway. Act III, the trip home; we sort of plan this one with all its sightseeing detours as we go along.

Our trip home will be circuitous, because Elaine wants to visit her son Chuck in Pocatello and her daughter Kathy in Boise (well, technically, Greenleaf, but who knows where that is!)

"Look at that sky," Elaine said as she stepped out of the motorhome early this morning when we set about to unhook our electrical and water connections. The sky was completely overcast and as we were unhooking a light drizzle began to fall.

I accepted the rain philosophically. After all, we had been running 18 days in New Mexico without any rain, and besides I had only 13 miles to go. It turned out that I ran every one of those 13 miles in rain.

Once underway I found the rainy weather refreshing compared to the 90-degree heat I usually experienced. Also the mindset of knowing that I had only 13 miles to go as opposed to the usual 22 or 23 made the going easier.

I even had a bike lane all the way. So I could not complain; no pain, no strain in the rain.

A short distance out of Jal I came across a sign that told me how the town got its name. In the 1880s, the Cowden brothers operated the largest cattle ranch in southeastern New Mexico. Their brand was JAL.

So in 1910, when a post office was established in this area, they decided to name the community Jal. What the sign failed to tell was what JAL stood for in the first place. However, I had to admit that Cowden was an appropriate name for two brothers in the cattle business.

This was an all-business day, and the business was running and finishing. Along the way we had no people encounters nor any scenic attractions.

Approaching the finish, I did experience a slight buzz or buoyancy from completing a run across another state. But I was not highly exhilarated and more or less accepted this finish somewhat matter of factly.

Maybe I should have been more excited. But actually I felt more grateful than anything – just thankful for being able to do it.

When I reached the Texas border and crossed into the state, I announced to Elaine, "I think I'll sing a chorus of 'Deep in the Heart of Texas'."

"Please don't," she replied. "You'll wake the coyotes. I don't want to hear them howl and excite the dogs."

Once again, no respect. The mere fact that I can't carry a tune has nothing to do with it.

When we were parked at the Texas border, marked only by the border signs and the monument, and no buildings, Elaine decided to take the dogs for a short walk – "So they can say they've been in Texas," she explained.

As I dwelt on the run, I thought it was interesting in retrospect to realize that when I planned the trip all the towns were just names on a map. But after I ran through them, each assumed a personality for Elaine and me, and most of them have a distinctive feature or two that we will remember.

Next stop: Grand Canyon. And thereafter the St. George Marathon. By the grace of God!

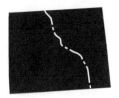

Overview of
WYOMING

June 11th to 27th, 1994
359.0 miles

Day	Overnight	Miles	Notes
1	Cheyenne	26.0	start at Wyoming/Colorado border
2	Chugwater	21.0	learn about "Black Jack" Pershing
3	Chugwater	21.0	exploring Chugwater
4	north of Wheatland	22.0	antelope come onto the scene
5	Glendo	21.0	Glendo State Park disappointing
6	Douglas	21.0	15 miles in rain
7	Glen Rock	21.0	assessing running on Interstate
8	Glen Rock	21.0	a snake encounter
9	Casper	21.0	running through Casper
10	Bar Nunn	21.0	kudos to the Wyoming Highway Patrol
11	Kaycee	21.0	first windless day in Wyoming
12	Kaycee	21.0	4660 feet, lowest elevation in Wyoming to date
13	Buffalo	21.0	entertained by prairie dogs
14	Buffalo	21.0	good time had by all in Buffalo
15	Sheridan	21.0	switch from I-25 (after 300 miles) to I-90
16	Sheridan	20.0	visit transcon biker
17	Billings, Montana	18.0	finish at Wyoming/ Montana border

Chapter 7

Wyoming:

Room for Roaming

DAY ONE. I had read so many varying descriptions of Wyoming roads that I did not know what to expect. The availability of facilities (gas, groceries, RV parks or camping) along the possible routes was of some concern.

Then there was the size of the state, the ninth largest in the nation. Unfortunately I had no source in the state – no people I knew and whom I could depend on – to give me reliable information.

All these considerations in mind, I decided the best way to plan Wyoming was to travel to the state and make a reconnaissance, not only of Wyoming but also of Montana. Affordable, because I had a free air ticket to Denver. So the battle plan was to fly to Denver, rent a car, drive to the Wyoming border and then begin the reconn.

This led to the decision to run Interstate 25 all through Wyoming, something I had never done in the previous 17 states run. Essentially the choice was made on safer road conditions (breakdown lane all the way and the Wyoming Interstates not being that heavily traveled) and more access to facilities.

The first day was critical for us in that we tested a couple of things: how I'd fare crossing the median, and how the Highway Patrol would react to Elaine parking in the breakdown lane for pit-stops. We were relieved to have no trouble on either count.

However, we remained a bit edgy about how different patrol officers would react on subsequent days when they saw Elaine parked in the breakdown lane. Only time would tell.

There was nothing distinctive about the area where we started this morning. Not the usual river or anything marking the boundary between Colorado and Wyoming. Only the border signs indicated the border for us.

It was not long before we knew we would be seeing plenty of antelope, which I am told the biologists prefer to call "pronghorns." From my April reconn, I was aware of this, but to Elaine it was a new-found delight. Seeing as many as she did, she asked me if this was unusual.

"I don't think so," I told her. "Wyoming has the third largest antelope population of any place in the world."

At the six-mile pit-stop, I told Elaine that instead of lingering in the motorhome I'd take the sandwich she had for me and hit the road, because a couple of Highway Patrol officers had gone past and we did not want any questions about the parked motorhome at this early stage. I had no sooner left the motorhome, crossed the median, and saw Elaine driving away than a Wyoming Highway Patrol officer pulled up in front of me.

Getting out of his car and approaching me, he said, "I just want to make sure you're okay."

"Doing fine," I answered, relieved that he seemed friendly and unconcerned about my running on the Interstate. I then told him I was just beginning a run across the state, all on I-25 and I-90.

"Geez, I can't recall that I've ever seen anyone doing that before," he said. "You mean all the way across the state, from here up to Montana, don't you?"

"Yeah, all 375 miles, or whatever it is."

"Well, good for you," he replied. "Take care, and maybe I'll see you on the road. Good luck."

As he left, I felt like we needed another Beatitude to add to the list: "Blessed be the Wyoming Highway Patrol."

As I approached central Cheyenne, I was somewhat apprehensive about running through some of the clover-leaf approaches and exits. Maybe that was why I goofed in rendezvousing with Elaine.

We had agreed to meet at the main gate of Warren Air Force Base so we could stop in at the base and make arrangements for overnighting at the family campground that had RV hookups. En route I took a wrong exit, which led to gate two instead of the main gate.

Realizing my mistake, I had the sentry call to confirm that Elaine was at the main gate and to instruct her to stay there if she were. That confirmed, I asked the sentry for the shortest distance to the main gate.

He pointed across some railroad tracks and grassy fields. Boldly I struck out on the shortcut route and on the way stupidly climbed through two different freight trains parked on parallel tracks. If either had moved, I would have gone into shock.

Next I sloshed through some tall grass that could have been infested with snakes. Luckily I made the rendezvous with Elaine unharmed except for being adorned with scratches and stickers.

Well, amend that to being *physically* unharmed. The verbal abuse that Elaine heaped on me for being so stupid as to take the wrong exit was a different matter. What hurt most of all was that she was right.

After all the planning and the long drive to Wyoming, I was geared to running, pumping adrenaline and wanting to get the show on the road. I guessed those were the main reasons why I hung in for 26 miles today. Well, there was one other reason: I wanted a little equity above our projected 21-mile-a-day average at the start.

It was a good feeling when we finished today to have an extra five miles in the bank, to come out of the day injury free and not to be more than reasonably tired.

One part of our recreation at Warren AFB consisted of driving around the historic base and seeing many of the red brick buildings that dated back to early in the century. Brudder and Rebel took a liking to the place after we let them swim in a pond near the Famcamp. They would have liked it more if we had turned them loose to chase some of the squirrels – or antelope, for that matter.

DAY TWO. I had not been out of bed for more than a couple of minutes when my body told me that I had overdone yesterday by going 26 miles. By now I've run enough states to know that the hardest running days in any state are the first three or four.

That's because when at home, training for any state run, I never go more than 10 miles a day. So it is understandable that when I up the daily mileage to 21, as I would here, I swim upstream the first few days when building a mileage base.

When I get violent and insist on 26 miles the first day, as yesterday, it's understandable that my 77-year-old body rebels. The good news is that after four days or so, I seem to get stronger.

As I ate breakfast in our camp spot in Warren Air Force Base, I reflected on a couple of things I learned last night about the base. For one, it was founded in 1867 and named Fort Russell after a general (David M. Russell) killed in the Civil War. It kept that name until 1930 when President Herbert Hoover changed it to Fort F.E. Warren, after the state's first governor who was a U.S. Senator for 37 years.

The base visitor guide also informed me that the Air Force acquired the base in 1947, that it was the country's first nuclear missile base and that it ranks as one of the most important intercontinental ballistic missile centers in America. That historical stuff was mildly interesting, but what I read about John J. "Black Jack" Pershing interested me much more.

I knew that General Pershing commanded the American troops in Europe in World War I and little else about the man. Well, it seems that, as a captain, he was stationed at this base in 1905 and met and married Helen Warren, the daughter of Senator Francis Emory Warren who happened to be the chairman of the Senate Military Affairs Committee.

And now the juicy part: Just six months after the marriage, President Theodore Roosevelt promoted Pershing to the rank of brigadier general, going over 862 senior officers in the process.

It was hard to understand how Senator Warren denied any involvement in this promotion. It was easy to understand why Pershing named his son Warren.

Until this trip, I never realized that Cheyenne sits so close to two other states, only 10 miles from Colorado and 40 from Nebraska. That's a lot closer than this state capital sits to most of the rest of Wyoming.

If I have the numbers right, the city's population is only around 50,000, yet it is the largest city in Wyoming. Well, maybe that was a bit more understandable when I learned that population for the entire state is under a half-million, making it the least populated state in the USA. One thing for sure, I won't be stumbling over people out here.

Getting underway, I discovered that I had a minor physical problem in addition to being tired from yesterday's marathon. When I moved my right hand, it was sore as a result of being hit yesterday by a rock kicked up by a passing semi. Such are the perils of passage. Could have been worse; the rock could have hit me in the eye.

At times on this Interstate, I could look two miles in either direction and see no vehicles. Just the grasslands, the wind, the antelope and me out here.

Except for the telephone poles, fences and highway, this land seemed untouched from pioneer days. Blank out the man-made intrusions, and I saw the land just as pioneers saw it. Slow as I was, I moved through it faster than they who were logistically burdened.

We finished seven miles south of Chugwater, and driving into this hamlet we were pleasantly surprised to find Pfizer's RV Park.

"How'd you find us? " the lady owner asked when I registered.

"We saw you listed in the Wyoming Tourist Bureau brochure on accommodations," I told her.

"I'm glad to hear that," she said, "because it costs me $150 to get listed there. And I also have to pay an annual fee of $64."

"That surprises me. I thought that was just a free service of the Wyoming Tourist Bureau."

"I wish it was," she said. "It could be a lot worse, though, if I was listed in a book like *Trailer Life Campgrounds*. They want $500 a year."

The thunder and lightning to the southeast provided entertainment much of the late afternoon and early evening for Elaine. The dogs would have been happier without it. I was too tired to care either way.

DAY THREE. In a day when not much happened, my most unusual experience came at 10 miles. Out of the corner of my eye, I saw something behind me, white and moving fast.

I turned to get a full look and saw a huge white jackrabbit running on the grass and headed straight for me. Still moving fast, he raced past me and impulsively I yelled, "Attaboy, Jack."

Whereupon he stopped 10 feet or so in front of me, turned, faced me and was brazen enough to stay there eyeing me as I passed. As I did, I had two thoughts:

Ye gods, I've been out here only three days, and already I'm talking to rabbits! And, in a more sobering vein, if that rabbit can sneak up on me like that, just think of what a cougar can do.

The major entertainment in Chugwater last night was rain, thunder and lightning. But we did get a chance to learn a bit more about the town.

What nurtured it in its early days was that it was headquarters for the Swan Land and Cattle Company, which owned over 113,000 head of cattle. The Company, with ownership in Scotland, operated for almost three-quarters of a century.

Today Chugwater is famous for the Chugwater Chili Cookoff held every June and attracting thousands of people. Actually the cookoff is held at a ranch about 15 miles out of town.

My plans to sample the famous Chugwater chili were sabotaged when I found that the restaurant on First Street featuring it was closed. At least I saved on Maalox.

The passage out of Chugwater offered a change in terrain as I ran through the Tyson Basin (or at least that is what I think I heard it called) studded with many trees. Each side of the basin, extending almost nine miles, was bracketed by a plateau. When I came atop a hill at the end of the basin, all I saw before me was the usual scenery of flat grasslands, though in the far distance I could, for the first time since leaving Cheyenne, see mountains.

All this day I struggled to get my sea legs. The battle was against the wind, the hills, the elevation (5500 feet was the lowest point) and low mileage in training. The thought that sustained me, this born of the experience of running through other states, was that as time goes on I will get stronger. Meanwhile when I struggle, the minutes go fast and the miles come slow.

One observation out here today was that I have learned I can now tell when a U-Haul truck is approaching, because most of the time I see a puff of black smoke in the distance. Or at least that has been the case the past three days when U-Hauls have signaled their presence.

The observation that disturbed me most was the graffiti I saw on a guard rail just out of Chugwater. The writing read, "Pedophile love is misunderstood."

To me, at least, this was completely unexpected in Wyoming. Are there no safe havens?

Elaine is always eager and enthusiastic to make these state runs, which she calls a vacation for her and the dogs. Sometimes I question "vacation," considering the chores she does each day.

Added to her list of chores should be the things she thinks up to raise my morale. Yesterday, for example, when I finished, she surprised me with a blackberry milkshake.

Again today, she presented me with the same treat. I am at a complete loss to figure out how I earned all these brownie points. Nice to savor the milkshake and all this love as we drove back again to Pfizer's RV park in Chugwater. We went back there mainly because Elaine was so enthralled with the town last night when she walked the dogs and met many friendly people, as well as a number of friendly dogs.

She went so far as to philosophically observe, "Any town loaded with friendly dogs has to be a good town."

DAY FOUR. One of my first thoughts on the road this morning was about angels. What I read about guardian angels in last night's newspaper added fuel to the feeling that I must have one.

The paper reported that last Sunday, the day after we left Cheyenne, an 84-mile-per-hour wind hit the city. At Warren AFB, where we had overnighted, many trees were blown about and some damage was done. A Cheyenne high school had a roof blown off one of its buildings.

On our original schedule we would have been in the midst of that. My guardian angel – or was it Elaine's – somehow got our schedule changed.

Maybe the most notable thing about today is what did not happen. When we started, the weather looked very threatening – impending storm, maybe lightning and likely rain. None of which materialized. In fact, the running was somewhat comfortable, and I felt strong at the finish – stronger than the previous three days.

More and more I am convinced that the only way to handle a run across a state – or across the country – is to take one day at a time. That is as true as it is trite.

If at this moment I were to dwell on the fact that I have about 300 miles of Wyoming to do – 300 miles, my God, 300 miles! – I might be inclined to quit. Survival is one day at a time.

Another thought occupied me early this morning: Why did I have an asthma setback last night? Nothing in my routine changed.

I didn't sleep more than half the night. As I fretted, I was consoled a bit by the knowledge that one of the quirks of asthma is that it is often an on/off thing, sometimes being triggered for no apparent reason.

My asthma sometimes has me upset when I see people smoke. They are blessed with no respiratory ailments, they can breathe normally – why screw that up by smoking?

Some signs and landmarks along the way today bore evidence of the presence of early French settlers in this area. I crossed Richelieu Creek, and down the road a short distance from it, Bordeaux Road.

And I was in Platte County. If my high school French stays with me, *platte* is the word for "flat." However, considering some of the hills I've negotiated, the guy who called this area flat must have been in dire need of an optometrist or sobriety test. In this "flat" country I ran through a number of *coulees* (ou, la, la, more Francais!).

I had a friendly encounter today with an antelope. After a 50-yard scamper he stopped and looked at me as if to say, What is this? I've never seen anything like this before – an old geezer running down the highway in his undies.

For all I knew, he might even have been thinking: Even the Indians wore more clothes, and they did not send their elders out on scouting missions. A changing world, indeed.

Of all the truckers I've encountered in 18 states, these in Wyoming are winning my vote as the most courteous. About 90 percent of them move from the slow to the fast lane when they see me. The 10 percent who don't are the national carriers such as Consolidated Freightways, whose drivers are uniformly devoid of any courtesy, and, with rare exceptions, the Wal-Mart drivers.

That sure in hell is a coincidence, I thought, when I saw this black guy on a motorcycle pass me in a construction zone. He was going slow enough for me to distinguish him and his motorcycle, and he was the same guy I'd talked with at a roadside rest stop on Highway 87 when I was in Wyoming in April checking out roads.

At that time he told me he was a musician – "On my way to play a gig," he said.

That April day was windy and bitterly cold, and I asked him how that affected him on the cycle.

"Oh, it's a pain," he said, "but a picnic compared to the stuff I ride in during the winter up here."

Today his passing by happened so fast and unexpectedly that I did not get a chance to greet him. Too bad; he was lively company.

The approach to the town of Wheatland was signaled by a series of farms that first appeared about four miles south of town. With a name like Wheatland, I expected a farming community and the main crop to be wheat. Wrong. Turned out that the main crops are barley, dried beans and sugar beets.

The Interstate actually splits this town of 5000 population. Mainly the school and residences and a few stores are on the west side, while most of the businesses and tourist hoopla (motels, restaurants, etc.) are on the east side.

Near the last pit-stop I saw a sign advertising the town of Guernsey. All I knew about the town was that wagon tracks of Oregon Trail pioneers are still visible nearby.

Elaine caught me off guard by extending the day to 22 miles, because she located a roadside rest stop at 22. She knew the extra mile was unwelcome, so she placated me with a root beer float – which was more than a fair trade.

DAY FIVE. I had not gone more than 100 yards this morning when I caught sight of a big antelope, only 50 yards away. He was an unusual fellow in that he just stood there, stayed his ground and stared at me instead of bolting away.

Whereupon I decided to immortalize him by taking his picture. Even my fuss in extracting the camera from my fanny pack and the click of the camera did not faze him. He flinched not at all. Why, I asked myself, is this guy so bold and brave, whereas every other antelope catching sight of me has sprinted away?

The incident furthered a resolve of mine. On my next run across a state, I will carry a camera with a zoom lens so I can zoom in on some of the wildlife. I would have liked to have captured the expression of that antelope as he stared boldly at me this morning.

Distractions like the antelope always help get my mind off mileage. Another distraction early morning as I climbed several hills was scanning the many caves in the alluvial clay hills for any animal activity.

I came up scoreless. Even birds were rare in this area, but at least the caves were a novelty.

I did, though, come across another dead deer, this one a two-pointer buck. By now I have noticed that the deer killed on the highway in Wyoming are treated differently from those I have seen in other states.

The practice here is to drag the deer five or more yards off the road, whereas in other states the deer are left where they fall. I'd vote for the Wyoming practice being a legal requirement.

The smell of the dead deer brought on echoes of what I had heard Frank Bacon say about the smells on Guadalcanal in World War II. Frank, a retired Marine Corps colonel, spent four long months on the Canal commanding an infantry platoon that he saw shrink from 44 men to fewer than a dozen through death, wounds and illness.

Frank described the nature smells of, in his words, "the dainty fragrance of a fragipani in the early morning ... the heavy smell of the deep jungle ... the stink from the stagnant water and decaying vegetation in the jungle ... the clean smells of the sea."

"Superimposed over these smells," Frank went on to say, "were the combat smells: the acrid smell of gunpowder ... the nauseating smell of diesel exhaust ... and the worst smells came from decaying human flesh because in the tropic heat and humidity the human body became a stinking mass of putrescence in hours."

Good Lord, I wished Frank's words were not so vivid. At the moment, my bacon and eggs weren't riding too well.

When we started today, we anticipated planning a pleasant night at Glendo State Park. Those plans were sabotaged when we visited the park and found that it had only 10 RV spots, all jammed together on the side of a hill, a facility that on a scale of one to 10 would be kindly treated with a rating of three. At the Collins RV Park on the south end of town, we again struck out when it turned out the facility was now defunct, being "in estate."

We were more than a little grateful when we discovered the Lakeview Motel and RV Park on the north end of town. Far from fancy, but quite adequate.

The town of Glendo, we discovered, was a has-been. At one time it had a number of stores when the highway went through town, but the freeway changed all that.

Now the stores are boarded and abandoned. Unlike Chugwater (population 200), unlike Wheatland (population 5000), Glendo (population 192) is a town without personality.

DAY SIX. Our good luck with the weather was torpedoed this morning when we awoke to rain. A rain that persisted through my first 15 miles and that saw me running in a Goretex rainsuit, haberdashery much less preferable to T-shirt and shorts, because it is heavier and bulkier, and that means I have to expend more energy when running in it.

During the last six miles it felt good to be stripped down to T-shirt and shorts and to have the wind breezing across my body. Contrastingly I sometimes get too warm and cozy in the Goretex and feel more inclined to siesta than running.

Since the weather was flaky, Elaine kept the radio on all day, hoping to get weather reports. But these reports were sparse, because news of O.J. Simpson being a suspect in the murder of his wife dominated the news and radio time.

For the first five miles of the Interstate today, railroad tracks paralleled the road. In that short distance five freight trains, each loaded with coal, went past. A guy did not have to be a rocket scientist to know coal mining was a big operation somewhere hereabouts.

I did not comprehend the scene when I first saw it: two guys in the grasslands, each separated by a short distance, each sitting at a table, each armed with a .22 rifle with telescopic sights. Curious, I waded through the grass to the fence line and asked them what they were doing.

They pointed to an area sprinkled with small mounds and said, "We're shooting prairie dogs. Damn things are a nuisance. They ruin a lot of farm land, and they populate like rabbits."

I scrutinized the area where they were shooting and saw hundreds of small mounds, each only a foot or so high, and beside each was a small hole leading to a prairie dog habitat. I lingered a dozen minutes watching the shooters.

Whenever a prairie dog would emerge from its hole and squat erect on its hind legs to sun itself, the shooters would try to eliminate him. From what I could see of the number of mounds and prairie dogs, to have a successful mission the shooters needed machine guns.

This was another of those days when road construction made the going tricky at times. For my part only the fast lane was open on my side of the road, the breakdown lane and slow lane being under construction. I was able to run through the construction in the fast lane but had to constantly look behind me to make sure no construction vehicles were bearing down on me from the rear.

For Elaine's part she had trouble finding places to park for three-mile pit-stops. One leg even stretched out to 6.5 miles. That sort of deprivation puts me in dire need of tea and sympathy.

On a normal day Elaine has trouble finding places for pit-stops. On a rainy day it is even tougher with bad road conditions and visibility.

Also on a rainy day when she, the dogs and I step into the motorhome, we tend to mess it up, and that spells cleanup work for her. Even on a good day her job is more difficult than mine, but she says she enjoys it.

She likes the family togetherness (dogs and husband in tow) and, in her words, likes "playing house in the motorhome." With that in mind, this might be an appropriate place to recite the chores that Elaine does every day. In sort of a shorthand listing they read like this:

• After rising, turn on hot water heater and coffee.
• Feed dogs.
• Get dressed and groomed.
• Walk dogs.
• Convert dogs' bed to dinette and make up our bed.
• Cook breakfast.
• Do dishes.
• Unhook motorhome and drive to start.
• Make three-mile pit-stops.
• For leisure, read Bible and practice guitar.
• Prepare food and drinks for pit-stops: sandwiches, pasta, beans, soups, iced tea, Koolaid, as needed.
• Conjure up dinner menu.
• At last pit-stop, vacuum day's dirt from motorhome.
• Grocery shop if a store is available.
• Drive to RV or overnight camping spot.
• Camped, take dogs for walk.
• Cook dinner; do dishes.
• Take dogs for their pre-bed walk, then bed them.
• Turn off water heater and prepare morning coffee.
• Shower.
• Climb into bed and, if not exhausted, read or watch TV, or – theatrics permitting – watch lightning.

And this, mind you, she calls, "playing house."

DAY SEVEN. The most unusual incident today came at one mile, when I was dive bombed by four big blackbirds with long tails and yellow eyes. Like fighter pilots in an attack, they peeled off individually and dived towards me coming within three feet of my face before banking sharply away.

I waved my arms and yelled, but that did not vary their pattern. They had formed an attack loop and were fully intent on attacking, keeping me fully occupied as I waved my arms and yelled as each descended at full power toward my face.

This went on for five minutes, during which I would have paid ransom money for a shotgun. Then as suddenly as they started, they ceased attacking and flew away. I was at a loss to figure out what brought on the problem.

The running itself went well today. Just a matter of chugging through another 21 miles.

It was a bit discouraging to be starting again in the rain. All part of the game, though.

I had logged seven miles before the wind came out of hiding. Once it appeared, it gradually increased in crescendo as the day wore on.

When Elaine and I talk with the Wyoming natives – in stores, RV parks, etc. – invariably they have the same comment: "You know, the wind is usually not this bad at this time of the year." I've heard that so often that I am bent to think these folks have been brainwashed by the state Chamber of Commerce.

At this stage of the game, I am using my asthma inhalants about 30 percent as much as I do at home. Much of this use is preventive medicine rather than to subdue an asthma episode.

Chances are that I could run without the inhalants. But I prefer to wait until I feel a bit stronger before attempting that.

Many times on these cross-state runs when I shake the asthma, I think that if I ran 10 miles or more a day at home, I'd be just about asthma free. Unfortunately there are so many diversions when I am home that I never come close to that mileage. Maybe I need to adjust my priorities.

Once we left Douglas, the terrain today was the same mile after mile. The scenario read like this: crest a hill, descend into a swoop or small valley of not quite a mile across, then another up and down. A cycle repeated so often I felt like I was on a roller-coaster.

A diversion came when I conducted a continuing experiment in my study of the sociology of I-25. This I did by counting the drivers of 20 cars and found 16 of them to be women, thus reaffirming my theory that 80 percent of the cars on I-25 are driven by women. Once again, though, despite this substantial data, I was at a loss to analyze the sociological significance of it.

Thinking came impulsively today when I was a half-mile past the North Platte River and looked west and saw the site of the World War II POW camp. I suddenly thought, These guys lived in barracks, they had toilets, they had running water. Damn ironic that they were more comfortable than the Americans who captured them.

For most of my 34 months in the South Pacific, I lived in a pyramidal tent, got water out of a Lister bag and availed myself of an outhouse commode with an overhanging canvas fly. I had a change of venue for the Bougainville operation when we lived in foxholes, drank from canteens and used slit trenches for a 45-day period. Then for a few days in each the Guam, Peleliu and Okinawa operations, I lived Hiltonesque aboard a small aircraft carrier when as an infantry officer I flew scouting missions in support of ground troops.

True, aboard the carriers I enjoyed more luxurious surroundings than the POWs. But still there was a major difference in their favor: They were out of harm's way – no bullets, no bombs buzzing around them. Again, the vanquished making out better than the victors.

Another luxury the POWs, being in a farming community, enjoyed over the combat Americans was three meals a day. Little wonder that the Italians were so enthusiastic about surrendering.

Momentarily today I thought about the similarity between a construction worker on a skyscraper and a runner on an Interstate. Both need confidence – the construction worker that he will not lose his balance, will not fall; the runner that none of the many drivers approaching him at high speeds will go berserk and steer into him and send him heavenward (all runners are ticketed for upward passage!).

On the radio today, we heard the shocking news of O.J. Simpson being charged with double homicide. From what I heard, it smacks of the fury of a man being scorned. From what I can guess, it will be one helluva drama when fully played out.

DAY EIGHT. This might be called "The Day of the Snake" because of an incident about halfway into today's run.

"Whooee!" I heard myself yelling as I jumped and saw out of the corner of my eye a four-foot snake. He was in an unexpected setting on the gravel under a metal guard rail.

Bravely I stopped to study him to see if he had the head shape of a viper. As I looked at him, my judgment and objectivity were warped by a bit (hell, quite a bit) of apprehension. I could not identify him.

All the while I was subconsciously commending myself for this new-found courage while facing a snake. My natural inclination is to run frantically.

Living recklessly, I decided to go one step further as I knelt to take his picture. That done, I awarded myself a medal of valor and continued on my journey, at the same time reminding myself to be doubly alert whenever I crossed the grass median for pit-stops, because this was one humongous snake.

I had gone but a few yards down the road when a lady driver who evidently had seen me taking the picture slowed down and yelled to ask if I was okay.

"I'm fine," I yelled back. As she drove away, I thought it would have been nice to have this kind of solicitude if I had been bitten by a rattlesnake.

I was not more than 10 or 15 minutes down the road when I saw two police vehicles – one Highway Patrol, the other sheriff department – going my way on the other side of the median and flashing red lights. Thirty yards or so ahead of me, they made a sudden turn across the median, then headed toward me.

I barely had time to question why before they stopped directly in front of me. Approaching me the deputy sheriff and Highway Patrolman asked almost in unison, "Did you have an encounter with a snake?"

Wondering how they knew that, I answered, "Well, I did see a snake, a big one, a short while ago."

"We had a report from a woman, "the deputy said, "who said she was a nurse and she thought she saw a snake strike you."

Ye gods, I'd told the woman I was fine. "She must have gotten mixed signals. I did kneel down to take a picture of the snake. That's probably where she got the idea that the snake struck me."

"So you're okay?" the Highway Patrolman asked.

"Yeah, I'm okay. You know, it's a funny thing. That woman asked if I was okay, and I told her I was fine. Anyway, I want to apologize to you guys for any inconvenience."

"No problem," the deputy said.

"Yeah, we get all kinds of calls," chimed in the Highway Patrolman.

When we parted, both of the officers – Les Paulsen of the Highway Patrol and Steve Menez of the sheriff's department – shook hands with me and wished me luck. Rethinking the incident after they left, I was impressed with their quick response time. On the road I rarely see a police officer; yet here when a situation was presented were two in a matter of a few minutes.

Today for the first time in eight days in Wyoming, I met a fellow pedestrian, a happening that took place three miles west of Glenrock. He was hitchhiking (perfectly legal in Wyoming) from Casper to Cheyenne and had just been dropped off by a farmer who lived nearby.

His first question was, "How far is the nearest town?"

I told him that Glenrock was three miles away to the east, in the direction he was headed.

When he saw me bring out my cassette recorder, he became very guarded, as if he had something to hide. He did tell me that his name was Dan, but he was reluctant to give me his full name.

In the course of our short conversation, though, he did loosen up enough to confide that his full name was Dan Bennett. He seemed a bit uneasy, in a hurry to move on and not to give much information about himself.

Not wanting to pry or make him uncomfortable, I wished him good luck and moved on and, yes, with a lot of questions in my mind. What was missing here, I thought, for a guy traveling from Casper to Cheyenne was any type of baggage.

Our 21 miles today brought us 175 miles into Wyoming. It was a good feeling to arrive at about the halfway mark and assume an all-downhill-from-here attitude.

Later we toured our home for the night, Glenrock. I was inclined to rate it as a typical American small town of modest homes in an oasis of trees here on the grasslands. But then as we saw a number of people staggering in and out of bars, I was not too sure.

DAY NINE. George Sheehan once wrote, "Being an athlete is not something I do an hour or so a day. It is something I am. Being a runner is something that informs my entire day. My 24 hours is lived as a runner. ... "

Paralleling that, I can say that dropping into a church for an hour on Sunday is conducive to being religious for one hour a week, whereas being out here is conducive to being religious 24 hours a day. While that may sound like heresy to some folks, it is simply meant as a statement that in a nature setting I feel the presence and power of God more than in a church setting.

Now, George, getting back to you. I too am a runner, but I have to plead guilty to not being one 24 hours a day.

One evidence of that is my diet that would be freakish for a 24-hour-a-day runner. Gimme hamburgers, milk shakes, candy, a Pepsi fix now and then, pizza, bacon and eggs, niblets of cheese – and okay if that takes me down the tubes some as a runner.

Another piece of evidence, George: When attired in dress clothes (as sport coat and slacks or a suit), I don't wear Nike or Reeboks or other running shoes as do some 24-hour runners.

Where we are more on frequency, George, is with your observation, "The decline of his [the runner's] ability does not interfere with the constant interchange between him, his solitude and the world and everyone around him."

There, George, you have touched on one of the main reasons why I so much enjoy running across states. Would that I could express it as eloquently as you.

How many times, George, have I read something you wrote and then said to myself, I've thought that a lot of times. But no way could I ever express it in words as eloquently as that.

Writing, someone once said, is turning blood into ink. Believe me, George, you bled beautifully.

At the six-mile pit-stop, I told Elaine, "You made the right decision. Good call."

She had just told me that when a Highway Patrol officer checked on her while she was parked roadside yesterday, she considered offering him some freshly baked brownies. But she balked because she thought he might issue her a citation for doing some baking while parked roadside.

I said "good call" for two reasons: The guy might have given her a ticket, and, hey, I didn't want anybody cutting into my supply of brownies.

The neon sign of the Flying J truck stop was flashing, "Happy Father's Day." When Elaine and I left home for this run, my children expressed regret that I'd be gone for Father's Day and not home for a dinner and gifts. That prompted me to send each of them a card today.

The card read, "So you think you didn't give me a Father's Day gift. Wrong. You gave the best of gifts: your love and a son/daughter of whom I am rightfully proud."

As I approached Casper, I thought of some of the battles that had been fought around this area. I'd read enough about the town to know that its name actually came from one of these battles.

The city is named after Lt. Caspar Collins who took a detachment of 25 soldiers out to rescue a wagon train and was killed in the ensuing conflict with Indians – understandably so since 2400 of them descended on him. A couple of peculiarities in this place naming: First the lieutenant's first name was used and not his surname. Secondly, in some paperwork processing, Caspar got changed to Casper.

The main impression I got while going through Casper was that it is a working-man's town with a focus on oil and ranching. As I left town, I-25 made a dramatic turn to the north. Now I was headed directly toward Montana, no wasted miles on the way.

Not only did the turn north on I-90 and the direct heading toward Montana raise my morale, but the turn took me out of the headwind I had been fighting and put me in a crosswind from the west. But that wind was so strong, I'd guess between 35 and 40 miles per hour, that I sometimes had to brace myself to keep from being blown into the slow lane. At a pit-stop Elaine told me she had to slow the motorhome to keep it from being blown eastward.

Not until I finished did it occur to me that, other than Elaine, I had not talked to a single person all day.

DAY 10. Soon after starting, I was a bit spooked when I slowed to a walk to adjust my fanny pack and discovered that I had a balance problem, some loss of equilibrium. When I stopped running and started to walk, my feet slid out from under me as if I were walking on ice. I was not in control and found it difficult to keep from staggering into the slow lane of traffic.

Could this be related to the ear ache I had last night? Could I be having an inner-ear problem?

The experience was frightening because I knew I was redlined. If I lost any more control, I would have to ground myself, because the risk of crashing into a vehicle would be too great.

It soon became apparent that while running I had no problem, but when I stopped to walk I lost control. In dealing with this problem, the best thing I had going for me was that it was not a new experience.

Back in 1990 while running across the USA, I was confronted with it on a half-dozen occasions. I handled it by being extremely cautious whenever I made a transition from running to walking or stopping. I would gradually decrease the tempo of the running to where I was almost at a walk pace. Then, as the imbalance set in, I would make a supreme effort to direct my body to the outside of the road and to stay away from the slow lane.

Then as now, I found the imbalance would come on for no apparent reason and disappear for no apparent reason. It was spooky then, and it was scary today.

I jokingly told myself, Maybe I need a transplant of some kind. That humor, if such it was, was probably a carryover from a newspaper article I read last night about a guy in England who had a six-organ transplant – new liver, kidney, stomach, duodenum, small intestine, and pancreas. Kind of made me wonder at just what point does a person cease to be himself and become somebody else.

I did have a human contact today, allowing me opportunity to talk with someone other than antelope, deer and rabbits. At the nine-mile pit-stop, a Wyoming Highway Patrol officer in a Camaro pulled up behind us.

I jumped out of the motorhome, approached the officer and said, "Hi, what's your name?"

The officer replied, "I'll tell you mine if you'll tell me yours." I laughed at his sense of humor and learned his name was Terry Vincent.

Trying to recover, I said, "I should say that the reason I asked your name is that I want it for the journal I keep."

And before he could ask, I volunteered, "We aren't broken down, and we don't have a problem. We're just running across the state." And I went on to explain that.

"Well, more power to you," he said.

Parting, we shook hands. As I returned to the motorhome, I was amused at the contrast between the two of us.

I had a scraggly beard of one week's growth, was desperately in need of an application of Right Guard, and was wearing shoes with the fronts cut out and my toes sticking out. By contrast, he was young, handsome, huskily built and well groomed.

As we drove back from our finish toward Casper, I found myself thinking about the Pony Express that passed through this area, the farthest north it got any place on its route. From Casper it dipped directly south to Salt Lake.

The Pony Express promised to deliver a letter in 10 days, pretty fast considering that the route from St. Joseph to Sacramento extended 2000 miles. Ye gods, they moved about 10 times faster than I! My kingdom for a horse!

DAY 11. The best thing that happened today came after we finished our day's run and not during the run itself, and it was, as Lawrence Welk would say, "a vunderful surprise." We had anticipated spending the night at some roadside spot, but when we drove 15 miles in Kaycee we found a small RV park (Sleigh's) with the amenities of water, electricity and even cable TV.

All of which is another way of saying that our day was completely uneventful. Probably the most distinguishing aspect was what did not happen, and that was for the first time in 11 days in Wyoming we had no wind. None. That's sort of like driving across Texas and seeing no armadillos.

Also unusual was the heavy fog that delayed our start this morning, because we decided that it would not be safe for Elaine to park the motorhome for pit-stops when visibility was so limited. My start was atop a hill that afforded me a view for 15 miles ahead.

As I looked at all the empty lands about me this day, as on other days in Wyoming, I could not help but think of the thousands of starving people in the world, and then entertained the thought that if all this land were properly irrigated and tended by farmers with the industry and ingenuity of the Japanese rice-paddy farmers, sufficient food could be produced here to feed several countries. Put a man on the moon, yes; feed starving humanity, no.

Because I met no people today and because I was not distracted dwelling on injuries or weather, I had no recourse but to spend my running day just observing and thinking. One thing I could not miss during the first half of my run was the abundance of wildlife. When I looked out onto the range I did not fail to see deer or antelope, so many that I was beginning to think I had stumbled into a convention.

Also I could not fail to notice the attention I was getting from truckers. Now that I have been on the road several days, many of the drivers recognize me and many toot their horns, flash their lights or wave in recognition as they pass by.

Elaine passed on an observation of her own: "Your beard is now beginning to make you look distinguished." Well, that would be welcomed from the scraggly appearance I've had with this 11-day growth. What I have observed most about the beard is the protection it affords from wind and sun.

I spent some time today thinking about the American jury system and concluded that it is screwed up. What set me to thinking was a reminder from a TV commentator last night, this in connection with the O.J. Simpson case, that it takes all 12 jurors to convict a person.

The more I thought about that, the more I concluded that it is idiotic and unfair to law-abiding citizens. On the theory of being overly fair to the accused, it makes mockery of justice.

Our democracy is based on a majority, not on 100 percent. How, I asked myself, did this business of a unanimous jury for criminal cases get started in the first place? What would be required to change it?

I hoped I could remember to ask the three lawyers in our family about this after we get home. To me, requiring a vote of 75 percent of jurors, as opposed to 100 percent, for conviction in criminal cases would be considerably more effective in controlling crime than gun control would be.

DAY 12. Last night the lady who owned Sleigh's RV Park in Kaycee and who went by the nickname "Tat," filled us in on the community. Kaycee, she said, was sort of a stomping ground for the Wild Bunch, and she told us that the Hole in the Wall where Robert Redford and Paul Newman – er, Butch Cassidy and the Sundance Kid – hung out is on private property a short distance southwest of Kaycee, but private tours to the site can be arranged.

"In these parts," she said, "Butch Cassidy and the Sundance Kid are remembered somewhat fondly. They were sort of like Robin Hood; they robbed from the rich and gave to the poor. They robbed banks in Idaho, Utah, and South Dakota and many trains."

Well, that answered one question, because I had been wondering what they could possibly find to rob in these parts. I was still left wondering about what they found to spend their money on here.

"The Hole in the Wall where they hung out, " she said," was in a pretty valley surrounded by huge red cliffs. Its attraction was that it was hard to get into."

She went on to tell us that, escaping after a gunfight, Cassidy and Sundance made their way to Argentina and lived there and in Bolivia for a while. From there, she said, the accounts get fuzzy, but most people around Kaycee believe they quietly returned to the USA and lived peaceful lives.

Like the accounts, my memory was fuzzy. But as I recalled, both of them were killed in the movie.

My Goretex rainsuit was worth its weight in gold today, because I was engulfed in rain from start to finish. But there are some mixed feelings here, because on the positive side the suit is warm/dry/cozy; on the negative side, it involves more weight than I prefer to carry and running in it is a bit cumbersome.

When I saw a big herd of cattle on both sides of the Interstate, my first thought was, Do they belong to the KC Ranch? Then, come to think of it, is the KC Ranch still in existence?

At one time more than 60,000 cattle roamed the ranch property. It was from the KC Ranch that the town of Kaycee took its name.

The running itself was routine today, just chugging along and logging miles, and – praise de lawd! – no problems with injuries. At times the rain was a refreshing contrast to the 95-degree heat of recent days. A half-dozen times I took off my hat and let the rain splash on my head and face.

I think that what sustained me the most today as I sloshed through the rain was knowing once the day was done we had but a short six-mile drive back to the comfort and security of the Sleigh RV Park. I was blessed with our timing today, because five minutes after I finished and was warmly and dryly ensconced in the motorhome, a deluge descended upon us.

This was more than heavy rain; this was flood condition. We were lucky in being parked roadside so that we could wait it out instead of trying to navigate midstream without a rudder.

DAY 13. George Billingsley calls it "a dead-ass day," and that's the kind of a day I had. Just to keep moving forward required undue effort and a strain of will-power.

This letdown was doubly disappointing after doing so well yesterday, because I had anticipated zipping along today, whereas at 18 miles I was tempted to tell myself, Let's call it a short day and quit. But I knew that if I did quit, I would come to regret it later.

It did not help that my asthma acted up and I had to resort to using inhalants to abate all the coughing and hacking. On top of that, I had a rebellious knee that threatened to sabotage running.

With asthma and knee problems I was anything but bubbly when starting. Luckily both problems evaporated after a half-dozen miles.

On the negative side this was the day of the "dead ass." On the positive side, the day of the deer and antelope.

At least 50 of them crossed the Interstate, in some instances narrowly missed by speeding cars. On one such crossing I acted as a traffic cop when some antelope crossed the Interstate in front of me, then ran across the median but stopped midway in the road on the other side.

Turning and seeing a trucker bearing down on them, I signaled to him by waving my hat and pointing. He instantly blared his horn to roust the deer from the road. Seeing them safely off the road gave me a good feeling.

At one point this morning when I stopped abruptly to unload some of the morning's coffee, my bladder was indeed grateful for the absence of traffic that permitted this pit-stop on the Interstate. As I slowed to this stop, I detected a trace of the imbalance that has worried me the past few days.

The difference now from when I had it stronger is it lasts for only two or three steps, then I recover. So I don't have much distance to get out of kilter, but I do have more than a little anxiety.

Elaine surprised me at the nine-mile pit-stop when she said that she is enjoying Wyoming more than Arizona or New Mexico. I had a hard time understanding that, considering the scenery of the three states and that we were not on an Interstate in Arizona or New Mexico.

Maybe she enjoys Wyoming more because she is a farm girl at heart and she identifies more with Wyoming. Or maybe she is more kindred to the pioneer spirit that still permeates Wyoming.

At 17 miles into my day, I came to a screeching halt to observe a colony of prairie dogs. Good lord, I thought, can I believe this? The colony is about a mile long and a half-mile wide.

I watched the action as prairie dogs emerged from their holes, sat on their hind quarters and basked in the sun. A riot, a damn riot, I thought, if Brudder and Rebel were turned loose here for a prairie dog safari.

Ever the prosaic one, I wondered where the grub and grog came from to sustain this prairie-dog population. Well, give them credit for providing a good floor show as I passed by.

On my last mile today, I made three unsuccessful efforts not to stampede three separate herds of cattle lying under trees along the river banks. In each case they left their comfort zone and stampeded out into the hot sun.

Coming to the end of my day, I saw Elaine parked ahead at the base of a hill that to me resembled the slope of an Olympic ski jump. Thank God, I won't have to negotiate that hill today. Tomorrow, yes.

DAY 14. At the start today, I did not feel zippy do-da. Immediately faced with a long hill, sloped like a ski jump, I tried to persuade my tired legs to get with the program, but they seemed to be advocating for a day off. Heresy, dammit, I told them. That opening ski-jump hill extended three miles. But it bothered me less than the insects that delighted in feasting on my legs.

At the nine-mile pit-stop, I sprayed my legs with the Avon goo Elaine touted and thereafter didn't have a single insect bite. Of such joyous little things is life made! Though I did feel a bit stupid for not trying the Avon at the three- or six-mile pit-stop.

All things considered, my running went fairly well today, but I did have problems to overcome. At 11 miles my right foot went gimpy.

I could not analyze whether the problem was the foot itself or the shoe. For a mile or so I varied from walking, to moving off the pavement onto the dirt, to a walk/jog while working my way to the 12-mile pit-stop and a shoe change.

When I started out of the motorhome after that pit-stop, it was as if I had a born-again foot. I made a mental note to get rid of the Nike Air Mariahs that caused the problem. I blamed myself more than the shoe; I kept trying to squeeze miles out of this pair of shoes long after they should have been given a dignified burial.

Another running problem today was that once again I had a trace of imbalance a couple of times. At 14 miles, about the time I was feeling lucky about overcoming my foot problem, my right knee suddenly went on the fritz.

At 15 miles I again changed shoes and magic followed. I was able to run the remaining six miles with no foot or knee problems. At this point I was wearing the same brand/model of shoe that I wore for 3192 miles across the USA and which I refuse to compliment by name here because I am still angry with the manufacturer for discontinuing the shoe.

My first visitor of the day said his name was George Slack, and he had stopped his RV to see if I needed help. I thanked him for his concern and told him that Wyoming is the 18th state I've run across, and in all those states he was only the second RV driver to stop to check on me.

He wanted to know how much farther I planned to run today, and I told him that he'd caught me midway in my day, that I had 10.5 miles to go.

"Well, take care of yourself, " he cautioned when parting.

Again today the truck drivers, those used to seeing me on the road, greeted me in different ways: some with a toot of their horn, others by turning on/off their lights, and a few by sticking out their arm and waving. Nice to have friends in high places.

Near the end of my running day when I went past the Buffalo fairgrounds, I was impressed with the track and grandstand and found myself thinking, What's this, the state fair in a town with a population of only 3500 or so?

Our running day concluded, Elaine and I set out to explore as much of Buffalo as the afternoon allowed. I had assumed this town got its name from the bison that once roamed the area.

When we visited the Jim Gatchell Museum – a two-story building downtown housing many historic artifacts – I learned differently. The town was named after Buffalo, New York.

I had forgotten that Buffalo was a setting in Owen Wister's novel, *The Virginian*. In the saloon of the Occidental Hotel, the Virginian meets up with the villain, Trampas, who challenges him to a gunfight. In the subsequent shootout on Main Street the Virginian kills Trampas.

These days the hotel is closed for business but open to public tours. I'd forgotten most of what I had read about the Virginian, but I could still hear Gary Cooper's famous line, "When you call me like that, smile."

Since there were three restaurants within two blocks of the RV park, we decided to give Elaine a night off from cooking by eating out. The dinner at Howard Johnson's was bush league compared to Elaine's culinary offerings.

DAY 15. The wind was my enemy today. At the start it was not less than 15 miles per hour, and as the day went on it increased in tempo to the point where most of my effort was spent battling a 30- to 35-MPH. wind.

Sheltered as we were before the start in the RV park, we had no awareness of today's prevailing wind, so it caught us by surprise. The strong headwind also played havoc with my cut lips.

Every time a semi passed, hitting me with a cold blast of arctic air, I turned my back to lessen the effect. And for sure the wind kept the many windmills whirling and doing so they emitted a loud clattering noise.

After almost 300 miles on I-25 it seemed like we were leaving an old friend when we took off on I-90 this morning. Two observations about I-90 were immediately evident: It was strewn with more litter than I-25, and the volume of traffic on 90 was up a few notches from 25.

After a mile's climb up a seven-percent grade from mile 10 to 11 in my day, I found myself at exit 44 leading to Fort Phil Kearny and wishing I had the time to detour and see that controversial site. This was the scene of many Indian attacks, because Red Cloud was incensed with the whites invading Sioux hunting grounds. Jim Bridger, eminent scout and mountain man, had warned the Army not to locate the fort at the site, but he was ignored.

As I passed the exit, I wondered what old Phil, a Union general killed in the Civil War, thought about the "e" being dropped from his name (Kearney) when the fort was named after him.

The most refreshing scene all day came around 13 miles when I found myself in hills and mountain passes and fascinated with a fast-flowing stream cascading down from the mountains. Once again, the antelope were all about. As contrasted with the brown, barren grasslands, this was like finding water on the desert.

Faced with a day like this when almost every step was a strain, when the cold air was cutting and the headwind was whipping me, I tell Elaine, "I'm doing penance for my sins."

Her typical reply goes something like this: "I'll never understand you Catholics."

It bothered me today, as we approached Sheridan, that I was in the town last April yet today could visualize very little of it. I did, though, vividly recall the night spent here, because the thunder tumbled right to the ground and, suddenly awakening, my first thought was that I was in a bomb attack.

Sheridan was another case of a western town being named after a Civil War general, in this case Philip H. Sheridan. We found this town of 15,000 somewhat devoid of personality. But it does harbor two major tourist attractions: the Sheridan Inn and Trail End Historic Center.

In its heyday, the Sheridan Inn hosted such important personages as Calvin Coolidge, Ernest Hemingway, Will Rogers and Buffalo Bill Cody. Today this rambling two-story wood-framed building still operates as a restaurant and lounge.

I was more impressed with what I read about the Trail End Historic Center than what I saw there. At a time when the average home sold for $1000, the cost to build this home for governor and senator John Hendrick was $168,000.

On a more prosaic level, when Elaine did her grocery shopping at Decker's and I saw the delicious tomatoes she purchased, I wondered how could this be: ideal tomatoes in Wyoming, whereas the ones we purchase in California are like rocks.

Got it made, got it made, I told myself as I snuggled into bed. Only 40 miles in two days. A comforting thought as sleep descended on me.

DAY 16. Underway smoothly today, buoyed in spirits by so few miles left in Wyoming, I stopped around two miles to study a fox – a casualty of the highway. Beautiful animal. I'd almost call him regal in appearance: fine coat, nice facial features, fluffy tail.

Just about every time I come across one of these road kills – fox, deer, antelope – I subconsciously remind myself, Be careful. Drivers have a fixation on speed, the almighty Getting There. Rare indeed is the driver who gives thought to the fact that we are invading the habitat of these animals who possess proprietary rights here.

Damn, I'm beginning to sound like one of those kooky activists. Nonetheless it always ticks me when I see a deer or antelope roadside and a driver approaching at high speed and making no effort to slow.

As I was thinking about thoughtless drivers and going past an exit at the same time, a maroon Mercedes in the middle lane suddenly swerved across the inside lane and raced onto the exit. Some contradiction here, I thought, because this guy has accrued enough money to buy that expensive car but insufficient brainpower to drive intelligently. Evidently he did not see me, or he did not care, because I had to jump to avoid being hit by him.

Highway construction played havoc with our routine today. But we did luck out in two respects here: First, we had driven into Sheridan yesterday after finishing our run and thus became aware of the construction and able to plan for it. Secondly, this being Sunday, the construction workers were not on site.

This was major construction for more than eight miles, with one side of the Interstate being closed entirely. On the other side was two-way traffic and no shoulder of any kind, which meant that I had to run the dirt and torn-up road, except for a couple of spots where bridges were being constructed and I was forced to edge slowly along the road in use and across the bridge there.

Worse yet, since there was no place for Elaine to park, I had to run the almost nine miles without pit-crew support. Luckily, as said, we knew what was coming, so I adjusted my fanny pack to carry enough water to sustain me for this distance.

As I started my solo trek, I could feel the weight of three water bottles and other supplies in my fanny pack as I carried three times my normal load. With the loaded fanny pack and wearing my big sacroiliac belt, I was carrying at least eight pounds of weight. It was also a nuisance because the pack kept slipping from the weight.

I was halfway through the construction zone when I first saw the pickup coming out from the construction headquarters site and heading toward me. Uh-oh, here comes trouble, I thought. They're going to tell me to stay out of the construction zone.

I could almost hear the words: "You can't run in this construction zone, because our liability insurance does not cover it."

Seeing that the pickup driver was an attractive blonde, early 20s I'd guess, and about 115 pounds at most, I concluded that at least I'd not be thrown bodily from the construction zone.

As she pulled alongside, she asked, "Whatever are you doing out here?"

I went into my song and dance about running across Wyoming. Then I asked about her. Her name was Mandy Bailey, and she was a nursing student at Sheridan College. Her parting words were, "Be careful. Don't get hurt."

"Good luck in school," I said. I was impressed with her outgoing personality and wholesome good looks and found myself thinking this girl will succeed in whatever she tries.

The last couple of miles through the construction were sheer luxury. The west side of the Interstate, two lanes and a breakdown lane, were closed off and I had them all to myself. I felt a bit smug as I looked across the median and saw all the highway traffic jammed into a two-lane, two-way traffic pattern.

Elaine was refreshed after a two-hour vacation from pit-stops, although she had expended energy and money shopping at a nearby supermarket and she had walked the environs with the dogs a couple times. She was now ready to get back on the road.

We limited our day to 20 miles, estimating that would leave us only about 18 miles to the finish tomorrow. After returning to the RV park, we pampered ourselves with a swim in the pool and a retreat to the air-conditioned motorhome, both appreciated in the 95-degree weather.

DAY 17. What mainly sustained me today was the exuberance of accomplishing our goal, of making it across Wyoming. I needed all the exuberance I could muster. The wind was my enemy again.

We got a taste last night of what was forthcoming today when a wind of 50 miles per hour hit our RV park around dinner time and continued to near midnight. Luckily our RV was parked next to a building that shielded us from the wind.

What came out of that today was a wind of 35 to 40 MPH. What saved me was that for the most part it was a crosswind. Nonetheless it drained a lot of my energy and made for unpleasant running.

Drivers approaching me had no idea, I was sure, of how marginal my directional control was in this crosswind. Much of the time I had to exert a lot of effort just to keep from being blown out of the breakdown lane into the slow traffic lane or onto the dirt shoulder, depending on the wind direction.

One effect the wind had was to sweep all the clouds from the sky, making this a rare day in Wyoming in that the sky was cloudless. Another effect of the wind was that whenever I tried to talk into my cassette recorder, the strong force of the wind overrode my voice. The resulting sound was a swooooosssssshhhh.

Already cantankerous from battling the wind, I decided to attack. I ran as hard as I could for as long as I could hold the pace, then I would walk a few steps to recover and again take off full blast. I had forgotten that I was running at elevation but got rudely reminded when I got a headache, the same type that I'd gotten in races such as the Lake Tahoe 72-miler and

Pike's Peak.

After a valiant struggle I arrived at the 12-mile pit-stop pooped and panting. With six miles yet to go I realized I had done a dumb stunt in overreacting to the wind and would now pay the price over the next six miles. And I did, because over the last six miles my elevation headache persisted and I started coughing and hacking, my arms and legs were heavy, and the hills seemed endless. Otherwise, I felt fine!

At one point today I found myself thinking for a few moments that I might be disoriented. I had passed mile marker 16, meaning 16 miles to the border, then three miles later when I should have been hitting mile marker 13, I saw mile marker 15.

Couldn't wait to come to the next marker, but when I did, disaster. It read 14, meaning I had actually run four miles but, by the mile markers, was credited only with two. Oh, adversity!

What ticked me here was that I had planned to make this a short day, only to find I now had two more miles than planned. Hey, Governor, tell your Transportation Department to clean up its act here.

Wyoming died hard, because the wind velocity continued right to the Montana border and our finish. To paraphrase Keats, I can call this, *Le windy day sans merci.*

The border was at a nondescript setting on a ridgeline in the boondocks. As I looked ahead, I could see a farm about a half-mile north and the Interstate working its way through a pass. No landmarks, just signs told us that we were finished with Wyoming.

After the run it was sheer luxury to get rid of the roar of the wind in my ears as I planted myself in the passenger seat of the motorhome and we drove to Little Big Horn and the site of Custer's debacle. Now there was a guy who really screwed up.

Following our usual procedure after finishing a state, Elaine and I sent to our family and a few friends a letter that capsuled the run. As we prepared the letter, Elaine and I talked about what a life-warming experience it is to be able to stop the world, to take time out and to adventure as we are doing, and in so doing to kindle our vibrancy for life. Damn lucky, we are.

Overview of
MONTANA

June 29th to July 17th, 1994
376.2 miles

Day	Overnight	Miles	Notes
1	north of Gardiner	22.3	start at Yellowstone Park on Montana-Wyoming border
2	north of Gardiner	19.0	enjoying a backroad
3	Bozeman	19.1	adventure on Trail Creek Road
4	Belgrade	19.1	a mistake, detouring to Highway 205
5	Three Forks	20.4	visiting Sacajawea Inn and Three Forks
6	Three Forks	19.1	Highway 287, adorned with crosses
7	Townsend	20.1	Townsend, a big city hereabouts
8	Helena	19.1	roadside meeting with Wes Underwood
9	Helena	21.8	Helena, a culture shock
10	Helena	21.4	Rebel bitten by rattlesnake
11	Dearborn	13.4	anxiety over ailing Rebel
12	Great Falls	22.0	tour of Great Falls
13	Great Falls	20.1	no wildlife sightings
14	Great Falls	21.4	meeting runner Rick Spady
15	Conrad	20.0	Henry talks about his prostate cancer
16	Conrad	20.6	setting cultivated fields
17	Shelby	21.8	maneuvering through construction zone
18	Shelby	20.9	Shelby, final city in state
19	Helena	14.6	finish at USA-Canada border

Chapter 8

Montana:

The West Ends Here

DAY ONE. I had several reasons to feel good as I stood in Yellowstone National Park at the 45th parallel that marks the boundary between Wyoming and Montana. One reason was that I did not feel tired after finishing Wyoming. Another was that we were on the last leg of running all states west of the Continental Divide.

I felt particularly good about the routing information I had received from James "Wes" Underwood of the Montana Department of Transportation. Sometimes when I correspond with agencies to get information about running across a state, I get no answer. Other times I get a perfunctory reply or maybe an inane answer, as the guy in New Mexico telling me I needed to be preceded and followed by vehicles with flashing yellow lights.

Once in a great while I get an answer from somebody who goes overboard and gives me extremely helpful information, as did Wes Underwood. In the 19 states I have corresponded with, no one did a better job than Wes in providing me with road, weather, terrain, crime, traffic and potential hazard information. An avid hunter and outdoorsman, Wes had driven over all my proposed routes within the past three months, so his information was entirely reliable.

"As a former artillery officer," he said, "I have some experience in providing support to Marines, and I am glad to send you this information."

Anxious to get underway, I paused at the border only long enough to whip out my trusty Olympus and take a picture of the border sign. On the way out of the park I was hampered from enjoying the absolutely beautiful scenery because I had to be alert for vehicles and jump off the road whenever one approached.

The fast-flowing Yellowstone River was enchanting, and I was delighted to see anglers midstream because I figured they were better bait for grizzlies than I, being younger and tender meat.

When I exited the park and passed by the woman ranger in the booth, I was in good spirits so I humorously remarked that I was an alien checking in from the 45th parallel. You know, the humor was that she seemed inclined to believe me.

I passed under the Roosevelt Arch and stopped to study it. An inscription read, "For the benefit and enjoyment of the people."

The arch has marked the north entrance to the park since 1903, and it's named after President Teddy Roosevelt.

Coming into Gardiner on Park Street, I was well oriented because we stayed there last night at the Rocky Mountain Campground. I knew that this town of 600 people has been a hub of tourist activity since 1872 when Yellowstone was first opened. And I knew that the park's north entrance here is the only one kept open year-round, a boon to the local economy.

Out from Helen's OK Corral came a kid about 12, carrying french fries, a hamburger and a milk shake.

"Boy, that smells good, " I told him.

"Tastes even better," he replied. The kid's an expert on torture, I concluded.

Passing Corwin Springs, I realized I was in the heart of a religious cult area. This I had learned from articles in recent issues of the local newspapers.

Somewhere I had read that the Church Universal and Triumphant (which the local folks called CUT) had purchased 12,000 acres or thereabouts in the Paradise Valley area. The seller was Malcolm Forbes, and I was left wondering how one man could accrue so much prime real estate.

In the area to the west of Corwin Springs CUT has built underground bunkers and storage tanks as one measure to survive the nuclear holocaust that CUT's spiritual leader, Elizabeth Claire Prophet, has predicted.

I concluded I was passing by the church headquarters when I saw a complex of buildings, many cars and six yellow buses. But, confusingly to me, the signs on the buses read "Royal Teton Ranch."

When a young couple came out from a building to their car, I went over to ask them if this was the church headquarters, and they confirmed that it was. That so, I decided that Royal Teton Ranch must be another CUT holding.

After counting over 60 cars and seeing a big complex of mobile-home-type dormitories, I also decided this was a big operation. Another conclusion: CUT is self-sufficient. It has cultivation, cattle, shops and stores.

We finished our day 19 miles north of Gardiner on Highway 89 and drove 18 miles farther north to overnight at the Yellowstone Edge RV Park. The Yellowstone River had not been out of our sight all day, and now our camping spot was directly on the river bank.

DAY TWO. After going across Wyoming entirely on an Interstate and knowing that in Montana we'd be on an Interstate from Helena to Canada, Elaine and I were more than ready for a fling at adventure. That's why we found ourselves on Highway 540 and Trail Creek Road today.

When I came to the junction of 540, the first thing I noticed was that it had its own mile markers and we were starting at zero. A sign read, "rough road."

I saw that 540 was just a notch over one lane wide, and it was practically deserted. I looked across the river and saw six deer taking in a morning drink. After facing the steady stream of traffic on 89, I welcomed the tranquillity of 540.

I was not more than five miles along on 540 when I saw a boy, about age 12 I'd guess, out in a cultivated field moving hoses. As I watched, the boy's dog caught sight of me and beelined for me.

Hope he's friendly, I was thinking just about the time he descended on me, wagging his tail and seeking attention. As I was petting him, I saw the boy climb through the fence, pick up his bike from the road and head toward me.

The boy and I talked, and he told me that his summer job was to keep this field irrigated. He yelled at his dog, Pepper, several times, trying to get him to quit jumping on me. But Pepper, thriving on attention, was deaf to these entreaties.

"I've been out here since 6:30, and I've got to get back and get busy to finish," the boy told me, breaking off our conversation. Leaving, he called to Pepper to follow.

The incident was not over. A quarter-mile down the road I again found Pepper on my heels.

I alternated between yelling, "Go home!" and going through the motions of throwing a rock at Pepper. Neither tactic discouraged him.

Then I heard a vehicle approaching from the rear and stepped off the road to let it pass. Instead it stopped abreast of me and Pepper's owner jumped out, grabbed the dog by the tail with one hand and paddled its butt with the other.

"I'm glad to see you," I said to the boy and driver. "I was beginning to think Pepper had adopted me."

"Aw, we have to watch him all the time," the driver replied. "He likes to travel." As they drove off, Pepper was too busy cowering to give me a farewell look.

Every time we made a pit-stop on the 12 miles along Highway 540, Elaine bubbled with enthusiasm over how much she enjoyed being on this road. She and the dogs took an adventurous walk at each pit-stop.

The last leg today was almost joyous. I felt fine, our navigation was flawless, we were out in the serenity of the boondocks, and the weather was comfortable. Just get over the hill to Interstate 90, which should happen tomorrow, and we'd be 20 miles ahead of schedule.

DAY THREE. We were startled last night by a sudden storm – thunder, lightning, a wind rocking the motorhome and stirring up dust. The lightning frightened the dogs, and they stirred restlessly.

What was that Fred Astaire song with the lines: "Thunder and lightning are frightening"? It's always a bit scary when the motorhome swings and sways with the wind.

When Elaine and I were driving to the start and listening to the radio, the newscasters were bombarding their listeners with reports of the O.J. Simpson case. My feeling, as I thought about the case as I started this morning, was that if this man is guilty – and it is hard to conclude otherwise – and if he buys his way to acquittal, there is little hope for the American justice system. And if he is acquitted, will a lot of young minds think, "If he got away with it, so can I."

Reflecting on the Simpson case almost got me into trouble, because it distracted me from watching the road for snakes. Only by pure luck did I catch sight of one when it was only three feet away from me. It was sort of an olive green with black markings.

I had been forewarned of Montana rattlers of this color, so I registered the appropriate reaction (at least for me): thumping heart, pumping adrenaline and goose pimples. Recovering from the shock of seeing him, I found myself thinking: The way he blends with the road makes it hard to see him.

The lesson learned here was: caution – snakes ahead. And that scenario developed because in the next six miles I saw two other rattlers. The snakes did motivate me to move along today, albeit with caution.

When I first saw the lady jump out of her car and run toward the fence, I thought she was making an emergency pit-stop. Then I saw her make her way to one of the many little boxes I'd been seeing posted along fences and trees. All the boxes had small holes in them.

"What are the boxes for?" I asked her.

"For blue birds," she said. "We catch them and then tag them for migration studies. We let them go after we tag them."

For a moment I questioned why the birds did not fly out of the boxes after entering them, then I saw that the hole was near the top of the box and realized that once in the box, the bird could not navigate up to the hole to escape.

Ah, henceforth when I saw one of those boxes, I could feel superior. I knew the what and why of them, having been so informed by Mary Hollis. All the time she was explaining this to me, she was holding a blue bird that she was in the process of tagging.

A little novelty after our nine-mile pit-stop. Elaine had gone less than 40 yards when she stopped, opened the driver's door, pointed to the ground and yelled, "Snake!"

And again, another 100 yards down the road, I saw her stop, open the door and point. No need to yell. I knew the routine by now.

When I arrived at I-90, there was no access. Trail Creek ran under I-90, then north into the hills. I turned west on a frontage road and followed it for one mile to the I-90 access and the end of our 19.1-mile day.

Finished with our run, we drove toward Bozeman and found an RV park on the south end of town. After registering, we drove into Bozeman to wash a very dirty motorhome, to replenish our supplies and to play tourist.

The downtown section of Bozeman appeared to be holding its own for a city of 23,000 or thereabouts. There was much evidence of its being a college town – for example, all the "Go Cats" signs decorating Main Street, Cats referring to the mascot of Montana State University teams.

I knew that the city was named after John Bozeman, the first person to lead a wagon train into the area. But I did not know that the Indians had called the area "The Valley of the Flowers."

That had a familiar ring to it. Then I remembered that the area around Lompoc, California, is also called "the Valley of the Flowers."

That was not too hard to remember, because I once ran the Valley of the Flowers Marathon in Lompoc. When we headed out for the drive to the race, Elaine had the impression (Lord knows why!) that Lompoc was only 100 miles away and she volunteered to drive her car.

In reality Lompoc was 400 miles, and Elaine has never let me forget it. Believe me, I did not remind her by informing her that we were again in the Valley of the Flowers.

DAY FOUR. After the exhilarating experience of pioneering a dirt backroad over a mountain yesterday, today was somewhat of a downer. For one thing starting on I-90 was almost a culture shock as I made the adjustment to a stream of fast-flowing traffic after the near solitude of yesterday's sojourn.

There was no breakdown lane on I-90, and the bike lane was too close to the oncoming 65-mile-per-hour or faster traffic. So I ran on the gravel shoulder, yearning as I did so for the isolation of Trail Creek Road.

Close to traffic, running the sloped gravel shoulder, I was on red alert and my anxiety mounted whenever I saw approaching drivers, sun in their eyes, squinting as they came toward me. Finally, spooked by the fast and close traffic on I-90, I departed the Interstate, went through the grass and weeds, and got onto the railroad tracks that paralleled the Interstate. Running the tracks was damned awkward but safe.

As I made my way down the tracks, I thought about an incident at the RV park this morning, and it sort of reinforced the idea that we seem to pick up a memory from each RV park we stay in. This morning Elaine was walking the dogs after breakfast and Rebel made a quick move, snatched a gopher, crunched and gulped it before Elaine could restrain him. She said she harbors a clear picture of that gopher momentarily half in, half out of Rebel's mouth.

Elaine and I, knowing that she could not make a pit-stop on this portion of I-90, had agreed to rendezvous at exit 313. I had studied the map enough to know that I could catch Bear Canyon Road and on it get to the exit.

On Bear Canyon, I encountered a man and his wife, both senior citizens, out for their morning walk.

"What are you doing out here?" they asked.

"Running across the state," I answered.

"Oh, that's nice," was the rejoinder. Hardly what I had expected to hear.

After introducing themselves as Mr. and Mrs. Stanley Freya, they moved rapidly away from me. Were they that intent on walking, I asked myself, or were they wary of the spooky-looking old man?

I'd had a shower this morning; so I did not think B.O. was the problem here. But my running shoes were getting a bit ripe, as in smelly.

Not much farther down the road, I came across an historical marker. Now for me, with my loneliness on the road, historical markers are like being at 42nd and Broadway.

The marker read: "Fort Ellis was located at this spot. A military post established on August 27th, 1867, and abandoned in 1886. Captain William Clark of the Lewis and Clark expedition camped at this location July 14th, 1806, while accompanied by his invaluable guide Sacajawea, nine of his men and Cahaponea, her husband, and their baby Baptiste, and York, the slave."

When I got back on I-90 on the southern outskirts of Bozeman, I was relieved to see that I again had the comfort of a breakdown lane. This was offset by facing the heaviest traffic yet in Montana. To escape I-90 traffic, I again made the decision to leave I-90 and follow 205 that paralleled it to Belgrade and beyond.

It turned out that while yesterday's decision to take Trail Creek Road was brilliant today's decision to take 205 was idiotic. This highway was woeful in many ways. The bike lane I started with petered out in one mile, the traffic seemed heavier than on I-90, and the aggressive drivers refused to give me any running room. I again took refuge on the railroad tracks.

In Belgrade I turned onto Highway 85 and headed for the Interstate. By the time I reached I-90, we had a 19.1-mile day and decided to quit there rather than to get on the Interstate and then not be able to find an exit when we wanted one.

Luck was with us in one respect today. We had to drive only a half-mile from the junction of 85 and I-90 to locate at the Lesley Acres RV Park overnight. I was glad to anchor for the night. The stress of 205 had drained me.

DAY FIVE. Today was much like that of the husband who returns home after work and his wife asks, "What happened at the office today, honey?" and he answers, "Nothing." Except for moving 20.4 miles down the road, we have a similarly uneventful day.

It was a case of shiver my timbers when I hit the road and a cold, cutting wind made the 32-degree temperature downright uncomfortable. When I started, the traffic was so light that I found it difficult to believe I was on I-90. But within an hour that changed as the Interstate became infested with traffic.

On the plus side, the air was so pure and clean that it was overwhelming. And having the breakdown lane to run in was sheer delight compared with the frenzy of yesterday's two-lane road.

I had a little trouble this morning with being a bit wobbly, whether from imbalance or light-headedness I was not sure. I was sure, though, that I sometimes make my own troubles.

A case in point: At the three-mile pit-stop, I stripped down to T-shirt and shorts, then as I ran the three to six leg I found myself chilled and cold, unnecessarily and stupidly so.

What saved me on that leg was that on the drive to the start this morning Elaine had stopped at a bakery and picked up some bear claws. I had one at the three-mile pit-stop. Who needs steroids? That sinning sugar fix kept me moving out down the road.

As I went through the Manhattan area, I saw that we were lucky because of the holiday weekend to be escaping the activity of a highway construction project. I also caught myself thinking that Manhattan was an inappropriate name for this tiny community located in all this open rural space. Manhattan and Logan were the only communities we passed through today.

When I came into the 12-mile pit-stop, Elaine was seething. She had just returned from taking Brudder and Rebel for a walk, and they had gone berserk trying to catch one of the many chipmunks about.

They were straining at their leashes, pulling her, and she was screaming, "Run for your lives, little chipmunks! Run for your lives!"

Meanwhile the dogs, drooling over chipmunk delight, were dragging her through the weeds. They kept missing chipmunks by one snap.

After a valiant struggle Elaine was able to regain control, paddle both dogs on their butts and return them to the motorhome. When I came into the motorhome, they both looked properly chastised. And Elaine looked properly frazzled.

Around 15 miles I stopped to read the only historical monument of the day. It told me about the Madison Buffalo State Monument, a cliff to the west where Indians (some say as long as 2000 years ago) killed buffalo by stampeding herds over the cliffs. The Indians used the buffalo for food, shelter, clothing and tools.

The thought most on my mind today, and the reason I was looking forward to reaching Three Forks, was that once there all our remaining route would be directly north to Canada and our goal. Today as we moved westward from Belgrade to Three Forks, our route did not advance us one inch northward toward Canada.

After finishing, we toured the town of Three Forks, which because of the town's size was a quick trip. Primarily we wanted to see the Sacajawea Inn, a local landmark built in 1882 and expanded in 1910.

By 1:30 P.M., we were registered at the KOA RV Park at the junction of Interstate 90 and Highway 287. Tomorrow we were slated to leave I-90 and follow 287 to Helena.

I knew 287 was a two-lane road with a marginal bike lane. I was hoping it would not be another Highway 205 fiasco.

The alternative would be to stick with I-90 to Butte, which would add 41 miles to our route. I decided I could, if necessary, stand a bit of agony on 287 to save all those miles. The question on my mind as I went to bed tonight was just how much agony would this entail.

DAY SIX. As I rousted from bed this Fourth of July morning, I realized that one of the most useless items I brought on this trip was an alarm clock. Why? Because at precisely five A.M. each and every day the dogs start to stir, then they get up, stretch, shake their collars and metal tags, and make more noise than any alarm clock.

They are signaling that it's time for them to go out and do their business and time for breakfast. Well, that's in inverse order: first, Elaine feeds them; then she puts their leashes on them and takes them out.

On Highway 287 today I soon became aware that I was seeing a cross about every mile to mark the spot of fatal accidents. Since a number of these crosses were in open, flat areas, it was evident the accident resulted from excessive speed or from someone passing illegally, or maybe from someone falling asleep.

It might help to replace the no passing yellow lines with cement barriers in the middle of the road. I could not go one mile without seeing someone passing over the double-yellow lines.

At one pit-stop Elaine told me she is enjoying this road because it is easier for her to park here than on the Interstate and because this backroad gives her more of a feeling of the outdoors than does being on the Interstate. I told her I'd enjoy it more if I did not feel such an affinity with the white crosses.

There should be an award for what I am seeing now, I told myself: an award for the outstanding farm, the best of all farms I have seen in Wyoming and Montana. And the award would go to Great Montana Farms, seven very well kept outbuildings, a sprawling ranch home located in a grove of trees, fields cultivated to the point of being manicured, everything neat as a pin. The place reeked of prosperity.

Seeing all the wheat and grain cultivation reminded me that in Montana I must try to buy some of the Montana Cream of the West hot cereal that our friends Hal and Darlene Stainbrook bring us from Montana. Major-league stuff that puts Quaker Oats and Cream of Wheat in the sandlot league.

An unusual experience today when I stepped aside for a man and a woman on bicycles and asked, "Are you going across the country?"

One answered, "Yes," and the other said, "Hello," but they kept going. First time I've been snubbed by transcon bicyclists in 19 states. Wonder why?

Guess I have joined the ranks of superstitious athletes, because I wore the same pair of running shorts all through Wyoming and as I start Montana I am still wearing them. That's not as bad as it sounds – I do wash them every night. Then again, those bicyclists did pass me by!

Most of my energy on 287 today was devoted to just staying alive, to avoiding getting hit by some speeding driver with his brain on vacation. Achieving that and this being the Fourth of July, I felt like singing a chorus of "Yankee Doodle Dandy" when I finished. Then I remembered those coyotes we heard howling last night, and afraid my singing might bring on more of that, I abstained.

DAY SEVEN. I was not overjoyed this morning as I thought about another day on Highway 287. By now I knew the scenario too well: no running space, much time in the weeds, aggressive drivers, apprehension about someone passing from the rear and clobbering me, and heavy traffic. And so went my day on the road.

I had not gone very far on this morning's run before I stopped to talk with a young guy attending to a field of russet potatoes. I asked him when they would be ready for harvest.

"About the end of September," he answered. "If all goes well."

He was hardly the portrait of a farmer: ball cap, almost shoulder-length hair, full beard, T-shirt, Levi's. He was working on the irrigation system.

Pointing to the symmetrical rows of potatoes, he said, "The crop is coming along great."

As he said that, I was curious about what this field of potatoes was worth, but I refrained from asking. I'm not an authority on measuring acres, but I was sure that there were at least 40 acres of spuds here.

When I studied the elaborate irrigation equipment and saw the combines and other mechanical equipment as I moved along the road today, I was left puzzling over how the farmers ever raised the money for all this capital outlay. Yet I knew the Catch-22 was that without this equipment they could not sustain the operation.

Radersburg. I had seen the name on the map and wondered what I'd see when I arrived there. The answer turned out to be very little – or more precisely a fire station, a grill and bar, and four mobile homes. My highlight here was crossing the Missouri River just north of town.

Usually I am the one who yaks about drivers, but at the 12-mile pit-stop it was Elaine who was fuming over the rudeness of a Montana driver. She was driving at 55 miles per hour when this Montana driver behind her, upset at her slow speed, suddenly passed her, sliced in front of the motorhome, then turned and flipped her the finger.

"I could expect this in a California city," she said. "But here in Montana, it amazes me. It's completely unexpected."

At 13 miles or so today I crossed paths with history when a sign pointed to the Lewis and Clark Trail. Judging from what I had read, members of one of the parties had camped several times along the route I was running.

As I ran through Townsend (population 1650), I found it to be characteristic of many small farming towns – grain elevators, trees, water tower, main drag. Penniless as I ran, I hoped I would not go past a donut shop, for if I did frustration would set in.

In the last 1.5 miles today I knew I had been on the road too long, knew I was losing my cool, knew that I had strayed from staying loose. I knew these things because of what happened when I saw an oversized motorhome, a Bounder, coming down a hill toward me and taking all the bike lane. I said, I'll show that sucker! and I planted myself on the fog line and started running it.

That left the Bounder with two choices: Move out from the bike lane and into the slow lane or hit me. Luckily for my mortality he elected to move.

After he passed, I realized how stupidly I had acted. Rather than take any more chances on beetle-brain actions, I moved out to the shoulder or dirt and grass and ran there the remaining distance.

We succeeded in logging 20.1 miles on this uneventful and not very pleasurable day. Routine-wise, though, it went much like any of our other days.

After we finished, Elaine did her grocery shopping on the north end of Townsend, then we drove to the south end to overnight at the Roadrunner RV Park. How could we pass by a place with a name like that?

DAY EIGHT. The miles this day came discouragingly slow and as a result of undue effort. My mind did not wander far from focusing on not getting hit by a car and on moving along with the best efficiency I could muster.

Actually I was not missing much by way of scenery, because the entire route was nothing but grain and wheat fields under cultivation.

I had more than my usual concerns about safety. For one thing, I worried about visibility in the rain: Could the drivers see me?

There was also the concerns with the way Montanans drive Highway 287. To them the double yellow lines indicating no passing do not exist. I've also noticed that immediately after passing another vehicle, the Montana driver will cut in and almost slice off the front fender of the vehicle passed.

Elaine heard on the radio that snow would fall on the mountains south of Helena today, and for some reason foreign to me this weather report drove her to making chocolate fudge candy. Seeing it at one pit-stop, I immediately wrote an Rx for same as a remedy for any and all things that might be ailing me. Nibbling on chocolate fudge as I trudged down the road getting splashed by passing cars did help offset some of the nastiness of the day.

So focused was I on running and surviving that only a couple of times did my mind wander to other things. One was kids.

This happy thinking related to probably the most heart-warming experience that resulted from the publication of our book, *Ten Million Steps*, the story of our run across the USA in 1990. That experience happened when I heard from Maureen Meyer, a fourth-grade teacher at W.F. Loomis School in Broomal, Pennsylvania. She told me that she had read passages of the book to her students and that they were impressed with our adventures to the point where they wanted to write to us.

She enclosed the letters they had written, and reading them brought smiles to Elaine and me. They had a wide range of questions: How are your Labradors, what kind of an insect was it that bit through the screen window of your motorhome, would you run across the country again, did you ever find a turtle for your wife, what state was the hardest and a dozen more that Elaine answered with pleasure.

Today I met Jim Bird of the Montana Fish, Game and Wildlife Department. He was intrigued with the idea of someone running across the state, and he bombarded me with questions. After a 10-minute conversation I left his warm pickup and felt fortified to make it to my next pit-stop.

At 15 miles my world changed. The rain stopped, the bike lane expanded to a breakdown lane, and the surface of the road changed to blacktop. Manna from heaven!

The highlight of my day occurred a mile later when a fellow standing along the road stopped me and said, "Seems like they let anybody on the Montana highways these days, don't they?"

Who's this guy? I thought. He seems to know me, but I don't know him.

I guessed it was my raised eyebrows and puzzled look that caused him to hastily add, "I'm Wes Underwood."

Instantly I was elated. This was the guy from the Montana Highway Department who had been so generous in giving me information about roads and routes.

"Hey, it's good to meet you," I said. "And thanks for all the help you gave me."

"Well, since I corresponded with you, there's been a big change in my life," he told me. "I quit the Highway Department. Just too much bureaucracy. I couldn't get things done."

"Does that mean you're out of a job now?" I asked.

"No, I'm just in between jobs. I'm going to teach at a high school over by Missoula. The school is on the Blackfoot River."

I was surprised when he told me that he was 44 years old. I would have judged him much younger. He was a big guy, about 6-2 and 230 pounds.

He said that at 39 he had a heart attack that caused him to change his lifestyle. He is now into walking and jogging. He thrives on outdoor activities, especially hunting and fishing.

"What will you be teaching?" I asked.

"American history and Montana state history. Both are required for all students."

He was enthusiastic about going into teaching. As I saw it, his job change was a plus for education and a minus for the Highway Department.

DAY NINE. Advertisements may spell relief as "R-O-L-A-I-D-S," but for me today it was spelled getting off Highway 287 and onto the much safer I-15. The Interstate also gave me an emotional and mental lift, for north we were headed directly to Canada, no more wasted miles going westward.

When I started running, the shakedown was a bit unnerving in that I had some traces of imbalance. Having been through this a number of times before, though, I was confident it would evaporate if I just took it easy for a while. I did, and it did.

An historical marker livened my morning. Investigating, I found that I was going past the Manlove Cabin, the first building in Pear Prickly Valley. I could get no closer than the wire fence surrounding the cabin, but that was close enough to see that it was surprisingly well preserved.

Coming into Helena, I took a shortcut and climbed up an embankment to get onto I-15. Doing so, I caught sight of the Overland Express Restaurant where I had dinner last time I was in Helena.

Great prime rib. I made a mental note to take Elaine there on our return from Canada.

Good Lord, I thought as I went through Helena, this city has a population of only somewhere around 25,000. So where does all this traffic come from?

It was almost a culture shock to run through Helena after being on the high plains so many days. On the northern edge of town, I had to step out of the breakdown lane to let a group of 20 bicyclists pass.

As we exchanged hellos, I noticed they were all senior citizens. Interesting to watch their facial expressions: some grim, some smiling, some fully concentrated on biking, some enjoying the scenery.

Since they were carrying no equipment, I concluded they were a local group out for a morning ride. They'd better enjoy, I thought, because there are not that many days in the year that they can bike in Montana.

Out of town and to the north, I stopped to look back toward Helena, and the three landmarks that stood out were the state capitol with its copper dome, the Cathedral of St. Helena with its twin spires and Carroll College that sits atop a bluff.

I was anxious to learn more about Helena, which we planned to visit on our return trip. I did know that its origins went back to the days when four ex-Confederate soldiers made a gold strike in an area called Last Chance Gulch, now a pedestrian mall in the city.

I had also read that in the late 1880s Helena had more millionaires per capita than any city in the USA. That one surprised me.

The closest RV park after we finished was back in Helena. As Elaine drove those 16 miles and I was comfortably lodged in the passenger seat, after evicting a somewhat protesting Rebel, I reviewed our day and was pleased that the 21.8 miles were relatively easy. Maybe it was the comparison with Highway 287 that made today's miles seem easy.

At any rate, we did not have any problems until we returned to Helena and I was filling the motorhome with gas and felt something drop on me. Then I saw that the window glass was shattered, and what was falling on me were pieces of glass.

Obviously the window had been broken by a rock from a passing vehicle, most likely a truck. When Elaine opened the bathroom door, she saw glass strewn all over the floor. Had one of us been in there when the rock hit, we would have been cut in a number of places.

Luck was with us, because we found Nicholas Glass only six miles from our RV park. They suggested a Plexiglas window instead of the single pane that was there.

"The manufacturer should not be allowed to get away with that single pane stuff," a worker told us. "It's too dangerous." We could not agree more.

DAY 10. Little did Elaine and I realize – as we started and finished this day's run – that this would be our most dramatic day in more than 4900 miles on the road to date in 19 states. Until the time we finished and had settled in for the night, we assessed this as a day fraught with danger because of road conditions and as a day of spectacular scenery.

The day also held much inherent danger for Elaine. Driving through the mountain passes and making her three-mile pit-stops, she often had to park in marginal spots, very close to the fog line, and hope that drivers would see her.

When finally in the last few miles I emerged from the gorge into open space and onto a regular breakdown lane, I celebrated by eating a piece of chocolate fudge Elaine had made yesterday. It felt yummy on top of the chili mac I had at the previous pit-stop.

We finished our 21.4-mile day just one mile north of the hamlet of Wolf Creek that had no RV park. We drove five miles to Holter Lake, only to find that all camping spots were filled.

We did not want to drive 40 miles back to Helena to overnight at an RV park, so we decided to explore Wolf Creek and find a spot to park overnight. We settled behind Wolf Creek Elementary School.

We had finished dinner and done our nightly chores and were about to settle in for the night. Elaine left the motorhome with Rebel and Brudder for their evening walk and last toilet stop for the night. She was gone less than three minutes when, crying and calling to me, I heard her running back to the motorhome.

Opening the motorhome door, she yelled, "A rattlesnake struck at us!"

As she pushed the dogs into the motorhome, I asked, "Did he bite you?"

"No, he didn't get me."

"How about the dogs?"

"I'm not sure, but I don't think so."

I looked at the dogs. Once he'd gotten into the motorhome, Brudder had jumped up onto his dinette bed and curled up contentedly. It seemed obvious that nothing was wrong with him.

But Rebel was a different story. He seemed sort of dazed, just standing still, his head hung slightly down. We had a suspicion he might have been bitten.

Hastily Elaine and I examined his legs but could find no evidence of a bite. But the way he was behaving was not normal – standing motionless, head hung down, ignoring his surroundings.

Over the course of an anxious 10 minutes, Elaine and I intensified our efforts, searching his legs for a bite. Inch by inch we rolled back his fur; then we got a flashlight and repeated the process. We found nothing.

By now he was quivering and appearing to go into shock. Then as Elaine tried to move him into a different position, she brushed against his chest and he whimpered in pain.

Gingerly rolling back the fur and using the flashlight, we probed his chest, and doing so we discovered a small red mark on his chest. It had to be a rattlesnake bite.

"We've got to get him to a vet," we both said almost in unison.

We decided to drive the half-mile into Wolf Creek to see if we could locate a vet there. The only place open in the dinky town was a cafe bar. I went inside to inquire about a vet while Elaine kept an eye on Rebel.

"I think our dog has been bitten by a rattlesnake," I told the bartender. "Is there a vet in town?"

"No," he said. "The closest one I know about is in Helena."

My God, 40 miles away! How will Rebel hold out until then, I was thinking.

"Where's the dog?" I heard someone ask. I looked up and saw two ladies sitting at the bar. They'd been having a sandwich and a drink.

"Oh, he's in our motorhome with my wife."

"I'll take a look at him," one of the ladies said. "I used to work for a vet."

She followed me to the motorhome, took a look at Rebel, then said, "That's a rattlesnake bite, for sure. You'll have to get him to a vet. I know a good one in Helena."

Taking the information she gave me, I phoned Helena, got an answering service, outlined the problem and told the operator that we had to drive from Wolf Creek. She told me that she would have the vet meet us at the Big Sky Animal Clinic at 10 P.M.

I knew Elaine was deeply affected. Face it, her love for Rebel was one step short of parenthood. As she drove, my job was to monitor and comfort Rebel as much as possible. Doing so, I wondered if the poor guy knew what had hit him.

Every so often, he would whimper as he sat on the floor beside me. Somehow he seemed to convey a confidence that he knew we would do what we could for him.

As we went down the road, I tried to reassure Elaine that Rebel was holding out okay. I had the feeling that she was worried he might drop over dead at any moment. I worked at keeping up a steady stream of conversation so that she could not dwell on Rebel.

When we arrived at the Big Sky Animal Clinic on the west edge of town, the building was unlighted, vacant. Good Lord, had something gone wrong? Didn't the vet get the word?

I hurried to a nearby phone and again called the answering service, being damn glad at the moment that I had kept the number. The operator assured me that the vet had been contacted and would be there.

Just as I hung up the phone and started the block back to the clinic, I saw a vehicle pull in. From the moment he greeted us, Dr. Gary Erickson radiated confidence. Elaine and I felt that Rebel was in good hands.

With some difficulty Rebel wobbled in to the clinic. Dr. Erickson placed him on an operating table and shaved the fur around the wound. Elaine and I were taken back by what we saw. What had been a small red dot when we first saw it was now an ugly purple-reddish discoloration spread all over his chest.

Elaine asked, "Is he going to die?"

"Well, in medicine you're never sure of anything," Dr. Erickson said. "But he's a very lucky dog. He was lucky to be bitten in his fatty chest area, because the fat will absorb much of the poison. If he'd been bitten a few inches higher, on the neck, the bite would have been fatal."

The doctor then gave him a number of shots of anesthetic. While we waited for them to take effect, he told us that Rebel would most likely live through this but that we would have one very sick dog on our hands for a few days. There would be not much we could do but comfort him and medicate him.

After the anesthetic took effect, Dr. Erickson excised the damaged tissue around the snake-bite wound. He then flushed it with water and with Betadine, and packed the wound with gauze strips so that Rebel's chest would drain. The operation completed, he gave Rebel shots of steroids, anesthetic, anti-shock medicine and antibiotics.

Though wounded and in much pain, Rebel was able to wobble back to the motorhome. He could not get up the step by himself, and Elaine and I lifted one leg at a time for him, being careful not to touch his chest area that was sensitive to the slightest pressure.

Once he was in the motorhome, he simply sat on the floor and hung his head. So tender was his chest area that he could not lie on it, not even on a soft bed.

Brudder got up from his bed, came over and sniffed Rebel, then returned to his bed instead of curling up alongside of Rebel as is often his want. We sensed that from that one sniff Brudder was aware that something unusual had happened and he then understood why we'd left him alone.

Rebel moved not an inch from his sitting position between the two front seats, his favorite spot in the motorhome (except when he was allowed to sit in the passenger seat). And that is where he stayed the rest of the night, a restless night for Elaine who got up several times to check on him.

She tried propping his head with pillows, which helped until he dozed off and changed position. Then he cried out in pain.

He did nothing all night but sit there, whimper in pain occasionally and drip blood onto the towel under him. Elaine was grateful that he was still alive but distressed that he hurt so much. Our hearts went out to him.

DAY 11. This morning blossomed bright in that Rebel had the strength to leave the motorhome, with Elaine's help, for a morning piddle. Then, after some hesitation, he accepted his morning food – that is, what was left of it after his five minutes of hesitation during which Brudder raided it.

Actually, though, Brudder had done a good deed, because it was best that Rebel had little food. An hour after eating, he upchucked.

Watching Elaine tend to Rebel, I recalled that the vet said that we would have a miserable three days with him and that it would take a lot of loving care. No problem. That's Elaine's forte.

After breakfast Elaine and I weighed what to do next. We decided that if we stayed in this RV park all day we'd just fret and stew. We'd be better off with a modified day.

When I went to the RV park office to check out, clerk Kim Harrison told me about a newly opened RV park only 10 miles from where we had finished yesterday. Oh my God, was my silent thought, if we'd known about that and stayed there, Rebel would not have been bitten last night.

Kim went to the trouble of making a reservation for us. Thus our battle plan when we left Helena and drove 40 miles back to Wolf Creek was to run about 10 miles today and then retreat to the RV park.

The only reluctance we had in leaving Helena was that if Rebel had a setback the vet would not be immediately accessible. On the other hand, as we understood it, if he did have a setback, it would probably be fatal.

By now we noticed that much of the swelling that was in Rebel's chest had moved to his stomach area. He was beginning to sag like a pregnant dog.

At the six-mile pit-stop Elaine reported that Rebel is still sitting, as he has been since the operation, and that his breathing is quite difficult. He does not seem to be quite aware of what is happening to him.

About all we can do is comfort him and administer the medicine the vet prescribed. I was sure that Elaine was supplementing that with bundles of prayers.

After my day's running ended, we spent the afternoon and evening trying to comfort Rebel as much as we could. Since being bitten, he had not slept. Since returning to the motorhome after the operation, he had been sitting because he could tolerate no other position.

After upchucking in the morning, he was now refusing food. And the sag and swelling beneath his stomach was increasing. We marveled at how stoically he endured his pain.

We felt lucky to log 11.5 miles today with no further disasters. We were now 45 miles south of Great Falls, where we had to take Rebel to a vet in two days.

DAY 12. Rebel was our main concern again today. We decided to play the day by ear, monitoring his health as we went along.

Elaine tried her best to make him comfortable. She had been able to get him to take all the pills the vet had prescribed and had followed his instructions by applying an ice pack every four hours.

On the minus side, Rebel did some vomiting around midnight. On the plus side, he did not cry or whimper as much as the previous night.

It was a blissful sight for us this morning when we saw that Rebel was able to tolerate lying down. But leaving the motorhome for his morning piddle was a severe strain for him in his weakened condition.

After he piddled, Elaine and I were heartened to see him sniffing around the tall grass as if searching for a gopher hole. We took that as a good sign.

I have to confess to committing an illegal act this morning by carrying a concealed weapon. I had my Colt .45 in a shoulder holster when I went through the cougar/bear area.

Frankly, though, I thought an attack by a cougar would be so swift and silent that I'd not get my .45 out of the holster before being attacked. Not only would I have to get the gun out of the holster, but also I had to insert a round in the chamber. I dared not carry it with a round in the chamber and run at the same time because of the inherent danger of an accidental discharge that could result in my demise.

The expensive shoulder holster I wore was comfortable, and the wind jacket I wore concealed it. Nonetheless the .45 was a weight burden added to the six pounds I was already carrying in my fanny pack.

After the bad luck we had been having, I dared not go into cougar/bear territory without some protection. Besides, still fresh in my mind was the memory of recently attending the funeral of Barbara Schoener, a running friend killed by a cougar.

I carried the .45 for only one three-mile leg. It was a load, a very welcomed and comforting load.

Today's journey took me through two small communities. The first was Dearborn, at our starting area. Besides the Dearborn Lodge and Inn, I counted 15 homes in this valley. About six miles into my day I was impressed with the small community of Hardy. About 40 homes, I estimated, sitting on the west bank of the Missouri River.

Overall, my running day went unexpectedly well. I was pleased to log 22 miles after we decided we'd try to get close to Great Falls, then drive there for two reasons: to find a vet and make an appointment for tomorrow, and to overnight at Dick's RV Park with which we were familiar.

I was mindful that today was Sunday and, yes, I was again observing the Sabbath by going to church out in this open air church God built. Beyond that, I was damn sure that if I had come eyeball to eyeball with a cougar or bear this morning, I would have swiftly made a desperate effort to get close to God.

After our day's run and while driving toward Great Falls, we decided to take time out for a short adventure, namely to see if we could take a shortcut tomorrow that would bypass Great Falls and save us 10 miles. On our maps we had seen a dirt road from the town of Ulm to Manchester.

There was no question that I could run the road. The question was: How would the motorhome fare on it?

Not well, we found out after only three miles of reconnoitering the road that was rough and rocky, involving too much inherent danger to the motorhome. Decision: no shortcut.

In Great Falls our first act was to check into Dick's RV Park. We were lucky enough to have the manager recommend a local vet in whom he had much confidence, and we called for an appointment, then after stocking up with gas and groceries, drove by the clinic to make sure we'd find it tomorrow without any delay.

During the day Rebel had given us some cause for concern. He was content to stay sprawled on the bed, he vomited a couple of times, and his appetite was zero. He had a mass of black, decaying matter around his chest and stomach.

By nightfall he seemed to perk up a bit. He was no longer vomiting, he accepted some food that he ate gingerly instead of in his usual gulps, and he showed some interest in his surroundings when he went out for his nightly toilet.

And he was no longer crying or whimpering. Maybe the angelic care Elaine was bestowing on him was paying off. We were anxious to get him to the vet tomorrow for a professional appraisal.

DAY 13. As I was eating breakfast, I knew Rebel had to be getting better because he squatted beside the table and assumed his usual beg for food stance and stare. We also noticed that the sagging of skin beneath his stomach had shrunk a bit.

Another encouraging sign occurred as we were driving to the start, and Rebel came to the front of the motorhome and assumed his usual position on the floor between Elaine in the driver's seat and me in the passenger seat. We seemed to be returning to SOP.

The loving, tender care that Elaine was lavishing on Rebel seemed to be paying off. Florence Nightingale was rough on the edges compared to Elaine's nursing. Her morale will hinge a lot on what the vet tells us today, I realized.

One offshoot of the attention we had given Rebel since his bite is that we had to be aware of Brudder's feelings. We tried to convey to him that Rebel was hurt and needed attention, that he was loved as much as Rebel and that he was not being rejected.

We were not sure how much he understood. Brudder is not the smartest kid on the block. That boy clearly understands only two things: food and affection.

Brudder and Rebel are the first dogs I've ever owned (well, actually they are Elaine's dogs!) in all my 70-plus years. From them I've learned two basic lessons about pets: They provide much company, pleasure and comfort, and owners become attached to them.

As I started running today, I found the air so fresh, so pure that I told myself, Hey, I might get dizzy from this. From the beginning the running was pleasant as I passed cultivated, open flatlands with some scattered ranch homes, easy going compared with yesterday's start through rocky passes. And with the exception of a couple of hills, each about a mile long and about a six-percent gradient, so the setting remained all day.

In our 20.1-mile day I went through only one community, the little town of Ulm that sits about a half-mile off the Missouri River about seven miles south of Great Falls. From what I could see, it appeared to be entirely a residential community with houses on both sides of the Interstate.

I was anxious to reach Great Falls today because we had a number of chores to do and also because, even though we would have about 122 miles from there to Canada, I sort of felt we would be on the home stretch once we left Great Falls.

Cresting a knoll just south of Great Falls, I was taken aback to see the city lying in a swoop and unfolding before me. It was easy to trace the Missouri River flowing through the area. Donna Deball, a highway worker who was planting foliage nearby, pointed out some landmarks, of which Great Falls College was the most distinguishable.

We finished in Great Falls and immediately drove to Dick's RV Park to clean up before setting out for our chores. At Gus and Jack's RV Repair, we plunked down $40 for a thermostat for the water heater, which did not do the trick.

We were told we would need a new control panel that would have to be ordered. Not being able to wait a day for it to arrive, we had a new agenda: no hot water, and buy a control panel soon as we can.

The repairman told us he thought we could get one in Conrad, 60 miles north, and it would cost us $180. We thanked him for the information and for serving us so fast so that we could make our appointment with Dr. Seekins at Skyline Veterinary Clinic.

Dr. Seekins was of a different mold than Dr. Erickson who had treated Rebel for his bite. He was, we guessed, in his mid-60s and he reminded Elaine and me of the type of doctor of the era of our youth who made house calls and who was almost an adjunct of the family.

Dr. Erickson was of the here-and-now generation, half the age of Dr. Seekins. His attire was sport shirt and Levi's. Dr. Seekins wore slacks, shirt and tie.

Both vets radiated these commonalities: They knew their business, they inspired confidence, and they liked animals.

Dr. Seekins removed the packing in Rebel's chest, examined him, then injected him with an antibiotic and gave us some pills.

"He's doing well," Dr. Seekins said. "Progressing fine. It's just going to take a little time for him to come around to normal."

I looked at Elaine. She was beaming so much I thought she might break into an Irish jig.

DAY 14. Helluva lot of traffic this morning, I told myself as I accessed I-15 in Great Falls and started running north. I suspected this was mostly commute traffic and that it would thin down later in the morning.

From what I saw of fast driving today, I had to agree with what I'd read on a Montana postcard last night: "This is Montana – you are going 75 miles per hour, and you are being passed by an 18-wheeler."

All the Montana people we've dealt with seem to be very friendly and helpful. However, put the same people behind the wheel of a car, and they all seem to be trying to qualify for Indianapolis.

The most interesting experience today occurred when I was approaching the motorhome for a pit-stop and from a half-mile away I saw a pickup parked behind the motorhome. My first thought was, Can some guy be giving Elaine trouble? I ran as hard as I could to get there.

Arriving at the motorhome, I saw an athletic-looking guy wearing a T-shirt, Levis, running shoes and ball cap. He stood on the shoulder and talked with Elaine who was in the motorhome.

I judged him to be in his 30s. When I saw that his T-shirt advertised a race, I relaxed a bit.

"Hi, Paul," he said. "I saw you running down the road and thought I'd stop for a visit. I'm Rick Spady."

Since we'd never met, I was wondering how he knew me. At the same time I heard him answering that "I read about your transcontinental run in *Ultrarunning*."

As runners are bent to do, we were soon talking about running and races. When he told me that he had run the 56-mile Comrades Marathon in South Africa in 7-1/2 hours, I realized I was talking to a world-class ultrarunner. We agreed that Comrades was the best ultra race we'd ever run and that Capetown ranks among the most beautiful of cities.

"What do you do about running here in the winter?" I asked him.

"Oh, I simply put on three or four layers of clothing," he responded. I shivered at the mere thought.

When I told Rick about Rebel getting bit by a rattlesnake, he replied, "I know this guy who got bit on the trail because he violated the cardinal rule. He was following three feet behind another runner instead of being 20 feet back."

The idea, he explained, is that the first gets past, the rattlesnake is alerted and scoots, and the second guy 20 feet back remains safe. Whereas if the second guy is only three feet back, the snake does not scoot.

It was evident as we talked that Rick was a baptized and confirmed member of the ultrarunning cult, the closest-knit group of all in running – and by many standards the most admirable. Much as I enjoyed our visit and would have liked to linger longer, the road beckoned. So I was not unduly disappointed when he said he had to leave and hurry to an appointment.

The most dramatic incident of the day happened not to me but to Elaine. Coming into the 12-mile pit-stop, I was taken aback to see tears in her eyes.

Before I could say anything, she said, "Let me tell you what happened. I knew the boys had to piddle, so I pulled of an exit ramp and got on a gravel road.

"I took them out, and when they finished I put Brudder back in first.

Then just as I was putting Rebel in, I heard this noise behind the motorhome door, the same cricket noise I had heard when Rebel was bitten.

"I looked toward the door and sound and saw a coiled rattlesnake, head up, rattling and ready to strike. Trying to stay calm, I gently lifted Rebel into the motorhome and heard myself saying, 'Be a good snakey, be a good snakey!'

"And at the same time, I jumped into the motorhome. I lay on my stomach on the floor, reached out through the open door, retracted the step and closed the door.

"Once safe inside, I found myself trembling, and I could hardly believe that the snake did not strike. I said a prayer of thanksgiving, and then I looked out the window and saw the snake was still there.

"He seemed to be saying, 'You stay in your territory, and I'll stay in mine.' I was still shaking when I drove back onto the Interstate." As I held her, I could tell she was still shaken.

It was somewhat upsetting at the end of the day when Elaine took the boys for their nightly piddle to see blood in Rebel's urine. We worried about poison getting into his bladder or kidneys.

DAY 15. By now I was pleased with the strategy Elaine and I had adopted of limiting our running day to not more than 21 miles. Maybe I was taking a lesson from John Stuart Mill

He wrote, "I have learned to seek my happiness by limiting my desires rather than in attempting to satisfy them." One thing for sure, John Stuart, if a person does not limit his desires when he grows old, he will build a heap of unhappiness.

After a mile on the road I looked to the west and saw the small community of Power that appeared almost like a painting – the granary, the homes, the greenery and even, unlike what I saw most of the day, a few trees. Power kicked in name-association again.

Back to Tyrone Power, movie actor, circa 1940s, old enough to avoid military service, but pulling a few political strings he got into the Marine Corps as a pilot flying transports. From all the reports I had, he turned out to be just one of the guys.

Once in Guam when three of us were in the showers, we were surprised to see him come in and shower. I chuckled, remembering one post-war talk I gave in which I mentioned it and some in the audience considered this the highlight of my war career. It was a shocker to me, many years later, to read that Tyrone Power died of a heart attack while filming a sword-fighting scene.

Uplifting today when I came in for pit-stops to see Rebel accepting treats. But it was obvious he was still in some pain.

His wound is open for drainage purposes, and we have to be on guard for infection. The tip of his penis is charcoal black, just like the area where he was bitten and much of his stomach area. He also has discoloration in various parts of his body.

Surprising in a way that he can urinate. But he does by the bucketful, which we take as a good sign.

There has been one somewhat humorous fallout from Rebel being bitten. Elaine often tells me to go light on the treats for the dogs.

"I don't want them to get too fat," she cautions.

When Dr. Erickson was operating on Rebel for the bite, he commented to Elaine and me, "What saved this dog's life, most likely, was that he was bitten on this fatty area on his chest." I since have taken up the battle cry by reminding Elaine every so often that my treats saved Rebel's life.

At the 15-mile pit-stop Elaine caught me off guard by asking, "Were you doing what I think you were doing out there?"

Ever the innocent one, I replied, "What do you mean?"

"I was looking through the binoculars and thought I saw you piddling as you walked along." Damn, caught red-handed!

"You sure were walking funny," she continued. Well, actually, I was trying to avoid backfire!

Caught, I could do naught but confess: "I was kind of bored, so I thought I'd try that and see how I fared."

"Well?" She really didn't have to ask that.

"Just barely passable – and I mean that in both senses."

The first thing we did after driving the 14 miles into Conrad when we finished was to find Weco RV Repair and check on the water-heater control panel for the motorhome. Tilt, life's little adversities; the one they had was the wrong type.

If we could return tomorrow, they could red-tag another one this afternoon and have it by tomorrow afternoon. Deal, we said.

When we arrived at the Pondera RV Park, the office sign said, "Park and pay later." Later, when Henry the proprietor returned, he explained that he had been in Great Falls where he had gone for radiation for prostate cancer.

"One of 36 treatments," he said.

Seeing that he seemed a bit despondent, I tried to encourage him by telling him about my experience: "That was seven years ago, and here I am today able to run across Montana."

He said, "If the radiation does not work, I will have to go through chemotherapy, and if that does not work I will have to have an operation."

Henry did demonstrate that he still had a sense of humor. After I registered, he handed me a sheet of paper and said, "These are our camp regulations. Please read them."

They read: "Pondera Travelers' Park. Free water, fresh air and conversation, and special areas to watch the grass grow. Please stay on the gravel, or you will bury your vehicle in the mud.

"Good spot for UFO observation, no trees. For you first-time patrons, we offer two seasons – winter and August. In the summer time, we farm and make love. In the winter, we can't farm."

DAY 16. There are days when a person feels like going to work and days when he doesn't. And my day was starting as a "doesn't."

My biggest problem when I hit the road this morning was that Elaine did the laundry last night and, among other things, she washed my running clothes. Because I was clad in them, the sanitation and sterility were killing me!

I would have appreciated more excitement, more spectacular scenery (a fast-flowing river, a majestic mountain, a forest, wildflowers, etc.), or Sheba doing the dance of the seven veils, and hopefully she, unlike Salome, would not ask for my head.

I did not even see any wildlife, nor was the Highway Patrol visible. I did, though, at about five miles see some highway workers on the other side of the Interstate, and as I went past one saluted me. Thirty years out of the Marine Corps, the best I could do was to return a rusty salute. I guessed the worker was respecting my vintage more than my running form.

Elaine was parked for a pit-stop on a side road leading into Brady. On the way to the motorhome, I met Rocky and Teresa Perry, two senior citizens out for their morning constitutional.

"We talked with your wife down the road, and she said you'd be coming along, " Rocky said. "She told us what you are doing. That's really something to be running all the way across the state."

"Well, we're not going very fast, and we don't go very far each day," I said.

"We used to walk a lot faster," Rocky told me. "But recently my wife had a blood clot in her leg, so we've slowed down a bit. But still enjoy getting out."

"How do you like life here in Brady?" I asked.

"Pretty nice," said Rocky. "We like this little town. We don't have much here, but it's a quiet town.

"We know everybody in the town. Just like a big family here. We used to live in Denver, but it has turned into a madhouse. We've been here almost 45 years."

Leaving them, I said, "Thanks for putting some variety into my day."

Finished, we retreated to Conrad and headed for Wesco RV Repair. There Larry Walter, one of the owners, took only 15 minutes to install a new hot-water control panel. When he turned it on and the propane purred, Elaine and I considered the moment the highlight of our day.

Larry spent more time telling us about the Little League team he was coaching than he did installing the panel. The team was a collection of all-stars from three area towns, Conrad, Brady and Dutton.

Tomorrow they would be leaving for a tournament in Canada, and it seemed that an exodus of spectators from the area would follow them. Big-league stuff in Conrad.

Back at the Pondera RV Park we learned that it was named after the county. But none of the half-dozen natives we talked to could tell us where the name Pondera (which they pronounced "pon-der-ray") came from.

Henry, the RV park's 76-year-old-owner caught sight of me when he returned from a radiation trip to Great Falls and approached to ask, "You did say, didn't you, that you had 37 radiation treatments for prostate cancer?"

"Yeah, 37. Four years ago."

"Well, that gives me some hope. You seem to be doing pretty well."

"I'd guess that you're managing pretty well, since you're able to drive all the way to Great Falls and back for treatments," I said, hoping to raise his confidence.

"Yeah, I guess so. But I do have a lot of pain in my bones." That scared the hell out of me, because the first thought it triggered was metastasis, but I said nothing.

Henry probed, "Do you have any bone aches or pains?"

I told myself, Be careful here. If you say none, it might shatter him.

"Oh sure, I have aches and pains all the time. I'm not worried about it, though. I think it's just part of the aging process, sort of goes with the territory."

"If you don't mind my saying so, I'm glad to hear that," Henry told me. "I was getting worried."

"No reason to worry," I said. "Besides, it doesn't help a thing."

"Yeah, you're right," he said. Leaving, he added, "Hope you enjoy your stay."

One of our final chores of the day was to give Rebel a bedtime check. It was disturbing to look into the open drain hole in his chest and see his muscles.

But his appetite was good, his bowel movements were regular, and his behavior was normal. Not to worry. Right, Henry?

DAY 17. Invariably when I near the end of one of these runs – at this point only three days left in Montana – I begin to get a bit edgy that some disaster might strike me (hit by an illness, a car, a snake) that would keep me from finishing. Today I again felt that so close/so far syndrome.

Concerned about finishing, I also focus on injuries and become almost unduly cautious. Speaking of which, running has an unfair reputation here with all the talk of how it will damage knees and bones.

I've now been running distances for more than 30 years and have logged more than 108,000 miles since starting at age 47. If running is so destructive, why hasn't it damaged my knees and bones?

An unexpected twist today when I saw a sign, "Construction next 11 miles." What now? I saw Elaine parked nearby. Evidently she was as much in doubt as I.

Seeing a worker, I asked, "How far does the construction extend?"

"All the way to Shelby," he answered.

The question now was, Would Elaine be able to stop anywhere along the way for a pit-stop, or would I be on my own for 11 miles? We did not know.

Taking no chances, I geared up to go 11 miles on my own. I loaded my fanny pack with two water bottles, a Powerbar and a package of Life Savers. Famine would not embrace me!

Studying the situation, I saw I had two choices: to cross the road and run in the breakdown lane in the direction of traffic, or run in the construction area that consisted of the fast lane still open to one-way traffic and the slow lane and breakdown lane closed to traffic and reduced to gravel in preparation for paving. Easy choice. I'd run the gravel.

Trudging along through the gravel was awkward but safer than running with traffic. Early on, a bit of variety was injected when I had to run across the road to avoid getting drenched by a water truck.

When I went past Jim Hahn, a flagman on the construction project, he yelled, "I saw you miles back when driving to work." Then, not too diplomatically, he added, "Why are you so crazy as to do this?"

I didn't have half an hour to explain it to him; so I replied by saying, "Well, you know, it takes all types."

It was obvious by now as I worked my way through the construction area that I was on my own, that I would not see Elaine until Shelby where the construction ended.

I did not need an 11-mile separation to remind me of how vital her support was to my cause, but I had no choice in the matter. Onward to Shelby.

For good reason the Shelby exit sign was to me the most beautiful sight of the day. Down the ramp and onto a street, which turned out to be Highway 2, I caught sight of Elaine.

After a quick stop for gas and groceries and a decision to leave a tour of downtown Shelby until tomorrow, we headed for the Lewis and Clark RV Park a mile north of town. The manager told us that there is not another RV park between Shelby and the Canadian border, now only 35 miles away. /

During the evening, I made two interesting discoveries about Shelby. The first was that its elevation was 3286 feet, the lowest elevation we've been at any point of our runs across Wyoming and Montana. The other was learning that the world heavyweight boxing championship between Jack Dempsey and Tom Gibbons was held here on July 4th, 1923.

An octagon-shaped wooden arena with a seating capacity of 40,208 was constructed for the event. But the fight was a financial fiasco, because only 7000 spectators showed. And, oh yes, need you be told Dempsey won?

DAY 18. I felt washed out the first three miles today. But I knew I had to plug on, unlike Roberto Duran who screamed *"No mas, no mas!"* and surrendered to Ray Leonard in their classic bout.

I was pulling for Duran but now realize, after meeting Leonard, that was a mistake. Ray Leonard is a gentleman.

He is a member of the California Governor's Council on Physical Fitness and Sports. We met when he presented me an award from the Council.

As we shook hands, I was glad that he was using that right hand to shake and not to deliver me a right cross that would send me into dreamland. I've since observed him at several Council meetings, and I repeat: The guy is a class act.

The day being uneventful and the scenery mostly unvarying, I was occupied only with running and with some mental meandering. I realized almost instantly what made the going easy today, that being I knew exactly where I was and how far I had to go.

I flashed back to World War II when not knowing was a major problem. We never knew how long we would be where we were; we never knew when we would get home, if indeed we would be lucky enough to get home. Little did I realize, for example, when I shipped out of San Diego that I would not return home for 35 months.

We were less than 15 miles from the Canadian border when we finished, so we drove to the area for two reasons. First we wanted to see how close Elaine could drive to the border without crossing it. We didn't want the motorhome subjected to a border inspector who might want to confiscate fruits and such or who could give us problems because of the dogs.

Secondly we wanted to find an area where we could rendezvous after I crossed the border and returned to Montana. We agreed upon a rest stop half a mile south of the border.

We then did a driving tour of Sweet Grass, the hamlet adjacent to the border. Pardon these unkind words, but we decided that the best thing that could happen to this town would be to raze it and start all over again.

DAY 19. It's gonna be a long 15 miles today if I can't shake these stomach cramps, was my thought as I started. Even walking was painful.

During the 21-mile drive to the start, both Elaine and I had stomach cramps. We decided that the chicken we had for dinner last night could have caused the problem.

As I fought the cramps in the early miles, I kept thinking, Damn, instead of celebrating on the home stretch, I've got a fight on my hands.

But the tide began to turn at the three-mile pit-stop when, after I had coffee and a sweet roll, the cramps diminished by about 50 percent. By the time I had done five miles, I no longer had any cramps.

Reveling in my good luck, I saw a Montana Highway Patrol officer stop just in front of me. After he got out of his car and approached me, I impulsively blurted, "Oh no, you've kept us from a record. We thought we'd get across the entire state without a patrol officer checking on us."

"How far have you come?" he asked.

"We started at the Wyoming border in Yellowstone, and we've come about 367 miles," I told the officer.

"I just came from checking on your wife in the motorhome and she said you were running across the state," he said. "But I wasn't quite sure what she meant. I think she was a little worried that I might be stopping to give her a citation.

"By the way, she told me your name. Mine's Jeff Douglas. I'm a runner myself, so I thought I'd check with you."

"Do they have physical conditioning standards that the Patrol officers have to meet?" I asked.

"Well, to get through the academy you have to be in good shape. But after that, it is sort of up to the individual officer.

"To me it's kind of a personal thing. I've ridden a bike for years, and the last couple of years I've gotten into weight lifting. I've never felt better in my life."

When we parted, I told him, "Hang in there with your running, and when you get to be a fossil like me, you'll really begin to appreciate that you did."

At the next pit-stop, Elaine told me that Officer Douglas had returned to have a second visit with her. He was curious about what I ate, about what she did pit-crewing.

As I approached the border, I was glad for yesterday's reconnaissance. I knew exactly what would unfold. No Mickey Mouse in finding Elaine.

At the U.S. customs station I asked a couple of agents if I could take their picture, or could we arrange a picture of one of them with me?

"You'll have to get the approval of the acting supervisor to do that," I was told.

On the Canadian side, as I approached a customs officer, he pointed to the cassette recorder in my fanny pack and asked, "Is that thing on?" He would not talk with me until I assured him it was off.

Between this and U.S. customs I was getting the impression that I was in an espionage zone. Why was this guy so fearful of me recording something? I felt lucky to escape the customs area without being arrested.

After the long drive back to Helena, I was able to talk Elaine into celebrating our run by having dinner at the Overland Express. She had to admit the prime rib was the best she had in years.

The dogs, gulping their tidbits, had to agree – and for good reason, because they'd never had prime rib before. They glowed over this baptism!

Back at the Lincoln RV Park and settling in for the night, I found myself thinking about how different this night was from our last night here when we arrived after Rebel's surgery. He was in such pain, and we were uncertain whether or not he would survive.

That was then. Tonight we had a frisky Rebel on our hands. On his walks, he was sniffing for gopher holes and he dug frantically when he found one.

He was drooling and begging for food when we ate. He did some frolicking with Brudder. He was again around to assuming his position in the passenger seat whenever it was empty and even sometimes insisting on being a 90-pound lap dog when I was sitting there.

Overview of
NEBRASKA

July 24th to August 1st, 1995
167.7 miles

Day	Overnight	Miles	Notes
1	Chadron	18.2	started at Nebraska-South Dakota border
2	Chadron	18.4	a quick look at Chadron
3	Bridgeport	21.3	visiting with six Nebraskans
4	Alliance	22.2	record 59-mile drive to start
5	Bridgeport	21.5	home of Carhenge
6	Bridgeport	22.0	passed 100 miles
7	Sidney	21.1	learning about the wheat crop
8	Sidney	21.6	tour of Sidney and Cabela's
9	Kearney	8.4	finished at Nebraska-Colorado border

Chapter 9

Nebraska:

Who Says It's Flat?

DAY ONE. As we drove to Nebraska, I worried about whether or not I would be able to complete my planned run across the state. I had run across 19 states; Nebraska would be number 20. But there will come a day, I told myself, when I will start one of these states runs and not be able to finish it.

Let's face it, I'm 78 and I am growing increasingly concerned about the steady erosion of my vitality. I would much like to know if that erosion is due to aging or to some medical problem.

Several times during the drive I found myself thinking that 1300 miles was a long distance to travel just to reach the starting point. Good Lord, I thought, the drive might be harder than the run.

Usually selecting a route to run across a state is a difficult task. Not so with Nebraska. Highway 385 jumped out as an obvious choice for a number of reasons.

First, the panhandle is the shortest distance across Nebraska, between 165 and 170 miles, I estimated. Second, a reasonable number of RV parks for overnighting lined the route. Third, on this route I would not have the problem of running through any major city.

This thinking was reinforced by Gary Meyer, race director of the Omaha Marathon, who told me, "If I were going to run across Nebraska, I'd run Highway 385."

Our route on 385 would take us from the South Dakota/Nebraska border south through Chadron, Alliance, Bridgeport, Sidney, and to the Nebraska/Colorado border. I decided to start by doing 10 miles or so the first afternoon as a gentle warm-up after five days of being a passenger in the motorhome.

At the start, I found myself in open grasslands, rolling hills, and 90-degree weather and humidity that immediately impressed me. Looking southward, I saw mountains in the distance.

I had gone only a half-mile when a senior couple in a Bounder RV stopped and asked, "What are you doing, just out for a jog?"

"No," I replied, thinking of the T-shirt I was wearing with "Run Across Nebraska" on the front of it, "I'm just starting a run across Nebraska."

"Oh, okay," they said as they drove off. Kind of a strange reply, I thought.

Later a farmer in a pickup stopped to ask, "Are you just out for a jog?" That left me again thinking that my run "Run Across Nebraska" T-shirt is a poor investment.

The only other encounter I had during the day was at 10 miles when a van slowed to a stop alongside of me and I was thinking, Lots of concerned people out here today. Then I heard the driver say, "Can you tell me where I am at?"

After he told me where he wanted to go, I told him he should be heading north on 385 toward South Dakota rather than going south on 385. When I pointed out his error on the map, his wife said, "I told you so."

Somehow, before planning this run, I – like many folks – had the impression that Nebraska is flat. Ha! There was not 10 yards of flat in the distance I ran today. From the map studies I did, I knew that during the entire run from north to south in the state no part of the route would be below 3300 feet in elevation.

I would have liked to have run farther than 11.2 miles today but backed off for several reasons. Primarily I wanted to ease into running after five days of being entrenched in the motorhome. Then there were a couple of practicalities: We wanted a little R&R time in Chadron, and we did not want to be too late with dinner.

As we finished seven miles north of Chadron, I felt good now that we had finally gotten the show on the road. I had been so engrossed with the scenery and running that I failed to notice the gathering of dark clouds that surrounded us at the finish. Those clouds and the lightning to the south forecast the storm that descended on us after we settled in at the S&L RV Park in Chadron.

DAY TWO. Last night Elaine insisted that I provide her with a menu of what I want at the various pit-stops. She said we would have breakfast at the three-mile pit-stop, but she needed a menu for the others.

Since we would usually have a 10- to 20- mile drive to the start, and since I'd need some energy to run the three miles to breakfast, I decided that while setting dressed each morning I'd have coffee, half a banana, and half a Powerbar – an arrangement favored by Rebel and Brudder, since the other half of the banana and Power Bar went in their direction. Then, without much reflection and to keep peace in the family, I gave this pit-stop menu to Elaine:

• Three miles – breakfast, as she had ordained.

• Six miles – coffee, sweet roll.

• Nine miles – iced tea, fruit, cookies.

• Twelve miles – iced tea, pasta or beans or potatoes.

• Fifteen miles – Pepsi, one-half sandwich, candy.

• Eighteen miles – Pepsi, other half of sandwich, and roll of Life Savers to eat on the road.

At one talk Elaine and I gave about our runs, a lady asked, "How long after eating do you wait before you start running again?" From the way her question was framed, I detected she was under the impression that I lingered after eating.

I answered, "Usually I head out the door as soon as I am finished. At most I hang around about five minutes." I did not know whether to read the look she save me as disapproval or astonishment.

Early in the day I was reminded that I was treading on history when I saw a historical marker about the Fort Pierre-Fort Laramie Trail which told me:

"From about 1837 until 1850, more than a quarter-million buffalo robes bought from Indians and 275 tons of fur company trade goods were hauled over the 300-mile long Fort Pierre-Fort Laramie Trail that followed the White River through this area. During the 1840s this trail was the shortest overland connection between trading posts on the Platte and steamboats plying the Missouri."

At seven miles into our day a sign told me I was in the city limits of Chadron and the population was 5598. Not very big considering that in its first four months back in 1885 the town's population was 2500.

We had toured the town yesterday after finishing our run. The most memorable building we saw was the Blaine Hotel, built in 1892.

It was the starting point for a horse race in 1893. Known as both "The Great 1000-Mile Horse Race" and "The Cowboy Endurance Race," it finished in Chicago and was not won by a cowboy but by railroad right-of-way agent, John Berry, age 40, in 13 days, 16 hours, 30 minutes.

I figured this to be an average of 60 miles a day – not bad, considering that each of the nine contestants was allowed only two horses. Victory was not altogether sweet for Berry, though, because according to reports the sheriff who held the $1000 purse lost it (a likely story).

We were told that on July 4, 1900, Teddy Roosevelt, who had come to the West primarily for his health, stood at the corner of Second and Main and delivered a speech. Roosevelt, who at one time in his career was police commissioner of New York City, might have been more useful in the early days of Chadron when it was flooded with saloons, gun fights and wild characters!

We also learned that there had been some confusion about the naming of Chadron. It's now conceded that it was named after Louis Chartran, a trader and trapper. But until as late as the 1970s, it was believed the town was named after Pierre Chadron, a French trapper.

Chadron hardly looks like a college town, but don't be deceived.

Chadron State College, dating back to 1910, is located in the southern part of the city.

I must have put my heart into my work today and gotten quite disheveled as a result of the dirt on the road and my sweating, because when I came in for the last pit-stop, Elaine remarked, "You look like a mess."

"What do you mean?" I replied. "I look like a hearty warrior."

"Oh no you don't," she said. "You look like one of the homeless."

I dismissed her remark as just another instance of her building my self-esteem!

DAY THREE. As I hit the road, I was attracted by the eerie sound of a motorcycle with its radio blasting as it roared along the highway in the quiet of the morning. Cycle and noise were completely out of place among these pine trees and mountains.

The featured attraction today was that six different people stopped to talk with me. The first of these was a farmer who drove out from a side road, saw me and asked, "Out for a jog?"

"A little more than that. I'm running across your state."

"Well, feature that. Good luck." And with that, he drove off in his Chrysler New Yorker.

Judging from his body language, he did not want to stick around for a conversation with a crazy old road runner. His bib overalls seemed out of place with the New Yorker and his "feature that" sounded more Hollywood than Nebraska.

My next conversation was with Sgt. Charles Buckingham of the Nebraska Highway Patrol. He had stopped to help a motorist with a stalled car.

"I recognize you," the sergeant said, "from talking with your wife yesterday."

"Yes, my wife told me an officer checked on her yesterday. She also said that from what she has seen the Nebraska Highway Patrol officers are as handsome as the Montana officers."

I detected that he was blushing ever so slightly, then he cautioned, "Don't get heat stroke," and added, "You're sensational for an old man."

I had gone only a couple of miles from the sergeant when a middle-aged man in a battered pickup pulled up alongside of me. He was wearing a cowboy straw hat that had a personality of its own, Levi's reflecting heavy usage and a shirt that appeared to be a fugitive from a laundry.

"Need any help?" asked Eric Nixon.

"No thanks, I'm in good shape. I have a pit crew up ahead."

He eyed me intently for a moment, then asked, "Is that shirt right? Are you really running across Nebraska."

"I am if all goes well."

His reaction: "Well, I'll be."

Next there was the fellow who said his name was Ray Edgecoe. He had stopped to ask if I needed help. I noticed he was an elderly gentleman, a bit on the paunchy side.

"Well, good luck," he added as he drove away in his Olds 98 but not before giving me a look up and down that said, "Ain't seen nothing like this before."

I had gone less than a half-mile when a man in a new Chevrolet stopped to tell me, "Do you know it's 100 degrees out here? Do you need help?"

"No, I'm okay," I told him.

Another mile or so down the road another farmer, Edgar Rector, stopped to confirm that I was alive and had blood flowing in my veins.

"Do you know how hot it is out here?" were his words. I assured him that I was okay and let him know that I'd come from California to run across the state.

"You know, I was born an raised in Nebraska but migrated to California as a young man," he said. "I lived in San Bernardino for many years, then I got fed up with the way things were going and came back here."

Laboring at running hills in the early part of today, I was reminded of how poorly prepared I am for this run. During the previous three months I had averaged a shade under five miles a day and had run no farther than 10 miles – and that only once.

And now I am shooting for a daily average of 21 miles. That certainly is not the textbook approach, but it should be character-building if nothing else.

After we finished our running day, things got complicated. We drove to Hemingford, about 20 miles, thinking we could get propane and camp there overnight.

We won with the propane, lost with the camping. The nearest RV park was in Bridgeport, meaning we would have 59 miles to drive to the start of tomorrow's run. As immortalized in so many sports happenings, "Them's the breaks."

DAY FOUR. When I hit the road at seven A.M., I found myself reflecting on how lucky we had been when Elaine was hurriedly driving through the bumpy brick streets of Alliance. Our TV bounced from the rack over the driver/passenger cab to the floor of the RV, a good five feet. Brudder was lying close to the drop zone and barely missed getting zonked.

As Elaine continued to drive, I said, "That's probably the death of the TV." Later, when we stopped in Alliance and I was making the RV reservation, Elaine tested the TV and it worked perfectly. We were both surprised and elated, and resolved that henceforth that the TV would be secured to the rack.

On the long drive this morning I told Elaine about how close the grain trucks came to me yesterday.

She said, "If you ever get hit and killed, I'm taking the body back to Auburn."

Now that's a morale booster, I thought. Going along with the gag, I asked, "How are you going to keep it?" You know, I told myself, I get the impression she has been thinking about this.

This exchange led me to some morbid thinking when I started running this morning, and as a result of it when I came in for an early pit-stop I told Elaine, "I've been thinking about it and I've found a better solution for getting my body back to Auburn if I am killed. Clean out the refrigerator and put me in it.

"I guarantee that would be more sanitary and less smelly than stashing me in the bed. You can buy an ice chest to hold your perishable foods."

Silently I complimented myself on this supreme contingency planning. This weird proposal was the opener for some subsequent in-house jokes Elaine and I tossed around about the refrigerator.

We extended our distance from 21 to 22.2 miles today to finish at a place called Carhenge, 2.5 miles north of Alliance. Actually Carhenge is an unusual exhibit put together, around the mid-1980s by a man named John Reinders.

What Reinders did was to take some old automobiles and arrange them in a configuration to resemble Stonehenge in England. After assembling all the cars, he painted them a dull gray.

Over the years his exhibit has attracted many tourists. The city of Alliance, with tourist dollars in its eyes, now calls itself "Alliance, the home of Carhenge." Besides bringing in the tourist dollars, Carhenge has made some people aware of a historic monument in England.

The day was unusual in that no one stopped to talk with me or to inquire what I was doing, and unusual in that we drove so far to get started. It was a day of flat, easy running and devoid of any eye-catching scenery. After yesterday's experience we were most appreciative of having to drive only five miles to overnight at the Sunset Motel and RV in Alliance.

DAY FIVE. Early today I went past a neatly kept cemetery. As I did so, it occurred to me that people in their sunset years become increasingly aware of cemeteries, poignant reminders that they are of things to come.

For most young people thoughts of death are a rarity; for older folks they are a commonality. Young, you are vibrant and healthy almost every day, and if you do get sick your resiliency is such that you bounce back soon. Old, you always seem to have some nagging ailment, and if you do get sick, you sometimes have considerable anxiety about whether you will weather the storm.

As an analogy, say you are a young person and sick, and wellness comes when you can find a tree to climb. It turns out that there are many trees around with branches easy to climb.

Whereas when you are an old person and sick, and wellness comes when you can find a tree to climb. It turns out that the trees are fewer and farther apart. As you age, the branches are fewer; next the trees are like telephone poles, and finally the poles are greased and you slide out of life.

What intrigues me, what scares the hell out of me as I grow older, is that one day I can feel healthy, run well and feel like I could go on forever, then the very next day I am felled with some illness and seem to be fighting every bit as much to survive as to get well. A giant today, a pygmy tomorrow.

Much as we think about death as we grow older, it's surprising how little we talk about it. But Elaine and I have talked about it recently, probably because even dying has become complicated with all the legal, medical, religious and financial considerations.

We both agree that we don't want to be plugged into any contraptions simply to lengthen our lives. We both agree that we can't afford the fantastic payments to ensure being institutionalized in some long-term care facility – whereas, almost conversely, if for religious or ethical reasons, neither of us is suicidal.

Because of these financial considerations, we both hope that death, when it comes, will be quick and kind. Whole damn thing is frightening if you dwell on it – and, for sure, inevitable, one way or the other.

Along with this affinity with death as you grow older comes the wisdom to distinguish between what is important in your life and what is not. Among other things you come to full realization that the most precious of God's gifts is love – to love, to be loved.

And, saying that, I sort of smile at some irony there, for I do have some male friends of whom I think dearly but cannot bring myself to say to one of them, "I love you." Yet because of their sterling qualities and enduring friendship, I do.

This thinking was disconnected when I entered Alliance from the north and began to focus on the town. All I saw at first was a farm implement sales lot, a couple of chiropractor clinics and a Kentucky Fried Chicken.

One sign downtown read, "Alliance, home of Carhenge," which seemed to be a bit of stretching for recognition. The only place in town that sold Carhenge postcards was McDonald's.

When I stopped there – adorned in running gear – my presence raised no eyebrows. As I stood in line, I was sort of surprised that my "Run Across Nebraska" T-shirt generated no questions.

With a population of almost 10,000 Alliance was metropolitan compared to most of the towns on our route. It seemed a bit strange to me that the town allied itself more with Carhenge than with the Knight Museum located downtown. The museum contains tools and equipment used by pioneers and exhibits that reflect their lifestyles.

About the time I finished today's run, it dawned on me that from the time I had left Alliance I had been accompanied by a horde of grasshoppers. No problem there. Not so with some flies that stuns with the ferocity of bees.

It also dawned on me that in five days on the road I have noticed remarkably little litter. Beer cans and soft-drink cans constitute the bulk of the scant refuse that does exist. Unlike most other states, there are no soiled Pampers.

When I came into the motorhome at the finish and Elaine handed me a root beer float, as she had done the previous four days, I said, "Well. I guess

I've got you pretty well trained by now."

Reading the look she gave me, I saw she was totally unappreciative of my jocularity and I thought, Oh no, don't tell me I've shot down the root beer program!

DAY SIX. At the breakfast pit-stop Elaine told me that the weather prediction for today was 105 degrees. At the moment it was only 70, and a slight breeze helped to offset the heat.

(It turned out that the forecaster erred by five degrees, but 100 was hot enough. However, contrary to the young runners whose blood percolates better than mine, I prefer 100 degrees to 35 degrees.)

"Angora, Unincorporated," the sign read. Another town that fast vehicles and better highways eliminated.

At one time, as still-standing evidence showed, there was a gas station, a restaurant and a small grocery store. Now only the post office, only about the size of a one car garage, survives as the hub of activity.

Leaving Angora, I found myself thinking about lifestyles and how we all seem to get our kicks in different ways. A lot of people would find it difficult to understand how Elaine and I enjoy puttering along the highway, 21 or so miles a day, while experiencing the country.

By contrast many of these same people would think the couple who parked beside us in the RV park last night were really living. Within five minutes after they hooked up their fifth-wheel, the woman brought out a card table and folding chair and set them up.

Then she returned to the fifth-wheel and came out with a big pitcher of martinis, which she placed on the table along with a package of Marlboros. She and her husband then spent the next hour chain-smoking and emptying the pitcher of martinis. Different folks, different strokes.

I spent some time today dwelling on my running. I get much exhilaration from just being on the road. But offsetting this is the discouraging fact that I am getting slow because my asthma will not permit a sustained run.

Every so often breathing problems force me to walk. My estimate is that these days I run 70 percent of the distance and walk the rest. Before beginning Nebraska, I had hoped for more running but realized I had to settle for what I could get.

Five years prior, averaging a marathon a day for 122 consecutive days while running across the USA, I had run 85 percent of the distance. Best as I can tell, the drop from 85 to 70 percent is due to asthma, which worsens with age.

On the one hand, the drop is discouraging. On the other hand, I realize I am extremely lucky just to be out here and moving at age 78. When I dwell on this, uppermost in my mind is: How long will I be able to continue doing these runs?

My Good Samaritan act today consisted of rescuing a grasshopper. Yes, grasshopper!

I saw that he had gotten into a glass container and could not figure or manipulate how to get out. I turned the container upside down and he escaped.

Realizing how hot it must have been inside that container, I concluded that grasshoppers must have remarkable heat endurance. Not very polite, though, because the little sucker hopped away without thanking me.

While atop a hill I stopped to look down into the verdant, fertile valley that housed the town of Bridgeport and which contrasted dramatically with the barren sandhills. The outline of the town was very distinct even though it had a population of only 1500 or thereabouts. Looking to the south beyond Bridgeport, I saw that my route would take me over a series of hills.

To the southwest, out in the flatlands, I saw a very distinctive rock formation. Later I learned I was looking at Courthouse Rock and Jailhouse Rock, important navigational landmarks for pioneers.

When I crossed the historic North Platte River on the northern edge of Bridgeport, I stopped to take a picture, photo journalist that I am. The river is historic in that some pioneer trails followed it. My impression of the river was that it was definitely fast flowing, definitely muddy and probably only about knee deep.

As I was about to exit Bridgeport, I discovered that, stupidly, I had not filled my water bottle at the 18-mile pit-stop. With the temperature hovering around 100 degrees, I knew that replenishment was in order. Luckily I was able to buy a Coke at a gas station on the south edge of town, and while drinking it I read the inscription on the Jailhouse Rock across the street:

"Old Oregon Trail, 1750 yards south, 1830-1869. Old Pony Express route, six miles south, 1860-61. First transcontinental railroad, 1861-70, six miles south. Old Deadwood Trail, four miles west, 1874-86. Old Mormon Road, one mile north, 1847-69. The Burlington Railroad, pioneer of the North Platte Valley, constructed its first line in 1899."

I was left with the impression that I was standing at a crossroads of American history. After we finished and returned to Bridgeport, we stopped to visit the Pioneer Trails Museum. There the young curator informed me that he was running a half-marathon tomorrow in Cheyenne.

DAY SEVEN. For some mysterious reason I awakened at 4:30 A.M., clogged with asthma and fighting for breath. I used an inhalant and within a few minutes it had the asthma under reasonable control.

Once I was no longer gasping, I looked out the motorhome window to check on weather conditions and saw a sky laced with dark clouds emitting the distinct impression that a storm was imminent. I had almost gotten back to sleep when the dogs started barking. Looking out the window I saw that the source of their concern was a farmer in an adjacent field gathering bales of hay as he drove his tractor with lights on in the morning darkness – one way to beat the heat.

As I trudged along this morning, I recalled a couple of things I had read in Nebraska newspapers last night. One article informed me that the University of Nebraska football stadium, which seats 100,000 spectators, has been sold out the past 33 years. Dollar signs somersaulted in front of my eyeballs.

The other article furthered my education on wheat farming. The article told how a bumper yield and the highest price in 14 years have combined to produce a record wheat crop.

The article went on to explain that farmers have a lot of expenses to pay in producing a crop. Harvest expenses include the "13-13-13" system of paying custom cutters to cut and haul the wheat.

Custom cutters generally receive 13 cents an acre for cutting, 13 cents a bushel for hauling and another 13 cents a bushel for hauling wheat from a field that produces more than 20 bushels an acre. The current selling price of wheat, $84.50 a bushel was the highest in 14 years.

Going along, I had a moment's flashback to the conversation yesterday with the young curator of the Pioneer Trails Museum in Bridgeport, the fellow who told me he was going to run the Cheyenne Half-Marathon.

At one point in our conversation, he asked, "How old are you anyway?"

I responded with, "You guess, and I'll tell."

"I'm not very good at this, but I'd guess about 75."

I thought, Fella, you're too damn good, but you should have been diplomatic and said about 65. Instead I said, "Pretty close – 78."

I was left thinking that I must be looking wizened these days since people are guessing so close to my actual age. Oh well, enter rationalization: Better to be looking wizened and out here on the road at 78 than to be 68, looking young but rooted to a rocking chair.

At times today I found myself thinking too much about mileage rather than milking the adventure. But, in truth, out here in the grassland, sage brush, sandhills and sprinkles of grazing cattle, it was hard to focus on the scenery. I try not to focus on the 100-degree weather because that only makes it hotter.

Harry Coffee from Bridgeport stopped to ask if I needed help. Dressed in white shirt, tie and slacks, he had actually gotten out of his Cadillac to check on me.

"My wife and I are just returning from church, and we wanted to make sure you're all right," he said. I went into my song and dance about what I was doing on the road.

"Well, you've certainly picked some warm weather for it," he replied. In the course of our conversation he told me that he farmed 750 acres nearby.

"That seems like quite a few to me," I told him.

"Not really," he said. "Where you are right now, all this is owned by one outfit that has 12,000 acres."

I reckoned that if a guy with 750 acres was driving a Cadillac, the 12,000-acre guys must travel in stretch limos.

Our last pit-stop today was in the hamlet of Dalton, population varying between 282 and 340, depending on which sign or atlas you read. In town I counted at least 30 homes, saw a good-sized church and the Prairie Schooner Museum.

We had hoped to stay in a peewee RV park there. But it was filled with harvesters, which translated to our having to overnight in Sidney, 21 miles to the south.

DAY EIGHT. The sky, which had been pouting most of yesterday with dark clouds threatening a storm, erupted with considerable force and noise just after we had settled in at the RV park in Sidney. The dramatic weather change brought rain, thunder and lightning.

The rain was so torrential that we became worried that the RV park might get flooded. After monitoring the situation for a while, we decided that the drainage system would handle the water and, at worst, we'd just have to contend with some puddles and some mud.

Confined to the motorhome because of the rain, we passed the time reading and watching television. I did some catching up on Nebraska lore.

I learned that the first wagon train bound for Oregon passed through in 1841, nothing startling there. What I did find startling was that 350,000 individuals crossed Nebraska in covered wagons between then and 1866.

When we left the RV park this morning, we noticed that none of the harvesters, who are usually gone before us, had stirred. The rain would keep them idle all day and force them to retune their schedules.

My first contact was shortly after I had started and a lady in a Ford Fiesta braked to ask, "Need any help? You look kind of wet out there?"

"No, no, I'm running across your state."

"You're what?"

Whereupon I told her my long story and in turn learned she was a nurse on a way to work in a nearby hospital. We pass but once in this life.

The second and only other contact came around 12 miles as I approached the motorhome for a pit-stop. A guy in a truck stopped. Ah, a Good Samaritan, I thought.

Then I heard him say, "Do you need any equipment?" Only then did I notice he was driving a tow truck. To him I was a potential sale, not a drenched and stranded runner possibly in need of help.

"No," I replied, "we're in good shape." And he sped away.

Around 7.5 miles I crossed the road, despite the foul weather, to read a historical marker. I had expected something out of the Old West. Instead I read about the Marathon Oil Company discovering oil here in 1949 after going down 4400 feet, which was something to cheer about because this was the first oil well in western Nebraska after 60 years of unsuccessful drilling.

Near the end of my running day I fell to thinking about a 166-mile race Dr. Ralph Paffenbarger and I ran alongside each other in 1987. I was 70; Paff, 65. We raced 41.5 miles a day for four days at elevations 5000 feet or above.

Now, by contrast, here I am eight years later, running 167 miles across Nebraska in seven full days and two half-days, 21 miles a day average, and I'm just as tired as when doing the 166-mile run. So I found myself with questions:

Is this slowdown due to aging? Is the tiredness due to some disease or ailment? Is the prostate cancer, or some fallout from it, getting to me? Let's face it, we're talking about a difference here of 20 miles a day.

There's a trace of irony here, because when an M.D. examines me these days and compares me with the average 78-year-old, he considers me a superman – whereas contrasted with my condition just eight years ago, I'm a panty-waist. End of today's medical report.

After finishing, we returned to the Cabela's factory outlet at the junction of I-80 and Highway 385. The place was impressive by nature of its size, architecture and landscaping.

Because we wanted to light out for Iowa immediately after finishing tomorrow, we toured Sidney after Cabela's. From my reading yesterday I knew that the town had grown up around Fort Sidney and that its growth mushroomed with the building of the railroad.

In fact, the town was named after Sidney Dillon, a railroad solicitor. The railroad made it a jumping-off place for gold seekers in the 1876 strike in the Black Hills.

In its formative days, Sidney was a wild town, abounding in saloons and shooting. Such colorful characters as Wyatt Earp, Doc Holiday and Bat Masterson stayed in Sidney.

We capped our Sidney tour by stocking up on groceries and gas. Then, overwhelmed with all this excitement, we took refuge in the Conestoga RV Park, luckily settling in just before the arrival of an ill-tempered storm.

DAY NINE. The first thought on my mind on awakening this morning was: With a scant 8.5 miles to go we should make it across Nebraska. Ah, the sweet taste of success!

What was it Henry James had said about success? "The only success worth one's powder was success in the line of one's idiosyncrasy." Well, I qualified on that one. Just how many 78-year-old men are running up and down state highways in T-shirts and nylon shorts?

The first thing I noticed on hitting the road was that I was uncomfortably cold, temperature in the 40s with a wind-chill factor making it much colder. I was wearing a nylon windsuit over my shorts and T-shirt, insufficient protection for my weary old bones, I soon found out. I should have known better.

The second thing I noticed was the heavy traffic, much of it from Colorado as indicated by license plates. Every two or three minutes I found myself in the weeds, waiting for cars to pass. I could not help but think how unhappy it would be if, in the process of invading the weeds, I were to meet up with a cantankerous rattlesnake.

I also thought that the Colorado drivers seemed unchanged from the time I ran across that state in 1990. They were – and still are – aggressive and unwilling to yield an inch of roadway to me. A notable exception was a pickup driver, name of Ray Jackson, who stopped to offer me a ride.

At six miles, when I made my last pit-stop in this state, I took time out to calculate (higher mathematics here!) that this was our 51st pit-stop in Nebraska. Bush-league stuff – as I recall, Elaine made around 1060 on our USA run.

It was only a small green marker, four inches by four inches, something most motorists would fail to see But I saw it, and the white lettering with "1" on it, which meant that I had but one mile left to reach the border. To preserve the fond memory, I stopped to take a picture of the sign.

When I saw Elaine parked a half-mile ahead at the border, I thought I should have been coming up roses. But instead I was smelling skunk, one close by.

The border itself was indistinct, marked only by cultivated fields. One farmer had two-thirds of one field in Colorado and the other third in Nebraska.

After finishing, we wasted no time in heading for Iowa and our next run. As Elaine drove the 222 miles to Kearney, where we overnighted, I had much time for reflection.

I thought about the luxury of being able to do what Elaine and I are doing with these states. A luxury in that we can afford the time to do it; a luxury in that we can afford the money to do it, albeit our expenses are not inordinate since they include only RV parks and gas, our food costs being about the same as if we were home; a luxury in that I am healthy enough to do it, and she is healthy enough to handle the motorhome; a luxury in that we get to experience different parts of the country together while traveling quite comfortably in the motorhome.

While we are experiencing, we are learning, and it's the sort of learning that makes us feel like we are achieving something, and at the same time contributes to our health and happiness. Maybe we feel so good because we are participants and not spectators as with some of our other vacations, good as they are.

I also reflected on how relatively easy the Nebraska run was, an observation tempered with the knowledge that often things are easier in retrospect. The key to it seeming easy, I suspected, was that we were reasonable and realistic in limiting our goal to 21 miles a day.

Another key was that Elaine and I worked well together. We each had a job to do.

By now, 20 states behind us, we knew most of the tricks of the trade. Most important of all we enjoy what we are doing.

Overview of
IOWA

August 3rd to 14th, 1995
240.1 miles

Day	Overnight	Miles	Notes
1	Ringgold Co. Park	15.0	started at Iowa-Missouri border
2	Green Valley State Park	21.0	dismal news: poisonous snakes in Iowa
3	Pammel State Park	20.0	visit to John Wayne's home in Winterset
4	Pammel State Park	21.0	Bridges of Madison County revisited
5	near Dexter	20.7	Adel, a cut above Winterset
6	Spring Lake State Pk.	21.0	passed 100 miles
7	near Fort Dodge	21.0	reluctant to leave Spring Lake State Park
8	near Fort Dodge	21.3	a look at Dodge City
9	near Fort Dodge	21.5	detour on Road 56
10	Ambrose Call State Pk.	21.2	passed 200 miles
11	Ambrose Call State Pk.	21.2	meeting Wesley Schultz in Algona
12	Jackson, MN	16.3	finished at Iowa-Minnesota border

Chapter 10

Iowa:

Treading in the Footsteps
of John Wayne

DAY ONE. I'd never spent any time in Iowa, except to pass through the state on a couple of transcon drives. So I reasoned this run should be adventurous since everything I would see would be new.

I knew little of Iowa's history, though I could still recall some facts from reading about it. I had been surprised to learn that some major glaciers had passed through the state, the last being 12,000 years ago.

I also found it interesting that Iowa is located between the Missouri and Mississippi Rivers. The name Iowa was easy to understand after learning that the Indian inhabitants of the area were the Ioway.

The fondest memory I had of Iowa (and Elaine won't appreciate this!) stemmed from my college days at University of California, Berkeley, when I dated an attractive and charming brunette, also a UCB student, from Des Moines. More than 55 years ago, that was, and I still remember her name: Kathy Else.

I must admit to some recent exposure to Iowa through reading the novel, *The Bridges of Madison County*, a bestseller that offers hope for any aspiring writer since it was rejected by 15 publishers. It's appealing that our Iowa route will take us directly through Madison County.

This route starts on Highway 169 at the Iowa/Missouri border and goes north to finish in Elmore, Minnesota. I did not select this route because of *Bridges* but rather because it was suggested by Tim Lane as the route best for us in Iowa. Tim is the Chairman of the Iowa Governor's Council on Physical Fitness and Sports.

Elaine and I had decided to limit the running day to 15 miles so that I could ease back into running. Thus facing an easy day, I was relaxed, despite starting in a slight drizzle.

As the day wore on, I discovered that my main adversary was the humidity, so thick you could shovel it with a pitchfork. I was more uncomfortable than during any one of the 100-plus-degree days in Nebraska.

What impressed me most this day was the neatness of the Iowa farms and residences, all freshly painted, invariably white, and all with well-manicured lawns. Each looked like a painting.

The first Iowan with whom I spoke was Jean Holly, a lady painting the white picket fence of her farm house. And, of course, snake coward that I am, the first question I asked was, "Are there any rattlesnakes in this area?"

"I think there might be some, but not that many," she said. "You don't have to worry about them."

Spoken like a pioneer, lady, but just one is too many for me. It takes but one.

When her neighbor from across the street came over to deposit some outgoing mail, I wished both ladies a good day and continued northward. I surely left them with something to talk about. Like, "Isn't he a little old to be running across the state? I wonder why he's doing it; is somebody paying him?"

I was completely unprepared for what I saw when I heard a clickedy-clack on the gravel behind me and turned around and saw an Amish man and his horse pulling a small buggy. As they passed me, I called, "Good morning. Sir."

He waved to me but said not a word. And my thought was, Friend, why speakest thou not to me?

As I was nearing 14 miles, Duane Schaffer and Lee Brand stopped to ask, "Are you in trouble?" Leading me to think, Do I look like a guy in trouble?

"No trouble. I'm just starting off on a run across Iowa on Highway 169."

They looked at each other, both with the same expression as if to say, "He's kidding, isn't he?"

Duane asked, "You mean all the way to the Minnesota border?"

"Yeah," I replied, nodding affirmatively.

Pointedly but not politely, Lee said, "Sure you can make it?"

"No problem as long as I don't get sick or injured."

We finished our day two miles south of Mt. Ayr and headed through town toward Highway 2 for the RV park Duane and Lee told us about. As we passed the Clinton Motel in Mt. Ayr, one of us made an obscene gesture, even though I told her not to do that!

DAY TWO. Last night when Rick Hawkins, a county employee, collected our camping fee, he got my full attention by reporting, "Iowa has 27 different species of snakes. Of those only four are poisonous: timber rattlesnake, massasauga, copperhead and prairie rattlesnake. The last three are on the state's endangered species list."

Question: Why in hell is a poisonous snake on an endangered species list? Haven't these guys ever heard of St. Patrick?

Still spooked today when thinking back on last night when Elaine picked three ticks off me. A bit frightening, Lyme disease being what it is. But Elaine says not to worry, because the ticks that transmit Lyme disease are so small they can hardly be seen by the human eye.

About halfway through my day, a young man, Robert Young by name, stopped to ask if I needed help.

"I'm doing okay, thanks," I told him.

He asked me what I was doing on the road, and I filled him in on our safari. He asked the usual questions.

"Your sidekick is too gabby," I kidded while referring to his two-year-old son silent all the time. What's that poetic phrase, "Silent on a peak in Darien"?

We chatted for a few minutes. Then, after saying, "Nice talking with you," Robert drove off.

By my estimate, he was around 27 years old and maybe a school teacher – certainly not a farmer.

As I neared the end of my day, I concluded that after a day on the road in this sultry weather, sweaty as I am, the pigs and I could have a smell-down, and it would be entirely possible that I would win.

As further proof of that, a horde of flies hovered around me as I finished. Their message: Get to the Lifebuoy, old man.

Our running day finished four miles south of Afton. Unfortunately the town had no RV parks.

But Green Valley State Park was only 10 miles away. This was our introduction to the Iowa State Park system, and a pleasant introduction it was.

We had a lakeside site under trees for only $12, along with a 30-amp electrical hookup that allowed us the creature comfort of running the air conditioner. Eat your hearts out, 0 Pioneers!

DAY THREE. I had anticipated, and correctly, that the highlight of this day would be visiting Winterset and the Madison County Courthouse. From reading *The Bridges of Madison County*, I had a vicarious acquaintance with both. Curious to see both firsthand, we headed directly for Winterset when we finished our day 13 miles south of the town.

The courthouse, the centerpiece of the town, is a landmark that can be seen from miles away. Built back in 1876, it is constructed of native limestone quarried in Madison County.

Impressive and majestic, the courthouse sits in the center of the town square. Contrastingly the stores on each of the four blocks that surround it border on being tacky.

The dominant theme, as I walked around and visited the Chamber of Commerce, was commercialization of the bridges. Buy a T-shirt, a sweat shirt, a book, a ball cap, or any of a dozen other trinkets.

The Madison County Courthouse records reflect that Marion Robert

Morrison was born in Winterset on May 26th, 1907. If you have to ask, "Who's he?" the answer is John Wayne.

The single-story, small frame home where he lived sits about a half-mile away from the courthouse. The home, loaded with mementos from Wayne's movies, is now a popular tourist attraction. Tours under the supervision of a guide (understandably they don't want any of those treasures to disappear) are conducted every half-hour.

The annex where the tours originate has every conceivable John Wayne souvenir (films, books, clothing, posters, pictures, T-shirts, sweat shirts, etc.) for sale. Here too commercialism is rampant. The Duke deserves better.

Much of the terrain today was rolling hills, grasslands, and an abundance of trees. At one point looking ahead, I thought, Can this be Iowa? That hill looks like a ski jump!

I had the annoyance of traffic being bumper to bumper for a while this morning. I kept wondering why so many cars until a motorist told me, "All these cars are on their way to the National Balloon Contest in Indianola." Later, checking a map, I saw that Indianola, Iowa, was about 12 miles away.

At the nine-mile pit-stop when I came into the motorhome, I found Elaine upset. "What's the matter?" I asked.

She pointed to the adjacent farm house and said, "The farmer in there is beating his dog. I've heard the dog cry several times, and I've seen him hitting it."

I knew it was upsetting to her. All I could think to say was, "I wish we could do something about it, but we can't."

Out in the middle of nowhere today I saw Beulah Cemetery and the question arose, What's it doing out here? A nearby sign told me that the historic Mormon Mount Pisgah cemetery was two miles west.

On the Mormon trek east Mount Pisgah (which the Mormons named after the biblical Pisgah, the mount from which Moses had viewed the promised land) was a major way station of the trail. Mormons occupied the Mount Pisgah area, as many as 2000 being there at one time, from 1846 to 1852. When they all moved westward, all that was left behind were the thousands buried in cemeteries there.

We cut our day to 20 miles to allow more time to play tourist in Winterset. We had hoped to overnight in the local RV park, but it was filled.

Luckily for us recovery was easy because Pammel State Park was only five miles to the south. Elaine and I felt lucky that the park was nearby. We felt even luckier in being able to find it, because once we left the highway navigation was a problem since along the three-mile gravel road leading to the park there were several turns, only one of which was marked with a sign.

DAY FOUR. It was no mystery to Elaine and me why there was only one other camper in Pammel State Park last night. Any other aspiring campers, hopelessly lost on the dirt road with its maze of unmarked turns, probably listened to Dante: "Abandon all hope ye who enter here."

For a while this morning as Elaine and I tried to find our way back out to the highway, it appeared that we might take up homesteading in the area since we twice made wrong turns. Eventually, though, after stopping at each turn and conferring, we worked our way back to the highway. Once again, the perils of passage.

I was about five miles into my day when the home of James and Mary Rohr caught my attention. In the middle of their front lawn was a huge rock, four feet or so in diameter, and atop the rock was mounted an ornamental eagle.

There was also a miniature windmill in the yard, and affixed to the top of it was a model of a World War II fighter plane. I had the impression that James knows every word to "Off We Go into the Wild Blue Yonder" whence he has gone many a time, I was sure.

Seeing the plane resurrected memories of my WW II flying days when, as an infantry officer, I scouted from torpedo bombers piloted by Navy officers off carriers. My job was covering the amphibious landings, reporting on friendly and enemy troop movements.

In the entire Marine Corps there were only 10 officers with this job. I admired the courage and skills of the Navy pilots, especially when they returned me safely aboard the carrier. Of the 91 missions I flew, all but 11 were piloted by Navy officers. The other 11, flown from ashore and not from a carrier, had Marine pilots, all also excellent except for one.

The exception was a Marine major. The command ship ordered us to descend on civilians on an Okinawa road and try to ascertain if Japanese soldiers were among them. To do that, we practically had to get on the deck, but the major refused to go below 500 feet.

As he stalled, command kept sending messages asking for reports, and my reply was, "Can't distinguish. Will try to get lower and take a closer look."

This went on three times. On each one I urged the major to drop down, and each time he had a different excuse for not doing so.

Dear God, I had flown with Navy pilots who had delighted in raising the dust on dirt roads. Now here I was with a fellow Marine who refused to go under 500 feet. I was torn between disgust and disappointment.

When command called again, I called it as it was: "Can't verify. Pilot says it's not safe to go under 500 feet."

There was a long pause, then command responded, "Understood." I hoped so.

About a third of the way through my day I met a young runner. Wearing only shorts and shoes and carrying a water bottle, he moved very fast toward me.

"Hello," he called when passing. "Was that you who I saw a few miles back while I was driving to Winterset?"

As he continued on, I answered, "Yeah, I guess so."

"I'm doing 18 today," he said while moving with the speed and elegance of a class runner. I would have liked to learn more about him, but that was not to be.

Often I think that if I had a companion out here, the miles would go easier, the time would pass faster. On the other hand, being solo I am blessed with much time to meditate, to ruminate, a luxury many folks never experience.

I became almost reverent for a moment of high drama as I approached the intersection of Highway 160 and Highway 2. As readers of *The Bridges of Madison County* will remember, this is the very spot where Francesca Johnson last saw Robert Kincaid – the very place where she restrained herself from calling to him and from running off with him.

I felt the need for a black mourning band to memorialize this moment. None being handy, I brushed back the tears and trod manfully forward.

The first thing Elaine wanted to do after we finished was to visit Roseman Covered Bridge, east of Winterset and off Highway 92. The attraction here for Elaine was that Roseman is featured in *Bridges*.

DAY FIVE. As long as I live, I will never wake up to an August 7th without thinking of Guadalcanal. For many reasons: I lived there for months; along with some natives, Australians and other Americans I made a five-day patrol across the island that is 90 miles long and as wide as 25 miles; several times I took refuge in a foxhole when Japanese bombed us there; I lost friends there; flying off Henderson Field in torpedo bombers, one of five infantry officers trained to scout from aircraft; it was home to my unit (3rd Battalion, 21st Marines) before and after we invaded Bougainville.

Yeah, I'll remember August 7th and Guadalcanal – the exotic beauty of the place, the deprivations and deaths of friends and the two bouts of malaria incurred there. I was secretly thankful that I was not in on the initial landing and fighting there, and I well could have been because when my class was commissioned in January 1942, half of us were sent to the West Coast and half to the East Coast. Those who went to the East Coast became part of the Guadalcanal invasion force.

My God, Guadalcanal was 53 years ago, and yet it hangs poignant as if only days or weeks ago. Many were the lessons I learned there. One, the luxury of an electric light. Another, an appreciation for indoor plumbing.

On our way out to run today, we stopped at Madison County Fairgrounds to attend to logistical matters. While we were waiting for the water tanks to fill, Elaine turned Rebel and Brudder loose to attend to their business.

Instead, finding themselves free spirits, they soared off into adventureland. Realizing they had taken off, Elaine and I set off in hot pursuit.

Elaine was in a tizzy, just sure that something disastrous would happen to her children. The energy I spent locating them would have gotten me two miles down the road.

This turned out to be just another day in Iowa – corn fields, soybean fields, sultry weather. Nothing unusual, just a smorgasbord of happenings and scenes sufficient to keep me entertained for the day.

All kinds of thoughts crossed my mind today. When I tired, I asked myself, How in hell was I able to average 26 miles a day for 122 consecutive days going across the country?

When the glare from the sun was strong on the gravel shoulder, I asked, How did I make it across the USA without ever wearing dark glasses?

When I saw my third dead snake on the road today: How come I'm so lucky that none of these snakes are alive?

And when a Highway Patrol car passed: Wonder why not one officer has been curious enough to check on me?

Then, on a somewhat different plane when thinking back on the visit yesterday to John Wayne's boyhood home: Does it attract more visitors each year than Thomas Jefferson's home in Monticello? I'd wager it does. After all, Disneyland attracts many more visitors than Yosemite. Such is American culture.

Highway 169 goes directly through the middle of Adel (population 2340), so I was able to get a first-hand look at the town and came away with a very favorable impression. Like Winterset its centerpiece was a magnificent courthouse.

Unlike Winterset, though, the stores on the blocks that bracketed the courthouse were not tacky. In a word, Adel had more class than Winterset.

I was impressed with the neatness of the city square, the downtown section, and of the homes along 169. By the way, "The Bridges of Madison County" was not playing at the local theater.

The KOA park on I-80 where we stayed tonight was upscale in amenities with water, electric and sewage hookups, albeit the setting was sterile compared to the woodsy state parks. Also upscale was the price, about four times what we paid in the state parks. Little wonder that the owner drove a Mercedes.

DAY SIX. It was still dark when Elaine drove the 20 miles to our start this morning. On the way I had my usual pre-breakfast fix – coffee, half a Powerbar and a small sweet roll – to sustain me until the three-mile breakfast pit-stop.

It was sufficiently light when I hit the road that I could make out the town of Minburn in the distance, about two miles by my estimate. It was distinguishable by its water tower, grain elevators and grove of trees.

When I arrived at Minburn, a sign there read, "Welcome to Minburn, a small town with a big heart." Its population, 390, verified it was small. Blazingly passing through afoot, I did not have time to verify "big heart."

Just before reaching the three-mile pit-stop and breakfast, I looked eastward and saw a cloud formation unlike one I had ever seen before. The sun was shining brightly on some silver clouds, and silhouetted in front of them were some dark clouds. The effect was that they appeared to be a mountain range in the sky.

At the breakfast pit-stop, Elaine and I talked about an item in yesterday's

Des Moines Register that told about a man who had been a teacher and coach at Ogden Middle School who for more than 10 years had been secretly videotaping girls and women as they undressed and dressed in a high school locker room. The town folks in Ogden, where we finished today's run, are quite naturally wondering just who among them appears in the videotapes.

The town folks are also trying to reconcile the man who took the videos with the good teacher and beloved coach they've come to know. Or maybe they *thought* they knew. The sad part of the story was that the man has a wife and three children.

Since only 1900 or so people live in Ogden, everyone there will know what happened. No Scarlet Letter is needed.

When I passed home after home flying the American flag, I concluded that 75 percent of the Iowa farm homes display the flag. The reason I was aware of this was that I was getting a sore arm from all the saluting.

Lucky for me, though, that the USMC flag was not alongside, else I'd have had to stop and sing a chorus of "The Halls of Montezuma." Now that would have been tragic, because my singing would have caused the corn to fall off the stalks prematurely and the hogs to become anorexic!

At one pit-stop a farmer's wife came out to talk with Elaine. The lady confirmed that Winterset area is indeed the rattlesnake convention center of Iowa.

She also told Elaine that I should exercise caution, because the TV and radio broadcasts today are stressing the dangers from heat and humidity. Paraphrasing a famous admiral, I later told Elaine, "Damn the heat and humidity, slow speed ahead."

Aw, that was a bit dramatic. Truth is, I honestly didn't think it was that dangerous out here for a person in reasonably good shape. The calamities befall those who try to do what they have not been doing.

The heat did get to me each time I left the motorhome after a pit-stop. That was understandable because the air conditioner was operating inside (after all, the dogs have to be comfortable!). So when I hit the road, I felt as if I were being tumbled in a dryer.

DAY SEVEN. Most people, I think, would be bored to tears out here doing what I am doing. Same thing, day after day.

For me, though, these days are filled with adventure and excitement. The adventure lies in not knowing what lies ahead, what will happen, what I will see, whom I will meet. The excitement lies in simply being able, at my age, to chug 20 or 21 miles every day.

Doing that would be a Lazarus experience for most people my age. To me it is exciting that I have the vitality to be able to experience and enjoy our daily routine.

Why I am so lucky, I am not sure. But I am sure to thank God every day that I am.

This morning I took the time to make a body assessment. The findings were that mechanically I was doing great; my ankles, knees, hips were just fine.

I am not quite sure to what our success is due. One factor should be the precautions I take, such as proper shoes and wearing a sacroiliac belt (for a back condition known as "spondylosis").

Another factor has to be the 10 hours in bed each night for recuperability. Too, Elaine's great meals, and tea and sympathy at three-mile pit-stops have to be added into the equation.

For the first time in 100 miles, if I remember correctly, someone stopped today to inquire if I needed help. Her name was Joan Erickson, and she was a nurse on her way to work. My first reaction was, Did her medical training tell her, "Here's a guy in trouble"?

I told her I was running across Iowa, and her response was to give me her card. Hey, Joan, you are not exactly building my confidence.

I did my usual meditative thinking as I went along today, and some of my thoughts were focused on Iowa. As when I passed an extremely well-kept farm, home and yard immaculate, the smell from pig pens was gagging. I asked myself, How are these farm folks, engulfed with this stench, able to live with it?

Another thought about Iowa was that until the exposure of this run I never realized the extent to which this state is a bread basket for America. And I had to honestly admit that, so far at least, Iowa has not been as much fun as Nebraska and Wyoming, and not as interesting as Nebraska had been.

At one pit-stop today Elaine reported on her observation of four state highway workers. For 40 minutes they were in the process of blowing debris out of holes in the road that they planned to seal later. Between coffee breaks, talk-ins and leaning on their shovels, they had moved down the road less than 60 yards in 40 minutes.

To Elaine and me the process seemed a bit futile in that they did not seal the holes immediately after cleaning them, which meant that more debris would accumulate in the holes before they were sealed at a later date. After that negativism I should quickly throw the positive switch and report that as we have traveled Highway 169, it is remarkably free of potholes.

The only town on today's route was Boxholm, and like most the towns on our route it appears in no tourist book. What businesses there are, and the Boone County Bank and Trust Company is the biggest of these, sit directly on the highway. In this hamlet of 267 people, I counted 19 buildings that once housed now-defunct businesses.

At day's end we faced the decision of whether to return 29 miles to Spring Lake State Park or to drive an equal distance to Fort Dodge and JFK Memorial Park. Since Elaine is the quarterback of our motorhome, I left the decision to her, though I was secretly hoping for a return to Spring Lake, a sure thing and a good one.

But such was not to be, because Elaine was curious to see Fort Dodge. Driving to JFK, and not sure we'd find it easily since it was miles off Highway 169, we decided we would wait until tomorrow to tour a town that the locals call "Fordodge."

DAY EIGHT. Our day started on a spirited note when the barking of the dogs awakened us at 4:30 A.M. The dogs were nervous, jumpy, restless.

Half-asleep, the first thing we saw was flashing lights. Our first thought was, Where are they coming from? We were puzzled only momentarily, because we soon realized they came from silent lightning. Traditional lightning streaks were descending from sky to ground, and the illumination was enough to light up the entire fairway of the adjacent golf course.

Thunder rumbled in the background, and a heavy rain pelted the motorhome. I could not help but wish that we were housed in something more substantial than the motorhome.

Seeing little to gain from roosting in the park, Elaine and I decided to drive to the start and, once there, to assess the situation. With lightning and thunder overhead and in a slashing rain Elaine drove cautiously, and as she did I tried to get in the mood to do my imitation of Gene Kelly's "Singing in the Rain." The problem here was that I can't sing and I'm a lousy dancer.

I began running in what was then a light rain but had not been on the road five minutes when a deluge hit me. Miserably wet and cold and not seeing Elaine in sight, I decided I had to keep my body temperature up. So, head down and plunging into the wind, I geared down to a 10-minute mile – blazing speed considering the rain, wind resistance, how bundled I was with clothing and my antiquity. By the time I had gone two miles, I had expended considerably more energy than desired.

About this time Elaine, realizing my predicament, returned to rescue me. Blessed are the merciful!

It soon became apparent that if I was going to log 21 miles today, I had no choice but to get out and get going. The net result was that I was drenched for the first 11 miles.

As I was trying to swim upstream in this muck all morning, Elaine said at one pit-stop, "I wish this trip would not get over. I love it out here, and I really don't want to go home."

Soaking wet and uncomfortable, I dared not comment. I have, though, told her several times that these trips are not primarily runs for me but vacations for her and the dogs.

Her rebuttal invariably is, "People tell me I should be canonized for the help I give you."

Even after the rain ceased, thunder rumbled off to the east, and dark clouds hung gloomily overhead. These clouds did not disappear until the last six miles, replaced by a blazing sun and sultry air that left me so uncomfortable that I would have voted for light rainfall.

Today I seemed to see more soybean fields than corn fields. If I could believe what I had been told, I now knew that an acre of corn was worth $450 and an acre of soybeans, $375.

That information came from Lyle Bikalith, the only Iowan with whom I talked all day. We chatted when he came out to his mailbox to pick up his mail. He attracted my attention because he was riding a four-wheel all terrain vehicle.

"This thing is fun," he said. "It belongs to my neighbor, and I'm just trying it out. But at $5600, it's too rich for my blood."

Approaching the environs of Fort Dodge, I had to negotiate a couple of hills of five-percent gradient and dash across a couple of bridges without bike lanes. Neither hills nor bridges demoralized me, because I was overjoyed to be logging 21.3 miles on a day when I had thought the weather might torpedo us.

It dawned on me as I went into the motorhome at the end of the day that Fort Dodge was the first semblance of a big city to date on our Highway 169 route in Iowa. Yet by most standards, with a population of only around 26,000, it was a peewee city covering only 30 square miles.

When we returned to our camp site at JFK Memorial Park, the elderly couple (eek, look who's talking!) next door visited for a short while.

At one point, the lady, a native Iowan like her husband, said, "Isn't this a pretty state?"

Detecting her native pride, and giving an honest answer, I replied, "I've never visited a state with so many well-kept homes and yards. And the state parks have better facilities and are less pricey than the California state parks."

Evidently I said the right things, because she beamed. Damn, couldn't help but think that I'm a scintillating conversationalist.

DAY NINE. Yesterday grasshoppers were my companions for much of the way. Today taking their place are squadrons of butterflies. Grasshoppers and butterflies, yeah, I'm rugged enough to handle them.

It's the snakes that give me the heebie-jeebies. Never can be too sure about snakes. That's why when Tim Bacon stopped to ask if I needed help, the first question I asked him was, "Any rattlesnakes around here?"

"No, once you get 10 miles past Winterset, there are no more rattlesnakes." Sweet confirmation.

I asked him if he liked living in Iowa and heard him say, "I love it."

"Even with the freezing weather in winter?"

"I can handle that," he said. "I work with my brother in a body shop, and I missed only one day from work last year because of weather."

He wanted to know what I was doing on the road, and I responded by giving him a broad brush sketch of what Elaine and I were up to.

Trying to get the focus back on him and Iowa, I commented, "You have some very nice parks in Iowa."

"Yes, we do," was the most I could set out of him. I wondered if his reticence was characteristic of Iowans. Maybe he was wondering if all Californians are as gabby as this old man.

At 14 miles signs from the Lions, the Kiwanis, and a host of churches welcomed me to Humboldt, the only town on our route today. This Humboldt, hot and sultry as it is, is one helluva contrast from California's

Humboldt with its majestic redwoods and chilly weather.

When unexpectedly I stumbled upon the Born Free Motorcoach Company, I made an instant decision to take time out and tour the small factory. Born Free is somewhat of an anomaly in today's market place in that, simply by calling, the customer can deal directly with the company's chief executive and in that all the service is personalized. The customer can be involved in the planning of the motorhome, check on it while it's being built, and expect good follow-up after the sale.

As I saw the product and was told of the company's policies, I thought that this small, Iowa-based manufacturer might be the source of our next motorhome. I jettisoned that idea when I noticed the prices are in the $50,000 range, a bit out of our league.

The major excitement of our day came when we returned to JFK Park and found an oversized Southwind motorhome parked in our space. I percolated because we had left signs saying the spot was reserved.

I knocked at the Southwind, but nobody was there. Across the road at another motorhome I saw three men and three women sitting in lawn chairs and visiting. I walked over there and asked if anyone knew about the Southwind.

One of the guys said. "It's mine."

"Well, you're parked in our space and you'll have to move," I said. "We had reserved signs on it."

He replied. "You left the space, and by camp rules it became open. It's mine now."

I assessed him: in his late 50s or early 60s, a bantamweight. I could handle this guy if push came to shove, but he did have two friends to reinforce him.

"Yeah, that's right," one of the other guys added. Once you leave the camp site, the space is no longer yours. I'm from Fort Dodge, and I camp here often and know these are the rules."

That left me thinking, Am I missing something here? Is that really the rule? After all, this guy is from Iowa, and from what I've seen Midwestern folks have a lot of integrity. He might be right.

I backed off and said, "I'm going to check on the rules." The easiest way to settle it, Elaine and I decided, was to track down the park ranger and get the straight story.

When we contacted the ranger, he exploded. "The guy's a damn liar. What's he think he's pulling?

"I'll take care of it. Follow me." So saying, he jumped into his pickup and drove back to our space.

Mincing no words, he told the intruder to get out of our space, and to get out *now*. Then he stood by to make sure the intruder obeyed his order and, beyond that, he even followed the intruder as he drove to a different place in the park to camp.

When the ranger returned to make sure Elaine and I were properly anchored, we thanked him profusely. Later I found myself wishing that our justice system would work as swiftly and fairly as that ranger's action.

DAY 10. Our day did not get off to the best of starts because, soon after leaving JFK in the morning darkness, we took a wrong turn, drove seven or eight miles out of our way, and wound up in the small town of Badger. There a kind soul gave us directions on how to get back to Highway 169.

The most discouraging part of our day was having to follow a detour, routed along road P56, because of a bridge being repaired on 169. The going on this narrow two-lane road was tough for me because there was no bike lane, no shoulder, just the fogline that bordered on the grass. For Elaine the problem was finding a place to park for pit-stops on this route that took us eight miles out of the way.

Along the way I talked with a couple of natives who bitterly complained that the bridge had been out over four months and that repair was proceeding at a snail's pace.

The detour did provide some diversity in that we went through the town of Livermore, population 450. As I went through town, I concluded that the citizens living along Ninth Avenue, the detour route, resented traffic being routed past their homes, which like all the homes in town were well-maintained middle-class structures.

At one pit-stop today I heard a radio report about two high school boys who got into a tangle about a girl. Subsequently one of these guys brought a gun to school and killed the other.

It took the jury 1.5 hours of deliberation to convict him. He was given a life sentence. My reaction: What a pity that O.J. Simpson did not have such a jury.

In my last six miles today I learned that Iowans take their concerns about heat seriously, because three different times (making this a record day for Iowa) people stopped to check on me.

At 19 miles a driver went past me, then stopped, turned around and drove back.

His first question: "Do you need help out here. It's pretty hot."

"You're right, it is hot. But I'm okay."

"You're sure?" he said.

"Yeah. I'm an old hand at this. Actually I'm running across your state." I could see that did not register with him.

"How far is it to Algona?" I then asked.

"About two miles. You know, it's kind of hot for you to be out here today," he added, again expressing his concern. Then wishing me good luck, he drove off.

As he did, I asked myself, With how many people like this man John Henck have I met with but a few brief moments on the road and with whom I'll never again meet?

We finished our 21.2-mile day at the south boundary of Algona and decided to immediately scout Ambrose A. Call State Park only about four miles away. We were aware that it was Friday and RV parks fill early on weekends.

Arriving at the 130-acre park of rolling timberlands, we were delighted to find space and hookups in this pleasant setting. Elaine and the dogs enjoyed exploring the place. I reveled in the tranquillity of the setting and the luxury of just sitting on my butt and relaxing.

As we settled in, no one else was in the camping area. But the serenity of that exploded about five P.M. when an invasion of Cub Scouts descended.

Let the games begin! Quietness did not again prevail until around 10 o'clock.

DAY 11. I had sworn that I'd never again be on the road in dark. But that vow was broken when, after the short drive to the start, I was on the road at 5:11 A.M., our earliest starting time in Iowa. At least I had the city lights of Algona to show the way.

I was surprised to catch sight of an elderly gentleman out walking. As I came upon him from behind, not wanting to startle him, I alerted him to my presence by announcing, "Good morning. If you wonder what I'm doing out here this early hour, I'm running across your state."

"Oh," he said in a tone that expressed mild surprise.

"Yeah, fact is, I'm just starting my 21-mile day. Judging from your pace, I'd say you do a lot of walking."

"Yes, I do this three-mile walk in town every morning. I used to own that place over there." He pointed to a car dealership.

"And I lived right back there," and he pointed to a side street. "There are three houses – one for my dad, one for my brother, and one for me. This used to be Schultz Street. My name's Wesley Schultz."

I again looked at the good-sized auto dealership to which he was referring.

He went on, "I used to sit here with 40 to 50 cars and a big gas station, and made a pretty good living. I sold out to a young guy, about 40 then, and he comes in and puts in 250 cars."

"He gets six salesmen and buys out the grocery store next door and puts it all in car showing. And he does a lot of business. He was a great advertiser, and I wasn't."

"How old are you now?" I wanted to know.

"Seventy-five."

"Aw, you're just a kid. I'm 78."

"Are you really?" he said. "The hell you are!"

"Seventy-eight and crazy enough to run across a state."

Realizing this extended conversation would make me late for the breakfast pit-stop and that Elaine would begin to get concerned, I said, "I better move on. My wife gets worried if I'm late."

Leaving him, I was sure he did more than just walk every morning. I suspect he does a heap of reminiscing as he goes past what is now the Flaherty Buick-Chevrolet-Pontiac-Cadillac dealership.

Out of Algona, onto the gravel shoulder, I was in the usual setting – corn fields, soybean fields, some hog and cattle farming. Despite the early hour, I was sweating profusely because of the humidity; and, pardner, out here I do mean *sweat* – no sissy perspiring for us.

I knew it was Sunday from observing the number of solitary women solemnly driving towards Algona and church. Where are the husbands, where are the children?

And isn't it ironic, I thought, that women – at least in the Catholic church – constitute the majority of the congregation, yet they can't be (change that to "aren't allowed to be") priests.

I guess I am getting real radical, or at least rapidly abandoning my Catholic upbringing, because I think the infusion of some highly qualified women priests would be preferable to some of the poorly qualified men priests I have seen in recent years.

Our day completed 4.5 miles north of Bancroft, Elaine handed me a root beer float with orders to drink it when she called home to retrieve our phone messages.

The only person who had called was Bob Spangler who said he and his wife Doris would like to get together with us for dinner. Bob is an old Marine buddy who has been farming extensively the past 50 years.

We first met in October 1941 when we were both on the same train from Sacramento heading for Marine Corps officer training in Quantico, Virginia. We were both 24 then, and 'tis funny how a person remembers small things.

I recall Bob had not a single filling in his teeth, whereas mine looked like a silver mine. He was a graduate of University California, Davis, where he was on the swimming team and he had the upper body torso to prove it.

All that a little over 50 years ago, and now just before this Nebraska/Iowa run Elaine and I had attended the 50th Anniversary of Bob and Doris' wedding.

DAY 12. Our last night in Iowa was a bit scary, made so because of menacing thunder, illuminating lightning and strong winds. Tucked in under the trees, we had reasonable protection from the wind, but we did worry about a tree or some big branches crashing onto the motorhome.

Driving through Algona this morning at 5:30 A.M. on our way to the start 25 miles away, we saw Wesley Schultz out for his morning walk. We stopped to greet him and to wish him good luck. He seemed genuinely pleased to see us.

Every morning in Nebraska, and now every morning in Iowa, to tide myself over until breakfast I've eaten half a banana and half a Powerbar as we drive to the start. The only problem here is that Rebel and Brudder have become fond of Powerbars, so I have to share with them.

I wonder what Brian Maxwell, the young entrepreneur who developed Powerbar, would think of that. Hey, Brian, maybe a whole new market awaits you – Pooch Powerbars. Go for it!

Assessing my condition as I left the motorhome to start the day's run, I had to admit I was a bit amazed at how well I have held up mechanically on the Nebraska and Iowa runs. Seems that if I could get a lung transplant or two, I could be a competitive athlete, he said as he hacked and coughed asthmatically.

I found it somewhat discouraging, shortly after starting, that when I came to the junction of Highways 169 and 9, the road went directly east for seven miles – miles which brought me no closer to the Minnesota border, out-of-my-way miles. Not until 169 again turned north did I begin to converge on Minnesota and get the feeling I was on the gun lap.

Early in the day I stopped to watch a farmer harvest corn. The forward part of his rig was like a lawn mower.

It just moved along chopping down corn and putting it into a machine that transported it to a conveyor belt and into a trailer following the farmer. Somehow the ears of corn were separated from the stalks. A truck followed the trailer which, when filled, was emptied into the truck.

Donald Shrader interrupted his work long enough to tell me this was the sweet-corn harvest season. The field corn is harvested at a different time. I asked him the name of the machinery I saw in operation

Smiling, he said, "It's called a corn picker." Simple as that, huh? He added that the same equipment is used to pick field corn when it comes into season.

This last day in Iowa was refreshingly easy. For one thing the distance was only 16.3 miles. Atop that, much of the road was newly surfaced blacktop, the gravel shoulder was as wide as four feet, the day was cool with the temperature hovering in the 70s, and the sun remained in obscurity until my last three miles.

Elaine was parked at a hilltop for the 15-mile pit-stop, and from there I could look ahead a little over a mile and see a clump of trees and a water tower. That thar is Elmore, I told myself. Ah, contentment.

I was torn between two moods: to walk the rest of the distance and to savor the experience or to shift into high gear, run the distance and get it over as fast as possible. I did neither. I simply jogged to the border and city limits of Elmore.

Elaine, parked at the city boundary of Elmore, exited the motorhome to give me a welcome hug as I finished. Then she reminded me our next move was to find the post office to pick up some tapes of 49er football games that my daughter Nancy and her husband Dan had mailed to us.

On the way to the post office, I found myself thinking about how the finishes of our state runs are always anticlimactic. There are no cameras, no cheering crowds – just Elaine and me there to feel the satisfaction of success.

We pour considerable planning, time, and effort into a state, then when we are involved in the actual doing of it it's all consuming. Then when it is over, as Iowa was at this moment, presto – no more day-to day association, it is gone, out of our lives except as a memory. And now that I think about that, the common denominator that runs through all our state runs is that we think back on each one fondly.

By dinner we were already talking about which states we would run next summer. We sort of favored the idea of completing all states west of the Mississippi River.

We had to run Minnesota, North Dakota, South Dakota, Texas and Louisiana. The question in my mind was, Could I run all these states in one summer?

I'd be 79 next summer and my warranty for such running, if not for longevity, is close to running out. For her part Elaine has made it clear that her favorite vacations are these on the road, seeing the country, having the dogs along and having me on a leash!

I have a strong suspicion that we will be embarked on an ambitious running safari in summer 1996. Time now to rest and to enjoy the trip home, and I need the rest because the thought of hoofing across five more states is tiring me.

Overview of
TEXAS

May 5th to 12th, 1996
180.5 miles

Day	Overnight	Miles	Notes
1	Vega	26.5	launching a five-state run
2	Vega	21.5	the lemon meringue tragedy
3	Amarillo	21.0	visit with Bobby Wilson
4	Amarillo	21.5	afoot in Amarillo
5	McLean	22.0	state trooper Gary Davis
6	McLean	22.0	"a young chick for a wife"
7	near Shamrock	23.5	Allenreed, McLean typical of Route 66 towns
8	Elk City, OK	22.5	Goodbye, Texas. Hello, Oklahoma.

Chapter 11

Texas:

Route 66 Revisited

DAY ONE. As Elaine and I – accompanied by our two Labradors, Rebel and Brudder – made the five-day motorhome trip from our home in Auburn, California, to the start of our run across Texas, I had plenty of time to think and much to think about. Primarily my thinking focused on our target: to run across Texas, Louisiana, South Dakota, Minnesota and North Dakota this spring and summer. If we could run across them, we would then have completed running across all 22 states west of the Mississippi River.

So read the scenario as I left the motorhome at the New Mexico/Texas border and ever so slowly strode east on Interstate 40: Starting on I-40, a divided highway with two lanes on each side separated by a grass median, I faced 70-mile-per-hour oncoming traffic. But protected by a nine-foot breakdown lane, I felt reasonably safe.

Immediately I noticed that 70 percent of the traffic on I-40 consisted of trucks. Semis were practically bumper to bumper, and the noise was deafening.

At one point, just to get the pulse of truck traffic, I counted the number that went past in one minute. Eleven just on my side of the median. – 660 in one hour.

After only 10 minutes of running I saw, 30 yards north of I-40 and paralleling it, a paved frontage road. Eager to escape heavy traffic, I crossed the grass and got onto this road. Soon a sign told me that I was on historic Route 66. At the moment I enjoyed a monopoly on it.

Unfortunately the route petered out after I'd been on it for 30 minutes or so, and it did not reappear until I'd logged 16 miles and was then able to get back on it for the rest of the day. Being on 66 was a tranquilizer compared to I-40.

In our planning Elaine and I had agreed on 21 miles as my daily mileage goal for the five states this summer. But I decided to launch today a bit more ambitiously with 26 miles. Two reasons:

First, after the five days of driving here, I was as rested as I'll ever be. With 26 miles I could build up a little equity.

Second, I was a bit inspired from watching runners in a hilly 100-kilometer (62-mile) race Hal Stainbrook and I had directed only a week ago. One of them, Ray Nicholl, age 59, had a hernia operation only 16 days before the race. Hell, I thought, 26 miles on this flat pavement is creampuff stuff comparatively.

The loneliness of the long-distance runner is the usual scenario that prevails when I am running across a state. That's why I welcome incidents like the one at 25 miles today when a fellow emerged from his station wagon parked on I-40 and jogged toward me. The first thing I noticed about him was that he moved like an experienced runner.

Catching up with me, he said, "I passed you a ways back, and decided to stop and talk with you since I'm a runner myself."

"Nice to have some company out here," I replied.

"I used to run for the Turkish national team many years ago before I came to the United States. I had to quit the team after a car accident." He pointed to the ugly scars on his legs. He went on to tell me that his name was Cahit Yeter. Well, actually he said it a couple of times and unable to get a handle on it, I asked him to spell it.

"I'm sort of surprised to see you running across a state," he said. "You must be almost 65."

If I were the Pope, I would have canonized him on the spot.

As he ran along effortlessly and carried on a conversation, I could easily detect he was a class runner. He told me he was a retired physical therapist, now 63 years old.

"I've got 165,000 miles on my legs," he said. On parting he insisted on giving me his address and phone number and asked that I contact him whenever in Phoenix.

Our 26-mile day closed out 10 miles west of Vega. As the curtain came down on this day, I disdained any modesty and applauded myself vigorously.

DAY TWO. Arriving at the day's start, we discovered a tragedy. Our frigidaire door had come open during the drive, and the lemon meringue pie Elaine had labored on long and diligently yesterday was splattered on the floor of the RV.

Because of the mess and because lemon meringue is her favorite pie, Elaine was in a tizzy. Understandably so, because just before leaving the RV park I had opened the fridge then failed to click the door firmly shut before we left.

When I left the motorhome to start running, the temperature outside was

40 degrees. Believe me, at the moment, it was much cooler inside. Getting underway, this old warrior knew he had two missions today: run 21 miles, and somehow restore myself to Elaine's good graces.

On the good graces bit, I knew I had my work cut out. Soon as the mess was discovered, I told Elaine, "I'll take you to dinner tonight at the Hickory Cafe in Vega to make up for this."

Her answer: "No deal. Even taking me to dinner at Sardi's would not make up for that one." The woman is unforgiving.

At each three-mile pit-stop I religiously followed all the prescribed rules: Before entering the motorhome, I dutifully wiped me feet; entering, I made a supreme effort to be upbeat and cheerful; before having a snack, I washed my hands and made sure to wipe them with a hand towel and not the dish towel (a sure entry to trouble); in the bathroom I always remembered to put the toilet seat down, and, believe me, I kept my paws off that frigidaire.

As the day wore on, I was left wondering if my angelicy would be recognized. Would forgiveness be in order?

Altogether this turned out to be somewhat of a dull day as indicated by the fact that the highlight was probably my being able to log 21 miles after yesterday's marathon. For the most part the setting today resembled that of yesterday – sand, barren grass plains, mesquite.

The major scenic attraction of the day was our passage through Vega on Route 66. As we entered town, one sign told us the population was 840, the elevation 4200 feet. An American Legion sign read, "For this we fought, for this we stand."

Exiting Vega, I saw another RV park and a gas/convenience store, but no continuation of 66. I reluctantly returned to I-40 until 66 again turned up within a couple of miles.

I was amused by a billboard advertising in large print, "FREE 72-OZ. STEAK," and in barely distinguishable type, "if you can eat it in one hour." Eating it, in this case, probably includes the bone.

I was left thinking, What's the gastronomical risk of eating a 72-ounce steak in one hour? Will have to ask my MD friend Ralph Paffenbarger.

I suffered the loss of an old friend today: my faithful water bottle that I've carried for more than 5700 miles on state runs. It was, I blush to admit, an eight-ounce baby bottle, chosen because it was the only size that would fit in the pocket of my fanny pack.

For reasons unknown, it sprang a leak and dripped water on me. Sayonara, Old Friend, as I retire you to the Great Baby Bottle Heaven.

As I neared the finish of my day, the thought uppermost in my mind was, Have I worked my way back in Elaine's good graces? The answer would come when I entered the motorhome. If she handed me a root beer float as she customarily does at the end of the day, I was forgiven. No float, no forgiveness.

Expecting denial but instead rewarded with a float, I had to admit it tasted especially good. To paraphrase Keats, *La Belle Dame Avec Merci!*

DAY THREE. In any direction that I looked today, all I saw was flat terrain with a smattering of rolling hills and an occasional tree. No mountains, no plateaus did I see. There was an increase, though, in the number of acres of cultivation.

At one point, this around four miles, I went past a stockyard on the south side of the road and, across the road on the north a herd of cattle grazed on the plains. Now this was Texas. The only thing missing from this picture was John Wayne.

My wanderings on Route 66 took me through one small town. Wildorado housed the Texan Motel, Jesse's Cafe, Texan Trading Post and three gas stations. Unlike the other small towns I had passed through, there were few defunct reminders of Route 66's heyday.

Had a thought today about a friend of mine, Al Baeta, for many years track and cross country coach at American River College, Sacramento. Singlehandedly he raised the funds from private sources to build an all-weather track at the college.

At this moment, while I'm playing out here, Al – a dynamo of energy at age 63 – is up to his arse in alligators at the Olympic swamp where he is team manager for the USA track and field team. Despite all the work and pressure he's happy doing his thing just as I am doing mine. His is more lofty than mine, and we are far apart in our ventures, yet we are allied in many ways.

I had another definite reminder today of being in Texas when I passed Happy Jack's Horse Motel. I counted 16 corrals, each with its own small stable. The place seemed to be doing a pretty good business. At least that was my conclusion judging from all the horse manure stacked out front.

As we began to approach Amarillo, Elaine and I were a bit apprehensive about finding our way through the city. It would be simple to get on I-40, but pedestrians were not permitted on I-40 within the city limits. We were told that the frontage road, which was more or less old 66, would take us through the city. That remained to be seen. We had our doubts.

Around 17.5 miles into our day I reached the city limits of Amarillo. Still on 66 and heading for downtown Amarillo I encountered a problem: 66 lost its tranquillity and became a one-way road eastbound with fast traffic, which meant I had my back to cars descending on me.

I almost passed by one novelty tourist attraction on the outskirts of Amarillo without even noticing it. And after seeing it, I felt I would have missed nothing if I had failed to take notice of it.

It's called Cadillac Ranch and consists of 10 Cadillacs, 1949-63 vintage, buried nose down in a field at the same angle. This was the idea of some rich Texan. If he were trying to convey a message, it evaded me. In my book, it registered as ricky-ticky, especially since all the cars were defaced with graffiti.

At our final pit-stop Elaine and I were parked in the lot of an apartment complex checking our maps when a young man in a pickup stopped near us. He's going to tell us to get out of the parking lot, we thought. I got out of the motorhome to talk with him.

When we approached each other, I could not make out what he first said, but I did hear, "I'm Bobby Wilson, and being a runner, I thought I'd stop and talk with you."

I introduced myself and asked, "Is there much running activity in Amarillo?"

"Oh yeah, quite a bit. We have the Lone Star Running Club with 300 members, and we have a number of races."

He went on to tell me that he considers himself a middle-of-the-pack runner; that while he has raced all distances from a 5-K to a marathon, his favorite distance is the half-marathon "because it allows me to run a challenging distance without sacrificing my whole life and body."

Before Bobby left, I asked if I'd be able to follow the frontage road we were on through Amarillo.

"You'll run into a problem on 66 when you come to the railroad tracks," he said. "You can run across them, but your wife will have to drive around."

Bobby had said it was four miles to the tracks. My guess was that we'd spend half of tomorrow just working our way through Amarillo and that we'd be lucky if we didn't encounter some navigational difficulty.

DAY FOUR. Just as Bobby Wilson had foretold, I found my way blocked by railroad tracks. He had said I could run across the tracks. But as I counted 10 tracks and saw trains on seven of them, I decided such a crossing could be fatal.

Now I was in navigational trouble, because I had planned on crossing the tracks and had no contingency routing. I climbed the steep embankment to the freeway and looked for the nearest railroad crossing, saw one about a half-mile away, scooted back down the embankment and ran to the overhead.

On it and across the tracks, my next problem was that I could not remember where Elaine and I had agreed to rendezvous. Was it just after the railroad crossing, or was it at the first exit she could take after crossing the tracks on I-40? Since she was nowhere in sight near the tracks, I followed the frontage road to the exit. Parked nearby, she was a welcome sight.

The rest of the way through Amarillo was somewhat routine. Once I came to the east city limit, I was again back in grasslands and cultivation. About half my day was in city surroundings, half in the open country.

Two things I can't resist checking when on the road are historical markers and tourist information centers. So understandably, 11 miles into my day, 80 miles into Texas, I detoured to visit a Texas Information Center.

I asked the lady at the counter for information about Route 66 to the east of Amarillo. She said it did not exist east of Amarillo.

Wrong, but I maintained a polite silence. Then I asked if she had any information about RV parks to the east.

"No, but I have information on many motels if you want that," was her answer. Seemed sort of obvious to me that in some way the motels subsidize the Center whereas RV parks don't.

Outside the Center I read a plaque about Texas. That is, I read this much, which was all I could stomach before I quit reading.

"Texas, land of contrasts. Land of cotton fields and citrus growth, mighty high mountains and semi-tropic valleys. Sand dunes and spring-fed lakes, huge ranches, plush resorts, ghost towns and booming oil fields. Texas, land of the drawling cowboy and city sophisticate, old-world charm and progressive ideas, thrill-packed rodeos and gay fiestas, modern as a moon flight, busy as its vibrant interests...."

Fell to thinking today of how much I would miss the annual reunion of our 7th ROC Marine Officer Class this year. It's scheduled for mid-September, and I'll miss it because of a schedule conflict.

We were all commissioned second lieutenants in the Corps in January 1942, and every one of us was in combat in World War II. When we are gathered in a room at the reunion, usually about 40 of us, I can almost reach out and feel the warmth and brotherhood camaraderie that permeates the room.

I will miss that along with much of the good humor that flows. W.E.B. Griffin, a friend of classmate Jim Barrett, will be aboard all three days of the reunion. I've read and enjoyed all his novels about the Corps and about the Philadelphia police department, so I am disappointed to miss the chance to meet the man and to talk with him.

DAY FIVE. Had a little trouble last night with Elaine who was making dire threats about washing my T-shirt, the one with "Run Across Texas" on the front of it. She's appalled that I vowed not to wash the shirt until we finish Texas.

Her very words were, "If it gets much riper, it'll be carrying you instead of you carrying it."

My rebuttal, "I hold old friends near and dear."

I was overcome this early morning with a feeling I'd never experienced before on one of these state runs. The feeling was one of guilt that I was out here enjoying all this, finding almost ecstatic pleasure in it, able to do all this at age 79 while so many other people, young and old, are suffering from infirmities. I knew that sort of thinking was somewhat oddball, but it did grip me for a while.

Going through Conway, I decided to end the discrimination that tourist books show by ignoring the town. Instead I would give a full recitation of what tourists would see in town: L.A. Motel, Shell gas station, Love's Travelstop, Motor Inn Restaurant, an area of modest homes, some huge grain elevators, clusters of trees, Phillips gas station and the S&S Restaurant that advertised biscuits and gravy, beans and corn bread, chicken fried steak and Mexican food. I suspected a quick snack there would beam me up for a fast five miles on the road.

The town has a population of less than 100 and an elevation of around 3500 feet to express it in round numbers.

Going through Conway, I made a name association: Jerry Conway, a friend, baseball coach at a community college in Sacramento, dynamic individual, fun loving, infatuated with baseball. Then, whammo, cancer in his early 30s and dead a short while later. Subjectively I asked myself, Why am I ordained to live twice as long as Jerry?

The same feeling I sometimes got in combat: Why did the guy nearby get zapped and I suffered not a scratch?

"You handle it," Elaine said today when we were at a pit-stop and a Texas Highway Patrol car pulled up behind us. I got out of the motorhome and approached the patrol car.

"Just wanted to make sure you are okay," the young patrol officer said.

"Oh, we're in good shape," I told him. Then after we introduced ourselves and I learned his name was Gary Davis, I briefed him on what we were up to.

"Well, more power to you," he commented.

Elaine and I, after listening to the CB, have become aware that the truckers are upset with the Texas Highway Patrol because of its diligence in trying to enforce the speed laws – a tough job on I-40 because the officers are so visible in all the open space and because the various truckers radio the presence of the officers.

Here I side with the police. A semi truck is a potentially dangerous weapon on the highways. I'd argue for unmarked police cars, for helicopter surveillance, for whatever gets the job done.

Listening to the CB, a person can learn a lot about truckers. For one thing they are a closely knit fraternity. For another they talk and behave as if the roads exist expressly for them, and they resent the presence of any driver or vehicle in their way.

They have a lingo of their own. Cars are "four wheelers," motorhomes are "campers," the fast lane is the "hammer lane," police are "bears" and so on.

I had the sort of monopoly on the road this morning that a trucker would envy. In my first 12 miles on the frontage road not a single car passed me in either direction.

Somewhat amusing to see written on the frontage road pavement "Start of 10,000," meaning that a 10-kilometer race must start here. My guess was that it finished in Groom, about six miles east. Good course, I decided – straight, flat, fast without any traffic.

Around 19 miles a couple stopped to ask if I needed help. When I saw their Oklahoma license plate, I asked what city they were from.

The wife replied, "We're from Oklahoma City, the friendly city."

Looking at her, I was tempted to reply, "And of attractive ladies," but remained silent not being sure whether her husband would beam or steam at the compliment.

DAY SIX. Our sense of adventure was tested to the hilt last night. First we had a tornado alert, and that developed into a tornado warning.

An alert, we learned, means to be prepared to find the best shelter available. A warning means hurry to the shelter.

It was one step short of frightening when we contemplated what would happen to the motorhome in a tornado. We could visualize it and everything in it flung over an area of miles.

When we became aware of the alert, I scouted around for a relatively save place for us (Elaine, me, the dogs) and decided, there being no shelters of any type nearby, we could crawl into the hole beneath a nearby cattle guard. We would be relatively safe. But the motorhome, parked on a barren knoll with no trees or buildings as protection, was highly vulnerable.

Luckily the tornado bypassed us. But strong winds did not. They buffeted and rocked the motorhome most of the night.

Come morning, we were far from being well rested. But we were at peace in that people, dogs and motorhome were alive and well.

By my last three miles today on I-40, the wind had increased to the point where I was in danger of being blown into oncoming cars. To avoid that, I crossed the median and ran with traffic because the crosswind then blew me away from cars and out onto the grass.

The major attraction was going through the town of Groom. I-40 bypasses the town, and we could have saved miles following it. But Elaine and I decided to follow 66 through town and pay the price of a little extra mileage to tread on history.

It was easy to recognize we were approaching Groom for two reasons. First its location is distinctly marked by a huge white cross. My guess is that the cross is close to 50 feet high and 30 wide, with the cross bar at least four feet in diameter.

The second indicator of the town's location: As with most small towns we saw in the Midwest, the telltale threesome of water tower, grain elevators, trees.

As I came into town, a sign told me the population is 613. The most bustling business in town was Alstrup's, a chain combination gas station/convenience store. My reaction to the big, sturdily built school in town was, good tornado shelter.

The most unexpected or surprising sight of the day came a couple miles east of Groom when I saw, about a quarter-mile off the road, an eye-catching mansion. I mean the place looked like a small hotel. Tudor architecture, if I had it identified correctly.

This guy seemed to be making a statement: "I'll live out here but on my own terms."

The other oddity about this building, other than this location, was that, despite its being in this farming area, not a single out building anywhere near it. It stood alone, a majestic mansion.

The day's entertainment was provided by truckers on the CB radio. And Elaine got an earful that she reported to me. They were talking about the old gray-haired guy running on the road.

She heard one trucker who'd seen her walking the dogs say, "He sure has a young chick for a wife." Made her day.

A couple of truckers were kind enough to say, "I'd like to be able to do that when I'm that old."

"You know, one of them said, "I don't want to get gray hair."

"You can dye it," was the reply.

Hearing that, I thought, Hey, fellas, better get your priorities straight. Gray hair and health are better than dyed locks and unhealthy.

Even at my last pit-stop Elaine reported the truckers were still talking about the old man running. One of them asked, "What's he doing out there in this weather anyway?"

Another: "He looks like the homeless type."

If proof was needed that I looked pitiful, it came near the end of my day when a lady driver, taking pity on me, pulled up alongside me and asked, "Do you need a ride?"

"No, but thank you very much for stopping," I said before explaining our mission.

"Well, ordinarily I don't stop," she said. More confirmation that I looked downright pitiful.

We talked briefly. I learned her name was Joan Graham and that she was on her way to a weekend at Greenbelt Lake. As she drove off, I again thought that I must indeed look a forlorn figure out here for this middle-aged lady traveling by herself to be brave enough to stop and offer help.

DAY SEVEN. Again the day started windy, chilly, overcast, temperature in the 40s, steadily climbing until it hit the low 80s. And once again I enjoyed the tranquillity and monopoly of Route 66 while 30 yards away on I-40 frenzied drivers raced the clock and jockeyed for road space.

There was some variation in scenery when I passed through the hamlet of Allenreed and the town of McLean. The most noteworthy aspect of Allenreed was that the area was lined with more trees than I had seen in the past 15 miles. The same was true of McLean, an area overflowing with trees – this contrasting distinctly with the grasslands, treeless for the most part.

Ironic, I thought, that this town so small, population only 849, had one-way streets. McLean was a typical Route 66 town in that it had a lot of unburied bodies (cafes, motels, gas stations, souvenir shops) from the heyday of 66.

I was told the town had a German POW camp during World War II but saw no evidence of it. I was also told that at one time it was referred to as "the uplift city" because of its being the location of a women's undergarment factory. McLean impressed me as a town still struggling to survive after the demise of Route 66 and after being bypassed by I-40.

Fell to thinking of two friends today. The first was Bobby Richardson. In my grammar school days Bobby was my summer companion when I came home from boarding school to Richardson Springs, where my mother worked.

Since the Richardsons owned the resort, the living was easy for Bobby and me – ponies, swimming pool, tennis courts, hiking trails, billiards. I still recall the racket we had with the *Saturday Evening Post*.

Only a limited supply of the magazine arrived at the Springs every week. Demand by guests far exceeded supply.

As a result Bobby and I, monopolistic owners of the *Post* concession, catered to the big tippers. We were able to get anywhere from 25 to 50 cents for this five-cent magazine.

My mother left the Springs when I started high school, and I saw Bobby (now Bob) only a couple times since. Close friends, they do drift apart.

The other person I thought about was Mike van Horn. The last time I saw him, he was 39 years old, seemingly vibrant, and he shocked me when he told me he had lung cancer.

It seemed inconceivable. Here was a guy who never smoked, who was an All-American cross-country runner in college. Less than six months after our meeting, he was dead, leaving a wife and two kids in high school. Thank God the whole family was bolstered by strong religious beliefs.

And the question that loomed for me again today was: Why am I out here at 79 and Mike is in his grave at 39? The man had so much more to give than I. Or maybe that was the answer: He had already given enough.

DAY EIGHT. When Elaine and I crawled out of our warm bed at five o'clock this brisk morning, I said, referring to our run, "Are you sure we're smart doing this?"

She thought about it a moment, then answered, "Well, it would be pretty humdrum around the house compared to this."

T.S. Eliot put it another way when he said, "Old men should be explorers." Well, as far as this Texas exploration went, I was beginning to feel pretty good, seven days down, one to go.

Just prior to starting Texas, I was apprehensive about being able to run across five states this summer, mainly because of my antiquity and because of my low mileage, less than a six-mile daily average over the past four months. Now with Texas almost in the bag, I felt confident we would complete our runs across the other four states on this current excursion.

The major attraction of the day was seeing the town of Shamrock, 7.5 miles into our day. As indicated by the name Best Western *Irish* Inn, the town is overboard with its Irish connection – the high school teams are "the fighting Irish," the school colors are green and white, the town name is painted in green on the water tower, and the town was named in honor of an Irish sheep rancher.

From what I saw, I was disappointed in Shamrock. It seemed to lack the vitality I've seen in towns of less population. I was surprised to learn that Shamrock contains some of the largest gas reserves in the USA.

The trucker chatter on the CB provided a heap of entertainment for Elaine again today. They kept referring to the local deputy sheriffs as the "county mounties" and to the Highway Patrol as "two stripers." They also kept asking each other for information about locations of police as they tried to get away with driving 80 to 85 MPH.

The big CB item today related to the tragic crash of the Valujet DC 9 in Florida. Approaching the Oklahoma border, only two miles or so away, they talked about outrunning the Texas troopers to the border. They talked considerably about how they liked Oklahoma and New Mexico but not Texas because it was strict in law enforcement. They had also passed word that the old man was finishing his Texas run today, and as a result during my last few miles a number of drivers tooted to me.

Remembering this was Sunday, I spent a few minutes, as is my habit on the Sabbath while on the road, focusing on religion. I thought of something I'd recently read, an account by a person who had a near-death experience and claimed to have seen Christ.

"What have you done with your life?" was the question Christ asked him. The man then named a couple of important accomplishments, and Christ answered, "But that glorified you."

Got me to thinking about what have I done with my life that has benefited people, made the world a better place to live. The conclusion was that I could use a lot more blue ink on that side of the ledger to balance off the load of red ink on the other side of the ledger.

Nearing the end of my day and Texas, I reviewed the adventure;

• During my 180.5 miles across the state, only one Texan stopped to offer help. Does that jibe with the state motto, "The Friendly State"?

• I talked with only one police officer, state trooper Gary Davis.

• Total wildlife seen amounted to two rattlesnakes, one skunk, one raccoon, one coyote, all dead, and a couple of rambunctious rabbits very much alive. Considering how uninviting the terrain was, the scarcity of wildlife was understandable. In fact, considering what they have to endure, the prairie cattle might even welcome a trip to McDonald Land.

• I found a total of seven cents and nothing else. Slimmest pickings of any state.

• The best part of the entire adventure was revisiting Route 66 and enjoying the tranquillity and monopoly of this road and of treading on history.

• All told, Texas was much easier than anticipated. Road conditions, availability of RV facilities, weather, were all better than expected. The threat of a tornado was the only major concern we had.

Elated when I reached the Oklahoma border, I told Elaine, "I'll sing a chorus of 'Oklahoma' if you want."

Since even George Burns would have ranked on par with Pavarotti compared to my singing, it was understandable to hear her say, "If you so much as open your mouth, you'll never get another root beer float when you finish your day's run."

Since I was already drooling over the float she was holding for me, I grabbed it and obediently maintained silence. So it was that we headed towards Louisiana without any musical accompaniment – and without any reason for the dogs to howl!

Overview of
LOUISIANA
May 15th to 24th, 1996
204.5 miles

Day	Overnight	Miles	Notes
1	Shreveport	17.0	introduction to Highway 80
2	Princeton	21.0	passage through Shreveport
3	Princeton	21.0	a tourist in Minden
4	Arcadia	22.0	tales of Bonnie and Clyde
5	Monroe	21.0	Ruston and Louisiana Tech University
6	Monroe	21.0	attacked by dogs
7	Rayville	21.5	Monroe and Northeast Louisiana University
8	Rayville	21.5	"white gold of South" territory
9	Vicksburg, MS	21.5	Tallulah ain't no lady
10	Greenville, MS	17.0	crossing the Mississippi again

Chapter 12

Louisiana:

Bayous, Boondocks, Bonnie and Clyde

DAY ONE. Louisiana was a puzzle. When I studied the state map, the shortest, most direct route across the state appeared to be Interstate 20. That route was my choice until the Department of Transportation told me pedestrians were not allowed on I-20.

I wrote to a friend, Maurice Raphael, who lives in Bestrop, Louisiana, for information. Maurice and I were classmates when we went through Marine officer training in 1941 and in 1954 when students at the Marine Corps Amphibious Warfare University. Maurice said, "Are you aware that you can run on Highway 80 that more or less parallels I-20? Highway 80 was the main west/east highway in northern Louisiana until it was replaced with I-20."

No, Maurice, I was not aware, and thank you. Our route across the state on Highway 80 started at the Texas/Louisiana border at a spot distinguishable only by the boundary markers. We would be on 80 until we finished in Vicksburg, Mississippi.

Starting, I immediately noticed the contrasts from our Texas run. In Texas, plains, grass, deserted Route 66 and just me on the road. In Louisiana, heavy traffic, businesses, residences, blaring boom boxes. From tranquillity to turmoil. Another contrast from west Texas was the heavy Louisiana forestation on both sides of the road for much of the day. As I looked at the forestation, I concluded the only way through it would be by using a machete to clear a path.

I had a momentary problem with dogs today, a pack of eight of them on the road. Six backed off when I yelled, "Stay!" When the other two kept coming, I had the presence of mind to remember I was in the South, so I yelled, "Stay, y'all!" And they then obeyed.

Elaine was in a different world all day. She was busy trying to assemble a new CB radio she had purchased. She was anxious to get back on the air and to listen to the trucker chatter.

Going past a sign telling me I was entering Caddo Parish, I thought, Well, that is one thing I do know about Louisiana. It's the only state that has parishes instead of counties.

Thinking about it, I was aware I really didn't know much about the state. Sure, I knew about the Mardi Gras and the French Quarter in New Orleans, knew about the Superdome and the Saints, about the state being the birthplace of jazz, about the antics of Huey Long, and about the Louisiana Purchase (one hell of a real estate deal). Which meant that just about everything that unfolded in Louisiana would be a learning experience.

I talked with only two people all day and both within the first five miles. A lady, waiting with her son for a school bus, told me school would be in session until the end of the month.

Charlie Elliott, a senior citizen driving a pickup, asked if I needed help. When I told him my wife was driving a motorhome and pit-crewing for me, he said, "Hope you enjoy your motorhome as much as we enjoy ours. Well, I just felt obliged to stop and see if you were all right." And with those words he drove off.

At around 15 miles when I began to edge into the western perimeter of Shreveport, the heavy traffic forced me to run the sidewalks. In this area I began to see evidence of the heyday and demise of Highway 80 as the main route across this part of the state. We decided to stop at 17 miles, because if we went farther we would be surrounded by traffic in downtown Shreveport. Elaine's big accomplishment of the day was to get her CB to function. Mine was to simply launch Louisiana by plodding through an unglamorous day.

DAY TWO. The first 10 miles of passage through the Shreveport/ Bossier areas kept this from being a humdrum day. All along the way I was gawking, and the sights took my mind off miles and time.

Striving to beat the downtown traffic, we were on the road shortly before six A.M. I'd gone less than a quarter-mile when I came across a black guy, mid 50s I'd guess, carrying a golf club for protection. I asked myself, What in hell am I doing out here?

Trudging through this questionable area, at about one mile I went past the Shreveport/Bossier Shelter and saw three big guys standing out in front. Felt a bit nervous and reminded myself I was built for flight, not fight. Then I almost rejoiced when one of them said, "Good morning, Sir!"

Nonetheless, must admit to being a bit apprehensive when two of them crossed the street and followed me through a three-block section where every storefront was deserted and boarded. Turned out they were on their way to the Rescue Mission where I saw a dining room full of people.

A bit of humor in this rough area, though, as I passed a fenced area with a sign, "Guard dogs on duty." Two dogs came to the fence, wagged their tails and exuded friendliness. I gave each a piece of the Powerbar I was munching, and they seemed delighted.

Two sights were commonplace in Shreveport: Every church, and there were a goodly number, had a historical marker in front of it. And many businesses had AR-LA-TX in their names, this stemming from northeast Texas, southwest Arkansas and Louisiana being joined at the hip.

Our timing was excellent, because we were out of downtown Shreveport before the influx of traffic. Actually once we crossed the Huey P. Long/Governor O.J. Allen Bridge over the Red River we were out of the Shreveport buildup area.

The Bossier area, contiguous to Shreveport, was ricky ticky – at least that part that I could see along Highway 80. Pawn shops, convenience stores, vacant store fronts and reminders of the demise of Highway 80, such as motels, bars, restaurants.

By 10 miles I was once again out in the boondocks with foliage on both sides of the road. Most of the time I was limited to running the grassy shoulder. The speed limit was 45 MPH, but the motorists drove as if they were heathens fleeing the Crusaders.

I had to do several wind sprints in the area in order to get across a half-dozen bridges 30 to 40 yards long – necessary to beat approaching cars. Since I was having a bad asthma day, they were not helpful.

Around 10.5 miles Highway 80 dipped under I-20. Shortly after it did, unfolding in front of me was the Louisiana Downs Racetrack. Even at this early morning hour cars were pouring into the parking lot.

Horse racing unleashed a flood of memories. My baptism into pari-mutuel betting came when I went to Hollywood Park, bet $2 on a horse named Iron Maiden that won and paid $88. Hooked!

Memories also popped to mind of summer employment as a college student selling pari-mutuel tickets at the State Fair races and the suspenseful moments after each race when our accounts were balanced and we had to pay for any shortages. Present day, my horse racing has been limited to reading a half -dozen of Dick Francis' novels with the sport as background.

I paused, around 15 miles, to talk with a guy named Richard Saunders who was repairing a culvert. Wearing only swimming trunks, a ball cap and no shoes, he was shoveling dirt out of a pickup bed. It was his ball cap that caused me to stop.

"I'm curious," I said. "Why are you wearing a 49er cap?"

His reply: "Because I used to live in California and there's no pro team near here that I like." He went on to tell me that he liked living in this area because of the low cost of living and because it was considerably less crowded than California.

In the last five miles we went through two small towns, Merry Woods and Princeton. Neither was overwhelming. Merry Woods had only a bank, gas station and elementary school; Princeton, a post office and used car lot.

The best thing that happened to us all day was discovering the Hilltop RV

Park in a delightful setting under pine trees and beside a small lake. The highlight of the evening for Elaine occurred when she took the dogs for a walk in the woods.

As they began to return to the motorhome a small fawn, showing no fear of the dogs or Elaine, started to follow them. Elaine got the impression that the fawn wanted to be adopted, but it scooted away once Elaine and the dogs reached the activity of the RV park area.

DAY THREE. Hundreds of people have the capability to run across the country or run across states as I have. They may even have the desire. But what they can't harness is the will power and unflinching resolve to do it.

Then, conversely, there are those who believe like the wheelchair athlete who, at a recent meeting of the Governor's Council on Physical Fitness and Sports (to which I'm a consultant), "Running across states like you do, I think you're in need of a psychiatrist."

We talked a while, and I tried to explain to this athlete (ye gods, he participates in wheelchair rugby!) reasons other than sheer enjoyment for my running. When I talked about being able to take time out from the daily cycle to meditate and think about life while running, I saw him light up.

"Well, I can understand that," he said. "About all I did for 10 years after my accident was to think about life. Meditate, I guess."

A variety of things remained static in today's run: The hot, humid weather, temperature in the high 80s prevailed; the road continued to be lined with thick forestation on both sides, except when we went through towns; no police officers looked in on us; we did not see any live wildlife, and Baptist churches continued to dot the landscape, but I could recall the names of only two (James Baptist and Antioch Baptist); no other denominations did I see, nor did we have any exciting experiences.

All told, this was sort of a yeoman day as we plowed through 21 miles, bringing our Louisiana total to 59 miles. The three diversions along the route were going through the towns of Fillmore, Dixie Inn and Minden.

After Fillmore and Dixie Inn, neither with more than 400 people, Minden, population almost 14,000 looked metropolitan. Maybe that population accounted for Smith's Marine Sales having an inventory of more than 100 boats with motors. The inventory indicated, in turn, that fishing and boating are big in these parts.

When I entered Minden, a sign told me it was voted Louisiana's cleanest city in 1983. This pilgrim's odyssey through town told me things have changed in the 14 years since, as evidenced by debris all over the streets and sidewalks.

Around 17 miles I went past one of the best residential areas yet encountered in Louisiana, and as I did so I met Jason Holloway, a high school sophomore out to pick up the family mail.

Jason told me he plans to attend Northeast Louisiana University in Monroe and that his brother would graduate from there tonight. In the 10-minute conversation we had, he interjected more "sirs" than a Marine Corps boot. What is it, I asked, that makes southern kids so respectful of age?

I had occasion today to think about O.J. Simpson, because yesterday's paper reported he had found religion. If you believe that, let me tell you that I am running six-minute miles out here, and along the way I am wrestling with a few alligators.

The nearest RV park, 18 miles away, had the glamorous (?) name of Bonnie and Clyde RV Park. We were lucky to get housed there, because the area was hosting the Bonnie and Clyde Trade Days that involved a hundred or more concessionaires selling such wares as antiques, jewelry, crafts, Bonnie and Clyde souvenirs, farm equipment and much more.

I was curious about how Bonnie and Clyde got tied into all this, but at the moment not curious enough to take the time and energy to find out.

DAY FOUR. A first in Louisiana today when a state trooper stopped to check on us as Elaine was parked for the three-mile pit-stop. When I left the motorhome to greet him, his first words were, "I just want to make sure you are not broken down."

I told him what we were up to, then pumped him for information dear to my heart: "What kind of poisonous snakes do you have hereabouts?" I refrained from adding, " ... that I might step on in the grass."

"Water moccasins, coral, copperheads and rattlesnakes," he replied. A depressing litany for me.

"I guess the rattler would be the most common one I'd see on the road?" I asked.

"No, the copperhead probably."

Still probing, I said, "Haven't seen any wildlife in the last 50 miles. I thought this was supposed to be the sportsman's paradise?"

"I don't know where all the deer are. They should be around."

The trooper sprinkled our 10-minute conversation that followed with a delightful southern accent and a heap of "sirs." Athletic in appearance, neat, well groomed and polite, he contrasted 180 degrees from the image of the southern police officer typically depicted in Hollywood movies.

Snake! roared my eyeballs a little later in the day. Pump went the adrenaline. Pop went the goose pimples. And just as quickly the snake slithered across the highway, through the grass and down the embankment.

Snakes got into the act again at the three-mile pit-stop when Elaine reported a trucker CB conversation she had listened in on.

A couple of truckers were talking about snakes and one said, "Snakes don't scare me, but spiders sure in hell do. I saw one in my living room last week and got scared as hell.

"You know what, I think I'm the only guy who ever shot a spider in his living room with a 12-gauge shotgun. Made one helluva mess!"

I got some insight to the Bonnie and Clyde thing when I went through the town of Gibsland. As I came to the downtown street, I saw the only modern building was the Gibsland Bank and Trust Company and that most of the brick store front buildings were defunct.

Then I saw the street was barricaded and that I had to detour on the truck route. Encountering a farmer, Phillip Hale, in town with his kids, I asked about the barricade.

"Oh, there's a Bonnie and Clyde festival," he said. "They have it every year. Gibsland is the first place that Bonnie and Clyde were brought after being shot. They were put on public display here."

I asked him, "Exactly where were Bonnie and Clyde shot?"

"Out on Route 154, about five miles south of Lebanon and just a few miles from here. There's a monument out there that marks the exact spot where they were ambushed in 1934."

I had not known that Clyde Barrow and Bonnie Parker were placed on public display. A grisly display it must have been, if I could believe another story I had read.

In one robbery the pair had taken a hostage who turned out to be a mortician. They released the hostage on one condition: that when they were killed (they had vowed never to be taken alive) he would restore them and "make us look good." Subsequently the mortician, hearing of their deaths, tried to keep his part of the bargain but could not because the bodies were beyond salvage.

DAY FIVE. There are times when I feel our days consist of the same rituals and routines just transposed from one setting to another, from one time frame to another. Every morning we go through the same routine of unhooking the motorhome and navigating to the start. Then we busy ourselves logging 21 miles punctuated with three-mile pit-stops.

The running day completed, we attend to any necessary logistics, locate an RV park and settle in for the night. In between rising and retiring lurks a sense of adventure – gawking and seeing country we've never seen before; going past a mansion and wondering how the residents sustain this type of living; passing a shack and pitying the people there in squalor; putting my foot in the grass and wondering if I'll antagonize a snake; being constantly aware of the weather; meeting people and hearing the tales they have to tell; never ceasing to wonder what we will see around the next corner.

The weirdest happening of the day was a trucker CB conversation that Elaine heard.

First trucker: "Is that girl in that car being raped? That's too bad."

Second: "She's stark naked. What da ya know!"

As the truck passed the moving car, the truckers continued to speculate as to what was happening and continued on without taking any action. Welcome to the USA, 1996!

The major diversion of the day was passage through Ruston, a community of 20,000 or so. Ruston was adorned with many of the stellar symbols of American culture – Taco Bell, Burger King, McDonald's, Baskin Robbins, Kentucky Fried Chicken, donut shops.

I took note that the main drag in town is called California Avenue and that the downtown section was quite active and minus any vacated buildings. Perhaps the main distinction of Ruston is that it is home to Louisiana Tech University.

The only other town I went through was Simsboro, population close to 700. From what I saw, I got the impression housing here was of three types: shacks, mobile homes, mansions. Facilities were limited to a combination gas station/convenience store, a Baptist church, hair salon and an elementary school.

Today being Sunday, I held my usual on-the-road church services. Rather than focus on one subject religious, I let my thoughts wander to an array of subjects pertaining to religion.

One thought: When a person is raised in one religion, it is hard when he comes to maturity to broaden his horizons wide enough to see the limitations and constrictions of that religion. Or, to put it another way, to concede that other religions may be as valid as his.

These days, as far as religions are concerned, I feel sure about one thing: I concede that all people adhering to any religion have an equal opportunity for heaven, eternal salvation, or call it what you will.

As the Indian chief Seattle said, "One thing we know, which the white man may one day discover, our God is the same God. He is the God of man and His compassion is equal for the red man and the white."

Another thought: I have come to recognize that people who are immersed in religion, absolutely convinced theirs is the way, are generally happier than those who dabble with religion.

And I concluded services with some radical thinking. The essence was: Why would God who created man want any man damned for eternity? For a man to be lost would be painful to the God who created him.

And as I thought about that, I concluded this was one damn strong argument for reincarnation: People keep coming back to earth until they get it right and are then qualified for heaven. If I understand reincarnation correctly, it is actually the kindest of spiritual doctrines.

After we finished our 21-mile day, we drove to the Shilo RV Park in Monroe where we ran smack into a comedy of errors. We proceeded to the spot that the manager assigned us, only to find it was already occupied.

Returning to the office, we got another assigned spot and once again after arriving there we found it taken. On our third try we found the spot taken over by a flock of geese. I told the manager, "Our dogs will eat those geese."

His reply was, "I don't give a damn if they do."

We balked, knowing the dogs would go absolutely berserk if turned loose near the geese. Since there was no other RV park nearby to which we could retreat, I resorted to diplomacy by telling the manager I could understand all the confusion since he was so busy.

As we talked, I detected he had been drinking, so I extended my diplomacy by offering tea and sympathy. Mission successful, because he said, "You go find an empty spot that you like, and then come back and tell me the number."

DAY SIX. The most dramatic incident of this day happened around mile

17 on the western outskirts of the city of West Monroe. Abstractly wondering about what I'd see in there, I paid no attention to the dogs barking nearby. Suddenly I was startled by two dogs emerging from the bushes five yards away, barking furiously and charging toward me from behind. I yelled "Stay!" "Git!" and a volley of other commands, but they kept heading toward me, snarling.

When within two or three feet, they started snapping, trying to bite me. Attempting to avoid them, I jumped about like a jitterbug dancer of the 1940s and at the same time shouting to them and looking about frantically for a weapon. My shouting, arm waving and kicking did confuse them a bit, but they were not dissuaded. Avoiding them, I was now in the traffic lane and worried about approaching cars, and at the same time trying to think of what I could use for a weapon. I was almost certain they would attack.

I did have the presence of mind to note that I was dealing with a couple of mongrels and not, thank God, a German Shepherd, a Doberman or a Pit Bull. And I also noticed that some drivers were detouring around me, paying little attention to my plight.

Damn dogs aren't going to keep retreating every time I kick in their direction, I told myself. I've got to think of something or they're going to bite me – maybe several times. As my hand brushed my fanny pack, I got an idea.

In one quick motion I unbuckled the pack and started swinging it as a weapon, knowing that the cassette recorder and filled water bottle in it hitting a dog might deter him. As a car came close, distracting one of the dogs, I was able to forcefully swing the pack, and the cassette recorder hit him in the area of an ear. He yelped and, trying to keep him scared, I waved the pack again. It worked because he started to run off and his companion, who had been backing away, decided to scamper off after him.

Today for the first time since day one that I got an offer of help. The Good Samaritan's name was Jeff Chandler, and he said he lived near Calhoun but worked in Ruston.

"Jeff Chandler, wasn't there a movie star by that name?" I asked him.

"Yes, and I've taken a lot of kidding because of it. But I'm not him."

"How do you like living in this area?"

"Enjoy it very much. Don't think I would want to be anyplace else."

Strange that, no matter where I am when I ask that question, about 90 percent of the respondents seem content to be living where they are.

After finishing in West Monroe, and because we had no other choice, we returned to the Shilo RV Park where we had troubles last night. Again, Mickey Mouse.

First we were assigned to a spot which we found already taken. At a second spot we started to hook up and found it had no sewer drain.

I hot-footed it to the office (just what I needed after a 21-mile day) and said, "Enough!" A young guy who seemed to know what he was doing took over and located us in a spot that was vacant and functional.

In two nights at this RV park we had more problems than we have had combined when dealing with 200 or more other RV parks. Despite its inefficiency, the place was operating at a 90-percent occupancy rate. What's the expression? "They came out smelling like a rose."

DAY SEVEN. The big deal today was seeing the city of Monroe. Among other things, I learned that Monroe sits on the Ouachita River. Formidable knowledge considering that until today I did not even know there was an Ouachita River, despite its being more than 600 miles long. Negotiating my way through the area was not easy. Alternately I was running through store lots, in grass or on narrow sidewalks in dire need of repair.

A few things I could not help but notice: Catfish Cabin Restaurant extended over an entire city block; though the city had a population of only 12,000 a Wal-Mart was located on both the west and east ends; in one five-mile stretch I saw 15 pawn shops.

The most uplifting sight in Monroe was Northeast Louisiana University. As I went past the university grounds, wending my way eastward along Highway 80, I kept expecting to see a sign identifying the university. But there was none.

The only sign I saw on the sprawling campus was one pointing to the stadium. The many old brick buildings and the new 14-story (if my count was right) dormitory added to the appeal of the campus. At its east boundary the campus was joined by a small lake.

Just as I passed the campus, I caught sight of an historical marker and small cemetery, fence enclosed and only about 20 yards by 35 yards in size. I detoured across the street to check it out.

The oldest grave was that of a sergeant who had fought in the Revolutionary War. Attesting to the short lifespan of the times, mid-1800s, were graves of people in their 20s, 30s and 40s.

I was nine miles into my day before I emerged from the built-up area. Out into the boondocks and noticing an 80-percent drop in traffic, I said, The road is all mine. C'mon, feet, get moving.

But they refused to change gears. This was a low-energy day, and I had to force myself down the road. One way to do this was by thinking of something besides the running. So I dwelled on an item some columnist had written about the 10 finest things in life. She listed:

"1. Dawn.
"2. Silent church before service begins.
"3. Love of a little child.
"4. The moment just before one is being sure of being loved.
"5. The moment of rescue from danger
"6. The understanding between friends.
"7. The mountains, the desert, and the sea.
"8. Two aged lovers going down the hill of life together.
"9. First love
"10. The joy of existence."

At first reading the list sounded pretty good. But the more I mulled it, the more I found fault with it.

For one thing it lumped together people and things – two separate considerations, to me at least. I had other objections. "First love" can be puppy love and, moreover, some second relationships are finer than firsts.

Next I wondered how a "silent church" ever got on the list. And I asked, is the understanding between friends finer than that between two people in love? How can dawn be listed and majestic sunsets omitted? Yeah, two aged lovers going down the hill of life together can be a beautiful happening, but not if they are both semi-vegetative and rusting away in a convalescent home.

If these are truly the finest things is life, where is mention of someone sacrificing his life for his country or to save another human being? That would be number one on my list.

Oh, what the hell, it was only a list. I must be getting to be a real curmudgeon to assail it. Hey, move over, Andy Rooney!

DAY EIGHT. Our route today took us through five communities, the most noteworthy of which was Rayville, population around 4500. The city sign read, "Welcome to Rayville, white gold capital of the south." A half-dozen large cotton sheds with many cotton trailers parked beside them gave evidence of that. Rayville is bracketed between Highway 80 on the north and I-20 on the south. When we drove through the town on our way to today's start, I found it hard to distinguish it from many small California towns. In fact, one large home of Spanish architecture smacked more of my home state than of Louisiana.

Rayville had two faces. The buildings sitting directly on Highway 90, many with vacant storefronts, seemed with a couple of exceptions to have died about 20 years ago. The second face, the downtown section, appeared to be doing a brisk business.

Elaine and I each had a people encounter today. Hers occurred when she was parked on a levee road for a pit-stop. A lady came out from her house across the street and told Elaine to park in her yard where it would be safer.

After Elaine explained what we were up to, the lady told her we could overnight in a vacant mobile home on her property if we desired. Elaine politely declined, telling the lady we would be down the road too far. In the conversation the lady told Elaine something she had heard from people in other states: "I'd never want to live in California. Too many earthquakes."

My encounter was with Theo McNeil, manager of the Holly Ridge Rice Plant. We met when he stopped at the plant entrance on Highway 80. In our 10-minute conversation I found out that one million bushels of rice were stored in the plant's bins.

I kiddingly asked if any of it was Uncle Ben's, and the joke was on me because some of it was. He told me that rice planting was down this year because many of the farmers went to corn, since it was paying a higher price than rice. He said there were no problems with irrigation in this area, since it was so close to the Mississippi.

I could not resist asking about alligators. He told me that some are about in the bayous, but they do not wander onto the highways.

On the sociological front I had a few questions today: Why are the drivers to the east of Monroe more courteous and considerate than those to the west? Why are there no sloppy yards and considerably less litter to the east of Monroe? How can the plethora of Baptist churches be supported by such a small population base? So many questions. So few answers.

In the evening when we went to dinner at the restaurant beside the Cottonland Motel and RV Park, I could have predicted Elaine would order the catfish. I settled for a rib eye steak, ordered medium rare and delivered cremated – which sort of tied in with the kind of a day I'd had.

DAY NINE. Last night I took inventory and confirmed that I have between 39 and 40 miles left to finish Louisiana. It never fails that when I have but a couple of days left I'm injected with a surge of energy and strength. And so it was today as I steadily jogged through 21.5 miles.

Despite my moving along steadily and strongly, the going was not without problems. For one thing I dared not plow into the 18-inch grassy shoulder, since I could not tell what lurked beneath it by way of surface – snakes, rocks, glass and other booby traps. My evasive action was to run to the other side of the road whenever a car approached, and this in turn demanded extra distance and energy.

The humidity hit harder because there was not a whisper of a wind. Another irritation was a muscle strain in my left calf for which I tried to compensate by wearing an elastic wrap over it.

My problems today brought on the thought that running across a state has one aspect of combat: When you are in it, it's a survival process and tough. But once it's over it does not seem so bad and you forget some of the fine points that made it so tough.

All day I talked with only two people. One was a native parked on a levee near where Elaine had stopped for a pit-stop. While parked, Elaine saw movement in the water and, grabbing her binoculars, saw two snakes swimming across the water. They appeared to be water moccasins.

After leaving the pit-stop there and getting back on the road, I told a man, "My wife saw two snakes swimming across that river."

His answer: "It's not a river. It's a runaway bayou." End of conversation.

The other encounter occurred when I was a mile or so away from Tallulah. A woman driving a Plymouth Voyager stopped to say she had seen me running through Delhi and asked if I would give an interview if a newspaper friend of hers was interested in writing about our run. I agreed but told her the reporter would have to track Elaine or me down on the road.

Then before departing she cautioned, "You watch yourself going through Tallulah. You could run into trouble if you are not careful."

When I'd seen Tallulah on the map, the name fascinated me. Was this city named after Tallulah Bankhead, famous actress and daughter or niece (I couldn't recall which) of a Speaker of the House of Representatives? Probably not named after her, since the Speaker was from Alabama.

My initial impression of Tallulah, the town, was that it could euphemistically be described as a dump. Entering, I went past about 15 shanties, all in various states of disrepair and with litter-strewn yards.

The Tallulah Correctional Facility for Youth was located mid-town. The fences with razor toppings extended to the edge of the city sidewalks.

Just east of town the story differed. Here I saw lovely homes, some just short of being mansions, many sitting on the river bank, and all with expansive grass yards. Nearby was a neat shopping center.

The only elevating sight all day was the community of comfortable homes here on the eastern edge of Tallulah. Typical of the day was the shack seen in my first mile with eight dogs running about the yard and yakking, leaving me to wonder how these folks can feed these eight dogs when it appears they can't afford to feed themselves.

I did something unusual today. I took time out to talk with the dead. I guess I got into this because there was not much to see on the road and because I wanted to disassociate from running. I told my mother how much I loved and appreciated her and how I wished I had taken more moments when she was alive to express this love and appreciation. I told my first wife, June, who died from cancer, what a great job she had done raising our three children and how proud she would be of them today. I said hello to Dub Carter, a devout Mormon and high school coach, whose hobby was cooking. And I let him know that Elaine and I missed the gourmet cheesecake he always gave us at Christmas. I thanked Brother Pius of the Christian Brothers for the guidance he gave me through three formative years of high school during which he turned my life around and was the closest person I had to a father figure.

"Not fair, Ben," I said to Marion Benedetti, fellow Marine and educator. Ben survived the Pacific War, winning a Navy Cross in the process, only to die from cancer in his early 50s at a time when he had much to live for.

From the sadness of Mike and Ben to a blossoming smile as, while thinking about death, I wondered how many girlfriends of years past were still alive, and if so what did they look like? Then I realized I was talking about ladies I had not seen in 60 or so years.

I could visualize them only as they were in their youthful years, meaning we could probably pass on the street and not recognize each other. From the blossoming smile to the sobering thought that I will be in deep doo-doo when Elaine finds out I've been thinking about past girlfriends.

DAY 10. Getting underway, I was elated to be finishing Louisiana, but only a bit so because there was the deflating thought that I had another 700 miles to go to finish South Dakota, North Dakota and Minnesota this summer. I had mixed emotions about getting five days off before we started South Dakota. Afraid mostly that I'd ease out of a running mood and mode.

The five days were necessary because we would spend two driving to Arkansas to visit a friend, Ray Mahannah, then a day with Ray, followed by two more to drive to the South Dakota start. Ray had worked with Hal Stainbrook and me for 20 years directing races in California. Last year he migrated to Arkansas. In his college days Ray was one of the best distance runners in the country. Several times he raced against Glenn Cunningham, the mile record holder, in Madison Square Garden.

To many people of my generation Cunningham was an inspiration, because as a boy whose legs were badly burned in a fire he was told he might never walk again. From that diagnosis he went on to hold the world record for the mile longer than any other runner ever has.

The scenery today consisted of seeing swampy water on both sides of the road and, if not that, fields under cultivation. It was a bit difficult at times to mosey straight down the road when my eyeballs were flashing right and left to keep the swampy water under surveillance.

I could not help but be aware of how much the humidity intensifies the stench of dead animals, such as armadillos, on the road. Sort of remindful of Bougainville patrols when we passed by, sometimes even over, dead Japanese bodies putrefying in the tropical heat.

The best entertainment I got all day was from watching a crop duster at work. I admired his flying, sharp turns, low passes over trees and fields, steep ascents to avoid trees and wires. I found myself thinking, This guy is probably getting less than $500 for this skill and for risking his life, whereas some chicken plucker who can warble a tune is getting $50,000 for a one-night stand or some basketball dunker is getting $30,000 for one game.

As I neared the end of my day, I took stock of what had happened and not happened in Louisiana. Notably I had run across the entire state wearing only a T-shirt and shoes – and, oh yeah, shorts – never once resorting to a windbreaker or sweats. That was a first for any state. Never once did it rain, putting Louisiana in a class with Texas, the only other state rainless when we ran across it. Once again I had worn racing flats, an 8.5-ounce shoe as opposed to heavier training shoes, across the entire state. Traveling through many swampy areas, I had expected to be devoured by mosquitoes, but not even one descended on me. Why their absence, I wondered?

And I decided I must be maturing (or could I be getting chicken?) because not once in Louisiana did I stand my ground on the highway and challenge a driver. Instead I took refuge in the grassy shoulder.

The battle plan after we parted at Delta on the Louisiana side of the Mississippi was that we would rendezvous at the Vicksburg Tourist Center on the other side of the bridge. Traffic on the bridge was practically non-existent, and the transit was a cakewalk.

All I could remember about Vicksburg was Grant's line, "I propose to fight it out on this line if it takes all summer," and the long siege of it by the Unionists in the Civil War. At the Tourist Information Center I picked up a brochure that told me quite a bit more. The shocker was learning that 16,650 Union soldiers are buried at the Vicksburg cemetery and, even more shocking, that 12,800 of these graves are marked "unknown."

Our only regret today was that we could not celebrate our finish in our usual manner – by having dinner out. To paraphrase Robert Frost, we had miles to go before we could eat.

Overview of
SOUTH DAKOTA
May 31st to June 10th, 1996
235.5 miles

Day	Overnight	Miles	Notes
1	Yankton	23.0	passage through Yankton
2	Salem	21.1	towns of Freeman and Marion
3	Salem	21.0	rain all day
4	Madison	21.0	chat with Bob Holman
5	Madison	21.0	Madison and Dan Bole; nice place, nice guy
6	Lake Poinsett	21.0	"Toughy" – and it fits!
7	Watertown	21.1	another rainy day
8	South Shore	21.0	onto Interstate 29
9	Sisseton	22.0	"a real Forrest Gump there"
10	Sisseton	22.0	"one will be taken"
11	Ortonville, MN	21.0	hottest and last day in SD

Chapter 13

South Dakota:

Nice People, Nasty Weather

DAY ONE. I really didn't know much about South Dakota, but what I did know I liked. For one thing we should not have to worry about crime, since only two other states have a lower crime rate. For another we should not have to worry about overcrowding anyplace, because 44 other states have a larger population.

Also I had it on good authority (a forest ranger) that no rattlesnakes would be in this eastern section of South Dakota. "They stay to the west of the Missouri," he assured me. We would hug the eastern edge of the state.

So that Elaine could park and safely debark me, I started about a quarter-mile south of the Nebraska/South Dakota border on Highway 81. Approaching the bridge over the Missouri River, I was immediately impressed with its narrowness and antiquity.

On closer look I saw it was two-tier, the lower road leading into Yankton, the upper road into Nebraska. Two things happened on the bridge to endear South Dakotans to me: Many drivers waved, most moved over to give me running room.

Immediately after crossing the bridge, I could see straight ahead a series of old brick buildings outlining downtown Yankton. Looked like a sturdy old town without semblance of modernization. As Highway 81 swerved west, to my left, I stopped to photograph the Yankton Courthouse – about my vintage, I guessed.

Around three miles I ran into a messy situation navigating through a three-mile construction zone where traffic was restricted to two lanes and vehicles more than 10 feet wide were not permitted. Much of the way there was a six-foot drop-off on my side and barrels to alert drivers to this.

The road was so narrow that I could run it only when a car was not approaching, and when one neared I took protection behind a barrel. This distraction I did not need, since I already had been contending with the rain ever since I started.

Out in the boondocks again, and thankfully so, one of my first acts was to rescue a worm on the highway by throwing him into the grass. I couldn't repeat this act when another thousand worms came across in the next mile or so.

In turn this made me aware of the recent flooding in the area. Later I was more aware of it when I descended into a small valley and saw the flood water within two feet of the road, and some roads leading to farms were washed out. Nearby was the James River, and I was at a loss to know whether it was named after King James, Jesse James or some other James.

Despite the rain, despite my asthma acting up, I found the route – with its bike lane, moderate traffic, farmlands – delightful.

Trying to equate this first day with Texas and Louisiana, my evaluation ran thusly: Texas was a desert, Louisiana a swamp, and this is an oasis.

The best happening of the day occurred around 11 miles when the rain ceased and the sun blossomed, causing me to sing a chorus of "Glory, Glory, Hallelujah!"

My intent on starting today had been to bang out a 26-mile marathon. But by the time I reached 23 miles, I was dragging and decided to quit for the day.

I was not inordinately tired but had drained enough energy from my reservoir. The trick now was to start refilling it for tomorrow.

DAY TWO. All signs and symptoms this morning pointed to this being a day of character building. When we went out to unhook the motorhome, we were greeted by a heavy overcast, chilly winds and a threat of rain. And my weary body resented leaving the comfortable motorhome bed for duty on the road.

"I understand you had your cap blow off and you were not happy about picking it up out in the weeds," Elaine said as she greeted me at the three-mile pit-stop. Instantly I knew she had been monitoring the CB. Seems the word is out to the truckers about "the old guy running on the road."

One trucker told Elaine, "If you're going up north, you better tell him to bring his overcoat and overshoes, because it's cold up there."

The event of the day was going through Freeman, although with a population of only 1300 or so it was not that big. Seeing that the elevation was 1500 feet, I realized this was more than three times any elevation I'd run in Louisiana.

The associations that Freeman stirred up occupied my mind more than the town itself. I shook my head in dismay when I thought about the FBI standoff with the Freemen in Montana. The nations that oppose us must look at the fracas and laugh.

It is absolutely ridiculous that 10 men with screwy ideas could cause the

U.S. government to spend so much money and manpower. And, among other things, this could result in other kooks springing up elsewhere to get attention.

Tender, loving concern by the U.S. government for 10 screwballs, while at the other end of the spectrum Air Force officers were relieved because of the Ron Brown plane crash. I suspect that someone in high authority, possibly Brown himself, told the young pilots, "The secretary must get there."

The pilots had no choice even though they knew the flight was marginal. The bottom line is that it should never have taken off in the first place, and the decision for it to take off was not made by the pilots.

The first thing I noticed about the lady who stopped to check on me today was that she appeared to be very upbeat. I guessed her to be in her late 30s.

"You're the first person in South Dakota who's stopped to offer help," I said.

"Oh, everybody in South Dakota stops."

Huh, lady? I said you were the first, and I've gone a little more than 30 miles.

"Well, a couple of pickup drivers did stop, but I waved them on," I told her.

"South Dakotans are very friendly people," she replied.

"They seem to be, judging from all the people who wave to me. This is the 24th state we've run across, so we're well acquainted with how people in different states behave."

"No kidding," she said. "Then you're out here running on purpose."

"Yeah, on our way to North Dakota. But we only go 21 miles a day."

"Then you don't need any help. Well, have fun now."

And as she drove off, I thanked her.

My passage through Marion, a town of almost 1200 folks, had me thinking about Sister Marion Irvine, a runner. Indelible in my mind is the first time I saw Marion in a race. Good Lord, a nun wearing a tank top and running shorts! Shocking to a guy who'd been raised seeing nuns fully covered from head to toe in habits.

Almost as shocking was the time she passed me in the last half-mile of a five-mile race. Of course, Marion shocked many people by being, at age 54, the oldest person ever to qualify for an Olympic Marathon Trial.

It wasn't too many years before then that she was 50 pounds overweight and a two-pack a day smoker. Great runner, tremendous sense of humor, a class act, Marion Irvine.

DAY THREE. Kind of a Catch-22 as I started this morning. I would have preferred to humor a wobbly metatarsal by starting gingerly with some walking. But with the 40-degree temperature and the wind-chill factor, I had to jog to keep warm, even though I was bundled in protective clothing.

By now my feet having expanded, all my shoes are too small, and some of my toenails are black and hurting from being jammed into the too-small shoes. I had to resort to a pair of beat-up New Balance 840s that I had worn some on the USA run. They "fit" because I had cut an opening in the toe box, and my toes wiggled in the breeze.

Except for the interlude of passing through the city of Salem, the scenery today was unvarying from the previous two days. Farms in all directions.

Today I came to realize why I was so taken back, so surprised at what I was seeing in South Dakota. I had expected to see the wild and woolly west, like Montana and Wyoming. Instead eastern South Dakota was tame and domesticated, given over entirely to agriculture.

What was not tame today was the weather. I had done only three miles when the rain began, and it never stopped the rest of the day. There were moments when I wondered why, instead of running, I had not taken up some avocation like chess, stamp collecting or even bridge.

The best feature of going through Salem was that it got my mind off the weather for a brief spell. Besides, the trees and buildings provided some shelter from the wind.

I was in somewhat of a meditative mood today, but my thoughts were all shotgun. I didn't seem able to focus on one subject and stay with it very long. Maybe it was the distraction of the weather.

My habit during Sundays on the road has been to focus a while on religion, but I simply failed to get very far while thinking about what was supposed to be today's sermon. This was a quotation from Seneca: "Religion is regarded by the common people as true, by the wise as false and by rulers as useful."

I had to agree that the common people generally accept their religion, whatever it is, on faith, unquestionably without any inquiry, and that rulers will use a religion if it will suit their purposes. I differed with Seneca's appraisal of wise men.

I agreed that many would consider some tenets and doctrines of religions false. But I would contend that all believe in the existence of an omnipotent, almighty God.

The Unabomber, I muttered today as I saw myself in a mirror at one pit-stop. I was wearing dark glasses (as eye protection against the wind), and the hood of my Goretex jacket covered my head. In this ensemble I greatly resembled the sketch portraits of the Unabomber.

Near the end of this trying day I kind of felt like I'd been in a boxing match, hit by the wind, knocked to the canvas a few times, got up every time and managed to finish all 21 rounds – er, miles.

Yet despite the weather, despite nagging injuries that could be potentially serious, I was finding South Dakota delightful running – a road with runnable shoulders, relatively light traffic, a pleasant albeit not spectacular agricultural setting, friendly folks and, thankfully, without the rattlesnake threat of Texas and Louisiana.

DAY FOUR. Damn, it's cold, I sputtered as I stepped out of the motorhome. The temperature was only in the low 40s, but the wind-chill factor made it feel much colder. And so it stayed all day, never getting above the low 50s.

There were, though, two gleeful recipients of this foul weather: the ducks swimming the ponds on the farmers' farms and our motorhome air conditioner, now on R&R, resting from severe workouts in the Texas and Louisiana heat.

About the time we started the radio carried a couple of contradictory weather reports. The National Weather Service said there would be no rain, whereas the local forecaster predicted rain. By the time we reached six miles, the local guy proved more accurate, because I began to get pelted with a heavy rainfall which continued for the remainder of the day.

Around 10 miles I had a brief conversation with Bob Holman, a local farmer, who stopped to see if I needed help. He told me that he has about 3000 acres and 300 cattle, that 1200 acres of his farm are under cultivation and the rest are given over to pasture. He said he loves the South Dakota area but hates the miserable weather. The meeting with Bob came when I was being whipped by the wind, soaked by the rain and burdened with a heavy load of clothing.

Ever since leaving Yankton we had been going north on Highway 81. That changed around 15 miles today when 81 made a turn eastward and joined up with Highway 34 for 13 miles before again turning north.

Highway 34 offered the worst running conditions so far, needing maintenance and having a gravel shoulder. At various spots flood water was within a foot of coming onto the road.

At day's end and after attending to some logistics (gas, groceries) we drove to Ron Holcomb State Park situated on Lake Herman near Madison. The setting was comfortable, but the park provided only electrical hookups (no water, no sewer).

The oddity here was, this being June and the summer season, the park had 60 camping spots and only two occupants, another couple and us. In California a reservation made three weeks in advance would be necessary to get accommodated in a park like this.

I've often heard military pilots say, "Any landing you can walk away from is a good landing." Guess that sort of applies to this day. Any day you can walk away from after running 21 miles is a good day. Seemed that was about the most memorable aspect of this day, simply covering 21 miles.

DAY FIVE. On the cheery side, when I started this morning there was no rain. In fact, not a whisper of wind, bright sun, not a cloud in sight – all so unlike the stormy South Dakota I'd fought the past couple of days.

On the dreary side I knew I faced 12 miles of a two-lane road along Highway 34 which had only a 12-inch gravel shoulder. From the short time I was on 34 yesterday, I already knew it was in need of some plastic surgery and that, unlike with Highway 81, the farm homes in the area were located very close to the road (translation: Watch out for dogs!). Unbelievably, at least to me, the speed limit along this narrow road was 65 MPH.

The first change I got from the agricultural scenery was when I entered the hamlet of Junius, consisting of a gas station, convenience store and about 10 residences. My presence was announced by four barking dogs – all restrained, thankfully.

Just as I was about to exit Junius, I saw a home and alongside it 10 hound dogs in cages. I was thinking, a lot of dogs for one family. when I saw the sign: Kellogg Kennels. Okay, so he raises hound dogs.

While Highway 34 itself was miserable for running, the pastoral setting was very pleasant. That, along with the weather, made the running too placid. I was having trouble grooving into a lean and mean mood.

This was evolving into a Rodney King, everybody love everybody, day. Whereas during the previous two days, fighting nasty weather, I was combative, running more aggressively.

Today I discovered that even South Dakota has some kooky drivers as I watched a guy come down the center of the road, see me, then head for the fog line. He drove as if I were running in Arkansas and wearing a Dole T-shirt.

The highlight of our day was meandering through Madison, population 6257. As I approached the city, I went past several comfortable homes and an attractive golf course on which I saw very few players. After seeing a number of portable potties at various locations on the course, I decided that many seniors with demanding bladders must play the course.

Shortly after passing the golf course, I came upon Prairie Village. The signs told me it was a recreation of a prairie village of the 1800s.

I could see a sod house, a church, a livery stable and, just past it, the opera house where, so I was told, Lawrence Welk got his start. There were a few other buildings, a railroad station and some train passenger cars. The most glaring falsity I saw here was that this prairie village sits on a hill with a neatly manicured lawn as versus the dirt, mud, dust of the actual prairie villages.

I began to realize that Madison must be a cut above when I read two signs. One stated that the Governor's award of excellence was given to Madison as the community of the year in 1995. The other sign stated that Madison was rated as a South Dakota Gold Community.

Madison impressed me as a well-preserved, vibrant small city. All the action was downtown. Shopping malls had not taken over.

When I asked one native if there was a Wal-Mart hereabouts, he replied, "No, we've been able to resist Wal-Mart. We think a Wal-Mart would weaken the integrity or structure, or whatever you want to call it, of our business community."

Madison was about halfway through my day, and I was just a mile or so out of town when a runner, passing me from behind, stopped to ask, "How are you doing? I noticed that elastic wrap on your calf."

"I'm okay. I'm just plodding through a 21-mile day," I replied.

"Twenty-one miles?" he asked.

Whereupon I launched in a description of what Elaine and I were doing. In turn I asked a couple of questions and learned that the runner's name was Dan Bole, that he taught English and coached wrestling and cross-country at nearby Chester High School, that he lived in Madison, that he was 51 years old (versus the 37 I would have guessed).

"How far are you running today, Dan?" I asked.

"I'm running my usual 10-mile loop."

"Ten miles? I don't see you carrying any water."

"That's right. I don't drink any on this 10-mile loop because I run sort of slow, around an eight-minute pace."

Leaving me to think, such a pace I would love to be running. I asked about his cross-country coaching.

He said, "I started running and coaching about 17 years ago when my own kids were in cross-country, one of the few chances I had to see them. I love coaching, working with kids is more fun than winning. I try to make it fun for the kids, and I tell them if they're not having fun, they should not be out here."

"Speaking of being out here," I said, "doesn't it get pretty cold sometimes for cross-country?"

"Sure does. One meet four years ago the chill factor was 10 degrees below zero. About all the kids could do was bundle up."

After Dan broke off running with me to follow his loop course, I found myself running in comfortable surroundings – on a five-foot paved shoulder over rolling hills and through an area given over entirely to agriculture. I encountered only one other person.

A highway maintenance man, whose name turned out to be Danny, braked to a stop near me, jumped out of his truck, ran over to me and started heaping praise on me. Seems that he'd been talking to Elaine, and she had told him what we were up to and had mentioned my antiquity.

"Just hope I'll be close to that active when I'm your age," Danny said a couple of times.

Our day done, we again returned to overnight at Lake Herman. A Chamber of Commerce brochure. mentioned that "beautiful Lake Herman is the second most visited state park in South Dakota."

That was not what we were seeing at the Lake Herman camping grounds, capacity 60 spots, which this night accommodated only one other couple and us. Couldn't argue, though, with the place being beautiful.

DAY SIX. While yesterday, with the entertainment of Madison and the powwow with Dan Bole, was somewhat lively, today was rather routine, enlivened only with talking with a 62-year-old farmer and seeing the town of Arlington.

I came across the farmer when, along with his son and 18-month-old grandson, he was parked roadside as his son, Danny, was repairing a tire on a tractor. The grandson, Justin, was content to just sit and watch his father change the tire.

When the grandfather told me his name was Toughy, my reaction was, damn appropriate for a chesty guy of at least 200 pounds and six feet in height. Some of us, like me, are built for flight while others, and number Toughy among them, are built for fight.

Toughy told me that he farms 1000 acres. The farm was passed from his grandfather to his father and now to him. He in turn will pass it to his son.

When I asked about the winters hereabouts, Toughy said that he's seen the temperature at 20 degrees below zero and down to minus 60 with the wind-chill factor. He told me that most of the towns in the state are five to seven miles apart because they were laid out by the railroads that wanted them so spaced.

"That's not true along Highway 81," he said, "because it came after the railroads."

Realizing he lived so close to Minnesota, I asked him about Highway 212 that I planned to run there.

"It's a good road," he reported, "with a pretty good shoulder and not many trucks. If you take a road farther south, you'll run into a lot of trucks."

The town of Arlington gave evidence of having been around for quite a while, of having weathered its share of storms. I thought of it as sort of a rough and tumble town. But there was a touch of class to the Red Fox Lounge and Restaurant on the west end of town and next to a Super 8.

Elaine was pleased with Arlington because there she was able to locate a vet and get some medicine for Rebel's eyes.

The vet cautioned her, "If the storms that are forecast hit, take cover. This town was almost leveled by a tornado four years ago."

Nice gesture, I thought somewhere around six miles, when three guys in business suits, obviously on their way to a meeting, stopped to ask if I needed help. Seeing me on the road probably gave them something to talk about for the next couple of miles.

One observation I made today was that South Dakotans seem to take their history seriously. By now I realized that every time I entered another county there was an historical marker about the county.

Today's example, the Kingsbury County marker which read, "A region of buffaloes and Indians in the 1870s. In 1818 the Nicolett/Fremont party skirted the northeast corner of the county. The county is 34 by 26 miles and contains five lakes – Spirit Lake, Henry Lake, Thompson Lake, Whitewood Lake and Albert Lake."

Again today I saw abundant evidence of recent flooding. Roads from the highway to farms were washed out, some barns were sitting in water, water was within a foot of some homes on knolls, at various spots the highway was shored with rocks, and at one point near the end of the day the road was nothing but a two-mile causeway.

Between seeing all the flooding and some lakes, I went past so much water that at one time I found myself reciting:

     "I want to go down to the sea again

     The lonely sea and sky

And all I ask is a tall ship
And a star to guide me by ... "

Who was that, Masefield? Funny thing about poetry: When I was in high school, I sort of regarded it as sissy stuff. Even when in college I did not have proper respect for it.

Not until I began teaching did I realize the power of poetry. Poetry, I decided, is to writing what the forward pass is to football. Ah, such literary eloquence!

DAY SEVEN. Now, after a week on the roads here, I am about to dub South Dakota "the you can't have your cake and eat it too state" because, on the plus side, road conditions are good for running and the natives are friendly but, on the minus side, the weather is miserable as witnessed by my sloshing through rain and wind for 17 miles today.

All the time the rain was falling, one local radio station was reporting, "There is a 30-percent chance of rain today."

Worse than the rain, the National Weather Service was cautioning, "Be alert and on the lookout today for funnel clouds in the Watertown area."

A new precaution for me today was watching out for ticks. Both Dan Bole and Toughy told me, "Be careful when stepping out in the grass because it is loaded with ticks."

No sooner had I hit the road this morning than I was dive bombed by squadrons of mosquitoes. If I can believe what I read lately, I must have been exhaling high levels of carbon dioxide.

According to a recent medical report, mosquitoes can – from a good distance – sense the carbon dioxide a person exhales. If the levels are high, you're mosquito bait.

When they get close, the mosquitoes recognize the lactic acid in a person's skin. Since a person exercising, enter me, has higher levels of carbon dioxide and lactic acid, he's a prime target for mosquitoes.

More than 50 years have passed since I have been in the jungles of the Solomon Islands and since my three malaria bouts there, but still to this day whenever I see or hear a mosquito, my mind goes back to the Solomons and malaria, chilled and chattering one minute, burning with fever the next. A full dose of malaria at the present age would most likely be fatal, I suspect.

In miserable weather all day and fighting nagging but not debilitating injuries, I fell to wondering if maybe I was overly ambitious in trying to run five states and somewhere around 1070 miles this summer. At the same time I realized that, human nature being what it is, next winter while comfortably ensconced at home I'll probably set about planning a similarly over-ambitious program for the summer of 1997.

The only settlement I passed through today was the hamlet of Poinsett that practically sits on the shores of Lake Albert, which I found a bit confusing since Lake Poinsett itself is reasonably close. The name Albert stirred up a memory of Albert J. Sessarego, my boss when I worked at Sacramento City Schools. The man was a sheer delight to work for because he knew his business, he stood behind his people, he was a pillar of integrity, and he had a tremendous sense of humor.

Often when Al and I had business to transact that we did not want aired around the office, we would sneak off to a local bakery and have coffee and sweet rolls, feeling a bit wicked for getting off the firing line a few moments. Even though Al was too old for combat duty in World War II, and could have avoided military duty altogether, he volunteered for the Marine Corps and spent the war in supply work.

All the years Al was an assistant superintendent and later the superintendent, he always met his wife, Helen, on Fridays for lunch at the Rosemount Restaurant that featured fish. This was a standing date in their marriage of more than 50 years. The man had his priorities right!

No wonder that Al and Helen's marriage is a model for Elaine and me. However, they are too zealous in their travels for us to emulate. Since Al has retired, they've taken more than 85 cruises!

Our day completed, we drove into Watertown to scout how we would get from Highway 81 tomorrow to Interstate 29. Lucky we did too, because there were no signs to guide us and we learned by trial and error. At least we were primed for the passage tomorrow.

DAY EIGHT. The big question in my mind today was how the action would go once we got on I-29 and headed north to the North Dakota border. Before I could even begin to get an answer to that question, I had to cover nine miles of Highways 81 and 212 to reach the Interstate.

Highway 212 through Watertown was a disaster zone because of construction. Traffic was restricted to two narrow lanes, no space for me to run there.

Nor were there any sidewalks. My only course of action was to run through store parking lots except for one stretch of a half-mile when I was on cemetery frontage.

While Watertown does have a downtown section, the shopping activity is along Highway 212. The whole nine yards is there: motels, restaurants, Penney's, K-Mart, Wal-Mart, video stores, fast-food franchises.

Traversing 212 was no easy task because I was continually dodging cars entering and exiting parking lots. Besides, I was receiving an inordinate amount of attention from drivers who were waving and sometimes tooting.

This actually resulted from a happening of yesterday when Elaine and I were at the last pit-stop. A reporter from a local radio station descended on us and interviewed us. Today the station played that interview several times, so Elaine reported after hearing it in the motorhome. The interview went like this:

"If you see an old man running through Watertown today, that's 79-year-old Paul Reese of Auburn, California. Back in 1990 Reese ran from California to South Carolina in four months. Since then he has been running across states he missed, running 21 miles each day to show that there is life after retirement."

"Reese said, 'That's one of the main reasons that we do this. There's too much of the concept that people over 60 or 65 should be in their rocking chairs, and that's not the way it should be.'

"So what advice does he have for those who reach retirement? 'Well, I would say first of all, when you go to the supermarket, don't drive to the front door. Drive to the end of the parking lot and then walk to the market. From that build up to a walking program.

" 'Walking, especially some vigorous walking, is all you need by way of an exercise program. It's okay to limit your ambition to walking; you don't have to run. Those of us who are running have been doing it for 30 years or more, so we are conditioned to it.' "

Why is it that every time after an interview when I hear myself quoted I feel I could have given a better response?

I-29 provided relief from earlier highways today: a breakdown lane all to myself, not worrying about anyone passing me from behind and paying little attention to the traffic flying toward me. One nice feature of the freeway was that I did not have to worry about dogs. One unpleasant feature of the Interstate was that I was hit with the full blast of a 30-MPH headwind, whereas in Watertown the buildings had done much to shelter me from the wind.

The dominant feeling I had once I got going on I-29 was that I was on the home stretch in South Dakota. Only 66 miles or thereabouts to go.

DAY NINE. What a relief last night to have no storm warnings, no tornado alerts, no funnel-cloud watches. And for an encore of good happenings this turned out to be the first time in South Dakota that we had clear, bright, sunny weather all day, nary a cloud in the sky and the temperature blossomed into the 80s. This was also the first time I could remember running comfortably all day in South Dakota.

From the moment I hit the Interstate, I should have known it would be a good day. The omen of that was when I looked down the road and did not see a single vehicle within a couple of miles. My kind of traffic.

But I was finding one aspect of I-29 unpleasant. About every 30 yards the breakdown lane had corrugated strips across, about one inch high, intended to alert drivers if they strayed from the slow lane. The problem with these one-inch ridges for me was that I had to be ever conscious of them because otherwise I might trip over them.

By now I was beginning to take note of another unattractive feature of the Interstate: The miles were hanging heavy. Analyzing that, I decided it resulted mainly from lack of contacts, both human and animal.

When I came upon Elaine parked for the six-mile pit-stop in front of an "Emergency Parking Only" sign, I said, "Kind of bold, aren't you, parking here?"

Her retort was, "I'm prepared to deal with that. If a trooper asks me why I'm parked here, I'll say it is an emergency because I am attending to a 79-year-old man who will collapse without my help."

My first instinct was to say, "Cheez, no respect!" But more diplomatically I replied, "I agree with you, and I'll testify in your defense."

Elaine's day was again enlivened somewhat by listening to the trucker chatter on the CB. She reported one conversation to me:

Trucker: "Didja see that old guy jogging on the Interstate? I could think of a lot better place to jog."

Unable to resist, Elaine told him what I was doing. Their reactions:

First trucker: "Holy hell, I can't imagine running 21 miles a day."

Second trucker: "Damn, you've got yourself a real Forrest Gump there!"

With naught much else to do but run and think, the Old Road Philosopher was busy grinding out thoughts, some of which were:

1. I read in yesterday's paper where the Chicago Bulls handily won the first game of the NBA playoffs. Superior athletes, those Bulls. Yet if the USA were committed to a war tomorrow, probably none of these athletes would pass a military physical, none would volunteer to serve his country. American heroes? So much for topsy turvy USA values circa 1996.

2. I should write the governor of South Dakota and suggest that each state park should have a tornado shelter.

3. Not enough good can be said about the commendable work the local radio and TV stations do to keep people informed of weather conditions. Very reassuring when they are tracking a tornado.

Needing propane, we had no choice after finishing today but to drive to the nearest town, Sisseton, 25 miles away. Sisseton has a population of barely 2000 people, but it has all the necessary facilities. Elaine was able to stock up on propane and groceries.

The singular most striking feature of the town was Roberts County Courthouse, an imposing two-story building with dome built in 1902 and renovated in 1975. We had the desire but not the energy to visit Fort Sisseton State Park, 25 miles to the west. The fort was build as a military outpost in 1864 and is one of the best-preserved cavalry forts in the nation.

Sisseton was an oasis because not only did it accommodate our logistical needs, but it also provided comfortable overnight accommodations at Camp Dakotah RV Park, located only a mile west of I-29, where we settled in for the night after a 22-mile day and 192.2 miles into South Dakota.

DAY 10. About halfway through this day I made a command decision; In North Dakota I would not run I-29 (from the South Dakota border to Canada) as planned. Instead I would start at the South Dakota border on Highway 281 and follow it north to the Canadian border.

The reason for the decision was that I was finding the Interstate sterile as compared with running a state highway. I missed the people and places encountered on a state highway and bypassed on the freeway. I thought I could get a better feeling for a state when running a state highway than when running an Interstate.

The only irony to my decision was that safety is one of my primary concerns and actually, in my thinking, the Interstate is safer than a state highway. Another major reason to abandon the Interstate was that Elaine decided the pit-stop parking is easier on a state road than on the Interstate.

At the start it was cold enough for me to be bundled in Sporthill pants, a polypro top, light windbreaker and a ball cap. An outfit I called "compromise attire" because if Dr. Ralph Paffenbarger were running with me, he'd be wearing a tank top and shorts, whereas if George Billingsley were with me he'd be wearing tights, Sporthill pants atop the tights, windbreaker pants over the Sporthills, a polypro top, sweat shirt and windbreaker, plus a knit cap with a ball cap over it and of course gloves.

Both the traffic volume and bundling changed in relatively short order. By the time I had reached six miles, the Interstate was a beehive of activity.

Likewise the temperature, which reached a high of 87, had risen. Joyfully for me, this turned out to be another clear, bright, sunny, cloudless day, albeit humid.

Over the 22.3 miles of the day the terrain – rolling hills the first dozen miles and flat the last 10 – remained as expected, given over largely to agriculture and to grazing on a small scale. There were many small ponds and three lakes during the last four miles, but nowhere did I see the evidence of flooding that I had seen so much of on Highway 81.

Remembering this was Sunday, I again held church services on the road. Today's theme was taken from the biblical quotation, "One will be taken" – a quotation first called to my attention by Otis Carney, a fellow Marine on Guadalcanal, who was writing a book by that title. Whether Otis ever got the book published, I don't know.

The plot revolved around the pilot of an SBD and his gunner/radioman. The SBD crashed and one survived, one didn't.

Injecting that theme into my personal life, the wonderment to me is that I have survived so often when others have been taken. For example, I flew 91 scouting missions without a scratch.

A Marine with the same job – Chuharski was his last name, and I could not recall his first – was on station only 15 minutes on his very first mission when he yelled, "I've been hit!" And he was, by a 50-caliber that destroyed one of his arms.

When we landed on Bougainville, my infantry scouting section was divided between two APDs. The one I was not on was sunk by a Japanese torpedo bomber, and my section lost 18-year-old Russell Simpson.

Even as late as when I was in my 50s and 60s, I did not expect to reach 79 and arrive there somewhat active with a healthy zest for life. Despite all this good luck, I can't pass a cemetery without thinking of my own rendezvous with death. I guess that's a quirk of old age.

In the last three miles today I was fully roused from any daydreaming when six cattle trucks, odiferously overwhelming, passed me. Those cattle, I thought, are either very nervous or very laxatived.

We stretched our day to 22.3 miles to arrive at Highway 10, which lead into Sisseston and back to the Camp Dakotah RV Park for another night. It was a good feeling to have to drive only one mile to the RV park as contrasted with the usual 20 to 25. It was even a better feeling to know that we had only 21 miles left to complete South Dakota.

DAY 11. I had barely gone up the exit ramp and onto the freeway when a car came down past me, braked suddenly and backed up toward me, rousing me from my slumber hangover when I saw the driver waving frantically to me. As he pulled alongside of me, I noticed the Texas license plates and the Mexican driver.

Obviously he was trying to ask me something. But we were at an impasse because I could not understand the Spanish he was sputtering, and he *no comprende* my English.

Listening intently and studying his body language, I was able to decipher that he wanted to know if the exit led anywhere, to food and gas I guessed. By sign language and a couple of *si's* I seemed to get the message across to him, and he nodded yes a couple of times, smiled broadly, and after a "*gracias*" drove off toward town.

The experience caused me to bemoan a shortcoming of my life, that being limited to speaking English only. If I had my life to live over again, I'd remedy that by being at least bilingual. My inadequacy is intensified when I compare myself with my five-year-old granddaughter, Jillian, who is fluent in English and German.

Found it somewhat ironic that finishing South Dakota today I should be buoyed up, even jubilant. But instead I was dragging and my legs were humming with tiredness. Even when I reached the 18-mile pit-stop – only three miles left in South Dakota – I was still plodding instead of jumping for joy.

All the way today the scenery was mostly cultivated fields. Early in the day when I looked at the serenity of the morning scene – the green pastures, the flowing creek, plowed fields, rows of trees – I could not help but think that the hand of God is much more evident out here than in the cities.

A couple of small lakes along the way enlivened the setting. Seeing a couple of ducks swimming on one of them, I yelled, "Which one of you guys is the runner and which one is the pit crew?"

They yelled back, "You've been out here too long, old man!"

I came close to being humanburger today as the result of one unthinking act. This happened when I saw Elaine parked ahead for a pit-stop, and instinctively started across the freeway and toward the grass median to get to her.

I was almost across the slow lane and starting into the fast lane when I became aware of a car in the fast lane descending on me. Luckily for me there still was no car in the slow lane, and I braked and lingered until the car passed.

Next time before starting into freeway lanes, engage brain, I told myself. The alternative is to be splattered all over the Interstate.

At one point today I came upon a three-mile construction zone that was a bonus to me because traffic was restricted to one lane and I had the other lane all to myself. In the closed lane I was running, I kept seeing holes about two feet long, three inches wide, seven inches deep. I counted about six of these holes very five yards.

After a while curiosity got the better of me, and I ran 100 yards out of my way to ask Jeremy Hawkins, the foreman, "What are these holes for?"

He patiently explained that the holes are filled with a certain material that strengthens the road and keeps one side of the cement slab from rising above the other. And for this vital information, I repeat, I ran 100 yards out of my way.

Besides talking with Jeremy, I talked with one other person today, Aas Pond. Yes, Aas.

When he introduced himself, I not only asked him to repeat his name but to spell it, and the result was my telling him, "You know, I've never heard that name before."

It turned out that Aas had driven out from Sisseton to meet us because he is a runner and Marsha, owner of the RV park in Sisseston, had told him about us. Aas said he has been running since the 1970s and has run a number of marathons.

"What's your favorite? " I asked.

"Grandma's," he said. Not a bad choice, since the race has an excellent reputation.

"My goal is to run New York City," he continued.

"Well, judging from the one time I ran it, that is a great experience. Another one you might consider is London, one of the very best I've run. What's your best marathon time?"

"I did 3:05 a few years ago," he said.

Silently I was thinking, damn fast for a guy who appears to be about six-feet-three inches tall and weigh about 195 pounds.

We talked a while longer, and I learned that Aas is a 56-year-old medical technician who had taken a few moments off from his job at the Sisseston Emergency Medical Center to visit with us. He had a number of questions about our run and seemed satisfied with the answers I gave him.

Fortunately for us, our last day in South Dakota was in clear, bright, sunny weather, albeit the 91-degree temperature was the hottest we experienced in this state. Finishing, we had the satisfaction of completing what we set out to do. But we were hardly exultant.

"Victory is a thing of will," Ferdinand Foch once said. He was commenting about war, but what he said could be applied to this run. I had the feeling that with two more states, Minnesota and North Dakota, to go this summer, will power would be playing a starring role.

Overview of
MINNESOTA

June 14th to 23rd, 1996
203.1 miles

Day	Overnight	Miles	Notes
1	Cambridge	20.7	"Well begun is half done"
2	Camp in the Woods	20.0	through Cambridge
3	Princeton	21.0	Father's Day on the road
4	St. Cloud	20.1	crossing the Mississippi – again
5	Paynesville	20.6	"What's for sale?"
6	New London	20.0	lost souls
7	Benson	20.5	surprise: courteous Minnesota drivers
8	Benson	21.7	help from a trucker
9	Ortonville	21.5	"How'd I get home last night?"
10	Sisseton, SD	17.3	Minnesota finish, somewhat déjà vu

Chapter 14

Minnesota:

Never Out of Sight of a Lake

DAY ONE. About to start Minnesota I made an assessment of where we were and decided divine intervention would be welcomed. Where we were with this summer's adventure added up to having run 620 miles across Texas, Louisiana and South Dakota, and having left about 440 miles to run to get across Minnesota and North Dakota.

Dipping my feet in the water, I started at the St. Croix River, ran up a dirt road for a quarter-mile and onto pavement leading out of Wild River State Park. Well, to report it a bit more accurately, once I started I was airborne out of the park by hordes of mosquitoes.

As protection against the mosquitoes I wore a long-sleeved shirt, windbreaker pants and a heavy sprinkling of Avon bath oil. Nonetheless I was a landing pad for mosquitoes, and a host of others buzzed around me thunderously waiting for a clearance to land.

Once out of the park and onto a state road, I was surrounded by agriculture. So what's new? I had to remind myself this is Minnesota, not South Dakota.

On this road, Highway 9, I immediately got a wake-up call when I had to trudge up a nine-percent gradient. Reaching Highway 95 at Amelund, I turned west to begin following the route Elaine and I had decided on across Minnesota. This would be our 25th state crossing.

As expected – after all, the license plates read "Minnesota, Land of 10,000 Lakes" – I immediately saw some lakes. I had thought the quotation of 10,000 lakes was hyperbole until I learned that the actual number is closer to 15,000.

One handicap I had in starting Minnesota was that I am now reduced to running in shoes with the toes cut out because my feet have swollen and all the shoes I have are too small. Actually it is not difficult to run in these shoes. The problem is that on the dirt and gravel road shoulders my shoes get invaded by small rocks and dirt clods, and my feet object rather strenuously to this invasion of their space.

Elaine had parked in midtown North Branch for the 15-mile pit-stop. When I was ready to hit the road, she decided to walk a couple of blocks with me because she wanted to see the local Rexall drug store and the Coast to Coast Hardware Store.

When she went into the hardware store, she told the manager, "I had to come in here because I've not been in one of these stores since I was a small child."

Somewhat undiplomatically, he replied, "That must have been a long time ago."

The highlight of North Branch for me was that I persuaded Elaine to buy me a donut at the local bakery.

"Why do you need a donut?" she asked. "You just finished a snack."

"Just trying to help the local economy," I replied. And I got away with it!

As I exited North Branch and crossed over I-35, I noticed the usual motels, gas stations and restaurants squatting alongside the freeway. And, within sight to the north, Factory Stores. Factory Stores! Whoops, if Elaine sees them, we're due for a return trip after finishing today.

After we finished, I was reminded of Willard Scott and his expression, "Well, you got that right." So reminded because I suspected Elaine would want to visit the Factory Stores, and when I heard her say, "What do you think about putting some excitement in our day by making a quick tour of the Factory Stores?"

DAY TWO. My costume changed. I was now wearing a new pair of black shorts, having shed my faded blue shorts that had adorned me across the past six states.

Also I was wearing a new fanny pack, having acquired it yesterday in Cambridge, instead of the tattered fanny pack, of late held together by safety pins, which I'd worn across 24 states. I felt as if I had lost two faithful friends.

Both the faded blue shorts and ragged fanny pack urged me to join them in retirement. But I patiently explained that somebody had to take Elaine and the dogs on their vacations.

Speaking of Elaine, my charm did not work on her this morning. Before hitting the road, we were having coffee and the two bakery-fresh sweet rolls bought in Cambridge yesterday and, sweet-roll freak that I am, I wolfishly devoured mine before she had barely tasted hers.

Drooling for a bite of hers, I tried an imitation of the Budweiser "I love you, dad" commercial wherein the son tries, unsuccessfully, to talk his dad out of a beer. Either because my acting was bad or because Elaine had a sweet-roll fixation, I failed miserably. She refused to give me even one bite.

The entire Highway 95 route through Cambridge was lined with flags, about 18 inches long, planted in the ground for Flag Day yesterday. The flags were spaced about every 15 yards.

I was impressed that none of these flags had been subjected to vandalism. Plant them in most California cities and the vandalism would be rampant.

Maybe this Minnesota respect for the flag ties in with the state's patriotism, going all the way back to the Civil War when the state was the first to volunteer troops, some of whom suffered heavy casualties. As one example, of the 262 members of the First Minnesota Regiment involved in the Gettysburg charge, only 47 escaped injury or death.

Near the west end of town I rescued a couple of the flags that had fallen to the ground and as I replanted them, I broke into a chorus of "Yankee Doodle Dandy," whereupon all the standing flags, hearing my melodious voice, wavered almost to the point of collapse.

My favorite sight of the day came when looking into the grass 30 yards off the road, I saw the ears of a deer. Then, as I looked closer, I saw a doe lying there raise her head to take a better look at me.

Evidently she decided I was of good intentions, because she put her head down and continued to lie there. In all my many years, including those as a boy when I hunted on my uncle's ranch, I have seen hundreds of deer. Never before this incident, though, had I seen a deer bedded down. The lady trusted me!

After finishing today, and feeling in desperate need for shoes, I phoned Nike with the intention of finding out where in Minnesota I could buy a pair of Nike Air Streak shoes, if anyplace. Because my need for shoes was acute, I hung on the Nike customer service line for 41 minutes with the only response being "All customer service lines are busy" or recorded music.

My conclusion: Nike should divert some of the money from the millions it pays Michael Jordan and invest it in better customer service. To which Phil Knight, Nike CEO, would probably reply, "Get lost, old man!"

Traveling different states, Elaine and I are always learning. Today's lesson focused on Minnesota liquor laws.

Trying to buy some non-alcoholic beer, we found out that it cannot be purchased in supermarkets but only from a liquor store. The liquor stores are controlled by the cities, each of which decides how many will operate within its jurisdiction. All this was related unto me by a clerk in a Cambridge liquor store when I was purchasing a case of Coors Cutter, a hard-to-find non-alcoholic beer.

DAY THREE. Somewhat of a surprise this morning at five o'clock when as I was enjoying coffee in bed, Elaine, saying "Happy Father's Day," handed me a box of candy and a card. Good Lord, she never forgets; even remembers the Marine Corps birthday. I was surprised, because I did not remember this was Father's Day.

Fatherhood, in some respects, has been a difficult role for me because I never had a father at home as a role model. In my 79 years I have spent only one year, that in infancy, in the same house as my father.

I didn't have a script on what a father should and shouldn't do, so I settled on treating my kids the way I would have wanted a father to treat me. At this stage in life, I realize in retrospect that I have stumbled with them in one respect: I have not told them often enough how much I love them, how proud I am of them.

Back to Elaine, one of her frequent remarks to me is, "I'm not cutting you any slack because of your age."

I appreciate that because there are a lot of mother hens who, on a rainy day like this, would say, "It's too wet out there. You'll get pneumonia. You better quit and wait until tomorrow." Forward progress is not made on *mañana*.

A few minutes after we launched this morning, the motorhome abruptly died as we were making our way down a foggy back road. After some coaxing, we got it started and, roaring noisily, it emitted a cloud of black smoke. Once the smoke stopped, we were able to drive to the start and begin our day.

Nonetheless Elaine was understandably nervous about the motorhome. This being Sunday, no mechanics available, we had no choice but to mush forward. It was an easy decision to make getting the motorhome repaired our number-one priority after finishing Minnesota, providing we could get through today and tomorrow.

The TV weather forecaster predicted no rain today until around six P.M. Well, I got news for you, fellow. That was not confetti falling on me from the start until mile 16.

The rain did not bother me, though, as much as did the Minnesota drivers. For years I had known that 3M was located here and that it stood for Minnesota Mining and Manufacturing.

Or at least I thought it did. After observing drivers here the past three days I'm not so sure that it doesn't stand for Minnesota motorized maniacs.

Never in the previous 24 states that I have run have I seen so many motorists driving with their wheels on or over the fog line. Some of them, seeing me, swerve even more over the fog line and I wonder if they are trying to read the lettering on my T-shirt.

Some seem downright aggressive, like the old guy I saw hunkered over the steering wheel of his pickup, already over the fog line. He caught sight of me and instantly moved another foot outside the fog line, causing me to scoot to the dirt and leaving me with the impression he resented my being on his road.

Every Minnesota native we have talked with has been pleasant, friendly. Contrastingly the majority of Minnesota drivers I've observed are discourteous.

Princeton was the only city on today's route. We had a close look at this city of 3719 residents when we stayed overnight at the local city park that is midtown.

"Small world" was my thought when just east of Princeton Highway 95 intersected Highway 169. Last summer I had run across Iowa on Highway 169. Ah yes, memories of *Bridges of Madison County* and of Marion Morrison (okay, John Wayne).

DAY FOUR. A high and a low as we drove to the start this morning. The high because we were anticipating crossing the Mississippi River and seeing St. Cloud, with 50,000 people by far the largest city on our Minnesota crossing. The low because we discovered that the drive to the start was actually 35 miles, 10 longer than estimated yesterday, which meant that just to find a place to overnight we had gone 70 miles out of our way, squandering time and about seven gallons of gas.

No, no, tell me not so, I said around 8.5 miles when I saw that the highway was undergoing extensive construction. The net result was that for the next four miles into St. Cloud I was dodging construction zones and equipment and getting pelted with bits of fine gravel flying off the gravel trucks.

Realizing this would happen, I turned my back every time a gravel truck approached. Never can understand, especially after having had a couple of windshields cracked by rocks from gravel trucks, why state law does not require these truck loads of gravel to be covered. Come to think of it, why don't the auto insurance companies lobby for this?

The dominant impression of St. Cloud was that the place was a traffic nightmare. The state has a population of only five million, but at times looking at the traffic jams I would have sworn that many drivers were in St. Cloud. Every place I looked, cars were clogging the roadways.

The diversion of the city's attractions made the time pass quickly. But with all the street crossings and traffic I was constantly on the alert.

When Elaine was parked for the six-mile pit-stop, a Minnesota state trooper stopped to check on her. Once she told him about our run, he was supportive and encouraging. Seems that the Highway Patrol officers in every state express some enthusiasm once they learn what we are doing. Maybe it's because of my vintage; maybe it's because they see so much negative stuff that seeing something positive is uplifting for them.

We stopped at 20.1 miles, then retreated to St. Cloud for two chores. Running through the city, I had stopped at Gilleland Chevrolet and asked the service manager, Gordy Roy, if he could check on our motorhome after we finished today. Listening to my tale of woe, he agreed.

That was the good news. The bad news was that they did not discover the problem.

Next we went to a couple of sporting goods stores where I attempted to buy a pair of running shoes that would fit me. Unable to find a lightweight shoe of any brand that would fit me, I succumbed to buy a pair of Nike Windrunners.

Time would prove this to be a foolhardy purchase, because the shoes were useless for me. I don't know if it was because of their construction, their weight or what, but I ran awkwardly in them and with much strain.

This I didn't need and wouldn't tolerate.

DAY FIVE. This was mostly a strictly business day. By that I mean plodding forward and being on full alert at all times. I could not indulge in the luxury of day-dreaming or spacing out.

The reason was simple: Minnesota drivers. I abhorred the thought of becoming a hood ornament for a car. By now I had come to realize there are things I will always remember about Minnesota: mosquitoes, lakes, ticks, maniacal drivers, nice people.

The scenery today was varied: agricultural, some grasslands, forestation and the cities of Rockville, Cold Springs and Richmond.

The most eye-catching sight in Rockville, population 579, was a gigantic rock quarry, the biggest I have ever seen. I saw a number of cranes and cables all about.

By my estimate the observation tower above one crane was at least 200 feet high. Fascinating experience to watch the operation and to see the mountain of granite slabs stacked about.

Wasn't hard to tell who owned the quarry. The answer came when, on the east end of town, I saw a huge mansion built of quarry rock, three-car quarry garage, manicured yard and a wrought-iron fence around the property.

Cold Springs appeared more diversified and, with a population of 2459, somewhat bigger than Rockville. It was similar in having a big granite plant, but in addition I saw that Unitex Company and Gold's Plumb Poultry contributed to the local economy.

Unlike Cold Springs, unlike Rockville, there was nothing distinctive about Richmond, a town of 906 people. All I saw, besides some residences, were gas stations, truck stops, liquor stores, a restaurant, a True Value Hardware and Casey's Convenience Store.

The most novel sight of the day was Mickville, or at least that is what the sign – Welcome to Mickville, population 14 – called it. The home's front yard was decorated with a menagerie of ceramics: a lighthouse, a covered wagon, a plow with two horses dragging it, a collection of dolls, a sleigh with reindeer and Santa, a red fire plug, a windmill and an authentic gas pump of 1930s vintage. That was some of the stuff; I could not remember the rest.

I have a good friend who steadfastly believes in angels and their powers. I am beginning to believe in my guardian angel, because more than once on the road an inner voice has cautioned me to an impending danger.

Like today when I saw a semi coming down a hill and an inner voice said, "Get out of the way." Luckily I had listened, because trailing the semi and entirely in the breakdown lane where I would have been had I not listened was a car driven by one of the 3M types.

A bit of drama on the high seas today at six miles. When Elaine left the pit-stop, the motorhome got temperamental and acted up, sputtering, emitting black smoke and balking.

We waited until it calmed down, then drove it three miles to make sure it would function okay. It did, and we returned to the six-mile spot and continued our safari.

This left us more anxious than ever to find a good mechanic. Meanwhile on the road our battle plan was that Elaine would always be ahead of me so that if she got into trouble I would eventually arrive to assist.

Except for the pit-stop visits with Elaine, I did not talk to a single person all day. She, by contrast, had a very interesting experience.

Or maybe weird is the word. While parked at the 18-mile pit-stop, she saw a guy in his mid-50s drive by, then suddenly brake and turn around and drive back to her.

"What's for sale?" he asked. "The dogs?"

"We don't have anything for sale," Elaine replied.

"Oh yes, you do," he insisted. "You have that sign in the back."

"I'm sorry, we don't have anything for sale," Elaine repeated.

"The sign says you do," the guy, obviously in a huff, yelled as he got back in his car and drove off.

All the time he was referring to the sign Elaine had posted in the back window of the motorhome and that read: "We are OK. Runner pit crew."

Oddly enough two state troopers who had stopped to check on Elaine had commended her for having the sign, saying it would save calls from motorists who otherwise would think she was in trouble.

DAY SIX. Call this the day of the lost souls. At different places and at different times, both Elaine and I got lost today. And each of us hit upon a novel way to rendezvous with the lost soulmate.

I got lost early in the day, around five or six miles when, ogling the sights in Paynesville, day-dreaming a bit, I missed the Highway 23 turn. I began to realize that something was wrong when I did not find Elaine waiting for a pit-stop that was due.

Then when I began to see Highway 55 signs, I definitely knew I had gone astray. More than 20 minutes late for the pit-stop by now, I knew Elaine would be worried, probably entertaining visions of me doing a Jim Fixx replay, sitting and leaning against a tree bodily while spiritually on my way to cross the Great Finish Line of life.

Meanwhile, realizing something had gone wrong, Elaine got on the CB and asked the truckers, "Have you seen an old man in red running shorts on the road?"

The responses were immediate: "He's on Highway 55 and headed back toward 23."

"He looks kinda tired."

"Just how old is he, anyway?"

Knowing I was on my way, Elaine waited for me at the junction of 55/23. She was forgiving of my mistake, probably because she understood how incensed I was about running two miles out of my way. But she was not forgiving enough to let me count those two miles as part of my total mileage.

Elaine's getting lost happened near the end of our day at a point where we were supposed to leave Highway 23 and take 9 west. When I came to this junction, I realized I had neglected to alert Elaine that it was coming up and that, since she was not around for a pit-stop due, I was reasonably certain she had missed the turn.

I was pondering how to handle this when just ahead of me I saw a Minnesota state trooper about to get back in his car after talking with a motorist. I ran to his car, and that was how I met Sgt. Mike Cruze of the Highway Patrol.

When I came up to him, he said, "Out here for a jog?" My cue to go into my song and dance about running across the state.

Getting to the problem that had brought me running to him, I asked if he'd do me a favor by finding Elaine when he drove ahead and asking her to return here, take Highway 9 west, and find me on it. Later when Elaine caught up with me, she reported that Sgt. Cruze not only found her but that he escorted her back to Highway 9 and made sure that she made the correct turn.

The city of Paynesville, which dates back to 1858, was the tourist attraction of the day. Highway 23 goes through a residential area of the city but misses the business district that is off to the north a block or two. The place appeared to be bigger than its population of 2375 would indicate.

A sign at the local high school proclaimed, "High school state wrestling champions, 1987." My thought: That was nine years ago. Seems to have been a drought with all sports since then.

It took me a while today to realize that something was missing: no mosquitoes buzzing about me. Another blessing: The motorhome purred contently, didn't act up one bit.

Coming in from the rain at a pit-stop, I told Elaine, "It's downright wet out there."

Her reply: "Rise above it. Remember, you're a Marine. Get tough!"

Then, after a pause, she added, "Oh, I love it!"

La dame sans mercy, she is.

DAY SEVEN. As we drove out of the RV park on Lake Kerns this morning, Elaine and I felt pitying compassion for the old man who owned the park and the beautiful 80 acres lakeside. When we went into his house yesterday to register, it reeked of smoke. Cigarette butts were scattered about in several trays.

The old man, hunched and walking with great difficulty, wore a soiled gray sweat suit and slippers. The seat of his pants was stained with a telltale brown.

The couple of opened cans of food were every bit as evident by smell as by sight. The room was in total disarray.

In stark contrast to the old man, his dog, a black Labrador, had a glossy coat and appeared to be in excellent condition.

Talking with us, the old man had to pause several times to cough and to catch his breath.

"You've got to pardon me," he said, "but I have emphysema. I'm supposed to use that thing, but I don't." He pointed to an inhaler.

He was struggling so much that we feared he could die any moment. Just as the old man was deteriorating, so was the park that stood in dire need of some heavy maintenance.

Despite his failing condition, or because of it, the old man was going out his way. A couple packs of cigarettes were on the table and, damn the consequences, he would enjoy smoking to his dying day.

Before us was a man who, robust at one time, had worked hard all his life, who had for years built and maintained this RV park and 85 acres. But a man now reduced to infirmity – skeletal, struggling for each breath, barely able to shuffle around. All he had left were his possessions, his independence – and his dog.

I could not find the words to express how lucky I felt after seeing the suffering and infirmity of the RV park owner, a man actually younger than I.

Had two people contacts today. The first was about halfway through my day when John Burns stopped to ask, "Are you just out jogging, or are you in trouble?"

I didn't want to detain him, so I answered, "Just out running." I admired his good intentions but almost gagged from his cigarette smoke when he pulled up alongside of me. Parting, he told me he was on his way to work.

The other contact, a couple miles later, came when I saw a high school girl on the other side of the road running toward me and I yelled, "Is this for fun or for cross-country?"

"It's for basketball," she yelled as she passed by. Lawdy me, how I envied that reservoir of youthful energy.

A bit of excitement around 15 miles when three police cars sped past, all with flashing lights, escorting a bus and a Cadillac. Reminded me of the William Jefferson Clinton convoy we saw last summer in Wyoming when he was vacationing at Jackson Hole.

Elaine and I had heard that Bob Dole was campaigning in Minnesota. Could this have been a Dole motorcade?

If I'd thought so at the time, I would have instinctively saluted. Had I thought it was Clinton, I'd have to restrain myself from my first act of mooning someone.

Years ago I heard Jack Foster, the great marathoner from New Zealand, say, "Wear the lightest shoes you can get away with." A practice that I've since followed. I run in the light shoes more comfortably, more efficiently and less tiredly than when wearing heavier training shoes.

That lesson was reinforced this morning when I tried the new Nike Windrunners for three miles. The damn things made running downright laborious. Rejuvenation when I switched back to the light shoes. Hear that, Jack?

DAY EIGHT. Ambush Park, our home last night, sits on the Chippewa River about a mile from downtown Benson. A sign in the park told me the origin of the name.

In 1838 a number of Sioux hunters left their wives and children here when they went off to a hunt. When they were gone, a group of Chippewa, led by Hole-in-the-Day, appeared and pretended to be friendly. But later in the night they killed all the wives and children except for one woman who escaped with her infant son and a young woman they kidnapped.

When the Sioux returned, they saw their mutilated loved ones and vowed vengeance that was realized two years later at the battle of Rum River where 70 Chippewa paid with their lives. And so it was that we camped on a historical site.

"Oh, no!" I yelled when we awoke and heard the rain beating on the motorhome. "Damn, another rain day," I muttered.

The rain seemed to increase in intensity as we went along. By the time we'd reached nine miles, some lightning with red streaks dead ahead got my full attention.

Rain I can handle. Lightning moves me to retreat to safety, which is what I did by roosting in the motorhome.

Waiting out the storm, we drove into Benson to see if some shoes I had ordered had arrived in the mail. All the streets of downtown Benson were flooded about one foot deep. I had to wade into the post office, only to find that we had no mail.

We then retreated to where I had stopped running and, the lightning no longer present, resumed running. Surprisingly by the time we returned to downtown Benson, all the flooding had disappeared.

When I passed the only grocery store in town and did not see Elaine parked there, my reaction was, Did she miss the turn onto Highway 12 from Highway 9? Twenty minutes later when I still had no sign of her, I went into action.

First I flagged down a pickup coming from the direction of Highway 9 and asked the driver if he had seen Elaine and the motorhome. The guy had a good memory, because he could recall exactly where he had seen Elaine parked on Highway 9.

When a county sheriff came along, I explained my problem. He offered no help. Fact is, baby-faced, overweight, chubby in appearance, sloppy in uniform, he looked like he needed help.

He acted confused and slow on the mental trigger when I explained my problem. I got the distinct impression he had his police job as a result of having a powerful relative.

My next move was to try to flag down a trucker and ask him to relay a message to Elaine on the CB. I was lucky enough to catch Rich Christian, a Western Coop driver, just as he was coming out of the plant and barely moving.

"Do you have a CB?" I yelled.

"Yes," he answered.

I pointed for him to pull over, and he obliged. I then asked him to put this message on his CB, "Lady, your runner is on Highway 12 just west of Benson."

Smiling, he did so. Almost instantly, Elaine answered, "Thank you. Thank you very much." In a few minutes she would catch up with me on Highway 12.

I thanked Rich Christian for his help, and as he drove away I thought about truckers. Driving, I sometimes get irritated with truckers who are aggressive on highways, especially when they tailgate. Running, I often appreciate the consideration many of them extend and their willingness to help when they are aware of a problem.

Our day done, we returned to Benson, seven miles east, to again overnight at Ambush Park. There we gave Rebel and Brudder strict orders to be on the alert for any invading Chippewa. The Chippewa must have know because we neither saw nor heard any.

DAY NINE. This was a day of all business. I simply hunkered down and plodded through 21.5 miles, about half of them in a heavy rain. The only person I talked with all day was Elaine.

No one stopped to ask, "Old man, do you need help? Old man, you broken down? Old man, whatcha doing out here? Old man, do the folks at Shady Pines know you are out here?"

Once again the motorhome got temperamental, balked, emitted smoke, refused for several moments to cooperate and get underway. Elaine's observation: "Kids usually get sick on weekends when no doctors are available. Seems that cars are like kids, sick on week-ends when no mechanics are around."

Road conditions on Highway 12 left much to be desired for running. But the saving factor was that the drivers were considerate. Wish someone could tell me the sociological significance of the drivers on Highways 9 and 12 being courteous and considerate, and those on Highways 95 and 23 driving like maniacs.

My lightest moments today came when I saw a mailbox with the name Erby on it. Up popped a World War II story that a Marine friend by that name told me when we were both captains.

It concerned his battalion commander, a lieutenant colonel, who was a wild man who habitually got rip roaring drunk at parties and the experiences Erby had at a couple of parties with the colonel. After the first party the colonel and Erby came to the CO's jeep to drive back to camp and the colonel said he would drive.

Erby replied, "Sir, you can't drive. You're drunk."

The colonel protested and Erby tried to talk him out of driving, but lost when the colonel said, "Dammit, Erby, I'm driving and that's an order."

Zigzagging all over the road, the colonel managed to get the jeep back to camp without incident.

The next morning the colonel called Erby to his office. "How'd I get home last night?"

Erby: "You drove, Sir."

"You mean you let me drive drunk?"

"Yes, Sir."

"Why'd you do that?"

"You ordered me to, Sir."

"You should not have paid attention to the order."

A few days later there was a second party and again a very drunk colonel. Returning to the jeep to go home, the colonel said he would drive.

Erby grabbed the colonel by the collar and yelled, "Dammit, Sir, you're not driving. I am. Get in." So saying, he shoved the colonel into the jeep.

The next morning the colonel called Erby to his quarters, and on his way there Erby feared the Colonel would chew on him for the way he manhandled him the previous night.

"How did I get home last night?" the colonel asked.

"Sir," Erby replied, "I drove you here."

"Good work, Erby."

Deployment for an amphibious operation and combat was next for Erby. Placid stuff compared to dealing with the colonel and parties.

Our day completed, we drove the 17 miles into Ortonville, closest place to overnight. We took advantage of being camped near a local beanery by having dinner out. Dessert was knowing that we had only 17 miles left in Minnesota.

DAY 10. Having seen today's route when driving into Ortonville yesterday and then again this morning while driving to the start, I knew before starting that the route was devoid of any spectacular scenery and replete with agriculture and naught else. Upon arrival at the start, Elaine dumped me somewhat unceremoniously out into the cold, windy, rainy weather. Uncomfortable but acceptable.

The only sounds on the road were the rustle of the wind, the rain beating on my Goretex and the pounding of my feet on pavement. The rain sloshing into my open-toed shoes chilled my exposed toes. After a few moments on the road I told myself, By the time a guy reaches 79, he should be smart enough not to be out in rain and cold like this.

Elaine took pity on me today and shortened the pit-stops from three to 2.5 miles. She was glad she did because of a scary incident that happened to her at the pit-stop on the outskirts of Ortonville.

A guy approached her and gave her a story about his equipment being stolen. Upon seeing him, see noticed he had a black eye and a cut on one ear.

When she asked him about his injuries, he said he had been attacked by some bikers. Elaine was parked in the vicinity of Hilltop Camping, and the guy said he was there because he was looking for a place to store the equipment he carried on his bike.

To Elaine that seemed a contradiction since he already had said his equipment had been stolen. Elaine's anxiety increased when he made a remark to the effect that she must have a lot of money because she owned a motorhome and came from California (which he deduced from the license plate) "where there are a lot of rich people."

He then began to move closer under the pretense of inspecting the motorhome. At this point Elaine informed him for the second or third time that her husband should arrive any minute. And just as she spoke, I came upon the scene and immediately saw the look of concern on Elaine's face blossom to relief.

Sizing up the situation, I saw why she was so glad to see me. Her concern was probably justified, because a couple minutes after I arrived the guy said he had to be on his way, and left. Elaine and I both decided that he was newly released from jail or prison.

Passing a sign reading "Welcome to Minnesota," I engaged in a bit of overkill by continuing another half-mile to finish at the boundary of Stone City, South Dakota. After finishing, Elaine and I found ourselves short on jubilation. The mood was almost *déjà vu*. Another state crossed.

Probably what kept us from feeling too celebrative was the dreary weather. Then too, heavy on our minds was the urgency to get the motorhome repaired. The question was where was the best place to take it for repair.

The closest big cities were Aberdeen and Fargo. But our experience in one big city, St. Cloud, reminded us that garages in most big cities would be loaded with urgent repairs and that, at best, we might get just a quick inspection and no remedial action.

We decided that we needed to find a small town with a good mechanic. But how?

Then, almost inspirationally, we thought of the friendly folks at Camp Dakotah, Gary and Marsha Valnes, and of the nearby town of Sisseton. Decision made, we drove from the finish to Camp Dakotah and there sang the motorhome blues to Gary and Marsha.

As a result the day after we finished Minnesota, Rick, the service manager, and Dale, the master mechanic, of Brooks Motor Company in Sisseton performed surgery on the motorhome and had it purring contently in a remarkably short time. A very happy sequel to Minnesota. (An even better sequel: In the weeks that followed the motorhome never faltered once.)

Overview of
NORTH DAKOTA
June 29th to July 10th, 1996
232.9 miles

Day	Overnight	Miles	Notes
1	Rolla	10.4	underway at Canadian border
2	Egeland	21.2	meeting Jamie Bradley
3	Cando	22.0	it's pronounced "Can-DO"
4	Wild Goose RV	20.7	meeting Tammy Roddy
5	New Rockford	22.1	it's spelled "Sheyenne"
6	New Rockford	22.2	Carrington and a 30-foot Indian
7	Jamestown	21.5	Melville and Edmunds
8	Jamestown	21.4	Bernie Allen and Bernard Steele
9	Jamestown	20.1	through Jamestown
10	Edgeley	20.0	Trooper Tracy Brunsfield
11	Ellendale	20.0	wheat fields left and right
12	Jamestown	11.2	Ellendale and "Mr. Merc"

Chapter 15

North Dakota:

During Which I Learned About Durum

DAY ONE. After arriving at the North Dakota/Canada border and while doing our usual photographing, I was surprised to hear Elaine say, "Maybe you'd like to run the 10 miles from here to Highway 281."

I was caught off guard because it was already early afternoon and I had not intended to start North Dakota until tomorrow. We had driven the last 120 miles on the Highway 281 route from Carrington to the Canadian border today primarily to check out the route.

"Well?" I heard Elaine saying.

"Sure, why not?" I replied. That decided, I saddled up in half-tights, a T-shirt and a pair of New Balance 110s, new lightweight shoes I had purchased in Fargo, the best feature of which was that they fit. Unlike in Minnesota I was no longer running with my toes sticking out of the shoes.

Back when we were home and planning our North Dakota route, we had decided to run I-29. But after running 70 miles on that Interstate in South Dakota, we decided that being on the Interstate drained some of the adventure (meeting people, seeing places and sights) from our trip.

This northern part of North Dakota was considerably more domesticated than I had anticipated. Northern Montana, just before we reached Canada, had been a bit wild and woolly.

Speaking of Canada, Elaine and I got a much better impression of USA customs at the North Dakota border than we did at the Montana border. The lady in charge at North Dakota was downright friendly, whereas at Montana the inspector simply tolerated us.

All told, I passed by only a half-dozen farms today and a total of approximately 20 cars went past me. No wildlife, no dogs, no police, no

Good Samaritans crossed my path.

Arriving at Highway 281 and completing our day, we drove into Rolla, 11 miles east, to the closest RV facility. We got the last spot of the 11 spots and, despite the surrounding mud, felt lucky to find a home for the night.

As we settled in for the night, the weather prediction was not too encouraging: 95 degrees and humid tomorrow. We were also told that a candy store in Fargo had been hit by lightning and that a funnel cloud had set down in Casselton. If nothing else, the weather in North Dakota should be interesting.

DAY TWO. Somewhat of an unspectacular day as I moved through an agricultural area of undulating hills. Invariably, wherever there was a depression in the terrain, it was filled with water, flooding, and ponds always in sight.

Which led to one of the major forms of entertainment – watching a couple hundred red ducks doing aquatics on the water. Another piece of entertainment was watching a crop duster, a daring guy who – much to my amazement – even flew under the telephone wires.

But the top entertainment act was by a small bird who was a gutsy little devil. He was fighting off a hawk trying to attack his nest. The little guy was like a fighter plane buzzing around a bomber.

Impressive watching him out-maneuver the hawk, even at one time riding on hawk's back and pecking him. Glad that I was not around long enough to witness the full scenario of that struggle, because I felt it to be futile for the valiant little guy in the long run. I left the scene wishing I had a shotgun so that I could even the odds.

What happened today endeared every driver to me, because all moved over for me and all except one waved. The exception was a guy in his 50s, full beard, probably an environmentalist who thought I was lousing up the area. Obviously a Clinton voter!

I was practically in shock when an oversized motorhome moved over, an occurrence never experienced by me before. Obviously a Dole supporter!

The only problem today was the wind, remindful of the strong, prevailing winds in Montana and Wyoming. Naturally it was a headwind.

A change in haberdashery today when for the first time in my running career I wore compression shorts. They're somewhat similar to half-tights but lighter in weight and the legs are shorter.

I found them to be a good buffer against the wind, protective of the hamstrings and groin muscles. Beginning to understand why so many professional athletes wear them.

We had to scratch our projected plans to stay at Graham Island State Park tonight because Highway 19 leading to the park was washed out. The *Jamestown Forum*, an outstanding newspaper for a community of 15,000, reported that campers in the park were stranded there.

Elaine, while parked for a pit-stop, had a brief visit with Jamie Bradley, a reporter for the *Record Herald*, out of Cando. He was on his way to an assignment but stopped to check on her after seeing the motorhome license plate RUNXUSA.

He told her that in the area we are crossing, elk, deer, moose, fox are seen and that sometimes a mountain lion strays into the area. From him she also learned that the durum wheat grown in North Dakota and used for pasta is the best quality grown in the USA. He told her that while in grocery stores she should look for Leonardo's and Farmer's Choice, two local brands.

The weather forecaster today was reasonably close with his prediction of 95 degrees. The actual reading was 91, with 66 percent humidity.

DAY THREE. We felt lucky to be on the road, unscathed and ready for action, especially after last night's heavy windstorm and rain and tornado warning. Actually we went through the tornado warning with minimum stress, because at the time it was happening we did not even know about it. About nine P.M. we turned on the radio and heard a report that the tornado warning of the past two hours for Towner County, which we were in the midst of, had just passed.

Cando, a town of nearly 1500 folks, was the change of pace in our setting today. Going through town on 281, about all I saw was the local school, a football field, the Zephyr Restaurant and Sportsman's Motel.

When we detoured for a trip to the business district, the cosmopolitan setting (considering what we had been seeing recently) was overwhelming – two drugstores, two bars, one restaurant, a hardware store, a bank, two insurance agencies and a bakery. I can testify that the bakery produces high-quality donuts, best I've tasted in years.

Cando, I learned, is the focal point for North Dakota's multi-county agricultural activity, producing 85 percent of the nation's durum. Leonardo's, a manufacturing plant that turns durum into semolina and semolina in turn into high-quality pasta, is located in Cando.

The town's name had its origin as a result of a debate over establishing the county seat there. One of the advocates for doing so said, "There has been much talk about our not having power to locate this county seat where we see fit. But we'll show you what we can do and furthermore, just to show you what we can do, we'll name this county seat 'Can-do'."

This name resurrected memories of the Seabees in WWII, because that was their motto. Ah yes, the Seabees for whom I hold fond memories, because on several occasions on Guadalcanal and Bougainville, when the Marine Corps chow was borderline, I wandered over to the Seabee mess hall for tasty food.

Kind of a sneaky maneuver, because I had to remove my officer insignia to get through the enlisted mess hall. The Seabees were well aware that we hungry Marines did not belong there, but they never failed to welcome us.

Three days now on the North Dakota roads, three days of drivers considerately moving to give me running space and often waving. But also three days without a single person stopping to inquire about my welfare.

Though minus human contacts I had some animal distractions. The first at three miles when a bull, atop a small knoll, stood staring at me and seemed to be saying, "Don't mess with my harem, Mac!" As I eased past his 30 or so cows, with only a flimsy fence between the bull and me and no trees about, my sole intent was to put distance between us.

The second animal encounter was frustrating, because I came across a calf that had somehow gotten through the fence and now roadside could not figure how to get back into the pasture.

The frustrating part for me was that, much as I wanted to help him, no way could I manhandle him back through the fence and no gate through which I could guide him was in sight. Sorry, fella, you're on your own, I thought while moving down the road.

But in a mile or so, when a farmer in a pickup approached me, I was able to stop him and explain the calf's plight. He said he knew the owner and would inform him. Mission accomplished!

As darkness fell at the RV park, three Indian teenage boys showed up and engaged in a game of lighting a firecracker, holding it a while, then running to a companion and throwing the cracker at him as he tried to dodge.

These antics went on for an hour or so, and we were less worried about the teenagers hurting each other (they were agile dodgers and had lousy aims with the crackers) than we were with their starting a fire in this highly inflammable area. During that hectic hour, while losing valuable sleep, we stood ready to evacuate at a moment's notice. Fortunately their game concluded with no dire consequences.

DAY FOUR. Brightening an otherwise routine day was a conversation with a 15-year-old girl I met when she walked out a quarter-mile from her home to pick up the family mail.

"Good Lord," I asked when we met at her mailbox, "do you walk all the way out here for the paper every morning?"

"Yes, except when it's snowing," she answered. "Then I drive out."

She was wearing a sweat shirt with the name of a Catholic organization on it. So I asked, "Do you go to a Catholic high school around here?"

"No, I go to a public high school in Leeds."

"What sports do you play there?" I asked. From her wholesome appearance I guessed she was involved in athletics.

"I'm on the basketball team."

"And I suppose you're enjoying school?"

"It's okay."

Before she left to return home, she told me her name was Tammy Roddy. I told her I was running across the state and kept a journal of my experiences, and that I was going to make a note that if all the girls in North Dakota were as pretty as Tammy Roddy, the state must be filled with pretty girls. Her reaction was a deep blush.

As I contrasted the world in which this bright, wholesome young lady was growing up with the one in which I grew up, I would not trade her places. With my generation there was less crime, the world moved slower, morals seemed higher, values were less materialistic, we had less and appreciated what he had more, and society was less splintered.

She was growing up in a world considerably more advanced technologically, yet I envied her not an iota. My generation, I truly felt, was indulged with the best of times.

Meandering through Minnewaukan was not very exciting, but it injected some variety into the day. As I entered town, one sign informed me that the town was the seat of Benson County, and another sign said that it's name meant "living waters." I must admit to some confusion here, because a bit later I saw another sign saying that it meant "spirit waters." At any rate, one thing I was sure of, both meanings came from the Indian language.

Elaine experienced a shaky moment this morning. A sheriff's car, red lights flashing, pulled up behind her and parked.

The officer stayed just long enough to read the sign she had posted on the back window of the motorhome, "We're okay – Runner pit crew." Then he drove off, much to her relief.

At one point today I found myself reflecting on some conclusions reached as a result of our travels. Among which:

• The closer we get to a metropolitan area, the more aggressive the drivers will be, the less polite people will be.

• In rural areas – as in North Dakota, South Dakota, Montana, Wyoming, Nebraska, Iowa – people seem to have more integrity, to reflect more patriotism, to cling to values that pioneers held dear.

• The decision of where to live for most people probably rests on where their job is or where their family members are. If the decision were based on values, the people would have to weigh what they prize most.

As but one example, if they want kind weather, the place is California, and the price is a high crime rate. Contrarily if they want a low crime rate, the place is North Dakota and the price is miserable winter weather. Come to think of it, I didn't have to leave home to come to that conclusion.

DAY FIVE. The minute I came into the motorhome for the nine-mile pit-stop, I saw Elaine was in a dither, and understandably so, I learned. Seems that on her walk with the dogs Rebel saw a snake, grabbed it and was trying to kill it.

She yelled, "No, no!" and Rebel obeyed by dropping the snake. Elaine was upset that a dog once bitten (on our Montana run) by a rattlesnake and barely living through the experience would be so dumb as to deliberately tangle with a snake.

She now realized that Rebel would not have the sense to stay away from rattlesnakes. Luckily for him, this slender snake, about three feet long and charcoal in color, was evidently not a viper.

Just three miles later Elaine and I had another disturbing experience. As I was nearing the 12-mile pit-stop, I saw a gravel truck driver, going uphill and across a double yellow line, pass Elaine as she was going uphill.

Coming into the pit-stop, I told her, "That truck driver must have been out of his mind passing you uphill and not knowing what was on the other side."

"You haven't heard the half of it," she replied. "He saw that I had a CB and said, 'You'd think you two could find a better place to play than out here on the highway."

For Elaine and me the sting of this truck driver's remark was that in more than 6000 miles of running across states this was the first and only negativism from a truck driver.

Routine as this 22.1-mile day was, it reminded me of what people sometimes ask me, "Isn't it dull out there? Doesn't it sometimes get boring?"

No, not for me. I'm always looking around and thinking. And thinking isn't bad.

Maybe what I do is more meditation than thinking. I don't know, but thoughts are always tumbling through my mind, many of them holding a mirror to my life. Too bad my thinking is so pedestrian, because otherwise I could possibly come up with a bright idea or two.

During much of this thinking – er, meditating – out here I usually come up with more questions than answers. Examples: I look at a crop and wonder what it is; I look at a tree and, fugitive from botany that I am, wonder about its name; I see a piece of farm equipment and usually recognize its purpose, but the question is how does it operate?

Going through this Indian reservation, our questions were: Who does all the cultivation here – Indians, or is the land leased to farmers? Does the government arbitrarily build this highway through here, or are negotiations with the Indians required?

And just where are the Indians; I don't see any scooting about? Sioux Reservation – wasn't Sitting Bull a Sioux?

The only town I passed through today was Sheyenne, and my reaction on first seeing it was, Sure looks like the old West. Later I learned that the citizens had made a deliberate effort, about 10 years ago, to refurbish the town in a western motif. The place was reported to have 300 citizens, but I saw none about. In fact, it somewhat resembled a ghost town.

Incidentally the name of the town is spelled *Sheyenne*, just as with the Sheyenne River, because the early explorers who intended to spell both after the Cheyenne Indians, were poor spellers.

DAY SIX. The dessert on today's menu was New Rockford – not merely passing through there on Highway 281 but after our running day was finished making a visit to the downtown business section.

Coming to the James River, I noticed it was about 45 yards across at this point and its location coincided with the northern boundary of New Rockford. I remembered seeing this same river near Yankton when we were running South Dakota and had somewhere read that it was about 700 miles long.

A sign extended welcome from seven churches. Not bad for a town of

1600 population. Let's see, on a per capita basis that would be about one church for every 230 people.

No end of signs here. One told me I was on the American Legion Highway. Wonder what the VFW reaction is to that?

Another sign told visitors that New Rockford is the home of astronaut James Buch. News to me on two counts, because I didn't even know there was an astronaut named James Buch. Sorry about that, Jim.

The most unusual sight in the environs of New Rockford appeared about a mile south of town when I came across a bison ranch and saw 40 or so bison grazing in a pasture. A sign told me that the big plant I was looking at was the North American Bison Cooperative, and that bison steaks, jerky and sausage were for sale.

Later in the day, playing tourist in New Rockford, I learned that this plant was built in 1993 at a cost of $1.47 million and that it's the world's first processing plant devoted exclusively to bison meat. The plant processes (to put it euphemistically) approximately 2600 animals a year.

Three miles after seeing the herd of bison, I came upon another source of entertainment: an ostrich farm. Some of these birds were running sprints and again, as when I've seen ostriches before, I marveled at their speed.

They brought back memory of my visit to South Africa in 1989 when Dr. Ralph Paffenbarger and I ran the Comrades Marathon, the country's famous 90-kilometer race. A tour guide told us that ostriches have a brain only the size of a walnut, that they mate for life, and that if antagonized they can kill with their claws.

Until I took time out to do some calculating today, I had not realized that six of the past seven years Elaine and I have been on the road running across states on July 4th. Some of these days have brought on more than the usual excitement – people throwing firecrackers at me, a couple beered-up guys in a pickup heading directly for me then swerving at the last moment, long drives to find an RV spot for the night.

The problem today was traffic – all headed north toward the lakes, as evidenced from most of the vehicles towing boats. In just one hour today I saw more traffic than I had seen in total my previous five days on the road.

A typical July 4th day in that the temperature was in the 90s. I talked Elaine into letting me extend the day to 22.2 miles so that we could finish at the Carrington city park and check on whether the eight RV spots there were occupied.

They were. Luckily we had reserved spots at the Bison in New Rockford.

After we had finished our day's run, I got a good chance to tour in the business district of New Rockford because Elaine had made a command decision to take time out and find a laundromat. I found a cafe and treated myself to a cup of coffee and a piece of pie.

The place was busy, with about 10 customers, all locals, none of whom said anything to me, though still wearing running clothes (nylon jacket, pants over my shorts and T-shirt) I was the source of a few curious looks. Reading the menu, I saw that bison burgers went for $3.65, and I knew from whence they came.

DAY SEVEN. Easing out of Carrington this morning, I was still a bit sleepy, because between fireworks and trains we lost a heap of sleep last night. The fireworks started around 9:30 and went on sporadically until almost midnight.

Then three times between 11 P.M. and five A.M. trains, three blocks from us, thundered through town. On each occasion the engineer blasted the train whistle several times. I got the impression these engineers got their kicks by rousing the natives.

Seemed strange to me too that both nights we stayed in New Rockford three trains came through. Yet during both days I never saw a train on the tracks that paralleled Highway 281.

The running itself was easy today, flatlands and an eight-foot breakdown lane. The problems were twofold: a 20-MPH headwind and a heavy fog.

Being out in this fog would be semi-suicidal if it were not for the wide breakdown lane, I realized, and I worried about Elaine being parked and waiting for me at a pit-stop. The weather sort of reminded me of being at sea, ship enshrouded in fog, wind flowing over the deck.

We passed through two hamlets today, Melville and Edmunds. Melville had a tie-in with Carrington in that they were both named after the same man, Melville Carrington, a major player in the Carrington and Casey Land Company. All I saw in Melville were a half-dozen residences, an old barn and 10 silos lined up like soldiers ready for inspection.

In Edmunds the sights consisted of 10 or so residences, a large-sized hall (Edmunds Hall, naturally), and next to the hall a deserted building that was once a general store. The remarkable thing about the abandoned store was that it had 14 (yes, I actually counted them!) windows, and every single one of them was intact. In an inner urban city that would rank as a miracle.

Because one of my running friends once went past a parked car and saw a hose from the exhaust pipe into the car, this resulting in the death of the occupant, I decided to look into the red Mazda parked roadside. What I saw was paper money on one front seat, a pile of CDs on the other, a set of golf clubs in the back, and a small cool chest.

I could see in almost all directions, but I saw no owner. I left concluding: This guy trusts people, or he has wandered off to do himself in.

As we near the end of our five-states run this summer, having about 82 miles left after today, Elaine and I are already talking about next summer. We've still got 21 states left to complete the Lower 48. Can we complete them in one summer, or will it take two?

Some motivating factors do say get it done in one summer. The main one: I'll be 80 next summer, and who even knows if I'll be around the following summer.

As we talked, the best battle plan we came up with was simply to start the 21 states next summer, go as far as we could, hopefully finishing all of them.

DAY EIGHT. The unusual feature of this day was that two different people actually stopped to ask if I needed help. The first offer came at two miles into my day when Bernie Allen played Good Samaritan.

"Are you okay, or do you need help?" he asked.

"I'm okay; but, you know, I've come all the way from Canada at the rate of 21 miles a day, and you're the first person who's stopped to ask if I needed help."

"No kiddin'."

"Do you farm around here?" I wanted to know.

"I farm some. I have around 2000 acres. My son and I work them."

"How do you like living in North Dakota?"

"I like it real good."

"You mean those cold winters don't bother you?"

"Don't bother me a bit."

Guessing him to be in late 60s or early 70s, I replied, "By golly, that's something because older people have trouble with the cold, and you're certainly over 39."

"Well, yeah," he said laughing, "I'm almost 39 turned around."

As he drove off and I plodded toward Pingree, I admired how upbeat and jovial he was, laughing, smiling most of the time we talked. He was a guy, I judged, who had little trouble dealing with the bumps on the highway of life.

In the words of the poets, it never rains but what it pours. No one stopping to offer help in 140 miles, then today comes Bernie Allen and now Bernard Steele.

"What's going on here?" he asked after stopping beside me.

I went into my routine about running across North Dakota from the Canada border to the South Dakota border.

"You mean, you're gonna run all the way to South Dakota? How old are you anyway?"

"I'm 79."

"The hell you are," he said. "I'm 75 myself."

"You look like you're in pretty good shape."

"Well, I do walk a couple of miles every day," he told me.

Remembering that earlier I had asked Bernie Allen if he liked living in North Dakota and then neglected to find out why he liked it, I asked, "Why do you like living in North Dakota?"

"I really don't," he said. "I was born and raised here, and I really never got enough money to get out."

Miles to go, I told him. "I'd better move on, because my wife gets nervous if I don't show up on time. Been nice talking with you."

So free of traffic was the road this early morning that I was calling it carless, and that sort of brought to mind something I had read someplace an eternity ago: car, caress, careless, carless. Four-word short story.

The only community besides Pingree that I saw today was Buchanan (named after James, not Pat, I presumed). Immediately south of town 281 became a divided highway. This meant that, facing traffic, I no longer had to worry about cars (on the other side of the median) approaching me from the rear. Relaxing thought.

Several times today I shook my head over a story in yesterday's paper about a guy in Fargo who restrained his wife with a dog collar and leash. Among other things, he made her drink from the toilet. He even offered his young kids a pony ride on his naked wife.

Brought to trial, the husband said the prosecution was making a big deal out of nothing. The judge didn't see it that way; he gave the guy a year in jail. Some folks would say the judge erred in not requiring the guy to take all his liquids from the jail toilet.

DAY NINE. From the time we left the Canadian border and headed south on Highway 281 for the South Dakota border, I always felt like Jamestown was an important milestone along the way. The feeling I had was, All downhill from Jamestown, albeit the distance from there to the South Dakota border was 64 miles. Both Elaine and I were experiencing the joyous feeling of closing in on the finish of North Dakota, another notch in our gun.

Because of its location Jamestown is the hub city of the south-central region of North Dakota. Jamestown owes its location to the railroads that needed maintenance crews every 100 miles. It's no coincidence that Fargo/Jamestown/Bismarck are spaced at 100-mile intervals.

Running the ridge line and looking toward Jamestown nestled in a valley below, all I could see of it were a huge white grain elevator, a couple of water towers and a forest of trees. On the flatlands, at the same time that I saw a sign reading "Welcome to Jamestown, Pride of the Prairie," I found myself crossing the James River – about 40 yards across at this point, slow moving and shallow.

From the time we spent in Jamestown, I got the distinct impression that it was bigger than 16,000. Maybe I was just seeing too much tourist activity because the city is a tourist mecca. That 16,000 population says something about North Dakota in light of the fact that Jamestown is the seventh largest city in the state.

At the southern edge of the business district I again crossed the James River, then trudged up a half-mile hill. Once on top of the hill I was smack into the I-94 complex.

This included the Buffalo Shopping Mall. I suspected that, our day finished, Elaine would succumb to temptation and exercise her Visa there.

The only problem I had running today was with the slant of the road. Since it was sharply slanted and since I ran facing traffic, this meant that my left leg was downhill more than usual.

The net result is that my left calf, already strained from too much downhill, was complaining bitterly. The best remedy I could think of was to tape it with Elastoplast tape, which provided some compression yet maintained flexibility.

Ever the pious one I took note of this being Sunday and tried, best I could, to meditate on things religious for a few minutes. I kept it pretty simple, though.

First I reflected on something Harry Truman had said: "A person who is fundamentally honest doesn't need a code of ethics. The Ten Commandments and the Sermon on the Mount are all the ethical code anybody needs."

Sounded good, I thought, but I wound up concluding that Harry was a bit provincial. What he said might pertain to Christians, but what about all the other sects?

Much more simple than what Truman said was an observation of William Penn: "Religion is nothing else but a love of God and man." Now that one, I decided, might work for all sects, though the nature of God might vary with each.

Carried to its ultimate, love of man should solve all society's problems. Loving someone, we would not rob, rape, murder, lie to or cheat that person. Probably oversimplification, but at least the way things should be.

Before returning to the RV place, we decided to tour the Buffalo Mall that was across 281 from where we were staying. Elaine bought three T-shirts with wolves on them and a pair of shoes.

I bought two post cards. Is there any doubt about who's the big spender in the family?

DAY 10. Our drought with North Dakota Highway Patrol ended today when trooper Tracy Brunsfield made contact with us. Elaine and I were parked for the nine-mile pit-stop when he pulled up and parked behind the motorhome.

"It's your job," Elaine said, "to go out and talk with him."

Even though I'd never read my job specs, I left the motorhome to talk with him. Doing so, I learned a number of things.

I learned that he works Highway 281 between Jamestown and the South Dakota border and that he's been a trooper for seven years. Hardly dry behind the ears compared to his father, a state trooper for 30 years.

"How do you like being a trooper?" I asked.

"It's all worthwhile," he said, "if I can save but one life. It often bothers me that most of the time when I stop people, they seem to be angry.

"Another problem is that the job is miserable in winter because of the wind and road conditions, and especially the way people drive. The biggest problem of all, though, is the lack of support police get from citizens."

When I returned to the motorhome, Elaine's first comment was, "Well, you two certainly talked long enough."

"Men talk," I replied. Let her juggle that one for a while!

Did get one offer of help today. This from a farmer in a pickup who came out from a side road, saw me and turned around to come check on me.

"Where ya' headed?" he asked.

"South Dakota border."

"Are you all right?"

"Yeah, fine."

"Okay, then. Good luck."

As he drove off, I thought, too bad Elaine was not around to see how short a men-talk conversation can be.

Elaine related an incident that happened to her. This came when she was walking the dogs. They and some horses spotted each other at the same time and excitedly ran to the fence to exchange greetings.

One horse and Brudder were so excited they both charged to the fence and, doing so, bumped noses. The experience did not seem to dampen their enthusiasm as they continued to cavort.

We were lucky to finish our 20-mile day in the town of Edgeley. Not enough good things can be said about some of these small towns (Edgeley's population is only 850) that maintain RV hookups in their city parks. Edgeley, Egeland, Carrington that I could think of offhand in North Dakota.

DAY 11. With Tennyson it was cannons to the left, cannons to the right. Here today it was wheat fields to the left, wheat fields to the right.

I saw but a scant number of homes contrasted with extensive acreage under cultivation, and I concluded the land holdings must be huge. During the last 10 miles of the day the most common sight was hundreds of round rolls of baled hay.

I did go through one small settlement, a place called Monango that consisted of a dozen or so residences, a grain elevator, shells of buildings belonging to defunct businesses and a small city park. None of the other sights were spectacular or startling.

It is always intriguing to me how many thoughts cascade through my mind when I am running the roads. A bombardment not experienced when I am inactive.

The thoughts tumble faster on a day like today when the running is easy because of light traffic, good weather and excellent road conditions (nine-foot breakdown lane all day). These thoughts usually weren't connected or sequential.

For instance, today I recalled my high school football days when I dropped a very catchable pass in the end zone. Even though we won, I have never been able to erase that memory.

The closest I came to any human contacts today was when Trooper Tracy Brunsfield sped past and tooted.

The day was so dull that with two miles to go, I said to Elaine, "How about me taking the boys with me the last couple of miles to liven up the day for them and me?"

The look I got was you-must-be-kidding. The words I heard were, "No way, no way. Do you really think I'd trust you with my children on the highway!"

Nice feeling as we wrapped up the day to know I had less than a dozen miles to go to finish North Dakota. The day over, we drove into Ellendale where Elaine stocked up on groceries and I descended on the local bakery. Never cease to marvel, as I munch some gooey pastry, how good the bakeries are in these small towns.

DAY 12. This 11.2-mile day, completing our run across North Dakota and five states this summer, felt almost like a victory lap. Not that I was smug about it because, somewhat the opposite, I was more inclined to gratitude and a touch of humility in being so blessed at being able to do the 1068 miles at age 79.

With every state we have crossed, Elaine has been very diligent to make sure that I cut no corners. Today was no exception. When we arrived at the starting point, she had to turn around to get pointed in the right direction, this being south.

Doing so, she wound up about five feet in front of our starting point, whereupon she said, "Don't get out. I've got to back up to get to the exact start."

Five lousy feet, whatta bean counter! Darn honest, though!

Only a 20-MPH headwind kept the day from being ideal for running. The temperature swung between the 50s and 60s, the breakdown lane was a protective nine feet, and the traffic was almost as scarce as an NFL title for the New Orleans Saints.

A thought today: There's always some guy (okay, ladies, or some *gal*) who can take a far-fetched idea and make a book out of it. These thoughts because I was thinking about *The North Dakota Joke Book*.

What the author has done is to cast North Dakotans as low-IQ types. He's done that by taking every joke he can find about people with low intelligence and associated these jokes with North Dakota. Here are samples:

• "Adam was a North Dakotan. He had to have been. Only a North Dakotan could eat an apple with a naked girl sitting next to him."

• "The other day a North Dakotan drove his new semi-truck off a cliff. He told the police he wanted to check his air brakes."

• "The North Dakotan was asked in the restaurant if he preferred red or white wine. 'It doesn't matter to me,' he said, 'I'm color blind.' "

• "Why does every North Dakotan shoe have 'TGIF' stamped on it? It's a reminder that 'Toes Go In First'."

The book does not square with my opinion of North Dakotans. Those I dealt with – on the road, in stores and other places – were intelligent, friendly and courteous. Considerate as they were as drivers, they did much to make the run across their state enjoyable.

Why in hell did the words, "*C'est fini!*" come to mind as I arrived at the "Welcome to South Dakota" sign, one-tenth of a mile south of the North Dakota border? True, though, we had finished North Dakota, finished our runs across five states this summer and now had finished all the contiguous states west of the Mississippi.

Toy with the words as I might – satisfaction, exhilaration, jubilation – none of them seemed quite right. I just knew for sure that it felt damn good to have done what we set out to do.

Epilogue

So let's see where we are today:

- We have run across 28 states.
- Spent 299 days on the road.
- Logged 6850 miles crossing states.

Now the question is: What have we learned from these experiences?

1. If you want to accomplish something *big*, you will have to do it bit by bit, piece by piece, a day at a time. You do not chop down a big tree with one whack of your axe.
2. If there is something major in your life that you want to do – say, build a boat, travel someplace, write a book, earn a degree – *do it*. Don't let it pass by, then live to regret.
3. If you have a dream, a burning desire to do something, plan to do it when you are physically and mentally able to do so.
4. If you are able to fulfill your dream, your life will be enriched.
5. Be aware that you can accomplish more than you, or others think possible.
6. In whatever you undertake, accentuate the positive, and that includes exercising your sense of humor.
7. Hopefully in whatever you do, you will be sharing it with someone, because sharing enhances the fun and satisfaction.
8. Above all, *enjoy*. If you are not enjoying, you could be doing the wrong thing – and life is too short for that.

Another question: Where do we go from here?

Well, at vintage 80, my first priority is to stay alive. And along those lines I must admit to being somewhat surprised and immensely pleased with my continued existence.

As to where we are going, the battle plan Elaine and I have is to *try to* (no guarantees here!) cross the remaining 22 states. Barring any disasters to Elaine, me or the motorhome, we think the time will come when we will be able to say we have run across all 50 states.

If that does happen, you can bet that we will be telling all about it in another book.

To order more copies of

Go East *Old* Man

Send $14.95 per copy ordered, plus $4 shipping per order, to:

Keokee Co. Publishing, Inc.
P.O. Box 722
Sandpoint, ID 83864

Visa or MasterCard orders by phone accepted toll-free at: 1-800-880-3573 from 8:30 a.m. to 5 p.m., Monday through Friday (Pacific Time). For orders by phone, please have at hand your credit card number and expiration date.